CHURCH SUPPERS

Church Suppers

722 FAVORITE RECIPES FROM OUR CHURCH COMMUNITIES

EDITED BY BARBARA GREENMAN

BLACK DOG
& LEVENTHAL
PUBLISHERS
NEW YORK

ISBN: 1-57912-453-4

Designed by Scot Covey

Manufactured in China

Published by Black Dog & Leventhal Publishers, Inc.
151 West 19th Street
New York, New York 10011

Distributed by Workman Publishing Company
708 Broadway
New York, New York 10003

Library of Congress Cataloging-in-Publication Data is available on file

g f e d c b a

TABLE OF CONTENTS

MY KITCHEN PRAYER

Bless my little kitchen, Lord,
I love its every nook.
And guide me as I do my work,
Especially when I cook.

May the food that I prepare
Be seasoned from above
With Thy blessings and Thy grace,
But most of all—Thy love.

INTRODUCTION

The tastiest recipes in America, tested and loved by generations, can be found in our church and community cookbooks. For this collection of over 700 favorites, we asked churches across the country to submit recipes—and what a generous response we had! More than fifty cookbooks arrived, from Oregon to Maine, Minnesota to Mississippi, proof that every corner of America, and perhaps every home, has its own perfect dish. Here, in *Church Suppers*, they are all yours to share.

The contributors are friends and neighbors, moms and dads and grandparents—some of them "celebrity chefs" in their own hometowns—who love to prepare delicious meals for their families and fellow parishioners. Most recipes serve an average family and can easily be doubled or quadrupled for large gatherings.

Inclusiveness, more than selectivity or personal taste, guided our choice of recipes. You'll find that the recipes our grandmothers loved (canned soup casseroles, molded salads) are still favorites today, along with newer ethnic dishes using garden-fresh produce. We felt that the more variations on chicken salad (five) and meat loaf (seven) the better. And if we don't like baked beans (we don't), those who do will find three baked bean recipes and even a 7 Bean Casserole. Missing are some foods no one seems to like today—whatever happened to turnips and mince pies?

Above all, we wanted to mirror the enduring diversity of regional food across the country, with Seafood Gumbo and Beef Jambalaya from Louisiana, and New England Boiled Dinner from Maine. And it's interesting how far local food has traveled; Vermont sent us Chicken Fajitas and Michigan sent us Honolulu Chicken. New York Cheesecake came from Mississippi and Key Lime Pie from Massachusetts.

Because cooking for and with children, is such a big part of family food preparation we have singled out particularly fun, kid-friendly recipes in boxes for easy identification. Reindeer Food, for example, makes a tasty appetizer for Santa's steeds at Christmas, and a warm Toll House cookie or gingersnap is welcome all year round.

To our many contributors: Thanks to all who recommended specific recipes and shared anecdotes with us on behalf of your church families. Please note that a number of recipes had exact duplicates in other books submitted, so to be fair we chose the first one we read. We have kept brand names as given in the recipes. When not available locally, just substitute with your own favorite.

To my bread and dessert expert, my husband John Greenman, my special thanks. It was a pleasure working with editors Lindley Boegehold and Kylie Foxx, who dealt patiently with a complicated manuscript. I also want to thank Christina McGrath, Carol Anderson, Scot Covey, and Alexandra Anderson.

BARBARA GREENMAN

APPETIZERS

For every comfort we enjoy
For food before us set
We thank thee Father
Through Thy love
Our needs are always met.

FIRST UNITED METHODIST CHURCH,
BELLEVILLE, MICHIGAN

DILL DIP

2/3 cup Hellmann's mayonnaise
2/3 cup sour cream
1 teaspoon seasoned salt
1/2 teaspoon Worcestershire sauce
1 tablespoon parsley flakes
1 tablespoon onion flakes
1 teaspoon dill seed
1 tablespoon chives
Dash of salt
Few drops of Tabasco sauce

Mix together all the ingredients. Refrigerate for 8 hours.

ROWENA METZGER
ASSEMBLY OF GOD
ESTÂNCIA, NEW MEXICO

MIXED HERB DIP

1 cup mayonnaise
1/2 cup sour cream
1 tablespoon snipped chives
1 tablespoon snipped parsley
1 1/2 teaspoons lemon juice
1 1/2 teaspoons snipped marjoram
1 1/2 teaspoons snipped oregano
1/2 teaspoon crushed rosemary
1/2 teaspoon curry powder

In small bowl, combine all the ingredients. Cover and chill. Serve as a dip for vegetables.

FAITH
FOREST AVENUE CONGREGATIONAL CHURCH
BANGOR, MAINE

ARTICHOKE DIP

Fresh Parmesan cheese
1 package cream cheese
2 garlic cloves, chopped
1 jar marinated artichokes, drained
1/2 cup mayonnaise
Paprika for color

Blend all the ingredients in a bowl. Let set overnight if you can. Warm in the oven and serve with crackers.

DONNA FEUILLET
DAMASCUS UNITED METHODIST CHURCH
DAMASCUS, MARYLAND

GUACAMOLE DIP

2 ripe avocados
1 teaspoon salt
1 1/2 teaspoons lemon juice
1 teaspoon Worcestershire sauce
1 clove garlic
1/2 teaspoon red pepper
1/2 tablespoon grated onion
3 dashes of hot pepper sauce (optional)

Peel and mash the avocados. Add the salt and lemon juice. Stir in the Worcestershire sauce, garlic, pepper, and onion. Add the hot pepper sauce, if desired. Serve with crackers. Makes 1 1/2 cups.

LOU BOXRZ
PITT COMMUNITY CHURCH
BAUDETTE, MINNESOTA

SALSA DIP

2 ripe avocados, peeled and pitted
Juice of 1 lemon
2 tablespoons medium salsa
1 cup sour cream
1/4 cup mayonnaise
Tabasco sauce to taste (optional)
2 cups shredded cheese (Jack or Cheddar)
10 to 12 chopped olives
1 bunch chopped scallions
1 cup chopped tomatoes

Mash the avocados with the lemon juice. Spread over the bottom of a 7 x 11-inch glass dish. Drain the salsa and mix with the sour cream, mayonnaise, and Tabasco sauce. Spread this mixture on top of the avocados. Sprinkle the cheese, chopped olives, onions, and tomatoes over the top of the salsa mixture. Serve with chips, crackers, pretzels, or raw vegetables.

GENEVIEVE LORD
PITT COMMUNITY CHURCH
BAUDETTE, MINNESOTA

BASIL PESTO

1 1/2 cups fresh basil leaves
2 to 5 garlic cloves, peeled
1/4 cup pine nuts
1/4 cup fresh Parmesan cheese, grated
1/4 cup freshly squeezed lemon juice

Combine the basil, garlic, pine nuts, and Parmesan cheese in a blender or food processor. Turn the machine on and drizzle in the lemon juice. Continue to puree until a smooth paste is formed. Serve as an hors d'oeuvre spread on a sliced baguette.

DEBRA HUTCHINSON
NORTHBROOK UNITED METHODIST CHURCH
ROSWELL, GEORGIA

HEARTY HUMMUS SPREAD

1 (19-ounce) can chickpeas, drained
3 tablespoons lemon juice
2 tablespoons water
1 tablespoon sesame oil
2 garlic cloves, crushed
1/2 teaspoon ground cumin
Dash of hot pepper sauce
Pinch of salt and black pepper

Puree all the ingredients together in a blender. Serve with pita slices. Makes 1 3/4 cups.

JANICE McCLEAN
NORTHBROOK UNITED METHODIST CHURCH
ROSWELL, GEORGIA

GOOD NEIGHBOR RECIPE

1 tongue, that does not slander
1 heart, generous and kind
2 ears, closed to gossip
1 mind, full of tolerance
1 dash of wit
1 sweet smile
2 eyes, overlooking other's faults
2 hands, extended to help others
1 dash of sunny disposition
1 dash of cheerfulness

Blend together and form into one being; serve generous portions to everyone you meet.

BRO. M. O. MADDEN
OAKMONT CHURCH OF GOD
SHREVEPORT, LOUISIANA

Baba Ghanoush (Eggplant Dip)

3 large eggplants
3 or 4 garlic cloves, crushed
Salt to taste
1/2 cup tahini (sesame paste)
Juice of 3 lemons
1/2 teaspoon ground cumin
2 tablespoons chopped fresh parsley

Pierce the eggplants in several places with a fork and roast over an open flame (or 4 inches under the broiler) until the skin blackens and blisters, turning them as necessary. When cool, peel and discard the charred skin. Mash the eggplants with a fork and add the crushed garlic and salt, stirring to a smooth, creamy puree. Add the tahini and lemon juice alternately, blending well between each addition. Add the cumin and parsley. Serve as an appetizer with Arab bread.

GAMILIE ISRAEL
TRINITY UNITED METHODIST CHURCH
YORK, PENNSYLVANIA

Curry Dip

2 cups mayonnaise
1/4 cup chopped onion (optional)
1 1/2 tablespoons curry powder
1/2 teaspoon dry mustard
1/4 teaspoon Tabasco sauce
Dash of salt

In a bowl, combine all the ingredients and mix well. Serve with raw vegetables like cauliflower, broccoli, and carrots.

MAURETA FUGATE
PRAIRIE CHAPEL UNITED METHODIST CHURCH
URBANA, MISSOURI

Creamy Cucumber Onion Dip

1 package dry onion soup mix
1 (8-ounce) package fat-free cream cheese, softened
1 cup fat-free plain yogurt
1 medium cucumber, peeled, seeded, and shredded
1/4 cup chopped pimiento
1/4 cup chopped scallions

Blend the soup mix, cream cheese and yogurt. Stir in the cucumber, pimiento and scallions. Cover and chill for 2 hours. Serve with chips or cut-up raw vegetables.

MARY WHITE
OAKMONT CHURCH OF GOD
SHREVEPORT, LOUISIANA

CAROLYN'S CRAB DIP

1 1/2 pounds crabmeat (imitation works
  just as well)
1 medium onion
6 ounces of sour cream
6 ounces of cream cheese
1/2 cup Kraft Parmesan cheese
Pinch of garlic salt
1 loaf French bread

Chop up the crabmeat and set it aside. Dice the onion. Mix all the ingredients except the bread in a medium saucepan over medium heat and stir until the Parmesan cheese melts. Cut the bread into cubes and serve.

Note: My mother-in-law, Carolyn, is a caterer. This is her most frequently requested appetizer.

MERRY DETRICK
NORTHBROOK UNITED METHODIST CHURCH
ROSWELL, GEORGIA

TANGY CRAB DIP

1/4 cup mayonnaise
1 tablespoon prepared mustard
1 tablespoon Worcestershire sauce
1 teaspoon lemon juice
Dash of seasoned salt
Dash of hot sauce
1/2 pound fresh crabmeat, drained and
  flaked

Combine the first 6 ingredients, mixing well. Stir in the crabmeat. Serve with assorted crackers. Makes 1 1/2 cups.

SUSAN STARLING
NORTHBROOK UNITED METHODIST CHURCH
ROSWELL, GEORGIA

CARAMEL APPLE DIP

1 (8-ounce) package cream cheese, softened
1 cup brown sugar
1 teaspoon vanilla
2 teaspoons milk
1/4 cup sugar

Combine all the ingredients in a blender or food processor and blend until smooth and creamy. It makes a great dip for tart apples.

KAROLYN MCFADDEN
CALVARY UNITED METHODIST CHURCH
TAYLOR, NEBRASKA

FRUIT DIP

1 cup sour cream
1/2 cup coconut
1/2 cup chopped pecans
1 cup raspberry yogurt

Combine all the ingredients in a bowl and serve with fresh fruit.

Note: This fruit dip recipe is from my good friend Debbie Meadows. She is one of the best cooks that I know!

MARY PAT TEMPLETON
NORTHBROOK UNITED METHODIST CHURCH
ROSWELL, GEORGIA

FRESH SALSA

2 ripe tomatoes, chopped
1/2 onion, chopped
1 tablespoon fresh cilantro, chopped
1/4 teaspoon basil leaves
Juice of 1/2 lime
1 tomatillo, chopped
1 jalapeño pepper, chopped

Chop all the ingredients in the order given. Mix. Keep refrigerated. Makes a cupful.

BONNIE EARL
MCCLAVE UNITED METHODIST CHURCH
MCCLAVE, COLORADO

CROSTINI WITH TAPENADE

1 (8-ounce) loaf baguette-style French bread
2 to 3 tablespoons olive oil
Freshly ground black pepper

TAPENADE:
1/2 cup pimiento-stuffed green olives
1/2 cup kalamata olives, pitted
1 tablespoon olive oil
1 tablespoon Dijon-style mustard
2 teaspoons balsamic vinegar
1 garlic clove, minced
1/2 cup tomatoes, finely chopped
2 tablespoons green onion, thinly sliced

Preheat the oven to 425 degrees. For the crostini, cut the bread into 1/2-inch slices. Lightly brush both sides of each slice with olive oil and sprinkle with pepper. Place on an ungreased baking sheet. Bake for 7 minutes or until crisp and slightly browned, turning once.

Place the first 6 tapenade ingredients in a blender or food processor. Cover and blend until nearly smooth, scraping down the sides of the container as necessary. Stir in the tomatoes and green onion. Top the toasted bread with the tapenade mixture. Serve immediately.

Note: Karen served them separately—"do it yourself style."

KAREN POPMA
SUBMITTED BY DOROTHY SANDERS
CROSS IN THE DESERT UNITED METHODIST CHURCH
PHOENIX, ARIZONA

CRACKER JACKS

just for kids!

2 sticks butter
2 cups brown sugar
1/2 cup Karo syrup
Pinch of salt
1/2 teaspoon soda
2 quarts popped corn

Mix butter, brown sugar, syrup, and salt. Stir and boil 5 minutes. Add soda. Pour over two quarts popped corn and bake 1 hour at 200 degrees.

MRS. ALMETA RUPPEL
CALVARY UNITED METHODIST CHURCH
TAYLOR, NEBRASKA

Savory Garlicky Popcorn

2 tablespoons honey
2 tablespoons tomato paste
1 teaspoon garlic powder
1/4 teaspoon chili powder
1/4 teaspoon paprika
6 cups air-popped popcorn

Preheat the oven to 200 degrees. In a 1-quart saucepan, combine the honey, tomato paste, garlic powder, chili powder, and paprika. Cook over medium heat, stirring frequently, until fragrant, about 3 minutes.

Place the popcorn in a large bowl. Drizzle with the honey mixture and toss to coat lightly. Spread the mixture on a large, ungreased, nonstick baking sheet. Bake for 15 minutes, stirring occasionally. Turn the oven off and let stand with door closed for 1 hour; this helps the coating to stick.

DENISE ORTON
TOWER HILL UNITED METHODIST CHURCH
TOWER HILL, ILLINOIS

Cheese Wafers

1/2 pound butter or margarine
1/2 pound grated sharp cheese
2 scant cups sifted all-purpose flour
Dash of red pepper
Dash of garlic salt
Dash of Worcestershire sauce

Preheat the oven to 375 degrees. Let the butter and grated cheese stand at room temperature for about an hour before mixing with the remainder of the ingredients into a stiff dough. You may use a cookie press or make small balls and flatten them to form wafers. Bake for 10 to 12 minutes.

KASI WALKER
CAVENDISH BAPTIST CHURCH
CAVENDISH, VERMONT

Party Cheese Ball

2 (8-ounce) packages cream cheese
1/2 cup crumbled blue cheese (about 4 ounces)
1 cup shredded sharp Cheddar cheese
1 small onion, finely chopped
1 tablespoon Worcestershire sauce
Chili powder or finely chopped fresh parsley

Place the cheeses in a small bowl. Let stand until soft. In a mixer, beat the onion and Worcestershire sauce on low speed until fluffy. Cover and refrigerate overnight. Shape the mixture into one large ball (or 2 small balls) and roll in chili powder or parsley.

VERA HOLMES
CALVARY UNITED METHODIST CHURCH
TAYLOR, NEBRASKA

CHEESE TOAST

1 slice bread
1 slice cheese

Put the cheese on the bread. Place the sandwich in the oven on broil. When the timer dings, take it out and eat it.

MARCUS BRISCO
FIRST GRADE
HOLUM BAPTIST CHURCH
GRAYSON, LOUISIANA

BOURSIN CHEESE BALLS (DELICIOUS CRACKER SPREAD)

8 ounces butter, unsalted
16 ounces cream cheese
2 garlic cloves
1/4 teaspoon salt
1 teaspoon dried oregano
1/4 teaspoon dried thyme
1/4 teaspoon dried marjoram
1/4 teaspoon dried dill
1/4 teaspoon black pepper
1/4 teaspoon dried basil

Let the cheese and butter soften to room temperature. Crush the garlic with the salt to form a paste. Stir in the herbs and spices. Chill before using. If using salted butter, omit the 1/4 teaspoon salt.

Note: I usually use even more garlic because I love the garlic flavor! You can also shape the cheese mixture into balls and freeze them for later use.

MARY PERRY
UNITED BAPTIST CHURCH OF POULTNEY
EAST POULTNEY, VERMONT

CHEESE STRAWS

1/2 pound sharp Cheddar cheese, grated
1/2 pound plus 2 tablespoons margarine or
   butter, softened
1/2 pound (2 1/2 cups) all-purpose flour
1/2 teaspoon salt
Cayenne pepper

Preheat the oven to 300 degrees. Cream the softened margarine. Add the grated cheese, then the flour and salt. Reduce the amount of flour if the mixture seems too dry. Roll out into a thin dough. Use fork tines to create a ridged texture. Cut into strips about 1 inch wide and 2 1/2 inches long. Carefully transfer the straws to a cookie sheet. Sprinkle with cayenne pepper. Bake for 20 minutes. Don't allow to brown. Be generous with the cayenne pepper if you like spicy snacks.

Note: These are a Christmas tradition at our house.

JAN OWENS
NORTHBROOK UNITED METHODIST CHURCH
ROSWELL, GEORGIA

CHEESY BACON BITES

1 (3-ounce) package cream cheese, softened
1/4 cup real bacon pieces
2 tablespoons chopped onion
1/8 teaspoon ground black pepper
1 (8-ounce) package refrigerated crescent
  rolls

Preheat the oven to 350 degrees. Combine the cream cheese, bacon, onion, and pepper in a bowl. Separate the crescent rolls into two rectangles. Pinch the seams together. Spread cheese mixture on each rectangle. Roll up, starting at the longest side, and seal. Cut each roll into 16 slices. Place the slices cut side down on ungreased cookie sheet. Bake for 15 minutes or until golden brown. Serve warm. Yields 32 appetizers.

MELISSA CLARK
WELLINGTON VILLAGE ASSEMBLY OF GOD
LITTLE ROCK, ARKANSAS

CHEESY POTATO SKINS

3 medium baking potatoes
Vegetable oil
Seasoned salt
1 cup (4 ounces) shredded Cheddar cheese
6 slices bacon, cooked and crumbled
Sour cream

Preheat the oven to 400 degrees. After scrubbing the potatoes well, rub the skins with oil. Bake at 400 degrees for 1 hour, or until done. Let the potatoes cool to the touch. Cut in half lengthwise. Carefully scoop out the pulp, leaving 1/4 to 1/8 inch shells. Cut the shells in half crosswise and deep-fry in hot oil at 375 degrees for 2 minutes, or until lightly browned. Drain on paper towels. Place the skins on a baking sheet. Sprinkle with salt, cheese, and bacon. Place under the broiler until the cheese melts. Serve with sour cream. Makes 1 dozen.

REBECCA HENSLEY
HIGHLAND HEIGHTS PRESBYTERIAN CHURCH
CORDOVA, TENNESSEE

DEVILED EGGS

6 hard-boiled eggs
1/2 teaspoon salt
1/4 teaspoon black pepper
1/2 teaspoon mustard
3 tablespoons mayonnaise
1/2 teaspoon vinegar
Paprika

Place the eggs in a saucepan and cover with cold water. Heat to boiling. Reduce the heat to a simmer and cook for 15 to 20 minutes. Immediately crack the shells and plunge the eggs into cold water to prevent further cooking and darkening of the yolks. Peel the eggs. Cut each egg in half lengthwise. Remove the yolks and mash them with a fork. Add the seasonings. Spoon the mixture back into the egg whites, heaping up slightly. Dust lightly with paprika.

BETTY GRAMLING
OAKMONT CHURCH OF GOD
SHREVEPORT, LOUISIANA

YOGURT DEVILED EGGS

6 hard-boiled eggs
1/4 cup plain yogurt
1 teaspoon dried minced onion
1 teaspoon dried parsley flakes
1 teaspoon lemon juice
3/4 teaspoon prepared mustard
1/4 teaspoon salt
1/4 teaspoon Worcestershire sauce
1/8 teaspoon black pepper
Paprika (optional)

Cut the hard-boiled eggs in half lengthwise. Remove the yolks and set the whites aside. In a small bowl, mash the yolks. Stir in the next eight ingredients. Refill the egg whites using about 1 tablespoon of yolk mixture for each. Sprinkle with paprika, if desired. Makes 1 dozen.

MCCLAVE UNITED METHODIST CHURCH
MCCLAVE, COLORADO

Fresh Tomato Parmesan Appetizer

1 loaf baguette-style French bread
Roma or another plum tomato
Parmesan cheese, grated
Salt and pepper
Garlic powder
Olive oil

Cut the bread into thin slices with a sharp serrated knife. On each slice, place one thin slice of tomato, grated Parmesan, salt and pepper to taste, and a dash of garlic powder. Drizzle a small amount of olive oil over the tops. Broil until warm and the cheese is heated. Serve warm.

Note: These appetizers are simple but delicious. You can top them with shredded basil or parsley, and substitute Mozzarella cheese for the Parmesan. They look nicest with thin round slices of tomato.

FAMILY HEIRLOOM
FOREST AVENUE CONGREGATIONAL CHURCH
BANGOR, MAINE

Veggie Sticks and Pesto Sauce

4 ribs celery, cut into sticks
4 carrots, peeled and cut into sticks
1 large red pepper, seeded and cut into strips
8 thin scallions, trimmed
1/2 zucchini, cut into strips
1/2 cup fresh basil leaves
1/2 cup parsley
1 garlic clove
Lemon juice
1/3 cup walnut pieces
1/4 cup grated Parmesan cheese
1 cup olive oil
Salt and pepper

Cut and arrange the veggie sticks on a platter. In a blender, combine the basil, parsley, garlic, and lemon juice. Grind into a paste. Add the nuts and cheese and mix. Pulse in the oil, a little at a time, until well combined. Add salt and pepper to taste. Put the mixture into a bowl and serve with the veggies.

FAITH
FOREST AVENUE CONGREGATIONAL CHURCH
BANGOR, MAINE

SEAFOOD-STUFFED MUSHROOMS

3/4 pound medium-large mushrooms
8 tablespoons melted butter or margarine
6 tablespoons soft bread crumbs
2 tablespoons chopped chives
1/8 teaspoon ground white pepper
2 eggs, lightly beaten
1/2 pound lump crabmeat
2 tablespoons chopped onion
2 tablespoons mayonnaise
1 teaspoon lemon juice

Preheat the oven to 375 degrees. Remove the stems from the mushrooms caps. Finely chop the stems and set aside. Brush the caps with 7 tablespoons of butter, reserving 1 tablespoon. Arrange the caps on a lightly greased baking sheet. In a small bowl, combine the remaining ingredients, reserving 2 tablespoons of the bread crumbs along with the remaining 1 tablespoon of butter. Fill each mushroom cap with the mixture. Combine the reserved butter and bread crumbs and sprinkle over the stuffed mushrooms. Bake for 15 minutes.

DOROTHY ROSS
MATTAPOISETT CONGREGATIONAL CHURCH
MATTAPOISETT, MASSACHUSETTS

SPINACH-STUFFED PORTOBELLO MUSHROOMS

4 fresh portobello mushrooms (3 to 4 inches)
1/4 cup chopped onion
1 package frozen spinach, thawed, drained, and squeezed dry
2 ounces Feta cheese
1 large egg
1/2 cup sour cream
1/2 teaspoon garlic salt
1/2 cup dry stuffing mix
Parmesan cheese

Clean the mushrooms and remove the stems. Set the caps aside. Chop the stems and place in a microwave-safe bowl. Add the onion and microwave on high for 2 minutes. Add the spinach and Feta cheese. Preheat the oven to 350 degrees.

In small bowl, beat together the egg, sour cream, and garlic salt. Add this to the mushroom mixture and stir. Stir in the stuffing mix. The mixture should be moist, not runny. Add slightly more stuffing if needed. Put 1/4 of the mixture into each mushroom cap. Place on a nonstick cookie sheet. Sprinkle with Parmesan cheese. Bake for 40 minutes.

AMY LUCIDI
FIRST UNITED METHODIST CHURCH
BELLEVILLE, MICHIGAN

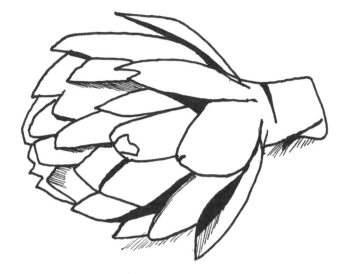

SHRIMP AND ARTICHOKE VINAIGRETTE

1 cup oil
1/2 cup olive oil
1/2 cup wine vinegar
2 tablespoons Dijon mustard
2 tablespoons chopped chives
2 tablespoons minced scallions
1/2 teaspoon salt
1/2 teaspoon sugar
Dash of pepper
1 1/2 pounds cooked shrimp
1 (15-ounce) can artichoke hearts, chopped

Blend the first 9 ingredients in a food processor. Pour over the shrimp and artichokes and marinate in the refrigerator for at least 6 hours. When ready to serve, drain off the marinade. Pour the mixture into a chilled bowl and have toothpicks to skewer the shrimp and artichokes.

Note: My mother has been making this appetizer for as long as I can remember.

SUSAN JONES
NORTHBROOK UNITED METHODIST CHURCH
ROSWELL, GEORGIA

BARBECUED SHRIMP WITH LEMON

3 large garlic cloves, sliced
4 tablespoons butter or margarine
12 ounces raw shrimp, cleaned (about 1 1/2 pounds in shell)
Salt and pepper to taste
1/2 lemon, sliced paper-thin
Snipped parsley

Cook the garlic in the butter for 2 or 3 minutes. Line a shallow pan with foil (or use a shallow foil/ware pan); arrange the shrimp in a layer on the bottom. Sprinkle with salt and pepper. Place lemon slices over the shrimp; drizzle with the garlic butter. Sprinkle with parsley. Cook over hot coals for 6 to 8 minutes, turning frequently. Serves 3.

ROQUELE JONES
GRIFFIN CHAPEL UNITED METHODIST CHURCH
STARKVILLE, MISSISSIPPI

Festive Meatballs

1 pound lean ground meat
1/2 cup finely crushed bread crumbs
1 garlic clove, crushed
2 tablespoons finely chopped parsley
1/4 cup evaporated milk
1 egg, slightly beaten
1/2 teaspoon salt
All-purpose flour
1 (7-ounce) can green chili salsa
1 cup beef bouillon

Mix the beef with the bread crumbs, garlic, parsley, evaporated milk, egg, and salt. Form into about 30 small balls and roll in flour. Brown over medium heat in hot oil. Pour off any excess fat. Pour the salsa and bouillon over the meatballs. Cover and simmer for 10 minutes. Serve on toothpicks, or thicken the sauce and serve as a main dish.

BILLY RUTH ELLIOTT
HOLUM BAPTIST CHURCH
GRAYSON, LOUISIANA

Barbecued Meatballs

2 pounds ground beef
3 eggs
3 teaspoons parsley flakes
1 cup Parmesan cheese
Salt and pepper
3/4 cup chopped onion

Mix all the ingredients well and shape into meatballs. Place in a baking pan and bake for 15 to 20 minutes.

SAUCE:
1 cup barbecue sauce
1/2 cup brown sugar
1 teaspoon vinegar
1 (small) can tomato sauce
1/2 teaspoon chili powder
3 or 4 drops Worcestershire sauce

Mix well by hand or in a mixer at low speed. Heat and pour over the meatballs.

MAGALENE NELSON
BETHEL AME CHURCH
AUGUSTA, GEORGIA

Life Recipe

1 cup of good thoughts
1 cup of kind deeds
1 cup of consideration of others
2 cups of sacrifice for others
3 cups of forgiveness
3 cups of well beaten faults

Mix all ingredients thoroughly. Add tears of joy, sorrow and sympathy for others. Flavor with a little bit of love. Fold in 4 cups of prayer and faith. Pour into daily life and bake well with the heat of human kindness. Serve with a smile.

BECKY HARRISON
WESTSIDE BAPTIST CHURCH
ANTLERS, OKLAHOMA

Hot Dogs in Coca-Cola

just for kids!

1 pound hot dogs cut into bite-size pieces
(or the miniature franks)
1 (16 ounce) bottle Coca-Cola

Put bite-size hot dogs/franks into a heavy-bottomed pan and pour Coke over. Cook slowly, covered, until tender and glazed. Serve with your favorite crazy mustard.

Note: This isn't diet food!

BECKY GAYLOR
CROSS IN THE DESERT UNITED METHODIST CHURCH
PHOENIX, ARIZONA

Liver Pâté

1 pound chicken livers
4 hard-boiled eggs
1/4 pound butter
1 onion, grated
Dash of cayenne pepper
1 teaspoon salt
1/2 teaspoon ground nutmeg
1/2 teaspoon ground allspice

In a small saucepan, simmer the livers in enough water to cover for 20 minutes. Drain and place in a food chopper along with the eggs. Chop the eggs and liver coarsely. In a small skillet, melt the butter and lightly sauté the onion. Do not brown. Add to the meat. Stir in the remaining ingredients and pour the mixture into an oiled mold; refrigerate. It will set in about 1 hour. Serve with crackers or party rye bread. Makes 12 servings.

PRINCE OF PEACE CHURCH
GRANTSVILLE, WEST VIRGINIA

Pickle Relish

16 cups finely chopped cucumbers
10 medium onions, finely chopped
1 green bell pepper, finely chopped
1 red bell pepper, finely chopped
1/2 cup salt
2 tablespoons mustard seed
2 trays ice
5 cups vinegar
5 cups sugar
1/2 teaspoon ground cloves
1 teaspoon celery seed

Place the chopped cucumbers, onions, and peppers in a large container. Sprinkle with salt. Add ice and cover. Let stand for 3 hours. Drain well. Add the remaining ingredients. Place over low heat and stir until the mixture comes to the scalding point. While the mixture is very hot, spoon it into hot jars and seal with lids that have been boiled and are hot. Makes 8 pints.

Note: Cucumbers and onions can be chopped to the desired size in a food processor. It is best if peppers are chopped by hand.

PAULA NEALY
HOLUM BAPTIST CHURCH
GRAYSON, LOUISIANA

Adrian's Trail Mix

just for kids!

1 cup pretzels
1 cup Honey Nut Cheerios
1 cup cheese crackers
1 cup M&M's
1 cup peanuts
1 cup Corn Chex
1 cup Wheat Chex
1 little boy's hands

Use one little boy's hands to mix all the ingredients. Sit back and enjoy.

MARTHA GUNTER
HIGHLAND HEIGHTS PRESBYTERIAN CHURCH
CORDOVA, TENNESSEE

Reindeer Food

20 ounces white chocolate
4 cups Crispix
4 cups Cheerios
4 cups pretzels
1 package semi-sweet mini M & M's

Melt white chocolate in a double boiler or microwave. Pour over dry ingredients. Toss well. Add M & M's when chocolate has cooled slightly so when mixed they won't melt. Spread on waxed paper to harden. Break apart.

Note: Great for a cookie exchange.

JILL JOHNSON
NORTHBROOK UNITED METHODIST CHURCH
ROSWELL, GEORGIA

Trash

1 box Cheerios
1 box Rice Chex
1 box very thin pretzels
2 cups pecans
Worcestershire sauce
Garlic salt
Tabasco sauce
1 pint (2 cups) cooking oil
2 cups peanuts

Empty all the dry ingredients except peanuts into a large roaster; season with the Worcestershire sauce, garlic salt, Tabasco sauce, and two-thirds of the oil. Toast in a slow oven at 200 degrees for 1 hour, stirring every 15 minutes. At the end of the hour, add the nuts and the rest of the oil and continue to toast for another hour. When cool, store in an airtight container. Great nibbles.

FREDIA B. GOON
GRIFFIN CHAPEL UNITED METHODIST CHURCH
STARKVILLE, MISSISSIPPI

AUNTIE ANN'S PRETZELS

PRETZELS:
1 1/2 cups warm water
1 1/8 teaspoons active yeast (1 1/2 packages)
2 tablespoons brown sugar
1 1/8 teaspoons salt
1 cup bread flour
3 cups all-purpose flour
2 cups warm water
2 tablespoons baking soda
2 to 4 tablespoons butter, melted

TOPPINGS:
Butter
Coarse salt
Cinnamon
Sugar

Preheat the oven to 450 degrees. Pour the warm water into a mixing bowl and sprinkle the yeast over it; stir to dissolve. Add the sugar, salt, and stir to dissolve; add flours and knead the dough until it is smooth and elastic. Let rise for at least 1/2 hour.

While the dough is rising, prepare a baking soda water bath with 2 cups of warm water and 2 tablespoons of baking soda. Be sure to stir often. After the dough has risen, pinch off bits of dough and roll into long ropes (about 1/2 inch or less thick) and shape. Dip the pretzels into the soda solution and place on a greased baking sheet. Allow the pretzels to rise again. Bake for about 10 minutes, or until golden. Brush with melted butter and enjoy!

After you brush the pretzels with butter sprinkle them with coarse salt. Or for Auntie Ann's famous cinnamon sugar, melt a stick of butter in a shallow bowl (big enough to fit the entire pretzel); in another bowl, make a mixture of cinnamon and sugar. Dip the pretzel into the butter, coating both sides generously, then dip again into the cinnamon mixture.

DONNA FOOR
TOWER HILL UNITED METHODIST CHURCH
TOWER HILL, ILLINOIS

Soups

We thank you, Lord, for happy hearts
For rain and sunny weather.
We thank you for the food we eat,
And that we are together.

First United Methodist Church,
Belleville, Michigan

CHICKEN NOODLE SOUP

1 medium green pepper, chopped
1/2 medium carrot, diced
1/2 medium onion, chopped fine
1/2 cup chopped celery
2 garlic cloves, chopped
3 tablespoons butter
2 quarts chicken broth
1/8 teaspoon hot sauce
1/2 teaspoon Worcestershire sauce
Salt and pepper to taste
1 cup raw egg noodles
2 tablespoons chopped pimiento
1 cup diced cooked chicken or 1 whole
   chicken

In a large saucepan, sauté the green pepper, carrot, onion, celery, and garlic in melted butter or margarine until tender. Add the chicken broth and seasonings; simmer for 10 minutes. Cook the noodles in boiling salted water till tender; drain and add to the chicken broth. Add pimiento and chicken; simmer for 10 minutes longer. Makes 8 to 10 servings.

ADDIE B. JONES
GRIFFIN CHAPEL UNITED METHODIST CHURCH
STARKVILLE, MISSISSIPPI

CHICKEN CURRY SOUP

1 tablespoon butter
1 teaspoon curry powder
3/4 tablespoon all-purpose flour
1 1/2 cups chicken broth
Paprika to taste
1 egg yolk
1/4 cup rich milk or cream
1/2 cup or so of cooked chicken, cut in slivers
Chopped chives for garnish

Melt the butter in a large saucepan. Add the curry powder. Add the flour and blend well. Slowly stir in the broth and bring to a boil. When boiling, add paprika. Reduce the heat to a simmer. Beat the egg yolk and milk together. When the broth mixture has stopped boiling, slowly whisk in the milk mixture. Stir over low heat until thickened. Add slivers of chicken. Can be served hot or cold, garnished with chives.

PAT FAST
UNITED BAPTIST CHURCH OF POULTNEY
EAST POULTNEY, VERMONT

ZESTY MEXICAN SOUP

2 cups cubed cooked chicken
1 large can chicken broth
1 (11.5-ounce) can tomato juice
1 large can Green Giant Mexicorn (whole-
    kernel golden sweet corn with red and
    green sweet peppers, undrained)
1 cup salsa
1 (4-ounce) can chopped green chilies,
    drained
1/4 cup chopped fresh cilantro

In a large saucepan, combine all the ingredients and bring to a boil. Reduce the heat and simmer for 10 minutes, or until the soup is thoroughly heated.

MIRACLE DELIVERANCE HOLINESS CHURCH
COLUMBIA, SOUTH CAROLINA

SPICY CHICKEN-TOMATO SOUP

2 (14 1/2-ounce) cans chicken broth
3 cups cubed cooked chicken
2 cups frozen corn
1 (10 3/4-ounce) can tomato puree
1 (10-ounce) can diced tomatoes and green
    chilies
1 large onion, chopped
2 garlic cloves, minced
1 teaspoon ground cumin
1 teaspoon salt
1 teaspoon chili powder
1/8 teaspoon black pepper
1/8 teaspoon cayenne pepper
1 bay leaf

Combine all the ingredients in a slow cooker. Cover and simmer for 4 hours. Discard the bay leaf when the soup is cooked. Serve with crackers, corn muffins, or cornbread. Makes 8 servings.

BETTY GRAMLING
OAKMONT CHURCH OF GOD
SHREVEPORT, LOUISIANA

CREAM OF CHICKEN AND WILD RICE SOUP

1 1/2 sticks butter
1 large onion, chopped
3 cups chopped celery
2 cups sliced mushrooms
1/4 cup all-purpose flour
Salt and pepper to taste
2 1/2 cups whole milk
1 1/2 cups half-and-half
1 package long-grain wild rice, cooked
1 1/2 cups chicken, cooked and shredded

In a large saucepan, sauté the onion and celery in 1 stick of butter until tender. Add the mushrooms and cook until tender. In a Dutch oven, melt the remaining butter and blend in the flour and the salt and pepper. Cook for 1 minute, stirring constantly. Slowly add the milk and half-and-half, cooking over medium heat until thickened. Add the mushroom mixture, rice, and the shredded chicken. Simmer for approximately 15 to 20 minutes.

Note: This soup is very rich and creamy.

SUSAN JONES
NORTHBROOK UNITED METHODIST CHURCH
ROSWELL, GEORGIA

TURKEY SOUP

2 medium carrots, sliced (about 2 cups)
2 medium celery stalks, sliced (about 1 cup)
1 medium yellow onion, chopped (about 1 cup)
4 garlic cloves, minced
1 medium tomato, seeded and chopped (about 1 cup)
4 cups chicken broth
1/2 cup frozen whole-kernel corn
1 teaspoon dried thyme
1/4 teaspoon black pepper
2 cups cubed cooked turkey
2 tablespoons chopped parsley

Spray a large saucepan with vegetable cooking spray; heat the saucepan over medium-high heat. Add the carrots, celery, and onion. Cook, stirring, until the vegetables are tender, about 7 minutes. Add the garlic, tomato, broth, corn, thyme, and black pepper to the saucepan. Bring to a boil. Reduce the heat to low and let the soup simmer until the vegetables are cooked through, about 15 minutes. Stir in the turkey and parsley. Cook, stirring, until heated through, about 5 minutes.

JEANNETTE VANOVER
NORTH MONROE STREET CHURCH OF GOD
MONROE, MICHIGAN

Happy Home Recipe

4 cups love
2 cups loyalty
4 quarts faith
2 tablespoons tenderness
2 tablespoons kindness
2 tablespoons understanding
3 cups forgiveness
1 cup friendship
5 tablespoons hope
1 barrel laughter

Take love and loyalty and mix them thoroughly with faith. Blend the mixture with tenderness, kindness, understanding, and forgiveness. Add friendship and hope. Sprinkle abundantly with laughter. Bake with sunshine and serve generous helpings daily.

SENIOR NEWSLETTER
HANOVER TOWNSHIP, PENNSYLVANIA

Grandma's Best Turkey Soup

1 turkey carcass
1 bouquet garni (6 peppercorns, 1 bay
  leaf, and 4 whole cloves tied in a piece of
  cheesecloth)
2 cups cubed cooked turkey
Water
1 to 2 chicken bouillon cubes
1 cup chopped celery
2 carrots, sliced
1 onion, sliced
Salt

Remove the meat from the turkey carcass and set aside. Crack the bones and place in a kettle with the skin and the bouquet garni. Cover with water, add the bouillon cubes, and simmer for 2 hours. Cool slightly. Remove the bones and bouquet garni by straining. Add the meat and vegetables to the stock and chill. Skim off the fat. Add salt to taste and simmer until hot.

Note: Chicken carcass and meat can be substituted for the turkey. For a heartier soup, increase the amount of celery and carrots, and add green beans and some cubed rutabaga.

SUE CLAIRE CALLESIS
UNITED BAPTIST CHURCH OF POULTNEY
EAST POULTNEY, VERMONT

CARROT SOUP

5 tablespoons butter
2 onions, chopped
2 medium potatoes, cubed
2 pounds carrots, sliced
6 cups chicken broth
3 teaspoons curry powder
Freshly ground black pepper to taste

In a large (4-quart) saucepan, melt half of the butter; add the onions and cook, stirring occasionally, for 10 minutes. Add the potatoes, carrots, broth, and curry powder. Bring to a boil and simmer for 45 minutes. Puree in a blender, adding pepper and the remaining butter. Serve immediately. Makes 8 to 10 servings.

PHIL POPE
UNITED BAPTIST CHURCH OF POULTNEY
EAST POULTNEY, VERMONT

BUTTERNUT SQUASH SOUP

4 tablespoons olive oil
4 tablespoons butter
6 shallots, minced
1 tablespoon fresh rosemary, chopped
3 1/2 pounds butternut squash, chopped (8 cups)
3/4 pound parsnips, chopped (2 1/2 cups)
7 cups chicken broth
1 cup heavy cream
Salt and pepper to taste

In a large saucepan, mix the oil and butter until the butter melts. Add the shallots and rosemary; sauté for 2 minutes. Add the squash and parsnips; cover and cook for 20 minutes. Stir thoroughly, add the broth, and bring to a boil. Reduce the heat to medium and cook, covered, until the vegetables are tender. Puree the soup in a food processor, add the cream and salt and pepper, and blend well. Reheat and serve.

CINDY WAGNER
UNITED BAPTIST CHURCH OF POULTNEY
EAST POULTNEY, VERMONT

HEARTY CORN CHOWDER

2 tablespoons bacon fat or cooking oil
1 large onion, chopped
4 medium potatoes, cut up
2 tablespoons all-purpose flour
2 teaspoons salt
1/4 teaspoon black pepper
1/2 teaspoon thyme
2 to 3 cups water
1 can whole-kernel corn
1 can creamed corn
1 can evaporated milk
Bacon bits

Put the fat in a heavy deep saucepan; add the onion and potatoes. Sprinkle with the flour, salt, pepper, and thyme and mix well. Add water to cover; bring to a boil and cook, stirring occasionally, until the onions and potatoes are tender. Stir in the corn and slowly add the milk. Heat but do not boil. Serve with bacon bits sprinkled on top.

MOLLIE HORTON
UNITED BAPTIST CHURCH OF POULTNEY
EAST POULTNEY, VERMONT

VEGETABLE BEEF SOUP

1 1/2 pounds beef stew meat
1 cup chopped celery
1/2 cup chopped onion
2 bay leaves
1 teaspoon salt
1/2 teaspoon black pepper
1 cup chopped cabbage
4 carrots, sliced into rounds
2 pounds canned Italian tomatoes
4 potatoes, cubed

Place the meat in a 3-quart saucepan and cover with water. Add the celery, onion, bay leaves, salt, and pepper. Bring to a boil, then reduce the heat to a simmer. Cook for 2 hours, adding more water if necessary. Test the beef for doneness and add the remaining vegetables, cooking until they are tender but not mushy.

GENEVIEVE LORD
PINEMOUNT BAPTIST CHURCH
MCALPIN, FLORIDA

Spicy Pumpkin Soup (with Mexican Cream and Toasted Pepitas)

3 tablespoons butter
3 cups finely chopped onions
1 1/2 (15-ounce) cans solid pack pumpkin
1 cup whole milk
3/4 teaspoon crushed red pepper flakes
2 1/2 cups chicken broth
Salt to taste
Sour cream
3/4 cup shelled pumpkin seeds (pepitas),
  toasted

In a large saucepan, melt the butter over medium heat. Add the onions and sauté for about 10 minutes. Add the pumpkin, milk, and red pepper and stir. Remove the pot from the stove, pour the mixture into a food processor, and puree. Return the pureed mixture to the pot and add the chicken broth. Simmer for 10 minutes to allow the flavors to blend, stirring occasionally. Season with salt and ladle soup into bowls. Add a dollop of sour cream and sprinkle with the pumpkin seeds. Makes 7 servings.

TRINITY UNITED METHODIST CHURCH
HUDSON, NEW YORK

Beef and Vegetable Soup

1 pound ground beef
1 cup chopped onion
6 cups water
1 (28-ounce) can diced tomatoes, undrained
1 cup chopped celery
1 cup chopped carrot
1 cup chopped turnip
1 cup chopped potato
1 tablespoon parsley flakes
2 beef bouillon cubes
1/4 teaspoon garlic powder
1 teaspoon oregano
1 teaspoon salt
1/2 teaspoon pepper
1/2 teaspoon basil
1/2 teaspoon Worcestershire sauce
1 cup macaroni, uncooked

In a Dutch oven or soup kettle, cook the beef and onion until the meat is no longer pink; drain if necessary. Add the water, vegetables, and seasonings; bring to a boil. Reduce the heat and simmer for 30 minutes, or until the vegetables are almost done. Add the macaroni and simmer for 15 minutes, or until the macaroni and vegetables are tender.

JOY STEWART
MEMORIAL BAPTIST CHURCH
TULSA, OKLAHOMA

MINESTRONE SOUP

1 large onion, chopped
2 tablespoons vegetable oil
8 (14-ounce) cans vegetable broth
1 package frozen green beans
3 carrots, sliced
2 small zucchini, halved and sliced
2 cups chopped green cabbage
1 (28-ounce) can chopped tomatoes in juice
1 teaspoon basil
1 teaspoon thyme
1 teaspoon oregano
1/2 teaspoon crushed red pepper flakes
Salt and pepper to taste
1 (15-ounce) can red kidney beans
1/4 cup dry barley

In a large saucepan, sauté the onion in the oil until its tender. Add the remaining ingredients, omitting the kidney beans. Bring to a boil. Reduce the heat to low. Cover and simmer for 20 minutes, or until the vegetables are tender. Add the kidney beans and heat through.

MARY GERGEL
FIRST UNITED METHODIST CHURCH
BELLEVILLE, MICHIGAN

MUSHROOM SOUP

1 quart mushrooms
1 1/2 quarts good, rich stock (veal or
    chicken)
1 tablespoon all-purpose flour
1 tablespoon butter, melted
1 teaspoon salt
1/2 teaspoon black pepper
Whipped cream (optional)
Croutons

Wash and dice the mushrooms. Place the mushrooms in a large saucepan and add the 1 1/2 quarts of stock. Thicken the stock by making a paste of the flour and butter; add the salt and pepper. At the last moment, add a bit of whipped cream, if desired, and the croutons.

DEBBIE VOLENTINE
HOLUM BAPTIST CHURCH
GRAYSON, LOUISIANA

CHILI SOUP

1 pound ground beef
1/2 cup chopped green pepper
1/2 cup chopped onion
1 tablespoon chili powder
2 cans Campbell's chili beef soup
1 soup can water
1 cup chopped canned tomatoes

In a large saucepan, brown the beef; add the green pepper, onion, and chili powder and cook until the vegetables are tender. Stir in the remaining ingredients. Heat through, stirring occasionally. Makes about 6 1/2 cups.

TOLLIE VOLENTINE
HOLUM BAPTIST CHURCH
GRAYSON, LOUISIANA

HUNGARIAN MUSHROOM SOUP

2 cups chopped onion
4 tablespoons butter
1 teaspoon salt
12 ounces sliced mushrooms
1 teaspoon dill weed
2 1/2 cups water
1 tablespoon soy sauce
3 tablespoons all-purpose flour
1 cup milk
2 tablespoons lemon juice
1/2 cup sour cream
1 tablespoon paprika
Salt and pepper to taste

In a large saucepan, sauté the onion in 2 tablespoons of butter, adding the salt. Add the mushrooms, dill, 1/2 cup of water, and soy sauce. Simmer for 15 minutes. In another pan, melt the remaining 2 tablespoons butter. Stir in the flour, then the milk. Heat until thickened. Add the flour mixture to the mushroom mixture, stirring in the remaining water. Cover and simmer for 10 to 15 minutes. Add the lemon juice, sour cream, paprika, and salt and pepper to taste.

RICHARD ARENDS
FIRST UNITED METHODIST CHURCH
BELLEVILLE, MICHIGAN

FRESH TOMATO SOUP WITH TORTELLINI

1 large onion, chopped
2 tablespoons margarine
2 pounds ripe tomatoes (about 6 medium),
    peeled, seeded, and chopped
3 cups chicken broth
1 (8-ounce) can tomato sauce
1 tablespoon fresh sage or 1 teaspoon dried
    sage, crushed
1/4 teaspoon salt
Dash of pepper
4 ounces dried tortellini or frozen cheese
    tortellini
1/4 cup finely shredded Parmesan cheese

In a large saucepan, sauté the onion in margarine until it's tender. Add the tomatoes, broth, tomato sauce, sage, salt, and pepper. Bring to a boil and reduce the heat. Cover and simmer for 30 minutes. Cool slightly. Meanwhile, cook the tortellini according to the package directions. Press the tomato mixture through a food mill or blend in a blender or food processor until smooth. Return the tomato mixture to the saucepan. Add the cooked and drained tortellini; heat through. Spoon the soup into bowls and sprinkle with Parmesan cheese. Makes 4 servings.

MARIANNE RAKER
NORTHBROOK UNITED METHODIST CHURCH
ROSWELL, GEORGIA

FRESH TOMATO SOUP

1 tablespoon oil
3/4 cup minced onion
2 garlic cloves, minced
1 tablespoon chopped basil
1 teaspoon minced thyme
5 cups diced tomatoes
1 1/2 cups vegetable or chicken broth
2 1/2 tablespoons tomato paste
2 teaspoons sugar
Salt and pepper to taste

In a large saucepan, heat the oil over medium heat. Add the onion, garlic, basil, and thyme. Cook, stirring frequently until the onions soften, about 5 minutes. Add the tomatoes and cook, for 5 minutes. Stir in the broth, tomato paste, and sugar. Season to taste with salt and pepper. Bring to a boil. Reduce the heat and simmer, uncovered, for 15 minutes. Blend the soup in a blender until smooth. Ladle into bowls and garnish with additional basil.

FAMILY HEIRLOOM
FOREST AVENUE CONGREGATIONAL CHURCH
BANGOR, MAINE

Hamburger Tomato Soup

1 to 2 pounds hamburger
1/2 cup onion, chopped
1/2 cup celery, chopped
1 large can tomato soup
1 can water
1/2 cup barley or oatmeal
1 can whole tomatoes

In a large saucepan, brown the hamburger with the onion and celery. Add the remaining ingredients and cook slowly until the barley is done.

Wendy Armstrong
Pitt Community Church
Baudette, Minnesota

Great Onion Soup

6 cups sliced onions
2 tablespoons olive oil
2 (14-ounce) cans beef broth
1 (14-ounce) can chicken broth
1/4 cup dry sherry
1 tablespoon Worcestershire sauce
1/2 teaspoon minced garlic
1/4 teaspoon thyme
Splash of burgundy
Croutons (optional)
Swiss cheese (optional)

Put the onions and olive oil in a Crock-Pot and cook on high for 8 to 10 hours. Add the remaining ingredients and heat to blend the flavors. Top with croutons and Swiss cheese, if desired.

Luanne Genga
First United Methodist Church
Belleville, Michigan

Onion Soup

10 large onions (2 1/2 pounds)
1/2 cup butter or margarine
1/4 cup all-purpose flour
4 quarts broth (beef or chicken)
1 cup dry white wine or 1/4 cup lemon juice
    plus 1/4 cup water
Salt and pepper

Condiments:
Shredded Gruyere or Swiss cheese
Seasoned croutons
Tomatoes, seeded and diced
Bacon, cooked and crumbled

Cut the onions in half vertically, then into thin vertical slices. Melt the butter in a large saucepan over medium-high heat. Add the onions, cover, and cook until limp, about 10 minutes. Uncover and cook, stirring often, until the onions are light brown, 20 to 25 minutes. If necessary, reduce the heat toward the end of cooking.

Sprinkle the flour over the onions; cook, stirring, for about 1 minute. Remove from the heat and add 2 quarts of broth. Return to the heat and add the wine, bring to boiling, and stir as needed. Cover, reduce the heat, and keep simmering for 30 to 40 minutes. If making ahead, cover and refrigerate.

Before serving, add the remaining broth and reheat slowly. Season to taste with salt and pepper. Serve. Offer your choice of condiments for each guest to add to his or her bowl of soup. Makes about 5 1/2 quarts.

Jan Wickliffe
Cross in the Desert United Methodist Church
Phoenix, Arizona

CURRIED CREAM OF ZUCCHINI SOUP

1 pound zucchini (about 1 medium)
2 tablespoons butter or margarine
1 garlic clove, minced
2 tablespoons finely chopped onion
1/2 teaspoon salt
1 to 2 teaspoons curry powder
1 cup chicken broth
1/2 cup milk or half-and-half
Chives or parsley, chopped

Scrub, then slice the unpeeled zucchini. Cook in the butter with the garlic, onion, salt, and curry powder until softish, about 20 minutes—but do not brown. Pour or spoon the mixture into a food processor with the chicken broth and process until smooth. Add the milk and heat again, but do not boil. Serve hot or chilled. Garnish with chopped chives or parsley.

NANCY BRAITMAYER
MATTAPOISETT CONGREGATIONAL CHURCH
MATTAPOISETT, MASSACHUSETTS

CREAM OF BROCCOLI SOUP

2 tablespoons butter
1 cup chopped onion
1/2 cup chopped celery
1 cup chicken stock
2 pounds frozen cut broccoli
1 pint whole milk
1 pint heavy cream
1/2 stick butter
2 bay leaves
Dash of Louisiana hot sauce
6 slices Canadian bacon, sliced into thin
    strips
2 tablespoons all-purpose flour
1/2 cup pepper cheese
Salt and pepper to taste

Heat the butter in a Dutch oven. Add the onion and celery; sauté until wilted. Add the chicken stock and bring to a boil. Add the broccoli. Cover and simmer for about 15 minutes. When the broccoli is tender, remove half of it and set aside. Add the milk, cream, and 1/2 stick butter. Stir constantly until it bubbles. Reduce the heat. Stir in the bay leaves, hot sauce, bacon, flour, and pepper cheese. When the soup is thoroughly blended, put the lid on and simmer for 45 minutes. Season with salt and pepper and add the reserved broccoli.

WAYNE LEVY
HUNGARIAN PRESBYTERIAN CHURCH
ALBANY, LOUISIANA

Loretta's Sweet Potato and Carrot Soup

4 tablespoons butter
1 large onion, finely chopped
2 large sweet potatoes, peeled and diced
5 large carrots, peeled and diced
1 tablespoon chopped fresh parsley
Juice of 1 lemon
3 3/4 cups vegetable stock
2 teaspoons salt
1 teaspoon black pepper
Sour cream (optional)

In a large saucepan, melt the butter and sauté the onion until it's transparent. Add the sweet potatoes and carrots. Reduce the heat to very low and cook for 10 to 15 minutes, stirring occasionally, until the vegetables are tender. Add the parsley, lemon juice, stock, and salt and pepper. Cover and simmer for 35 to 40 minutes. Allow to cool slightly, then pour into a blender or food processor and blend until the soup is fairly smooth but retains some texture. Return the soup to the pan and reheat it over very low heat until it's piping hot. Pour into bowls. Top each serving with a dollop of sour cream, if desired. Serve immediately. Makes 6 servings.

CHARLOTTE SNYDER
CAVENDISH BAPTIST CHURCH
CAVENDISH, VERMONT

Strawberry Soup

2 cups strawberries (cold)
1 cup low-fat buttermilk
1 tablespoon plus 1 teaspoon sugar
Mint leaves (optional)

In a food processor, blend the first three ingredients reserving mint leaves. Serve immediately or chill in the refrigerator. Garnish with mint leaves, if desired.

BERTHA DICKERMAN
CAVENDISH BAPTIST CHURCH
CAVENDISH, VERMONT

Gazpacho

4 cups tomato juice
1/2 medium onion, peeled and coarsely chopped
1 small green pepper, peeled, cored, seeded, and coarsely chopped
1 small cucumber, peeled, pared, seeded, and coarsely chopped
1/2 teaspoon Worcestershire sauce
1 garlic clove
1 drop hot pepper sauce
1/8 teaspoon cayenne pepper
1/4 teaspoon black pepper
2 tablespoons olive oil
1 large tomato, finely diced
2 tablespoons minced chives or scallion tops
1 lemon, cut into 6 wedges

Put 2 cups of tomato juice and the next 9 ingredients into a blender and puree. Slowly add the remaining 2 cups of tomato juice to the pureed mixture. Add the chopped tomato. Chill. Serve ice-cold in individual bowls garnished with chopped chives and lemon wedges.

EVELYN WOLFE
OAKMONT CHURCH OF GOD
SHREVEPORT, LOUISIANA

Onion Soup

1 quart beef bouillon or brown stock
3 tablespoons butter
3 cups thinly sliced yellow onions
1 teaspoon salt
1 tablespoon sugar
2 tablespoons all-purpose flour
1 cup shredded sharp cheese

Pour the bouillon into a Crock-Pot and turn on high. Cook covered. In the meantime, melt the butter in a large skillet and cook the onions, covered, for about 15 minutes, or until they are wilted. Uncover and add the salt, sugar, and flour. Stir well. Add the onion mixture to the bouillon. Cover and cook on low for 6 to 8 hours or on high for 3 hours. Before serving, add the shredded cheese. Allow the soup to cool before pouring it into bowls.

GARY MYERS
OAKMONT CHURCH OF GOD
SHREVEPORT, LOUISIANA

Pea and Ham Bone Soup

3 cups dried split peas
1 large onion
2 tablespoons bacon fat
1 ham bone (or ham chopped into bite-size
   pieces)
4 cups chicken stock
Salt and pepper to taste
1 1/2 cups milk
4 tablespoons chopped fresh mint (optional)

Cover the peas with water and leave them to soak overnight.

The next day, drain the peas and discard the water. Coarsely chop the onion. In a large saucepan, fry the chopped onion in the bacon fat for 3 minutes, or until soft (do not burn). Add the ham bone and pour in the stock. Bring to a boil and reduce the heat to a simmer. Now add the split peas. Bring to a boil again, and again reduce the heat. Simmer for 1 1/2 to 2 hours, stirring occasionally. Stir in the salt and pepper and the milk, and continue to simmer for another 10 minutes. Serve hot with garnish, if desired. Makes 6 to 8 servings.

KATHRYN TOBIN
CROSS IN THE DESERT UNITED METHODIST CHURCH
PHOENIX, ARIZONA

BLACK BEAN SOUP

1 medium onion, chopped
4 garlic cloves, minced
1 teaspoon red pepper flakes, or more to taste
2 tablespoons oil
3 cans black beans, with liquid
1 can chicken broth
3 cups chunky salsa

In a large saucepan, sauté the onion, garlic, and red pepper flakes in the oil until the onions are tender. In the meantime, add 1 can of beans to a blender with half of the broth and puree. Add to the onion mixture. Repeat this procedure with another can of beans and the rest of the chicken broth. Add the last can of beans and the salsa to the pot; stir. Bring the mixture to a boil, stirring constantly. Lower the heat and simmer for 1/2 hour. If you like, add a dollop of sour cream or yogurt after serving. Serve with chips or crackers.

GWEN SEPMOREE
BUCKINGHAM UNITED METHODIST CHURCH
GARLAND, TEXAS

GARDEN-FRESH CORN CHOWDER

3 slices bacon
1 cup sweet onion, chopped
1 tablespoon butter
1 tablespoon self-rising flour
1 teaspoon salt
1/4 teaspoon black pepper
1 cup chicken broth
1 cup water
2 cups red potatoes, diced
2 to 3 ears sweet corn
    kernels
1/2 cup evaporated
    milk

In a large saucepan, cook the bacon until crisp. Remove the bacon, drain and crumble it, and set it aside. Measure 2 tablespoons of bacon drippings into the pan. Add the onion and cook over medium heat until it's transparent. Add the butter, flour, salt, and pepper and stir until the mixture begins to simmer. Add the broth, water, and potatoes; cook until the potatoes are tender. Add the corn kernels and simmer for 10 minutes. Remove the chowder from the heat and add the milk and crumbled bacon.

PINEMOUNT BAPTIST CHURCH
MCALPIN, FLORIDA

CLAM CHOWDER

1 can condensed cream of potato soup
1 soup can of milk
1 tablespoon butter
1 can condensed New England clam
  chowder
1 can chopped or minced clams

In a medium saucepan, combine all the ingredients and heat and serve.

ARLENE GLICK
TOWER HILL UNITED METHODIST CHURCH
TOWER HILL, ILLINOIS

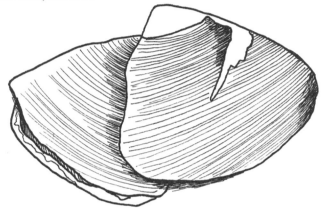

SEAFOOD CHOWDER

2 pounds fish (grouper, halibut)
4 slices bacon
1 small onion, diced
4 celery stalks, diced
1 large can diced tomatoes
10 large potatoes, diced
1 cup ketchup
1 lemon
4 pounds shelled, deveined shrimp
2 cans crab-claw meat
1 tablespoon cayenne
1 teaspoon garlic salt
1 tablespoon Worcestershire sauce
1 tablespoon Tabasco sauce
Pepper
1 teaspoon celery salt

In a 6-quart saucepan, boil the fish for about 10 to 15 minutes. Cool the fish, reserving the fish water for later use. Flake the fish. Fry the bacon until crisp and set aside. In the same pot, sauté the onion and celery until limp. Add the tomatoes, potatoes, ketchup, and fish water plus 2 additional cups of water. Cut half of the lemon into thin slices and add to the mixture. Squeeze the juice of the remaining lemon half into the mixture. Add the shrimp, crabmeat, flaked fish, crumbled bacon, and seasonings. Simmer for about 30 minutes to enhance flavoring. Serve with a salad and French bread. Makes 8 servings.

ANN GILL
MCCLAVE UNITED METHODIST CHURCH
MCCLAVE, COLORADO

SHELLFISH CHOWDER WITH FRESH THYME

2 (6.5-ounce) cans chopped clams with juice
3 ounces (1/2 cup) salt pork, chopped into
    small pieces
1 large onion, chopped
2 tablespoons all-purpose flour
1 cup water
1 pound red-skinned potatoes, unpeeled and
    cut in 1/2-inch pieces
2 tablespoons chopped fresh thyme, or 1
    tablespoon dried
1 bay leaf, broken in half
3 1/2 cups whole milk
10 ounces bay scallops
Salt to taste
1/2 teaspoon white pepper

Drain the clams and reserve the juice. Sauté the salt pork for about 7 minutes; drain on a paper towel. Sauté the onion in a small amount of fat for about 10 minutes until tender. Add the flour and stir for 1 minute. Gradually add the water and clam juice; bring to a boil. Stirring, add the potatoes, thyme, and bay leaf. Reduce the heat, cover, and simmer for about 15 minutes until the potatoes are tender. Discard the bay leaf. (This mixture can be made a day ahead by covering and chilling the chowder and salt pork separately.) If stored, bring the chowder to a simmer before continuing. Add the milk and bring back to a simmer while stirring. Add the scallops and reserved clams; cook for 2 minutes until opaque. Add the salt and pepper and garnish with salt pork.

DOROTHY ROSS
MATTAPOISETT CONGREGATIONAL CHURCH
MATTAPOISETT, MASSACHUSETTS

MAINE SEAFOOD CHOWDER

4 large potatoes, diced
1 onion, diced
1 teaspoon salt
1/4 cup butter
1/4 pound salt pork
1 1/2 pounds fresh scallops
2 pounds shelled, deveined shrimp
2 cups shucked clams
1 cup crabmeat
2 pounds haddock
1 can evaporated milk
Salt and pepper to taste

In a large saucepan, set the potatoes and onions to boil in enough water to cover. Add 1 teaspoon salt. Melt the butter on a low flame. Fry the salt pork and add the grease to the butter. Add the scallops, shrimp, clams, crab, and haddock to the butter and grease mixture. Simmer until all the seafood is cooked. Pour in the potatoes, onions, and evaporated milk. Season with salt and pepper to taste. Serve.

MARGIE LOBLEY
FOREST AVENUE CONGREGATIONAL CHURCH
BANGOR, MAINE

Shrimp and Corn Soup

1 (10-ounce) can diced tomatoes and green
    chilies
1 large onion, chopped
1 teaspoon minced garlic
1/2 cup all-purpose flour
4 cups water
2 pounds medium shrimp, shelled and
    coarsely chopped
1 (16-ounce) package frozen corn
1 (15-ounce) can cream-style corn
1 bunch scallions, sliced
1/4 cup chopped parsley
Salt and pepper to taste

Puree the tomatoes and green chilies in a food processor. In a large saucepan coated with nonstick cooking spray, sauté the onion and garlic over medium heat until tender, about 5 minutes. Sprinkle the flour over the mixture and stir. Gradually add the pureed tomatoes and chilies and the water, stirring to mix. Add the shrimp and corn. Bring to a boil. Lower the heat and continue cooking, stirring occasionally, for 5 to 7 minutes, or until the shrimp turn pink. Add the green onions and parsley. Season with salt and pepper.

Barbara Bolinger
Hungarian Presbyterian Church
Albany, Louisiana

Shrimp Gumbo

1 medium onion, chopped
3 tablespoons bacon drippings
3 tablespoons all-purpose flour
1 can tomato sauce
1/2 pound okra (frozen, fresh, or 1/2 can
    canned)
1/2 cup chopped celery
Few sprigs parsley
1 quart water
1 pound shrimp, shelled
1/2 teaspoon poultry seasoning
1/4 teaspoon pepper
1 teaspoon salt
2 teaspoons Worcestershire sauce

In a skillet, sauté the onion in the bacon drippings until the onion is limp. Add the flour and brown. Add the tomato sauce, okra (ends removed), celery, and parsley, stirring occasionally until the mixture is very thick. In the meantime, boil the water in a large saucepan. Pour the contents of the skillet into the boiling water. Add the shrimp and seasonings. Cook slowly for about 1 hour. Serve with cooked rice. More water may be added if necessary. Crabmeat may be added if desired. Makes 4 servings.

Note: This recipe belongs to my mother, Mrs. W. H. Pettey (Jeanel) of Gulfport, Mississippi.

Elizabeth Hubby
Northbrook United Methodist Church
Roswell, Georgia

CROCK-POT TACO SOUP

1 pound ground meat
1 (16-ounce) can whole tomatoes
1 (16-ounce) can corn
1 (16-ounce) can V-8 juice
1 (16-ounce) can red beans
1 package taco seasoning
1 large onion, chopped

Place all the ingredients in a Crock-Pot, put heat on low, and leave overnight or all day. This makes a "good meal" served on rice or with Fritos.

DURELLE DAVIS
HOLUM BAPTIST CHURCH
GRAYSON, LOUISIANA

TACO SOUP

1 pound ground chuck (optional)
1 can corn
2 (16-ounce) cans diced tomatoes
2 (8-ounce) cans tomato sauce
2 cans beans, chili hot
1 package taco seasoning
1 can Ro-Tel

Brown the ground chuck. Add the remaining ingredients and stir well. Simmer for about 30 minutes. Serve.

Note: You can add noodles, sour cream, green onions, grated cheese, or Fritos. It's impossible to botch this. It's a great recipe for Dad to cook, and it's perfect for potlucks or big crowds!

DANITA ZELINSKI
HIGHLAND HEIGHTS PRESBYTERIAN CHURCH
CORDOVA, TENNESSEE

COLD TOMATO SOUP

5 to 6 medium tomatoes, very ripe
1/2 to 3/4 Vidalia onion, thoroughly
  chopped
1/4 cup capers, with juice
1/3 cup balsamic vinegar
1/4 cup vegetable oil
Salt and pepper to taste
1/2 packet Sweet 'n Low or 1 teaspoon
  sugar

Core the tomatoes. Place them in a food processor and pulse until you get them chunky, not soupy. Pour the tomatoes into a large serving bowl and add the onion and capers. Mix well. Add the remaining ingredients and mix. Add more vinegar or pepper if necessary. Let sit overnight. Cover and refrigerate.

Note: For a different twist, add chopped cilantro.

BARBARA WHITAKER
NORTHBROOK UNITED METHODIST CHURCH
ROSWELL, GEORGIA

GREEK EGG LEMON SOUP

1 (10 1/2-ounce) can condensed chicken
  broth soup
1 soup can water
2 eggs
2 to 3 tablespoons lemon juice
1/2 to 3/4 cup cooked rice

In a saucepan, heat the soup and water to boiling. Reduce the heat to a low flame. In a small bowl, beat the eggs and lemon juice together. Pour a little of the soup into the egg mixture, stirring constantly. Add the rice. (The eggs will curdle if you stir too quickly.) Serve at once. Makes 3 cups of soup.

ESTHER SAMAKOURIS
DAMASCUS UNITED METHODIST CHURCH
DAMASCUS, MARYLAND

CRÈME VICHYSSOISE

3 medium leeks
3 tablespoons butter
3 medium potatoes, peeled and thinly sliced
3 cups water
2 chicken-flavored bouillon cubes
1 cup heavy cream
1 cup milk
1 teaspoon salt
1/4 teaspoon pepper

Cut the roots off the leeks and discard the tough leaves. Cut each leek lengthwise in half and rinse under cold running water to remove sand. Cut the white part of the leeks and enough of the green tops crosswise into 1/4-inch slices to make 2 cups. In a 2-quart saucepan over medium heat, melt the butter and cook the leeks for 5 minutes. Add the potatoes, water, and bouillon; heat to boiling. Reduce the heat to low; cover and simmer for 30 minutes. In a blender on low speed, blend half of the leek mixture until smooth; pour into a 3-quart saucepan. Repeat with the remaining leek mixture. Stir the remaining ingredients into the leek mixture and cook the soup on a low flame just until heated through. Pour the soup into a large bowl; cover and refrigerate until chilled.

Note: This soup is also wonderful served hot.

MARIANNE RAKER
NORTHBROOK UNITED METHODIST CHURCH
ROSWELL, GEORGIA

COLD PEACH SOUP

5 large peaches, peeled and quartered
1/4 cup sugar (or less)
1 cup sour cream
1/4 cup lemon juice
1/4 cup sweet sherry (cream sherry)
2 tablespoons thawed orange juice
   concentrate
Fresh peaches, peeled and sliced for garnish

In a blender, puree the peaches with the sugar. Stir in the sour cream. Add the lemon juice, sherry, and orange juice. Blend until smooth. Transfer the mixture to a bowl. Cover and refrigerate until well chilled. Garnish each bowl with sliced peaches and serve.

JAN WICKLIFFE
CROSS IN THE DESERT UNITED METHODIST CHURCH
PHOENIX, ARIZONA

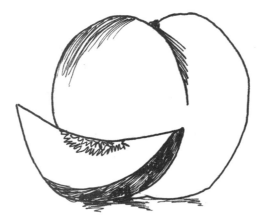

SALADS

Thank You for this nice day:
Bless our food, our work, our play.

FIRST UNITED METHODIST CHURCH,
BELLEVILLE, MICHIGAN

CREAMY POTATO SALAD

10 medium potatoes
1 cup celery, chopped
1/2 cup onion, finely chopped
1/3 cup sweet pickles, chopped
1 1/4 cups mayonnaise
3 teaspoons sugar
2 1/2 teaspoons vinegar
2 teaspoons yellow mustard
2 to 3 teaspoons salt
5 hard-boiled eggs, coarsely chopped
Paprika

In a covered saucepan, cook the potatoes in boiling salted water for 25 to 30 minutes, or until tender; drain well and transfer to a large bowl. Peel and cube the potatoes. Add the celery, onion, and sweet pickles. In a separate bowl, combine the mayonnaise, sugar, vinegar, mustard, and salt. Add the mayonnaise mixture to the potatoes and toss lightly to coat. Carefully fold in the chopped eggs. (Sometimes I save one egg, thin sliced, to decorate the top of the salad with it.) Sprinkle with paprika. Cover and chill thoroughly before serving.

SHANNA GRUBBS
NORTH MONROE STREET CHURCH OF GOD
MONROE, MICHIGAN

GERMAN POTATO SALAD

1/2 pound cooked bacon, diced
1/3 cup bacon drippings
1 tablespoon all-purpose flour
1 tablespoon sugar
1/2 teaspoon salt
1 teaspoon celery seed
1/4 teaspoon freshly ground black pepper
1/2 cup chicken broth
1/2 cup white vinegar
6 cups sliced and cooked potatoes (about 3 pounds)

In a medium skillet, cook the bacon until crisp; drain and set aside. Heat the drippings, blending in the flour, sugar, salt, celery seed, and pepper. Gradually blend in the broth and vinegar. Cook, stirring constantly, until the mixture thickens slightly. Combine the potatoes and bacon bits. Pour sauce over, toss gently, and spoon into a serving dish. Before serving, heat for 1/2 hour in a 325 degree oven.

GRIFFIN CHAPEL UNITED METHODIST CHURCH
STARKVILLE, MISSISSIPPI

Hot German Potato Salad

6 baking potatoes
1/3 cup vinegar
2 teaspoons salt
1/4 teaspoon black pepper
1 pound bacon, fried (reserve 1 to 2
    tablespoons of fat)
6 hard-boiled eggs (4 minutes)
3/4 cup chopped scallions (or 1/2 cup regular
    onion, chopped)

In a large saucepan, cook the potatoes in boiling water until done. Transfer them to a large bowl. While the potatoes are still hot, peel and dice (or slice thick) them, and add the vinegar and seasonings; stir gently. Fry the bacon quickly and break it into pieces. Add the bacon pieces and hard-boiled eggs to the potatoes while everything is still hot; add the onions and reserved bacon fat (optional). Stir well and serve.

Note: This recipe is submitted in memory of my paternal grandmother, Grandma Tittes.

GRIFFIN CHAPEL UNITED METHODIST CHURCH
STARKVILLE, MISSISSIPPI

It's Better-Than-Potato Salad

1 cup uncooked rice
2 cups mayonnaise
2 cups sliced celery
1 medium onion, finely chopped
4 teaspoons prepared mustard
1/2 teaspoon salt
4 hard-boiled eggs, chopped
8 radishes, sliced
1 cucumber, pared and diced

Cook the rice according to the package directions. Chill. In a large bowl, combine the mayonnaise, celery, onion, mustard, and salt. Mix well and chill. Add the rice and stir in the eggs, radishes, and cucumbers just before serving. Makes 6 to 8 servings.

LINDA FERRON
HIGHLAND HEIGHTS PRESBYTERIAN CHURCH
CORDOVA, TENNESSEE

SWEET POTATO–APPLE SALAD

6 medium sweet potatoes
1/2 cup vegetable oil
1/4 cup orange juice
1 tablespoon sugar
1 tablespoon cider vinegar
1 tablespoon Dijon mustard
1 tablespoon onion, finely chopped
1 1/2 teaspoons poppy seeds
1 teaspoon grated orange peel
1/2 teaspoon grated lemon peel
2 medium Granny Smith apples, chopped
2 scallions, thinly sliced

In a large saucepan, cook the sweet potatoes in boiling water until just tender; cool completely. While the potatoes are cooling, combine the next 9 ingredients in a jar and shake well. Peel the potatoes and cut them in half lengthwise, then into 1/2-inch slices. In a 4-quart bowl, layer one-fourth of the sweet potatoes, apples, and onions. Drizzle with one-fourth of the dressing. Repeat layers and dressing three times. Refrigerate for 1 to 2 hours. Toss just before serving.

PRINCE OF PEACE CHURCH
GRANTSVILLE, WEST VIRGINIA

PRETZEL SALAD   just for kids!

2 cups crushed pretzels (not too fine)
3/4 cup melted butter or margarine
1 tablespoon sugar
1 package (8-ounce) cream cheese,
    softened
1/2 cup sugar
1 small container whipped cream
1 (6-ounce) package strawberry Jell-O
2 cups boiling water
1 (10-ounce) package frozen strawberries
    (sweetened)

Preheat the oven to 400 degrees. Combine the pretzels, butter, and 1 tablespoon sugar and place in a 9 x 13-inch pan. Bake at 400 degrees for 8 minutes. Let cool. Beat together the softened cream cheese and 1/2 cup sugar and stir in the whipped cream. Spread this mixture over the baked pretzels and chill.

Dissolve the Jell-O in the hot water and add the frozen strawberries. Mix and let stand for 10 minutes. Pour the Jell-O mixture over the chilled pretzel and cream cheese mixture and chill until firm.

PAM HUNTER
UNITED BAPTIST CHURCH OF POULTNEY
EAST POULTNEY, VERMONT

CORNBREAD SALAD

1 medium pan cornbread, crumbled (not too fine)
1 pound cooked bacon, crumbled
6 scallions, chopped (tops and all)
1 green pepper, chopped
4 medium tomatoes, chopped
1/2 cup sweet pickles, chopped, or 1/2 cup relish
Salt and pepper to taste
Grated Cheddar cheese (optional)
4 hard-boiled eggs, chopped (optional)
1 small can English peas (optional)
1 cup celery, chopped (optional)

DRESSING:
2 cups mayonnaise
1 teaspoon sugar
1/4 cup sweet pickles

Layer all the ingredients in a large bowl, beginning with the cornbread. Mix dressing ingredients. Drizzle the dressing on top. Do not mix the salad until you are ready to serve it. Add salt and pepper to taste.

Options: Top with grated Cheddar cheese, hard-boiled eggs, English peas, or celery.

MARIE JONES
NORTH MONROE STREET CHURCH OF GOD
MONROE, MICHIGAN

CORNBREAD SALAD FOR TWENTY

2 (6-ounce) packages Mexican cornbread mix
1 (15-ounce) can whole-kernel corn, drained
1 onion, chopped
1 1/2 cups fresh tomatoes, chopped
1 cup Monterey Jack cheese with peppers, grated
2 tablespoons Italian seasoning
1 tablespoon Ranch dressing mix
1 whole green pepper, chopped
1/4 teaspoon celery seed
1 (10-ounce) package frozen peas, thawed
3 hard-boiled eggs, chopped
1 cup Cheddar cheese, grated
6 slices bacon, fried and crumbled
Salt and pepper to taste
1 cup reduced-calorie Ranch salad dressing
1/2 tablespoon whole milk

Make the cornbread according to the package directions. Cool the cornbread and crumble it into small pieces; divide them between 2 small bowls. In a large serving bowl, layer the first bowl of cornbread crumbs, corn, onion, tomatoes, Monterey Jack cheese with peppers, 1 tablespoon Italian seasoning, and 1 teaspoon Ranch dressing mix. Continue to layer with the second bowl of cornbread crumbs, green pepper, celery seed, peas, 1 tablespoon Italian seasoning, the boiled eggs, Cheddar cheese, bacon, salt, and pepper. In a separate bowl, combine the 1 cup salad dressing and milk and pour over the salad. With a small knife, open holes in the salad to allow the dressing to trickle down to the bottom. Chill overnight. Serve cold. Makes 20 servings.

Note: I like to serve this recipe as a layered salad, but it also tastes great tossed.

DEBORAH DANIEL
NORTHBROOK UNITED METHODIST CHURCH
ROSWELL, GEORGIA

Light Italian Pasta Salad

1/4 cup chicken broth
3 tablespoons wine vinegar
2 tablespoons olive oil
1 garlic clove, minced
1 teaspoon dried basil, or 1 tablespoon
    chopped fresh basil
1/2 teaspoon salt
1/8 teaspoon crushed red pepper flakes
    (optional)
6 ounces (1/2 box) tricolor pasta, cooked,
    rinsed, and drained
1/4 cup Parmesan cheese
2 cups broccoli florets, blanched
1 large red pepper, cut into strips
1/4 cup chopped black olives

In a large bowl, combine the chicken broth, vinegar, oil, garlic, basil, and salt and red pepper. Add the pasta and Parmesan; toss to coat well. Stir in the broccoli, red pepper strips, and olives. Serve at room temperature. Makes 8 servings.

Variations: Cauliflower may be added or substituted.

JoAnne Swanson
St. Paul Church
Waterford, Connecticut

Cold Spaghetti Salad

1 pound cooked spaghetti, cooled
1 bunch scallions, chopped
1 green pepper, chopped
3/4 cup celery, chopped
Black olives
1 pint cherry tomatoes, quartered
8 ounces Wish-Bone Italian dressing
1/2 cup Parmesan cheese
2 tablespoons parsley flakes
Garlic powder to taste
Salt and pepper to taste

Combine all the ingredients and mix well. Let the flavors blend overnight. Before serving, add salt and pepper to taste.

SHERI COOPER
MEMORIAL BAPTIST CHURCH
TULSA, OKLAHOMA

Shells and Tuna Garden Salad

1 (7-ounce) package pasta shells (uncooked)
1 large firm tomato, chopped
1 small zucchini, chopped
1/2 cup chopped celery
1/4 cup chopped green pepper
1/4 cup chopped scallions
2 (7-ounce) cans tuna, drained and flaked
1 cup mayonnaise or salad dressing
1/2 cup bottled Italian salad dressing
2 teaspoons prepared mustard
1 teaspoon dill weed
1/2 teaspoon salt
1/8 teaspoon pepper

Cook the shells according to the package directions; drain. In a large bowl, combine the shells, tomato, zucchini, celery, green pepper, onions, and tuna; mix well. In a small bowl, stir together the remaining ingredients. Add this to the shell mixture; mix well. Cover and chill thoroughly before serving. Refrigerate any leftovers.

PRINCE OF PEACE CHURCH
GRANTSVILLE, WEST VIRGINIA

Macaroni Salad

2 cups macaroni
2 cups celery, finely chopped
2 tablespoons onion, finely chopped
2 tablespoons green pepper, finely chopped
10 ripe olives, finely chopped
1 (6-ounce) can tuna fish, flaked
1 teaspoon mustard
1 1/4 cups mayonnaise
Salt and pepper to taste

Cook the macaroni according to the package directions, drain, and rinse in cold water. Add the celery, onion, green pepper, olives, and tuna fish. Toss with the mustard and mayonnaise. Season with salt and pepper.

PAULINE SUMMERS
TRINITY PRESBYTERIAN CHURCH
WILMINGTON, DELAWARE

MARY JO'S CLASSIC MACARONI SALAD

3/4 cup mayonnaise or other dressing
2 tablespoons cider vinegar
2 tablespoons prepared mustard
1/4 teaspoon black pepper
2 tablespoons sugar
8 ounces macaroni, cooked until tender
1/4 cup onion, chopped
1/4 cup pickle relish
1/4 cup celery, chopped
*1/2 cup bell pepper (red, yellow, or green),
  chopped*
1/4 cup Cheddar cheese
1/4 cup diced ham or crumbled bacon
1/4 cup hard-boiled egg, chopped

In a large bowl, combine all the ingredients and mix well. Refrigerate overnight if possible to let the ingredients flavor the macaroni.

PINEMOUNT BAPTIST CHURCH
MCALPIN, FLORIDA

SUMMER PASTA SALAD

4 ounces pasta shells
4 teaspoons olive oil
1/4 cup minced fresh parsley
1/8 teaspoon pepper
1 small onion, diced
1 medium cucumber, chopped
1 large tomato, cubed

Cook the pasta according to the package directions and drain. Add the olive oil, parsley, and pepper. Toss. Add the onion, cucumber, and tomato and toss well. Makes 4 servings.

ALEX
FOREST AVENUE
CONGREGATIONAL CHURCH
BANGOR, MAINE

DIANNE'S PENNE PASTA SALAD

1 pound penne pasta, cooked until tender
1 cup vinegar
1 cup sugar
1 tablespoon parsley flakes
1 1/2 teaspoons salt
3/4 teaspoon black pepper
1/2 cup thinly sliced onion
1 cup thinly sliced cucumber
1 cup tomatoes, chopped
1 green or red pepper, sliced
1 teaspoon mustard
1/2 teaspoon celery seed
1/2 cup olive or vegetable oil

In a large bowl, mix all the ingredients together and refrigerate overnight.

PINEMOUNT BAPTIST CHURCH
MCALPIN, FLORIDA

WARM CHICKPEA SALAD

1 (16-ounce) can chickpeas
3 tablespoons olive oil
12 ounces button mushrooms
2 garlic cloves, minced
1 red serrano chile, seeded and chopped
2 teaspoons ground cumin
Juice of 1 lemon
3/4 cup plain yogurt
Handful of mint leaves, chopped
Sea salt to taste
Freshly ground black pepper to taste
About 5 cups baby spinach

Drain and rinse the chickpeas, then drain them again. Heat 2 tablespoons of the olive oil in a skillet. Add the mushrooms, season with salt, and cook until softened. Reduce the heat and add the garlic, chile, and chickpeas. Sauté for 2 minutes, then add the cumin and half of the lemon juice. Cook until the juices in the skillet evaporate, then set aside.

In a large bowl, combine the yogurt, mint leaves, and the remaining lemon juice and olive oil. Season with salt and pepper and mix until blended. Divide the spinach among 4 plates. Add the chickpea and mushroom mixture, then pour the yogurt dressing over the top and serve.

Note: This salad can also be served in couscous or bulgur wheat to make it more substantial. Even our nonvegetarian friends like it. And it's both easy and foolproof.

CHIARA GARTHWAITE
NORTHBROOK UNITED METHODIST CHURCH
ROSWELL, GEORGIA

GREEN BEAN SALAD

1 pound green beans
2 tomatoes, chopped
1 red onion, sliced
Ripe olives, sliced (optional)
1/4 cup Parmesan cheese (freshly grated)

DRESSING:
1/3 cup olive oil
2 tablespoons red wine vinegar
1 garlic clove, minced
1 teaspoon salt
1 teaspoon dark mustard
Pepper

In a medium saucepan, cook the beans uncovered in 1 cup of boiling water for 5 minutes. Cover and cook for a few minutes longer, but the beans should still be a little crunchy.

In a small bowl, whisk together all the ingredients for the dressing. Pour the dressing over the warm beans and refrigerate for at least 2 hours. Just before serving, add the tomatoes, onion, and olives, if desired. Toss lightly. Sprinkle the Parmesan on top.

STEVE SCHANK
FIRST UNITED METHODIST CHURCH
BELLEVILLE, MICHIGAN

GREAT THREE-BEAN SALAD

1/2 cup canola oil
1/2 cup cider vinegar
3/4 cup sugar
1 medium onion, chopped
1 green pepper, chopped
1 can kidney beans, drained
1 can cut yellow wax beans, drained
1 can cut canned green beans, drained

In a large bowl, combine all the ingredients and mix. Refrigerator overnight. Mix well before serving.

KAY ANDREWS
ST. PAUL CHURCH
WATERFORD, CONNECTICUT

TOTALLY AWESOME THREE-BEAN SALAD

2/3 cup vinegar
3/4 cup sugar
1 teaspoon salt
1/3 cup salad oil
1/2 teaspoon black pepper
1 can wax beans
1 can green beans
1 can kidney beans
1/2 cup onion, chopped
1/4 cup green pepper, chopped

In a small skillet, heat the vinegar, sugar, and salt. Stir until the liquid dissolves. Pour the mixture into a large bowl and add the salad oil and pepper. Mix well. Drain the beans thoroughly. Add the drained beans, onion, and green pepper. Gently blend so that the beans do not break. Cover and refrigerate at least overnight. This recipe gets better with age!

MARTA LITTLE
TRINITY UNITED METHODIST CHURCH
YORK, PENNSYLVANIA

PAINTED-DESERT ROASTED PEPPER SALAD

1/2 cup extra-virgin olive oil
1/4 cup vegetable oil
2 garlic cloves
1 tablespoon chopped onion
1/4 cup cider vinegar
1/2 teaspoon salt
1/2 teaspoon sugar
1/8 teaspoon dried Mexican oregano
Freshly ground black pepper
Combination of 3 mild green chilies
    (poblano, New Mexico, and Anaheim),
    roasted
1 red pepper, roasted
1 green pepper, roasted
1 yellow pepper, roasted
Crumbled Cotija or aged Monterey
Jack cheese, grated
Romaine or other sturdy lettuce leaves, for
    garnish

Combine the oils, garlic, and onion in a blender and puree. Pour the mixture through a strainer into a large jar with a lid. Combine with the remaining ingredients and shake well. Refrigerate the mixture for 30 minutes. Slice the chilies and bell peppers into ribbons about 1/2-inch thick and arrange them decoratively on a serving platter. Pour the dressing over the chilies and bell peppers. Scatter the cheeses on top. Garnish with lettuce around the plate's edge.

PINEMOUNT BAPTIST CHURCH
MCALPIN, FLORIDA

SPINACH SALAD

1 bunch spinach
Scallions, chopped
Water chestnuts, chopped
Hard-boiled eggs, chopped
Bacon, crumbled

DRESSING:
1/2 cup oil
1/2 cup sugar
1/4 cup ketchup
1/4 cup red wine vinegar
2 tablespoons Worcestershire sauce

In a large bowl, combine all the salad ingredients and mix well. Combine the ingredients for the dressing in a saucepan over low heat. Do *not* boil. Pour the warm dressing over the salad.

Note: My mom, Carolyn Thieman, gave me this recipe. The dressing is the best part!

JENNY MAJOR
NORTHBROOK UNITED METHODIST CHURCH
ROSWELL, GEORGIA

TABBOULEH (PARSLEY, MINT, AND CRACKED WHEAT SALAD)

1 cup fine bulgur (crushed wheat)
1 cup finely chopped mint
3 cups finely chopped large-leaf parsley
   (about 3 bundles)
1 cup finely chopped scallion
1/4 cup finely chopped yellow onion
3/4 cup finely chopped tomatoes
1/2 cup olive oil
1/2 cup fresh lemon juice, or to taste
Salt and pepper
Dash of ground cinnamon
Chopped tomatoes, for garnish
Parsley sprigs, for garnish

Soften the bulgur in water for 1 hour. Using a cheesecloth in a collander, drain the bulgur and press out the excess water. In a large bowl, combine the mint, parsley, and onions. In a separate bowl, whisk together the olive oil, lemon juice, salt and pepper, and cinnamon. Just before serving, add the parsley mixture to the bulgur and stir in the tomatoes. Pour the dressing over the bulgur mixture and toss thoroughly with a fork. Garnish with chopped tomatoes and parsley sprigs. Makes 6 to 8 servings.

Note: Do not use dried herbs with this recipe.

GAMILIE ISRAEL
TRINITY UNITED METHODIST CHURCH
YORK, PENNSYLVANIA

Marinated Vegetable Salad

1/4 cup vegetable oil
1/2 cup vinegar
1/4 to 1/2 cup sugar
1 cup water
1 cup sliced water chestnuts
1 cup French green beans
1 green pepper, diced (optional)
Small jar chopped pimientos
1 cup petits pois
1 cup diced celery
1 chopped onion
2 carrots, grated
1 cup baby corn (white)

In a large skillet, heat the oil, vinegar, sugar, and water. Pour this mixture over the vegetables and chill.

JOY STEWART
MEMORIAL BAPTIST CHURCH
TULSA, OKLAHOMA

Chunky Greek Salad

2 tablespoons olive oil
2 tablespoons lemon juice
3/4 teaspoon salt
1/3 teaspoon black pepper
1 pint grape tomatoes, cut in half
6 cucumbers, cut into 1 x 1/2-inch chunks
1 red pepper, cut into 1-inch pieces
1 onion, thinly sliced
1/2 cup olives, coarsely chopped
1/4 cup chopped mint leaves
3/4 cup crumbled Feta cheese

In a large bowl, combine the oil, lemon juice, salt, and pepper. Add the tomatoes, cucumbers, red pepper, onion, olives, and mint. Toss until evenly mixed. The salad can be refrigerated for up to 6 hours. Sprinkle with the Feta cheese before serving. Makes 12 servings.

PAPOO
FOREST AVENUE CONGREGATIONAL CHURCH
BANGOR, MAINE

ANTIPASTO SALAD

1 jar marinated mushrooms
1 jar pimientos
1 jar artichoke hearts
1 can black olives, drained
Some provolone and mozzarella cheese, cut up
Parmesan or Romano cheese
Italian dressing

In a large bowl, combine all the ingredients and mix well. You may substitute ingredients of your choice.

HELEN TAGLIANETTI
ST. PAUL CHURCH
WATERFORD, CONNECTICUT

BEET SALAD

1 (No. 202) jar julienned beets, drained
    (save juice)
1 (3-ounce) package lemon Jell-O
1 small can frozen lemonade, or 1/2 cup
    lemon juice and 1/2 cup sugar
1/2 teaspoon salt
1 1/2 cups chopped celery
4 scallions, chopped
1 tablespoon mustard seeds

In a large saucepan, add enough water to the beet juice to make a cup; bring to a boil and dissolve the Jell-O. Add the lemonade and salt; chill slightly. Add the remaining ingredients and pour the mixture into a mold. Refrigerate until firm. Serves 8.

DAMASCUS UNITED METHODIST CHURCH
DAMASCUS, MARYLAND

SPINACH-ORANGE SALAD (WITH HONEY VINAIGRETTE DRESSING)

4 cups spinach leaves, torn
1 (11-ounce) can mandarin oranges,
    drained
1/2 cup sliced, red onion
3 tablespoons distilled white vinegar
2 tablespoons vegetable oil
1 tablespoon honey
1/2 teaspoon salt
Few grindings black pepper
2 tablespoons slivered almonds (optional)

Remove the coarse stems from the spinach, then wash and dry the leaves. Transfer the spinach to a large bowl and tear it into bite-size pieces; add the orange slices and onion; toss gently to mix. In a separate bowl, mix together the vinegar, oil, honey, salt, and pepper; pour over the spinach mixture. Sprinkle almonds over the top, if desired. Makes 4 servings.

GRIFFIN CHAPEL UNITED METHODIST CHURCH
STARKVILLE, MISSISSIPPI

SALAT KHYAR BI LABAN (CUCUMBER WITH YOGURT)

2 1/2 cups yogurt, or laban
1 cup peeled, chopped cucumbers
3 garlic cloves, minced
1 teaspoon dried mint
1 tablespoon fresh lemon juice
Salt and pepper to taste

In a large bowl, smooth the yogurt by stirring it with a spoon. Add the cucumbers. Mash the garlic into a paste with a little salt and mix it with a spoonful of yogurt before adding it to the cucumber mixture. Add the mint and lemon juice. Serve as a salad with any meal.

Note: Variations on this dish include using the above mixture as a dressing on a salad of lettuce, tomatoes, and onions or simply adding onions and tomatoes to the recipe. The use of laban in salads is only one of the many delights of this dairy product. In the Arab world, it is added to such dishes as hot soups, or used as a cooking liquid in meat and vegetable dishes. It is also added to rice while it is being cooked.

GAMILIE ISRAEL
TRINITY UNITED METHODIST CHURCH
YORK, PENNSYLVANIA

BROCCOLI DELIGHT SALAD

5 cups chopped fresh broccoli
1/2 cup raisins
1/4 cup chopped red onion
2 tablespoons sugar
3 tablespoons vinegar
1 cup mayonnaise
10 bacon slices, cooked and crumbled
1 cup sunflower seeds

In a large bowl, combine the broccoli, raisins, and onion. In a small bowl, combine the sugar, vinegar, and mayonnaise. Pour the dressing over the broccoli mixture and toss to coat. Refrigerate. Just before serving, sprinkle with bacon and sunflower seeds; toss. Makes 6 to 8 servings.

BILLIE JO SNIFF
MCCLAVE UNITED METHODIST CHURCH
MCCLAVE, COLORADO

Broccoli-Tomato Salad

5 cups broccoli florets
1 tablespoon water
1 pint cherry tomatoes, cut in half
2 tablespoons chopped scallions
1/4 cup fat-free mayonnaise
1/2 cup reduced-fat sour cream
1 tablespoon lemon juice
1/2 teaspoon salt
1/4 teaspoon pepper

Place the broccoli and water in a microwave-safe bowl. Cover and microwave on high for 3 minutes; drain and cool completely. Transfer the broccoli to a serving bowl and gently stir in the tomatoes and green onions. In a small bowl, mix the mayonnaise, sour cream, lemon juice, salt, and pepper; pour over the vegetables and stir gently. Cover and chill for at least 1 hour. Makes about 6 servings.

BETTY FULTON
FIRST UNITED METHODIST CHURCH
BELLEVILLE, MICHIGAN

Tomato Refresher

2 small green peppers, diced
2/3 cup diced celery
2 small onions, diced
1 tablespoon salt
1/4 teaspoon black pepper
1/4 cup vinegar
1/4 cup sugar
1 cup cold water
6 medium tomatoes, sliced about 1/2-inch thick

In a large bowl, combine the peppers, celery, onions, salt, black pepper, vinegar, sugar, and water. Pour the mixture over the tomatoes. Cover and chill for 3 to 4 hours (can set overnight). Makes 8 to 10 servings.

Note: This is really good in the summer, when there is an abundance of fresh tomatoes.

AUDREY MONROE
MEMORIAL BAPTIST CHURCH
TULSA, OKLAHOMA

Tomato-Mozzarella Salad

3 medium tomatoes, sliced
1/2 pound part-skim mozzarella cheese, thinly sliced
1/3 cup safflower oil
3 tablespoons red wine vinegar
3 tablespoons chopped fresh parsley
3 tablespoons finely chopped onion
1 tablespoon finely chopped fresh basil, or 1/2 teaspoon dried
Dash of salt
Dash of pepper

Layer the tomatoes and cheese in a shallow dish. In a small jar with a tight-fitting lid, combine the oil, vinegar, parsley, onion, basil, salt, and pepper. Cover and shake well. Pour the mixture over the tomatoes and cheese. Cover and refrigerate for several hours, occasionally spooning the dressing over the salad. Makes 4 servings.

GRIFFIN CHAPEL UNITED METHODIST CHURCH
STARKVILLE, MISSISSIPPI

EVERLASTING COLE SLAW

1 medium head cabbage, chopped
1 red pepper
1 green pepper
1 small onion
1 cup celery
1 cup sugar
1/2 cup white vinegar
1/4 cup oil
1 teaspoon mustard seed
1 teaspoon celery seed
1 teaspoon salt

Combine the cabbage, peppers, onion, and celery in a saucepan and warm on low heat. Do not boil. Add the remaining ingredients. Mix well. Remove from the heat and refrigerate.

Note: This dish will last up to 1 week if refrigerated. It tastes great if it's made at least 24 hours before the event.

JoAnn Glaab
North Monroe Street Church of God, Monroe, Michigan

MEMPHIS-STYLE COLESLAW

1 medium green cabbage, shredded (remove core and tough leaves)
2 medium carrots, peeled and grated
1 green pepper, cored, seeded, and diced
2 tablespoons grated onion
2 cups mayonnaise
3/4 cup granulated sugar
1/4 cup Dijon-style mustard
1/4 cup cider vinegar
2 tablespoons celery seed
1 tablespoon salt
1/8 teaspoon white pepper

Place the vegetables in a large bowl and set aside. Combine the remaining ingredients in another bowl. Add this mixture to the vegetables and toss well. Cover the coleslaw and refrigerate for 3 to 4 hours before serving to allow the flavors to meld.

Rex Morris
Buckingham United Methodist Church
Garland, Texas

APPLE-CABBAGE SLAW

1 cup plain yogurt
1/2 cup sour cream
1 tablespoon honey (optional)
1/2 cup chopped fresh parsley
2 cups shredded napa cabbage
2 cups shredded red cabbage
2 to 3 carrots, shredded
1/3 cup raisins
2 medium apples (Granny Smith or another tart apple), peeled, cored, and finely chopped or grated
3 tablespoons dried minced onion
Salt and pepper to taste

In a large bowl, whisk together the yogurt, sour cream, honey (if desired), and chopped parsley. Add the cabbages, carrots, raisins, apples, onion, and salt and pepper to taste. Mix well. Cover and chill until you are ready to enjoy. Serve on chilled plates.

Donna Crusi
North Monroe Street Church of God
Monroe, Michigan

CHICKEN SALAD

1 quart cooked chopped chicken
1 cup seedless grapes (white; whole or cut
    in 1/2)
1 1/2 cups slivered almonds
1 cup diced celery
1 cup mayonnaise
1 1/2 teaspoons curry powder
1 tablespoon lemon juice
1 tablespoon soy sauce
Pineapple slices

In a large bowl, combine the chicken, grapes, almonds, and celery. In a separate bowl, mix the mayonnaise, curry powder, lemon juice, and soy sauce. Pour the dressing over the chicken mixture. Serve over pineapple slices.

CARLOTTA GREGORY
MEMORIAL BAPTIST CHURCH
TULSA, OKLAHOMA

Curried Chicken Salad

1/4 cup slivered almonds
12 ounces cooked boneless, skinless chicken
1/4 cup mango chutney
1/4 cup sour cream or plain yogurt
1 teaspoon curry powder
1/2 cup red or green seedless grapes, cut in
   half

Preheat the oven to 350 degrees. Spread the almonds on a baking sheet and toast them in the oven for 6 to 8 minutes, or until golden brown. Remove from the oven and cool. Cut the chicken into 1/2-inch pieces. Combine the chutney, sour cream, and curry powder in a large bowl, mixing until smooth. Add the grape halves and chicken to the bowl and mix well. Stir in the almonds. Serve in pita bread or on a bed of lettuce.

Cindy Johnson
Mattapoisett Congregational Church
Mattapoisett, Massachusetts

Ann and Jim's Gourmet Chicken Salad

4 cups cooked chicken, diced
1 cup celery, diced
1 cup grapes, halved
1 cup diced apple
1/4 cup pecans, chopped
1/2 teaspoon curry powder
1/2 teaspoon salt

In a large bowl, combine all the ingredients and mix.

Dressing:
1 cup mayonnaise
2 tablespoons sour cream

Combine the ingredients in a small bowl and pour over the salad, mixing well. Serve on lettuce leaves.

Ann Jeffery
First United Methodist Church
Belleville, Michigan

ITALIAN CHICKEN SALAD

3/4 cup plus 1 tablespoon vegetable oil
1/2 cup lemon juice concentrate
2 tablespoons grated Parmesan cheese
3 teaspoons chicken-flavor instant bouillon
1 teaspoon sugar
1/2 teaspoon dried oregano
1 garlic clove, minced
1/8 teaspoon black pepper
1 pound chicken strips
1 pound linguine, cooked and drained
1 cup sliced mushrooms
1/2 cup chopped red peppers
1/4 cup sliced olives, pitted

In a large bowl, combine 3/4 cup of the oil, lemon juice, cheese, 2 teaspoons of the bouillon, sugar, oregano, garlic, and pepper; mix well. In a large skillet, heat the remaining 1 tablespoon oil on medium heat. Add the chicken and the remaining teaspoon bouillon. Brown the chicken until it becomes tender, stirring occasionally. Add the chicken, pasta, and the remaining ingredients to the oil mixture; mix lightly to coat. Cover and chill. Serve on lettuce leaves.

DENBOW FAMILY
FOREST AVENUE CONGREGATIONAL CHURCH
BANGOR, MAINE

CHICKEN PASTA SALAD

1 1/2 pounds cooked boneless chicken
    breasts, diced
1-pound box rotini pasta, cooked and
    drained
1 medium-size bottle Kraft Zesty Italian
    dressing
2 large tomatoes, diced
1 large cucumber, diced
1/2 cup Parmesan cheese
1/4 cup onion, finely diced

Mix all the ingredients in a large bowl. Refrigerate until cool.

SABRINA WISE
BETHEL AME CHURCH
AUGUSTA, GEORGIA

CRUNCHY CHICKEN SALAD

1/3 cup vegetable oil
1/4 cup cider or white wine vinegar
2 tablespoons honey
2 tablespoons sesame seeds, toasted
2 tablespoons soy sauce
1 tablespoon dried parsley flakes
1/2 teaspoon ground ginger
1/2 teaspoon ground mustard
3 cups coarsely chopped cooked chicken
2 cups shredded cabbage
1 cup fresh snow peas, halved
1 cup sliced carrots
1/2 cup sliced scallions
1/2 cup sliced radishes
Salted peanuts (optional)

In a large bowl, combine the first 8 ingredients and mix well. Stir in the chicken. Cover and refrigerate for at least 1 hour. Just before serving, toss the cabbage, peas, carrots, onions, and radishes in a serving bowl. Top with the chicken mixture. Sprinkle with peanuts, if desired.

TONYA BOWMAN
FOREST AVENUE CONGREGATIONAL CHURCH
BANGOR, MAINE

CAJUN CHICKEN SALAD

Use prepared Cajun spice seasoning or mix together the following:
   1/2 teaspoon onion powder
   1/2 teaspoon garlic powder
   1/2 teaspoon ground white pepper
   1/2 teaspoon ground red pepper
   1/2 teaspoon ground black pepper
   1/2 teaspoon dried thyme, crushed
   1/4 teaspoon salt

Melted margarine
4 boneless chicken breast halves
Lettuce
Sliced fresh mushrooms
Tomatoes, cut into sections
Tops of scallions
Shredded Cheddar cheese
Ranch dressing

Combine the seasonings in a small bowl. Brush the chicken breasts with the melted margarine and coat with the seasonings. Cook the chicken in a skillet until it's done. Make a bed of lettuce and top with the remaining vegetables and the cheese. Cut the hot chicken into bite-size pieces and arrange on the salad. Top with Ranch dressing.

Note: This is the first recipe that I "created" after having something similar at a restaurant.

VALERIE NORRIS
NORTHBROOK UNITED METHODIST CHURCH
ROSWELL, GEORGIA

CHICKEN AND WILD RICE WALDORF SALAD

6-ounce box long-grain wild rice
3 cups cubed cooked, skinless, boneless
   chicken breast
3 celery stalks, finely chopped
2 tart green apples, cored and cubed
1 cup seedless green or red grapes, cut in half
2 tablespoons minced fresh parsley
1 teaspoon grated lemon peel
1/2 cup toasted walnuts, chopped

DRESSING:
1/2 cup lite mayonnaise
4 tablespoons cider vinegar
2 tablespoons fresh lemon juice
1 tablespoon whole grain mustard
1 tablespoon honey
1/4 teaspoon thyme or tarragon
Fresh parsley sprigs, for garnish

Cook the rice according to the package directions, omitting the butter. Remove from the heat and transfer to a large bowl; cool to room temperature. Combine all the other ingredients with the cooled rice.

In a separate bowl, combine all the ingredients for the dressing and mix well. Pour over the rice and other ingredients, mixing well. Refrigerate for 2 hours. Serve on a large lettuce leaf and garnish with the parsley sprigs. Makes 9 servings.

NANCY HENDERSON
FIRST UNITED METHODIST CHURCH
BELLEVILLE, MICHIGAN

COBB SALAD

2 boneless chicken breasts
3 tablespoons olive oil
1 teaspoon poultry seasoning
Salt and pepper to taste
4 eggs
8 bacon slices, cut into 1/2-inch pieces
3 hearts romaine lettuce
Juice of 2 lemons
2 ripe avocados, scooped and diced
2 tomatoes, diced
1 red onion, chopped
2 cups white Cheddar or Monterey Jack
   cheese, shredded

Heat the grill over medium heat. Coat the chicken with 1 tablespoon of the olive oil, the poultry seasoning and salt and pepper. Grill for 6 to 7 minutes on each side. Remove and let rest for 5 minutes

In a small saucepan, boil the eggs for 10 minutes. Cool, peel, and chop the eggs. Brown the bacon (chopped) on medium. Remove and let drain on paper towels.

Chop the 3 hearts of romaine lettuce and place them in a bowl. Dress with the juice of 1 1/2 lemons and drizzle with the remaining olive oil. Season the greens with salt and pepper. Toss the avocados with the remaining lemon juice. Chop the chicken and arrange the chicken pieces, eggs, bacon, avocadoes, tomatoes, onion, and cheese in the bowl. Serve.

FOREST AVENUE CONGREGATIONAL CHURCH
BANGOR, MAINE

Shrimp Salad

1 (16-ounce) box macaroni, cooked, drained,
    and cooled
1/2 to 1 pound shrimp, cooked and shelled
4 hard-boiled eggs, chopped
1/2 cup chopped yellow onion
1/4 cup chopped celery
1/2 cup chopped black olives
1/2 cup chopped dill pickles
1 cup mayonnaise
2 tablespoons olive oil
1 teaspoon fresh lemon juice
2 teaspoons Worcestershire sauce
1 tablespoon Dijon mustard
1/2 cup ketchup
Hot sauce to taste

In a large mixing bowl, combine the first 7 ingredients. In a separate bowl, whisk the remaining ingredients together to make a dressing. Pour the dressing over the other ingredients. Allow the salad to marinate in the refrigerator for a couple of hours before serving.

PINEMOUNT BAPTIST CHURCH
MCALPIN, FLORIDA

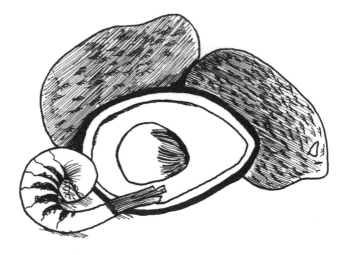

Avocado and Shrimp Salad

3 medium avocados
3 teaspoons fresh lemon juice
1/4 teaspoon minced garlic
1/4 teaspoon ground turmeric
1/4 teaspoon poultry seasoning
1/8 teaspoon black pepper
1/16 teaspoon ground red pepper
1 teaspoon salt
1 teaspoon cider vinegar
1 teaspoon salad oil
1 1/2 cups cooked, deveined shrimp
1 1/2 cups diced tomatoes
2 tablespoons mayonnaise
Watercress or parsley, for garnish

Halve and pit the avocados. Scoop out the avocados and make large cavities. Combine all the ingredients and spoon the mixture into the avocado halves. Garnish with watercress or parsley.

JANET CARLSON
BUCKINGHAM UNITED METHODIST CHURCH
GARLAND, TEXAS

ORIENTAL SALAD

SALAD:
1 head Chinese napa cabbage
1/2 cup butter or margarine
1/2 cup sesame seeds
1 cup sliced almonds
2 packages ramen noodles, broken into small
  pieces (do not use flavor packets)
8 scallions, chopped
dressing (recipe below)

DRESSING:
2 tablespoons soy sauce
1/2 cup white vinegar
1 cup sugar
1 cup canola oil

Wash, core, and cut up the cabbage. Set it aside, or cover with plastic wrap and refrigerate to keep it crisp. Melt the butter in a skillet over low heat. Combine the sesame seeds, almonds, and noodles; add the mixture to the butter and brown slowly, stirring constantly to avoid scorching. When the seeds and nuts are evenly toasted, remove the mixture from the heat and cool. To serve, toss together the green onions, cabbage, and browned noodle mixture. Pour the dressing over the salad and toss lightly. Serves 12 to 15 people.

(Prepare several hours ahead):

Combine all the ingredients in a blender and refrigerate for several hours. Just before serving, blend again quickly and pour over the salad.

Note: I obtained this delicious recipe from a potluck supper in Arizona.

RUTH ALEXANDER
UNITED BAPTIST CHURCH OF POULTNEY
EAST POULTNEY, VERMONT

FRUITY CRUNCH SALAD

just for kids!

2 1/2 cups strawberry yogurt
1/4 cup honey
1/2 teaspoon ground cinnamon
4 ounces chopped almonds
1/2 cup chopped cashews
1/3 cup raisins
1/4 cup M&M's candy-coated chocolate
  pieces
2 large oranges (peeled, sectioned, and cut
  into bite-sized pieces)
3 bananas, peeled and sliced
2 cups chopped pears
2 cups chopped grapefruit

In a large bowl, mix together the yogurt, honey, cinnamon, almonds, cashews, raisins, candy pieces, oranges, bananas, pears, and grapefruit. Cover and chill until you're ready to serve. Sprinkle with nutmeg and cloves before serving, if desired.

PINEMOUNT BAPTIST CHURCH
McALPIN, FLORIDA

Taco Salad

1 pound hamburger
1 small onion, diced
2 tomatoes, diced
2 avocados, diced
1 can red kidney beans, drained
1 can black olives, chopped
1 pound medium or sharp Cheddar cheese,
   grated
1 large head romaine lettuce

In a skillet on medium heat, brown the hamburger and drain. (You can brown the beef and the onion together or add the raw onion to the salad.) Combine all the ingredients. Pour in the dressing. Crush 1 bag of Doritos taco chips and add it to the salad, mixing well. Serve on a bed of lettuce.

Dressing:
1 cup mayonnaise
1/8 cup vinegar
1 tablespoon cumin
1/4 cup ketchup
Dash of Tabasco
Dash of Worcestershire

In a small bowl, combine the ingredients for the dressing and mix into the salad.

Linda Smith
Buckingham United Methodist Church
Garland, Texas

SAVORY FRUIT SALAD (A FRUIT SALSA)

1 pound peaches, cut into chunks
1 pound plums, cut into chunks
1 pound nectarines, cut into chunks
1/2 cup coarsely chopped fresh basil
1 large red pepper, seeded and diced
1/2 cup chopped red onion
1/2 cup herbed white wine vinegar
1/4 cup olive oil
2 tablespoons sugar
1/2 teaspoon crushed rosemary
1/2 teaspoon crushed thyme
1/2 teaspoon crushed marjoram
1/2 teaspoon ground black pepper

In a medium bowl, combine the fruit, basil, red pepper, and onion. Mix well and set aside. In a separate bowl, combine the vinegar, olive oil, sugar, crushed herbs, and black pepper. Pour this mixture over the fruit and toss to coat. Refrigerate for 1 hour to blend flavors. Toss the salad fruit before serving.

CROSS IN THE DESERT UNITED METHODIST CHURCH
PHOENIX, ARIZONA

SUMMERTIME FRUIT SALAD

1/2 cup orange juice
1/4 cup honey
2 cups strawberries, sliced
2 cups raspberries
2 cups blueberries
1 cup cantaloupe, cut into bite-size pieces
Mint leaves, for garnish

In a large bowl, whisk together the orange juice and honey. Add the rest of the ingredients and toss gently. Chill for 1 hour. Garnish with mint leaves. Makes 4 servings.

FOREST AVENUE CONGREGATIONAL CHURCH
BANGOR, MAINE

SUMMERTIME FRUIT MEDLEY

2 large ripe peaches, peeled and sliced
2 large ripe nectarines, sliced
1 large mango, peeled and cut into 1-inch
  chunks
1 cup blueberries
2 cups orange juice
1/4 cup amaretto, or 1/2 teaspoon almond
  extract
2 tablespoons sugar
Mint leaves, for garnish

Combine the peaches, nectarines, mango, and blueberries in a large bowl. In a small bowl, whisk together the orange juice, amaretto, and sugar until the sugar dissolves. Pour over the fruit mixture and toss. Marinate the salad for 1 hour at room temperature, gently stirring occasionally. Garnish with mint, if desired.

ETHEL GRIFFIN
CROSS IN THE DESERT UNITED METHODIST CHURCH
PHOENIX, ARIZONA

Fruited Tossed Salad

8 cups mixed greens
2 cups strawberries, sliced
1 can mandarine oranges, drained
1 medium sweet onion, sliced
1/3 cup almonds, toasted
4 bacon strips, fried and crumbled

Dressing:
1/4 cup sugar
2 tablespoons cider vinegar
1 tablespoon honey
1 1/4 teaspoons lemon juice
1/2 teaspoon paprika
1/2 teaspoon ground mustard
1/2 teaspoon onion, grated
1/4 teaspoon celery seed
Dash of salt
1/3 cup vegetable oil

Combine the salad ingredients in a large bowl. In a separate, microwave-safe bowl, heat all the dressing ingredients except the oil in the microwave for 1 1/2 to 2 minutes. Stir until the sugar dissolves. Whisk in the oil. Cool. Just before serving, pour over the salad and toss.

Kathy Myers
Cross in the Desert United Methodist Church
Phoenix, Arizona

Sinful Salad

1 (6-ounce) package strawberry Jell-O
1 cup boiling water
3 medium bananas, mashed
1 cup walnuts, finely chopped
2 (10-ounce) packages frozen strawberries,
    thawed and drained
1 (20-ounce) can crushed pineapple, drained
1 pint (2 cups) sour cream

Make the Jell-O using only 1 cup water, and set aside to cool. In a large bowl, combine the bananas, walnuts, strawberries, and pineapple. Add the cooled Jell-O and mix thoroughly. Pour half the mixture into a 12 x 18- or 13 x 9-inch pan and refrigerate until set (30 minutes to an hour). Keep the remaining Jell-O mixture at room temperature. Spread sour cream over the set layer of Jell-O mixture. Carefully spoon and spread the remaining half of the Jell-O mixture over the sour cream layer. Cover and refrigerate for at least 1 1/2 hours, but it is much better to let salad set overnight before serving.

Beverly Moore and Ruth Souza
Mattapoisett Congregational Church
Mattapoisett, Massachusetts

Classic Waldorf Salad

1/2 cup mayonnaise
1 tablespoon sugar
1 tablespoon lemon juice
1/8 teaspoon salt
3 medium apples, diced
1 cup sliced celery
1/2 cup walnuts, chopped

In a large bowl, combine the mayonnaise, sugar, lemon juice, and salt; stir in the apples, celery, and walnuts. Cover and chill.

LEE MINOR
MEMORIAL BAPTIST CHURCH
TULSA, OKLAHOMA

Orange-Jicama Salad

4 cups jicama, peeled and julienned
2 oranges, peeled and sectioned
2 tablespoons fresh cilantro, chopped
1/3 cup fresh orange juice
2 tablespoons balsamic vinegar
1 tablespoon extra-virgin olive oil
Salt and pepper to taste

In a large bowl, combine the jicama, orange sections, and cilantro and mix. In a separate bowl, whisk together the remaining ingredients and toss with the jicama-orange mixture. Season with salt and pepper and serve.

BECKY GAYLOR
CROSS IN THE DESERT UNITED METHODIST CHURCH
PHOENIX, ARIZONA

CRANBERRY–JELL-O SALAD

1 (6-ounce) package cranberry Jell-O
1 3/4 cups boiling water
1 (16-ounce) can whole-cranberry sauce
1 (20-ounce) can crushed pineapple,
    including juice
1 cup sour cream
Whipped cream

In a large bowl, dissolve the Jell-O in the hot water. Add the cranberry sauce and stir until it dissolves. Add the pineapple. Pour half of the mixture into a 2-quart bowl or mold and chill until firm. When the mixture is firm, spread with the sour cream and gently pour the remaining mixture over the top. Return to the refrigerator and chill until it's completely firm. Top with whipped cream and serve.

PENNY ILLSELY
UNITED BAPTIST CHURCH OF POULTNEY
EAST POULTNEY, VERMONT

CRANBERRY-ORANGE SALAD

1 (3-ounce) package cherry or orange Jell-O
1 1/2 cups hot water
3/4 cup sugar
1 tablespoon lemon juice
1/2 cup pineapple juice
1 cup ground fresh cranberries
1 orange, finely ground
1 cup crushed pineapple
1/2 cup chopped celery
1/2 cup pecans (optional)

In a large bowl, combine the Jell-O and hot water; mix until it dissolves. Add the sugar, lemon juice, and pineapple juice. Then add the cranberries, orange, pineapple, celery, and pecans (if desired). Chill the mixture until it is firm.

PAT ARGANBRIGHT
MEMORIAL BAPTIST CHURCH
TULSA, OKLAHOMA

CHRISTMAS CRANBERRY SALAD

1 1/4 cups boiling water
1 (6-ounce) package raspberry Jell-O
1 cup whole-berry cranberry sauce
1 (20-ounce) can crushed pineapple
3/4 cup cranberry juice
8 ounces cream cheese
8 ounces sour cream
1/2 cup sugar

In a large bowl or mold, combine the boiling water, Jell-O, cranberry sauce, pineapple, and cranberry juice. In a separate bowl, mix the cream cheese, sour cream, and sugar. Combine the two mixtures and stir well. Chill until set.

LEE FONTENOT
HOLUM BAPTIST CHURCH
GRAYSON, LOUISIANA

BANANA SPLIT SALAD

2 sticks butter
2 cups crushed graham cracker crumbs
2 eggs
1 box powdered sugar
5 bananas
1 can crushed pineapple, drained
1 large container Cool Whip
1 cup nuts, chopped
1 small jar maraschino cherries,
   cut up and drained

In a small skillet on low heat, melt 1 stick butter. Mix the melted butter with the graham cracker crumbs, reserving about 1/4 cup. Pat the mixture into a pan and bake at 325 degrees for 10 minutes. Let cool.

In a mixer, beat the eggs, powdered sugar, and the remaining stick of butter for 10 to 12 minutes, or until creamy. Spread the mixture over the crumbs. Cover with the sliced bananas. Spread with the pineapple and then the Cool Whip. Sprinkle with the nuts, reserved crumbs, and cherries. Refrigerate overnight.

Note: This is my Bo Bo's main dish of salad.

JOYCE FREELOVE
WESTSIDE BAPTIST CHURCH
ANTLERS, OKLAHOMA

SALAD DRESSING

1 cup olive oil
1/4 cup red wine vinegar
1 teaspoon salt
1/3 cup ketchup
1/2 cup sugar
1 to 2 garlic cloves, pressed
1 tablespoon Worcestershire sauce

Combine the ingredients in a jar with a tight-fitting lid. Shake well and pour over the salad.

VIRGINIA NEW
MOSCA UNITED METHODIST CHURCH
MOSCA, COLORADO

SALAD DRESSING

1 cup salad oil
1/3 cup vinegar
2/3 cup sugar
1/4 teaspoon dry mustard
1 teaspoon salt
1/4 teaspoon celery seed
Dash of finely ground onion (optional)

In a mixer or blender, mix all the ingredients together well; keep refrigerated.

Note: I love this dressing on a tossed lettuce salad.

BONNIE GRUND
PITT COMMUNITY CHURCH
BAUDETTE, MINNESOTA

HONEY-MUSTARD DRESSING

1 1/4 cups mayonnaise
1/3 cup honey
1 tablespoon vinegar
2/3 cup oil
1 teaspoon onion flakes
2 tablespoons minced parsley
2 tablespoons mustard

Whisk together all the ingredients and refrigerate.

CHRISTINE WALKER
CAVENDISH BAPTIST CHURCH
CAVENDISH, VERMONT

SALAD DRESSING FOR FRUIT

2 eggs
1 cup pineapple juice
1/4 teaspoon salt
1 tablespoon all-purpose flour
2/3 cups sugar
1 tablespoon butter
1/4 cup cream

In a small bowl, beat the eggs. In a saucepan over medium heat, combine all the ingredients except the butter and cream and cook until the mixture thickens. Remove the pan from the heat and add the butter and cream. After the mixture cools, serve it over a bowl of fresh or canned fruit.

LOIS PURDUM
DAMASCUS UNITED METHODIST CHURCH
DAMASCUS, MARYLAND

Russian Salad Dressing

1 cup mayonnaise
2 to 3 tablespoons chili sauce
4 tablespoons milk
4 tablespoons chopped stuffed olives
2 tablespoons chopped onion
2 tablespoons chopped green pepper
4 tablespoons lemon juice
1/2 teaspoon salt
1/4 teaspoon black pepper
Dash of Tabasco sauce

In a bowl, combine all the ingredients and stir well. Makes 1 1/2 cups dressing.

Carole Bishop
St. Paul Church
Waterford, Connecticut

Bleu Cheese Dressing

3/4 cup sour cream
1/2 teaspoon dry mustard
1/2 teaspoon black pepper
1/2 teaspoon salt
1/2 teaspoon garlic powder
1 teaspoon Worcestershire sauce
1 1/3 cups mayonnaise
4 ounces Danish Bleu cheese

In a blender or electric mixer, blend the first 6 ingredients for 2 minutes at low speed. Add the mayonnaise and blend in the cheese. Refrigerate. The dressing must sit for 24 hours before it is used. Makes 2 1/2 cups.

Kay Andrews
St. Paul Church
Waterford, Connecticut

SEASONED CROUTONS

Loaf of baguette or Italian bread, sliced
Margarine or butter
Italian seasoning
Parmesan cheese, grated

Preheat the oven to 400 degrees. Cut the crusts off the bread slices. Brush both sides of the bread with the margarine. Sprinkle the Italian seasoning and grated Parmesan cheese on the buttered surfaces. Cut the bread into 1/2- to 3/4-inch cubes. Bake in an ungreased pan, stirring every 5 minutes, until golden brown, 10 to 15 minutes. Use as a garnish on salads or soups when cool.

Note: This is an excellent way to use up stale French or Italian bread. My family nibbles the croutons as a snack.

LESLIE LAWRENCE
TRINITY PRESBYTERIAN CHURCH
WILMINGTON, DELAWARE

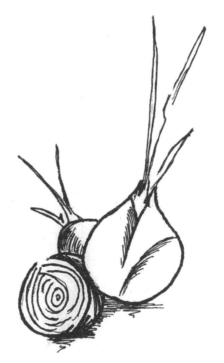

BREADS

We thank thee, Lord, for this our food,
For health and strength and every good.
Let manna to our souls be given,
The Bread of Life sent down from heaven.

FLORENCE PORTER WINTERS, 2000

White Bread

1 package dry yeast
1/4 cup warm water
2 cups scalded milk
2 tablespoons sugar
2 teaspoons salt
1 tablespoon shortening
2 cups all-purpose flour
4 1/4 cups all-purpose flour

Dissolve the yeast in the warm water. In a large bowl, combine the milk, sugar, salt, and shortening. Stir in 2 cups of flour and beat well. Add the softened yeast and the remaining 4 1/4 cups of flour. Turn out onto a floured bread board and knead well, about 8 to 10 minutes. Shape the dough into a ball. Place in a lightly greased bowl, cover, and let rise in a warm place until doubled in size (about 1 1/2 hours).

Shape the dough into loaves. Place the loaves in 2 greased (9 x 5 x 3) pans. Let rise until doubled, 45 to 60 minutes. Toward the end of this time, preheat the oven to 375 degrees. Bake for 40 minutes, or until golden brown. Cool on a wire rack.

Note: This recipe can also be used to make rolls.

Delina Karlson
Forest Avenue Congregational Church
Bangor, Maine

No-Knead Bread

2 packages dry yeast
3 cups warm water
8 cups all-purpose flour
2 eggs, slightly beaten
1/4 cup oil
1/2 teaspoon salt
3 tablespoons sugar

In a large mixing bowl containing the warm water, dissolve the yeast. Add 4 cups of the flour and mix well. Add the eggs, oil, salt, and sugar; mix together. Add the remaining flour and mix until smooth. Let the mixture stand until doubled in size, about 60 minutes. Punch the dough down and divide it into two well-greased 8-inch loaf pans. Let rise again just to the tops of the pans. Preheat the oven to 375 degrees. Bake for about 35 minutes.

Note: Two cups of Miller's bran can be substituted for 2 cups of flour for a high-fiber bread.

Joyce Baldwin
Memorial Baptist Church
Tulsa, Oklahoma

IRISH SODA BREAD

4 cups all-purpose flour
2/3 to 1 cup sugar
1/2 teaspoon salt
4 teaspoons baking powder
6 tablespoons butter
2 eggs, slightly beaten
1 teaspoon baking soda
1 1/2 cups buttermilk
2 cups raisins
2 teaspoons caraway seeds

Blend the first 5 ingredients with a fork. Combine the eggs, baking soda, and buttermilk and add to the flour mixture. Add the raisins and caraway seeds. Place in heavy pan that has been greased and floured. Pat the dough down with a floured hand; make a cross with a sharp knife. Preheat the oven to 375 degrees. Bake for 45 minutes to 1 hour.

Traditional Irish Toast: Health and long life to you; land without rent to you; children without end to you; and may you die in Ireland.

MRS. MAUREEN E. FORD
PRINCE OF PEACE CHURCH
GRANTSVILLE, WEST VIRGINIA

FRENCH BREAD

1 package yeast
2 cups warm water
1 tablespoon sugar
2 teaspoons salt
5 3/4 cups all-purpose flour
1 egg white, unbeaten

Sprinkle the yeast over the water. Add the sugar, salt, and 3 cups of the flour. Beat until smooth and shiny. Stir in 2 1/2 cups more flour. Sprinkle the remaining flour on a bread board. Knead 5 to 7 minutes. Let the dough rise for 1 hour. Divide it into 2 balls. Set aside for 5 minutes. Roll the balls into long rolls, placing them 4 inches apart on a cookie sheet. Cut 3/4-inch slashes in the tops. Set aside for 1 hour. Toward the end of this time, preheat the oven to 375 degrees. Bake for 30 to 35 minutes. Brush the loaves with the egg white and return to the oven for 2 minutes.

MRS. WALTER PAULSON
MOSCA UNITED METHODIST CHURCH
MOSCA, COLORADO

Batter Bread

Plain Bread:
1 1/4 cups warm water (105 to 115 degrees)
1 package dry yeast
2 tablespoons soft margarine
2 tablespoons sugar
2 teaspoons salt
3 cups all-purpose flour

Measure the warm water into a large warm mixing bowl. Sprinkle the yeast over the water, stir until it dissolves. Add the margarine, sugar, salt, and 2 cups of the flour. Beat in a mixer for 2 minutes at medium speed (or 300 vigorous strokes by hand). Scrape the sides and bottom of the bowl frequently. Blend in the remaining flour with a spoon until smooth. Cover and let rise in a warm place, free from draft, until doubled in size, about 30 minutes. Stir the batter down by beating about 25 strokes. Spread evenly in a greased 9 x 5 x 3-inch loaf pan. Smooth the loaf by flouring your hand and patting the top into shape. Cover and let rise again until doubled in size, about 40 minutes. Toward the end of this time, preheat the oven to 375 degrees. Bake for 45 minutes, or until the loaf sounds hollow when tapped. Makes 1 loaf. No kneading, no shaping; your mixer does the work and you collect the compliments.

Fruited Batter Bread:
1/4 cup raisins
1/2 cup mixed candied fruit
1/4 teaspoon cinnamon
1/4 teaspoon nutmeg

Prepare Batter Bread as directed, but during the first rising period combine the raisins, candied fruit, cinnamon, and nutmeg. Add this mixture to the batter when you stir it down. Beat until blended. Divide the batter into 2 greased 1-pound coffee cans. Let the batter rise until it reaches 3/4 inch from the tops of the pans, about 40 minutes. Toward the end of this time, preheat the oven to 375 degrees. Bake for about 40 minutes. Ice with white frosting, if desired.

Ceola Adams
Trinity Presbyterian Church
Wilmington, Delaware

Baked Brown Bread

1/2 cup cornmeal
2 cups all-purpose flour
1/2 cup sugar
1/2 teaspoon salt
1 teaspoon baking powder
1 teaspoon baking soda
1 1/2 cups milk
1/2 cup molasses
1 egg, beaten
1 tablespoon shortening, melted

Preheat the oven to 350 degrees. Mix together the cornmeal, flour, sugar, salt, baking powder, and baking soda. Add the milk and molasses to the beaten egg. Blend the milk mixture into the dry ingredients. Add the shortening. Pour into a greased loaf pan and bake for about 1 hour, or until firm.

Mabel Wescott
United Baptist Church of Poultney
East Poultney, Vermont

Oatmeal Bread

2 cups boiling water
1 cup oatmeal
1/4 cup warm water
1 teaspoon sugar
2 packages dry yeast
1/2 cup brown sugar
1 teaspoon salt
2 tablespoons butter
1/2 cup whole wheat flour
5 cups all-purpose flour

In a large bowl, cool the boiling water slightly and add the oatmeal. In a small bowl, combine the warm water, sugar, and yeast and let sit for no more than 10 minutes. Add the yeast mixture to the oatmeal mixture and add the remaining ingredients. Knead the dough on a floured surface for 10 minutes. Place in an oiled bowl, cover with plastic wrap or a clean towel, and let rise until doubled in size. Punch down, divide, and shape into 2 loaves. Place in 2 5 x 9-inch pans and let rise again until doubled in size. Preheat the oven to 350 degrees. Bake for 35 to 40 minutes. Remove the loaves from the pans and brush the tops with butter. Cool on a wire rack. Makes 2 loaves.

ANNE RIGGS
FIRST UNITED METHODIST CHURCH
BELLEVILLE, MICHIGAN

Honey Whole Wheat Bread

3 cups whole wheat flour
1/2 cup nonfat dry milk
2 packages dry yeast
1 tablespoon salt
1 cup Honey Crunch Wheat Germ
3 cups warm water
1/2 cup honey
2 tablespoons cooking oil
crunched nuts
1 cup whole wheat flour
4 to 4 1/2 cups all-purpose flour

Mix together the whole wheat flour, dry milk, yeast, salt, and wheat germ. Add the water, honey, oil, and nuts. Blend in a mixer at low speed for 1 minute and at medium speed for 2 more minutes. By hand, stir in 1 cup additional whole wheat flour and add 4 to 4 1/2 cups all-purpose flour. Knead on a floured surface for about 5 minutes. Place the dough in a greased bowl; cover and let rise 45 to 60 minutes, or until doubled in size. Punch the dough down and divide it in half. Shape each half into a loaf. Place in two 9 x 5-inch loaf pans. Cover and let rise 30 to 45 minutes. Toward the end of this time, preheat the oven to 375 degrees. Bake for 40 to 45 minutes, or until the loaves sounds hollow when tapped. To soften the crust, brush with butter immediately.

BRUCE LEE
CROSS IN THE DESERT UNITED METHODIST CHURCH
PHOENIX, ARIZONA

CHEESE BREAD

1/2 cup milk
1 egg, beaten
1 1/2 cups biscuit mix
1 tablespoon minced onion
1 cup shredded Cheddar cheese, divided
2 tablespoons chopped parsley
1/4 cup margarine, melted

Preheat the oven to 350 degrees. In a large bowl, combine the milk and egg. Add the biscuit mix, onion, 1/2 cup cheese, and parsley. Pour into a greased 8- or 9-inch round pan. Sprinkle the remaining 1/2 cup cheese over the batter. Pour the melted margarine over the top. Bake for 25 minutes, or until golden brown.

STEFANI WILSON
HIGHLAND HEIGHTS PRESBYTERIAN CHURCH
CORDOVA, TENNESSEE

HOT GARLIC BREAD

1 garlic clove, peeled
4 tablespoons butter
1 (8- to 10-inch) loaf Italian bread
2 tablespoons grated Parmesan cheese

Mince the garlic. Melt the butter over low heat, add the minced garlic, and cool for 4 minutes. Divide the loaf of bread lengthwise in half. Spread the melted garlic butter evenly over the cut faces of the bread. Sprinkle 1 tablespoon of Parmesan cheese over each loaf half. Place the bread under the broiler for about 2 minutes, or until the bread toasts to a golden brown and the cheese sizzles but does not burn. Serve in a basket covered with a cloth to keep warm.

MERRY R. JONES
GRIFFIN CHAPEL UNITED METHODIST CHURCH
STARKVILLE, MISSISSIPPI

MEXICAN CORNBREAD

1 cup yellow cornmeal
1/2 teaspoon salt
1/2 teaspoon baking soda
1/3 cup shortening, melted
1 cup sour cream
1 (8-ounce) can cream-style corn
2 eggs, beaten
1 (4-ounce) can chopped green chile peppers, drained
1 cup shredded Cheddar cheese

Preheat the oven to 375 degrees. Combine the cornmeal, salt, and baking soda and blend. Stir in the shortening, sour cream, corn, and eggs and mix well. Add the green chilies and cheese and stir. Pour into a greased 9 x 13-inch pan and bake for 35 to 40 minutes.

FLO WYLES
HOLUM BAPTIST CHURCH
GRAYSON, LOUISIANA

JOHNNYCAKE

1 cup cornmeal
2 cups pancake mix
1 teaspoon baking powder
1 tablespoon sugar
1 egg
1/4 cup oil or butter
1 cup water

Preheat the oven to 350 degrees. Combine all the ingredients and mix well. Pour the batter into a greased 9-inch pan and bake for 35 minutes. Makes enough for 8 to 10 people.

Note: The pancake mix makes this recipe light and nice.

KATE LYSTAD
PITT COMMUNITY CHURCH
BAUDETTE, MINNESOTA

HUSH PUPPIES

2 cups cornmeal
1 cup all-purpose flour
2 tablespoons minced onion
1 egg
2 tablespoons bacon grease
Creole seasoning to taste
2 tablespoons baking powder
milk

Combine all the ingredients with just enough milk to make a thick mixture. Wet your hands and shape the mixture into 1 1/2-inch balls. Drop into deep fat and remove when brown. Drain on absorbent paper.

BARBARA BOLING
HUNGARIAN PRESBYTERIAN CHURCH
ALBANY, LOUISIANA

CORN FRITTERS

1 1/2 cups self-rising flour
1 1/2 teaspoons baking powder
1 teaspoon salt
1 (16-ounce) can cream-style corn
1 egg, slightly beaten
1 cup corn oil
powdered sugar (optional)

Sift together all the dry ingredients. Combine the corn and egg. Add the dry ingredients to the egg mixture, stirring slowly. Heat the oil in a large skillet over medium heat. Drop the batter by tablespoonfuls into the hot oil, one layer at a time. Fry on each side for about 2 minutes until golden brown. Drain on absorbent paper and dust with powdered sugar, if desired. Makes 16 fritters.

PINEMOUNT BAPTIST CHURCH
McALPIN, FLORIDA

DINNER ROLLS

3/4 cup lukewarm water
3 packages dry yeast
2 1/4 cups lukewarm milk
1/4 cup cooking oil
1/4 cup sugar
3 teaspoons salt
3 eggs
9 1/4 cups all-purpose flour, divided in half

Measure the water into a mixing bowl. Add the yeast, stirring to dissolve. Stir in the remaining ingredients (half of the flour). Mix with a spoon until smooth. Add enough flour to handle easily, but keep the dough as soft as possible. Mix by hand. Turn out onto a floured board. Knead until smooth, about 5 minutes. Place the dough in a greased bowl, turning to coat with the oil. Cover with a damp cloth. Let rise until almost doubled in size. Divide the dough and shape as desired. Preheat the oven to 400 degrees. Let the dough rise again and bake for 12 to 15 minutes, or until browned.

MAXINE KASZA
MCCLAVE UNITED METHODIST CHURCH
MCCLAVE, COLORADO

LAST-MINUTE ROLLS

1 1/4 cups scalded milk
2 1/2 tablespoons sugar
1 1/2 teaspoons salt
1/4 cup soft shortening
2 packages dry yeast or cakes
1/4 cup warm water
3 1/4 cups all-purpose flour, sifted

About 1 1/2 hours before dinner: In a large bowl, combine the milk, sugar, salt, and shortening. Cool until lukewarm. In a small bowl, sprinkle or crumble the yeast into the warm water and stir until dissolved. Stir into the lukewarm milk mixture. Add the flour; stir until well blended, about 1 minute. Cover with a towel and let rise until doubled in size. Stir the batter well to deflate, then beat vigorously for about 1/2 minute. Preheat the oven to 400 degrees. Fill greased muffin pan cups or pinch off pieces of dough and arrange in a pan. Bake for about 25 minutes. Makes 1 dozen.

DONNA SHAFER
NORTH MONROE STREET CHURCH OF GOD
MONROE, MICHIGAN

NICE AND EASY ROLLS

2 cups self-rising flour
1 cup sweet milk
1/4 cup regular mayonnaise

Preheat the oven to 425 degrees. Grease 12 (about 2 1/2-inch) muffin cups. Combine the flour, milk, and mayonnaise in a medium bowl. Stir just until the dry ingredients are moistened. Divide the dough equally among the muffin cups. Bake for 20 minutes. Serve warm or at room temperature.

ROQUELE JONES
GRIFFIN CHAPEL UNITED METHODIST CHURCH
STARKVILLE, MISSISSIPPI

GIVE US THIS DAY OUR DAILY BREAD

Back of the loaf is the snowy flour,
And back of the flour, the mill ...
And back of the mill are the wheat and the shower
And the sun, and the Father's will.

This is from "Our Favorite Recipes", St. John's, Newfoundland Jaycettes, 1968-69

SUBMITTED BY ANNE CHAPMAN
UNITED BAPTIST CHURCH OF POULTNEY
EAST POULTNEY, VERMONT

SOURDOUGH ROLLS

6 cups self-rising flour
1/4 cup sugar
3/4 cup oil
2 cups buttermilk
1 package yeast in 1 cup lukewarm water

Preheat the oven to 425 degrees. Combine the dry ingredients, then add the oil, buttermilk, and yeast to the mixture. Store in the refrigerator. Pinch off as needed for rolls. (Keeps in the refrigerator for up to 3 weeks.) Bake for 10 to 12 minutes.

CLARA MILLER
WESTSIDE BAPTIST CHURCH
ANTLERS, OKLAHOMA

REFRIGERATOR ROLLS

1/4 cup sugar
1 teaspoon salt
6 tablespoons Wesson oil
1 cup warm water
1 egg
1 package dry yeast
3 1/2 to 4 cups all-purpose flour

Mix the first 4 ingredients. Add the egg. Dissolve the yeast in 2 tablespoons of warm water, then add it to the mixture. Add the flour. Refrigerate and let sit for several hours or overnight.

Dip your hands in the flour and roll the dough into small pieces; put pieces into an oiled muffin ring. Let rise 2 to 3 hours. Preheat the oven to 450 degrees. Put 3 or 4 pieces of dough into each muffin ring. Bake for about 8 minutes.

JEANIE MOORE
HIGHLAND HEIGHTS PRESBYTERIAN CHURCH
CORDOVA, TENNESSEE

LIGHT TASTY BISCUITS

2 cups all-purpose flour
2 1/2 teaspoons baking powder
1/4 cup sugar
1/3 cup shortening
1/4 cup milk

Preheat the oven to 475 degrees. Sift together the flour, baking powder, and sugar. Cut in the shortening with a fork. The mixture should resemble coarse cornmeal. Add the milk and lightly blend until the flour is moistened and the dough pulls away from the sides of the bowl. Turn out onto a floured board. Knead lightly, about 30 seconds, and roll to 3/4-inch thickness. Cut the dough with a biscuit cutter, dipping the cutter into the flour between cuts. Place on lightly greased pans. Brush the tops of the biscuits with butter. Bake for 12 to 15 minutes, or until golden brown.

MICHELLE FLETCHER
HOLUM BAPTIST CHURCH
GRAYSON, LOUISIANA

TINY CREAM CHEESE BISCUITS

1 (8-ounce) package cream cheese, softened
1/2 cup margarine, softened
1 cup self-rising flour

Preheat the oven to 400 degrees. Beat the cream cheese and margarine in a mixer on medium speed for 2 minutes or until creamy. Gradually add the flour, beating on low speed just until blended. Spoon the dough into ungreased miniature muffin pans, filling full. Bake for 15 minutes, or until golden. Serve immediately. Makes 1 1/2 dozen.

RENATA MARTIN
NORTHBROOK UNITED METHODIST CHURCH
ROSWELL, GEORGIA

CHEESE-GARLIC BISCUITS

2 cups Bisquick
2/3 cup milk
1/2 cup shredded Cheddar cheese (2 ounces)
1/4 teaspoon garlic powder
1/4 cup margarine or butter, melted

Preheat the oven to 450 degrees. Mix the Bisquick, milk, and cheese until a soft dough forms; beat vigorously for 30 seconds. Drop the dough by spoonfuls onto an ungreased cookie sheet. Bake for 8 to 10 minutes, or until golden brown. Mix the garlic powder and margarine; brush over the warm biscuits before removing them from the cookie sheet. Serve warm.

MAGALENE NELSON
BETHEL AME CHURCH
AUGUSTA, GEORGIA

POPOVERS

2 cups self-rising flour
3 tablespoons mayonnaise
1 cup milk
1 teaspoon sugar

Preheat the oven to 350 degrees. Combine all the ingredients. Drop by teaspoonfuls onto a well-greased cookie sheet. Bake for 10 to 12 minutes. Will be crispy.

SHELBY FLETCHER
HOLUM BAPTIST CHURCH
GRAYSON, LOUISIANA

You Won't Tire of This Recipe

just for kids!

Take two or more children, wash well in warm water and tuck into bed early. Leave for 10 or 12 hours with windows open. Next morning, dress them lightly and set at the cheeriest place at the breakfast table. To each child add juice of 1 orange, 1 soft boiled egg mixed with 2 tablespoons cream and salt to taste, several slices whole wheat bread, a glass of milk.

Remove to the yard, add some garden seeds, toys, a sand pile and mix thoroughly. Leave in the sun until brown.

DELPHIA STONE
CALVARY UNITED METHODIST CHURCH
TAYLOR, NEBRASKA

Banana-Nut Bread

1 cup mashed ripe bananas
1/3 cup low-fat buttermilk
1/2 cup packed brown sugar
1/4 cup margarine
1 egg
2 cups all-purpose flour
1 teaspoon baking powder
1/4 teaspoon baking soda
1/2 teaspoon salt
1/2 cup chopped pecans

Preheat the oven to 350 degrees. Lightly oil a 9 x 5-inch loaf pan. Stir together the mashed bananas and buttermilk; set aside. Cream the sugar and margarine together until light. Beat in the egg. Add the banana mixture; beat well. Sift together the flour, baking powder, baking soda, and salt; add all at once to the liquid ingredients. Stir until well blended. Stir in the nuts and turn into a prepared pan. Bake for 50 to 55 minutes, or until a toothpick inserted into the center comes out clean. Cool for 5 minutes in the pan. Remove from the pan and complete cooling on a wire rack before slicing.

MARY WHITE
OAKMONT CHURCH OF GOD
SHREVEPORT, LOUISIANA

FRESH BLUEBERRY-BANANA BREAD

1 cup fresh blueberries, washed and drained
    well
1 3/4 cups all-purpose flour, divided
2 teaspoons baking powder
1/4 teaspoon baking soda
1/2 teaspoon salt
1/3 cup butter
2/3 cup sugar
2 eggs
1 cup mashed ripe bananas

Preheat the oven to 350 degrees. In a small bowl, toss the berries with 2 tablespoons flour. Sift together the remaining flour, baking powder, baking soda, and salt. In a separate bowl, cream the butter; gradually beat in the sugar until light and fluffy. Beat in the eggs, one at a time. Add the flour mixture and bananas alternately in 3 parts. Stir in the blueberries. Spoon the mixture into a greased and floured 9 x 5 x 3-inch pan. Bake for 50 minutes, or until done. Cool for 10 to 15 minutes; remove from the pan and finish cooling. Makes 1 loaf.

JAMIE KLEINDL
TRINITY UNITED METHODIST CHURCH
YORK, PENNSYLVANIA

PUMPKIN-NUT BREAD

2 cups all-purpose flour
2 teaspoons baking powder
1/2 teaspoon baking soda
1 teaspoon ground cinnamon
1/2 teaspoon ground nutmeg
1/2 teaspoon salt
1 cup canned pumpkin
1 cup granulated sugar
1/2 cup milk
2 eggs
1/4 cup butter or margarine, softened
1/2 cup chopped nuts
Confectioners' sugar

Preheat the oven to 350 degrees. Grease a 9 x 5 x 3-inch loaf pan. On a sheet of waxed paper, sift together the flour, baking powder, soda, cinnamon, nutmeg, and salt; set aside. In a large bowl, combine the pumpkin, sugar, milk, eggs, and butter; beat until well blended. Add the flour mixture, beating just until smooth. Stir in the nuts. Pour the batter into the prepared pan. Bake for 50 to 60 minutes, or until a cake tester inserted in the center comes out clean. Cool in the pan for 10 minutes. Remove from the pan; cool completely. Before serving, sprinkle with confectioners' sugar and cut into thin slices.

MARGARET W. DECKER
TRINITY UNITED METHODIST CHURCH
YORK, PENNSYLVANIA

Amish Friendship Bread

Do not use a metal spoon on bowl for mixing.

Do not refrigerate.

If air gets in the bag, let it out.

It is normal for batter to ferment and thicken.

Day 1: This is the day you receive the batter. Do nothing.

Day 2: Squeeze the bag.

Day 3: Squeeze the bag.

Day 4: Squeeze the bag.

Day 5: Squeeze the bag.

Day 6: Add 1 cup flour, 1 cup sugar, 1 cup milk & squeeze the bag.

Day 7: Squeeze the bag.

Day 8: Squeeze the bag.

Day 9: Squeeze the bag.

Day 10: Combine in a large bowl, the batter, 1 cup flour, 1 cup sugar, and 1 cup milk. Mix with a wooden spoon or spatula. Put four (4) 1 cup starters in zip lock bags. Keep 1 starter for yourself and give the others to your friends with these instructions.

To the remaining batter in bowl, add: 1 cup oil, 1 cup sugar, 1 teaspoon vanilla, 3 large eggs, 1/2 teaspoon salt, 2 teaspoons cinnamon, 2 cups flour, 1/2 cup milk, 1/2 teaspoon baking soda, 1 large box instant vanilla pudding, 1 1/2 teaspoons baking powder. Mix all.

Pour into 2 large well-greased sugared (mix cinnamon and sugar) loaf pans.

You can sprinkle extra sugar and cinnamon on top.

Bake at 350 degrees for 1 hour. Let cool in pans before removing.

Optional: Add 1 cup chopped pecans and/or 1/2 cups raisins or dried cherries.

A GIFT FROM A FRIEND
GALE JAMES
MIRACLE DELIVERANCE HOLINESS CHURCH
COLUMBIA, SOUTH CAROLINA

Zucchini Bread

3 eggs, beaten
2 cups sugar
1 cup oil
2 teaspoons vanilla
2 cups grated zucchini
3 cups all-purpose flour
1 teaspoon baking soda
1/4 teaspoon baking powder
1 teaspoon salt
3 teaspoons cinnamon
1 cup chopped nuts (optional)

Preheat the oven to 325 degrees. Mix the eggs, sugar, oil, and vanilla until blended. Add the zucchini, flour, baking soda, baking powder, salt, and cinnamon. Mix well. Add the nuts, if desired. Pour into a greased bread pan and bake for 1 hour, or until done.

Note: The bread can be frozen for later use.

PAM LAMBERT
UNITED METHODIST CHURCH
ESTÂNCIA, NEW MEXICO

APPLE BREAD

2/3 cup sugar
1/3 cup soft shortening
2 eggs
3 tablespoons sour milk mixed with 1
    tablespoon vinegar
1 cup grated, unpared apples
2 cups all-purpose flour
1 teaspoon baking powder
1/2 teaspoon baking soda
1/3 teaspoon salt
1/2 cup chopped nuts

In a large bowl, mix the sugar, shortening, and eggs until creamy. Stir in the milk mixture and apples. In a separate bowl, stir together the flour, baking powder, baking soda, salt, and chopped nuts. Add the dry mixture to the creamed mixture. Pour into a 9 x 5 x 3-inch greased loaf pan. Let stand for 20 minutes, preheating the oven to 350 degrees toward the end of this time. Bake for 50 to 60 minutes. The apples can be chopped in a food processor (Red says she hates graters because she always gets her fingers.)

RED LESTER
MATTAPOISETT CONGREGATIONAL CHURCH
MATTAPOISETT, MASSACHUSETTS

CANADIAN LEMON BREAD

6 tablespoons shortening
1 cup sugar
2 eggs, beaten
1 1/2 cups all-purpose flour
2 teaspoons baking powder
1/2 cup milk
Juice and rind of 1 lemon
1/2 cup sugar

Preheat the oven to 350 degrees. In a large bowl, mix the shortening and the 1 cup sugar. Add the eggs. Combine the flour and baking powder and add to the mixture, alternating with the milk. Add the lemon rind. Pour into a loaf pan and bake for about 1 hour. Before removing the bread from the pan, and while it is still hot, pour a mixture of 1/2 cup sugar and 1/4 cup lemon juice over the top. Let cool. Makes 1 loaf.

LINDA LAPLANTE
CAVENDISH BAPTIST CHURCH
CAVENDISH, VERMONT

EGGNOG BREAD

1/2 cup melted butter
1 1/2 cups sugar
4 eggs, beaten
2 cups eggnog
4 1/2 cups all-purpose flour
4 teaspoons baking powder
2 teaspoons salt
1 cup chopped pecans
1 cup chopped cherries
1 cup raisins
1 cup dates

Preheat the oven to 350 degrees. In a large mixing bowl, using a fork blend the butter and sugar together. Stir in the eggs, then gradually stir in the eggnog. Mix well. In a separate bowl, combine the flour, baking powder, and salt. Gradually add the dry mixture to the eggnog mixture. (Do not use an electric beater.) Fold in the pecans, cherries, raisins, and dates. Fill loaf pans three-fourth full (I recommend 6 small 6 x 3 1/2 x 2-inch pans or one 9 x 5 x 3-inch pan). Bake for 25 minutes.

GLORIA OLSON
CROSS IN THE DESERT UNITED METHODIST CHURCH
PHOENIX, ARIZONA

Babka for Easter (Grandma Koller)

4 eggs
1 teaspoon salt
1 cup sugar
1 teaspoon vanilla extract
1 teaspoon Grand Marnier
2 cups milk
2 sticks butter, melted
1 cake yeast
1/2 cup warm water
8 cups all-purpose flour
2 oranges, chopped
1 lemon, chopped
1 cup almonds
1 cup dark raisins
1 1/2 cups golden raisins

In a mixing bowl, beat together the eggs, salt, sugar, vanilla, and Grand Marnier. Scald the milk with the butter and cool to lukewarm. Dissolve the yeast in the warm water and add to the milk mixture. Into a large bowl, sift the flour. Combine the milk mixture with the egg mixture and slowly stir in the flour. Add the citrus fruits, almonds, and raisins. Mix with a wooden spoon until smooth. Form the dough into a mound and place it in a greased bowl. Cover with a towel and let rise until doubled in size. Punch down; let rise again. In the meantime preheat the oven to 350 degrees. Grease a 9-inch tube pan and scatter crumbs made of 1 stick butter, sugar, cinnamon, and flour on the bottom. Punch the dough down again and arrange it on top of the crumbs. Bake until light brown and hollow-sounding.

This is my Grandmother's recipe.

GRACE LeLORENZO
PRINCE OF PEACE CHURCH
GRANTSVILLE, WEST VIRGINIA

Christmas Braid

DOUGH:
1 1/2 cups scalded milk, cooled to lukewarm
1/2 cup butter or margarine
2 packages dry yeast
1/2 cup warm water
1/2 cup sugar
2 teaspoons salt
2 teaspoons grated lemon rind
3 eggs, slightly beaten
1/4 teaspoon mace
1 cup raisins
1 cup chopped nuts (almonds, pecans, walnuts, or a combination)
1 cup chopped mixed candied fruit (such as an 8-ounce container of fruitcake mixture)
7 to 7 1/2 cups sifted all-purpose flour

Scald the milk and add the butter (to melt the butter and help cool the milk). In a large mixing bowl, dissolve the yeast in the warm water. Add the next 9 ingredients and half of the flour, mixing well with a spoon. Continue adding flour until the dough can be handled easily. Turn out onto a lightly floured board and knead for 5 minutes, or until smooth and elastic. Form the dough into a ball and place it in a greased bowl; cover with a damp cloth and let rise in a warm place until doubled in size, about 1 1/2 to 2 hours. Punch down and let rise again until almost double, about 30 minutes. Punch down again. Divide the dough in half. Divide each half into 3 equal portions and roll and stretch each into a long strand. Braid the strands, tucking the ends under. Place on a greased cookie sheet. Cover again and let rise until doubled in size, 45 to 60 minutes. Toward the end of this time, preheat the oven to 350 degrees. Bake for 30 to 40 minutes. When cool, use a pastry brush to brush on Quick White Icing (see below). Makes 2 generous loaves.

QUICK WHITE ICING:
1 cup powdered sugar
1 teaspoon vanilla
small amount of milk

Sift the sugar into a bowl; add the vanilla and then the milk, a little bit at a time, until the icing is of spreading consistency.

PEGGY OLNEY
MATTAPOISETT CONGREGATIONAL CHURCH
MATTAPOISETT, MASSACHUSETTS

CHRISTMAS STOLLEN

12 cups all-purpose flour
3 cups milk
1 pound butter, melted
6 eggs
1 pound seedless raisins
1 pound currants
2 cups sugar
1/2 teaspoon mace
1 tablespoon grated lemon zest
3 tablespoons lemon juice
1 tablespoon cognac (plus more to sprinkle
    on top)
2 1/2 cups blanched almonds, chopped
1/2 pound finely chopped citron
1 1/2 teaspoons salt
2 cakes compressed yeast, dissolved in 1/2
    cup lukewarm water
1/2 teaspoon grated nutmeg
Melted butter
Powdered sugar

Preheat the oven to 350 degrees. Sift the flour into a large mixing bowl. Make a hollow in the center and work in the milk, butter, and eggs until almost everything is mixed. Wash and drain the raisins and currants, soaking them for a few minutes. Drain and combine with the other ingredients. Work everything into the dough by hand until the ingredients are evenly mixed. (The dough should be stiff.) Knead and fold the dough over on itself repeatedly until it is smooth and all the ingredients have been evenly distributed. Cover the bowl lightly with a folded towel and let it stand in a warm place (not hot) for 12 hours. Turn the dough out onto a lightly floured bread board. Divide it in half and shape each half into a loaf with slightly pointed ends. Place them in greased baking pans. Cover the loaves lightly with the folded towel and let them stand in a warm place (not hot) until they have doubled in size. Bake for about 1 hour. While the bread is still hot, spread it with melted butter and sprinkle with the cognac and powdered sugar. Makes 2 loaves. Serves 16.

TRINITY UNITED METHODIST CHURCH
HUDSON, NEW YORK

JEAN GALLANT'S COFFEE CAKE

1/2 cup butter
1 cup sugar
2 eggs
1 teaspoon vanilla extract
2 cups all-purpose flour
1/2 teaspoon salt
1 teaspoon baking powder
1 teaspoon baking soda
1/2 pint sour cream

TOPPING:
1/4 to 1/2 cup sugar and cinnamon
1/4 to 1/2 cup chopped nuts

Preheat the oven to 350 degrees. In the bowl of an electric mixer, cream the butter, sugar, and eggs; add the vanilla. In a separate bowl, combine the dry ingredients and add to the liquid mixture alternately with the sour cream. Mix together the topping ingredients. Spread half of the batter in a tube pan and sprinkle with half of the topping. Add the remaining batter then the remaining topping. Bake the cake for 40 minutes.

HAZEL JONES
DAMASCUS UNITED METHODIST CHURCH
DAMASCUS, MARYLAND

German Coffee Cake

2 cups all-purpose flour
3/4 cup sugar
1/4 teaspoon cinnamon
1 teaspoon salt
4 teaspoons baking powder
1/4 cup shortening
3 eggs
1 cup milk
1/4 cup chopped nuts
1 cup chopped apples
brown sugar (optional)

Preheat the oven to 350 degrees. Sift the dry ingredients together. Work in the shortening, then add eggs and milk. Stir until smooth. Stir in the nuts. Pour the batter into a greased 8 x 12-inch pan. Cover with the chopped apples. Sprinkle with brown sugar, if desired. Bake for 30 minutes.

Madlyn Rosel
Highland Heights Presbyterian Church
Cordova, Tennessee

Sour Cream Coffee Cake

1/2 cup butter
1 cup sugar
2 eggs
1 cup sour cream
2 cups all-purpose flour
1 teaspoon baking powder
1 teaspoon baking soda

Filling:
1/2 cup sugar
1 teaspoon ground cinnamon
1/2 cup chopped nuts

Preheat the oven to 350 degrees. Grease a tube or Bundt pan. In the bowl of an electric mixer, cream the butter and sugar. Add the eggs and sour cream, mixing well. Sift the dry ingredients together and add to the butter mixture; beat, mixing until well blended.

In a bowl, combine all the ingredients and mix well. Spread half of the cake batter in the baking pan (the batter will be thick). Top with half of the filling. Top this with the other half of the batter, ending with the remaining filling. Bake the cake for 30 to 40 minutes or until a wooden toothpick inserted into the center comes out clean.

Cindy Bersch
Arlene Baker
Trinity United Methodist Church
Hudson, New York

CRANBERRY COFFEE CAKE

CAKE:
1 cup softened butter (no substitution!)
1 cup sugar
2 eggs
2 cups all-purpose flour
1 teaspoon baking powder
1 teaspoon baking soda
1/2 teaspoon salt
1 cup sour cream (8 ounces)
1 teaspoon almond extract
1 (16-ounce) can whole-berry cranberry
   sauce
1/2 cup chopped walnuts

GLAZE:
1/3 cup confectioners' sugar
5 teaspoons warm water
1/2 teaspoon almond extract

Preheat the oven to 350 degrees. In a mixing bowl, cream the butter and sugar. Add the eggs and mix well. Combine the flour, baking powder, baking soda, and salt; add to the creamed mixture, alternating with the sour cream. Add the extract. Spoon a third of the batter into a greased 9-inch square baking pan. Top with a third of the cranberry sauce. Repeat layers twice. Sprinkle with walnuts. Bake for 55 to 60 minutes, or until a toothpick inserted into the center comes out clean.

Combine all the ingredients and mix until smooth. Drizzle over the warm coffee cake.

MARTHA ANN EDMINSTER
MATTAPOISETT CONGREGATIONAL CHURCH
MATTAPOISETT, MASSACHUSETTS

CINNAMON ROLLS

2 cakes yeast
2 tablespoons sugar
1 cup warm water
1 cup milk, scalded and cooled (can use
   powdered milk)
6 tablespoons butter
1/2 cup sugar
7 cups all-purpose flour
2 eggs
1 teaspoon salt
cinnamon and brown sugar
raisins and nuts (optional)

Dissolve the yeast in the warm water with 2 tablespoons sugar. Add the milk, butter, 1/2 cup sugar, and 3 cups flour and beat until smooth. Add the eggs, salt, and enough of the remaining flour to make a soft dough. Turn out onto a floured board and knead lightly adding flour as needed to prevent the dough from sticking. Place in a greased bowl. Cover and let raise in a warm place for about 2 hours. Roll out to 1/4-inch thickness. Brush with the melted butter. Sprinkle with cinnamon and brown sugar. Add nuts or raisins, if desired. Roll up the dough and cut it into 1 1/2-inch slices. Place in a well-greased pan. Cover and let rise for about 1 hour. Toward the end of this time, preheat the oven to 375 degrees. Bake for about 40 minutes. Frost with powdered sugar frosting.

Note: For longer-lasting rolls, add 1/2 cup mashed potatoes to the batter.

MARY JANE FLOYD
UNITED METHODIST CHURCH
ESTÂNCIA, NEW MEXICO

STICKY BUNS

1/2 to 3/4 cup chopped nuts
1 (18- to 24-ounce) package frozen dinner
  rolls
1 (3-ounce) package butterscotch pudding
  (not instant)
3/4 cup granulated sugar
3/4 cup brown sugar
1 teaspoon cinnamon
1/3 cup butter, melted

Coat a tube pan with cooking spray. Scatter the chopped nuts on the bottom of the pan. Separate the dinner rolls and arrange them on top of the nuts. Mix the dry ingredients together and sprinkle over the rolls. Drizzle the melted butter over the top of the rolls. Put the pan in the cold oven and leave overnight. Do not remove the rolls from the oven. Bake at 350 degrees for 30 to 35 minutes.

When the rolls have browned on top, remove them from the oven and turn them upside down on a plate. Remove the pan carefully, as it will be very hot.

FRANCES CHAMBLEE
CROSS IN THE DESERT UNITED METHODIST CHURCH
PHOENIX, ARIZONA

BLUEBERRY MUFFINS

1 cup all-purpose flour
1 cup whole wheat flour
1/4 cup granulated sugar
3/4 teaspoon baking powder
3/4 teaspoon baking soda
1/2 teaspoon ground cinnamon
1/4 teaspoon ground allspice
1 egg white
1 cup buttermilk
1 1/2 tablespoons vegetable oil
1 1/4 cups fresh or frozen blueberries

Preheat the oven to 375 degrees. Coat a 12-cup muffin pan with cooking spray or line with paper liners. Set aside. In a medium bowl, combine the flours, sugar, baking powder, baking soda, and spices. Mix well. In a small bowl, whisk together the egg white, buttermilk, and oil. Add the liquid mixture to the dry ingredients and stir until just blended. Gently fold in the blueberries. Divide the batter among the prepared muffin pans, filling each two-thirds full. Bake until the tops are lightly golden, about 20 minutes. Place the pan on a wire rack and cool for 5 minutes. Turn the muffins out onto a rack and cool completely. Makes 12 muffins.

Note: If you are using frozen blueberries, do not thaw them before adding them to the batter.

ROSE VANOVER
GRIFFIN CHAPEL UNITED METHODIST CHURCH
STARKVILLE, MISSISSIPPI

ORANGE-PUMPKIN MUFFINS

1 3/4 cups all-purpose flour
1 1/2 teaspoons pumpkin allspice
1/2 teaspoon baking powder
1 teaspoon baking soda
1/2 teaspoon salt
1 cup sugar
1/2 cup packed brown sugar
2 eggs
1/3 cup oil
1 cup canned pumpkin
1/3 cup orange juice
1 tablespoon grated orange zest
1/2 cup chopped walnuts

Preheat the oven to 350 degrees. In a small bowl, combine the flour, pumpkin allspice, baking powder, baking soda, and salt. In a large bowl, combine the sugars, eggs, and oil. Add the pumpkin, orange juice, and orange zest to the sugar mixture. Beat until well blended. Stir in the dry ingredients until just blended. Line a 6-cup muffin pan with paper baking cups and fill two-thirds full. Sprinkle the walnuts on top. Bake for 20 to 25 minutes, or until a toothpick inserted into the center comes out clean. Cool. Makes 6 muffins.

DOROTHY VALDEZ
UNITED METHODIST CHURCH
ESTÂNCIA, NEW MEXICO

CORN MUFFINS

2 tablespoons sugar
1 1/2 cups Bisquick
1/2 cup cornmeal
2 eggs
2/3 cup milk

Preheat the oven to 400 degrees. Mix all the ingredients in a medium bowl. Preheat a greased 12-cup muffin pan in the hot oven until it's hot. Spoon the mixture into the muffin cups and bake for 15 minutes. Makes 12 muffins.

Note: These muffins can also be cooked in a hot, greased 10-inch skillet. Bake for 20 to 25 minutes at 400 degrees.

ANN CURTIS
BUCKINGHAM UNITED METHODIST CHURCH
GARLAND, TEXAS

BRAN MUFFINS

2 cups bran flakes
1 cup milk
1/2 cup vegetable oil
2 eggs, slightly beaten
1/3 cup sugar
1 1/2 cups all-purpose flour
1/2 teaspoon salt
2 teaspoons baking powder

In a medium bowl, combine the bran flakes, milk, oil, and eggs. Mix briefly by hand. Add the next 4 ingredients and stir until just blended. Place about 2 heaping tablespoons of the mixture into muffin pans. Makes approximately 18 muffins.

Note: We have these for breakfast, crumbling them into a big glass, then pouring milk over and eating with a spoon.

LINDA THOMAS
IMMANUEL BAPTIST CHURCH
ESTÂNCIA, NEW MEXICO

MORNING GLORY MUFFINS

2 cups all-purpose flour
1 1/4 cups sugar
2 teaspoons baking soda
1/2 teaspoon salt
2 teaspoons cinnamon
2 cups grated carrots
1/2 cup raisins
1/2 cup shredded coconut
1/2 cup chopped pecans
3 eggs
1 cup vegetable oil
2 teaspoons vanilla extract
1 apple, cored and shredded

Preheat the oven to 350 degrees. In a large mixing bowl, combine the flour, sugar, baking soda, salt, and cinnamon. Stir in the carrots, raisins, coconut, and pecans. In a separate bowl, combine the eggs, oil, vanilla, and apple. Add to the flour mixture. Stir only until combined. Spoon into greased muffin cups. Bake for 15 to 18 minutes. Makes 18 muffins.

MARTHA YEARY
NORTH MONROE STREET CHURCH OF GOD
MONROE, MICHIGAN

WHOLE WHEAT–MAPLE MUFFINS

1 cup sugar
1/2 cup butter or margarine
3 cups whole wheat flour
5 teaspoons baking powder
3 eggs
1 cup milk
2 tablespoons maple syrup

Preheat the oven to 400 degrees. In the bowl of a mixer, cream the butter and sugar; blend in the flour and baking powder. In a separate bowl, beat the eggs, milk, and syrup. Make a hole in the center of the dry ingredients and add the liquid mixture. Mix with a fork until just blended. Fill 12 greased muffin cups about one-half full. Bake for about 20 minutes. Makes 12 muffins.

CINDY GENNES
PITT COMMUNITY CHURCH
BAUDETTE, MINNESOTA

STRAWBERRY MUFFINS

1 1/2 cups all-purpose flour
1/2 teaspoon baking soda
1/2 teaspoon salt
1 cup sugar
1 teaspoon vanilla extract
1 teaspoon butter-flavored extract
1 1/4 cups fresh sliced strawberries
2 eggs, well beaten
2/3 cup Mazola oil
1/2 cup chopped pecans (optional)

Preheat the oven to 375 degrees. Sift the dry ingredients together into a large bowl. Mix the remaining ingredients and add to the dry ingredients. Mix just until the dry ingredients are moist; do not overmix. Pour into a greased 12-cup muffin tin (or line the ungreased muffin cups with baking cups) and bake for 25 minutes. The muffins are best if they are removed from the tin immediately.

Note: You can make a loaf if you prefer. Pour the batter into a greased 9 x 5-inch loaf pan and bake for about 60 minutes at 350 degrees. Serves 12.

FRANCES RADEMACHER
DAMASCUS UNITED METHODIST CHURCH
DAMASCUS, MARYLAND

PECAN FRENCH TOAST

4 eggs
2/3 cup orange juice
1/3 cup milk
1/4 cup sugar
1/4 teaspoon ground nutmeg
1/4 teaspoon vanilla extract
1/2 loaf Italian bread, cut into 1-inch slices
1/3 cup melted butter
1/2 cup pecan pieces
Grated orange peel to taste
Maple or Orange Syrup

ORANGE SYRUP:
1/2 cup sugar
1/2 cup butter
1 cup orange juice

For the toast: Combine the first 6 ingredients in a medium bowl and beat with a wire whisk. Place the bread, edges touching, in a single layer in a large flat baking dish or cookie sheet. Pour the egg mixture over the bread, cover, and refrigerate overnight, turning once. When ready to cook, preheat the oven to 400 degrees. Pour the melted butter on a cookie sheet or jellyroll pan, spreading evenly. Arrange soaked bread slices on the pan in a single layer. Sprinkle with the pecans and orange peel. Bake until golden, 20 to 25 minutes. Check slices during the last 10 minutes of baking time to avoid burning. Serve with syrup, butter, or fresh fruit. Serves 4.

For the syrup: Combine the 3 ingredients and cook over low heat for 10 minutes. Do not boil. Serve warm.

JAN WICKLIFFE
CROSS IN THE DESERT UNITED METHODIST CHURCH
PHOENIX, ARIZONA

BLUEBERRY-SOUR CREAM PANCAKES

1 1/3 cup all-purpose flour
1/2 teaspoon baking soda
1 teaspoon salt
1 tablespoon sugar
1/4 teaspoon ground nutmeg or cinnamon
1 egg, beaten
1 cup sour cream
1 cup milk
1 cup fresh blueberries

Sift the dry ingredients together. Combine the egg, sour cream, and milk and mix until blended; add to the dry ingredients. Fold in the blueberries and stir just until mixed. Spoon about 1/4 cup of the batter onto a hot nonstick griddle or skillet and cook until the edges look done. These pancakes take a little longer than usual to cook, but they're really light.

JAN WICKLIFFE
CROSS IN THE DESERT UNITED METHODIST CHURCH
PHOENIX, ARIZONA

BLUEBERRY FRENCH TOAST BAKE

FRENCH TOAST BAKE
12 slices of bread, cubed
2 (8- ounce) packages cream cheese
1 cup blueberries
12 eggs
1/3 cup maple syrup
2 cups milk

BLUEBERRY SYRUP
1 cup sugar
2 tablespoons cornstarch
1 cup water
1 tablespoon butter
1 cup blueberries

Arrange the bread cubes in the bottom of 13 x 9- inch baking pan. Dot with cream cheese and pour the blueberries over the bread cubes. Beat the eggs, add maple syrup and milk. Pour over the bread mixture and cover tightly with foil. Refrigerate overnight or at least 3 to 4 hours. Preheat the oven to 350 degrees. Bake for 30 minutes covered, then uncover and bake for an additional 30 minutes.

Stir sugar, cornstarch and water over high heat in a saucepan. Add butter and blueberries and cook until the blueberries pop. Serve warm over French Toast Bake.

REBECCA MCCULLOUGH
MATTAPOISETT CONGREGATIONAL CHURCH
MATTAPOISETT, MASSACHUSETTS

GINGERBREAD WAFFLES

2 cups all-purpose flour
1 1/2 teaspoons ground ginger
1/2 teaspoon ground cinnamon
1/2 teaspoon salt
1/3 cup butter
1 cup molasses
1 1/2 teaspoon soda
1/2 cup sour milk
1 egg, beaten

Sift together the flour, spices, and salt. Heat the butter and molasses to the boiling point, but do not boil. Beat in the baking soda. Add the sour milk, egg, and sifted dry ingredients. Serve hot with whipped cream. A combination of spiced peaches and gingerbread waffles makes a nice dessert.

MRS. HARRY STAHL
MOSCA UNITED METHODIST CHURCH
MOSCA, COLORADO

CHEESE DANISH

2 packages crescent rolls
2 (8-ounce) packages cream cheese
1 cup sugar
1 teaspoon vanilla extract
1 egg
1 egg white

GLAZE:
1 cup sugar
1 tablespoon milk
1/2 teaspoon vanilla extract

Preheat the oven to 350 degrees and grease a 13 x 9-inch pan. Lay a pack of crescent rolls in the pan and pinch the openings together. Beat the cream cheese, sugar, vanilla, and egg. Spread the mixture over the rolls, then lay a second pack of rolls on top; brush with egg white. Bake for 30 minutes. Top with the glaze.

MARLENE BURROW
BUCKINGHAM UNITED METHODIST CHURCH
GARLAND, TEXAS

DOUGHNUTS

One cup sugar, one cup milk
Two eggs beaten, fine as silk.
Salt and nutmeg (lemon will do)
Of baking powder, teaspoons two
Lightly stir the flour in.
Roll on a pie board, not too thin,
Cut in diamonds, twists or rings

Drip with care the doughy things
Into fat that briskly swells
Evenly the spongy cells;
Watch with care the time for turning
Fry them brown, just short of burning.
Roll in sugar, serve when cool,
Price a quarter for this rule.

This recipe is from a cookbook published in 1925.

DORIS M. POPE
DAMASCUS UNITED METHODIST CHURCH
DAMASCUS, MARYLAND

DOUGHNUTS

1 cup sugar
1/4 cup lard or shortening
2 eggs
1 cup buttermilk
1 teaspoon baking powder
1 teaspoon baking soda
1 teaspoon nutmeg
1 teaspoon ginger
1/4 teaspoon salt
4 cups all-purpose flour (about)

Cream the sugar and lard; add the eggs and beat. Add the next 6 ingredients. Beat until well mixed. Add enough flour to prevent the dough from sticking. Let stand, covered, in the refrigerator overnight. The next morning, roll the dough out onto a floured surface, cut (using a double cutter), and fry in deep fat.

ISABELLE BRIGGS
CAVENDISH BAPTIST CHURCH
CAVENDISH, VERMONT

BEIGNETS

2 cups all-purpose flour
1 tablespoon sugar
1 cup milk
1 egg

Sift the flour and sugar into bowl. Add the milk and egg; mix well. Drop by spoonfuls into deep fat heated at 375 degrees. Fry until golden brown. Drain on paper towels. Serve with syrup and butter.

CADE LYONS
HOLUM BAPTIST CHURCH
GRAYSON, LOUISIANA

SCONES

2 cups all-purpose flour
Pinch of salt
4 heaping teaspoons baking powder
1 tablespoon butter (1 ounce)
1 egg
Milk
Cheese
Raisins

Preheat the oven to 450 degrees. Combine the first 6 ingredients and mix. If you like textured scones, use a generous amount of milk. The mixture will be wettish and doughy. If you prefer to roll out the mixture and cut the scones into rounds with a cutter, it should be more like a bread dough and you would use less milk. I also grate cheese and sprinkle on the top of the scones before baking, or you can add 1 cup of grated cheese to the mixture. If you do not want cheese scones, leave out the cheese. If you want a sweet scone, add about 1 tablespoon of sugar and a few raisins. Bake for 12 to 15 minutes.

ETTA NEETHLING, PASTOR JOHANN'S MOTHER (SOUTH AFRICA)
UNITED METHODIST CHURCH
ESTÂNCIA, NEW MEXICO

YOGURT AND FRUIT SCONES

3 cups whole wheat flour
2 teaspoons baking powder
2 teaspoons baking soda
1/2 teaspoon salt
6 tablespoons butter or margarine
2 tablespoons brown sugar
1 1/4 cups low-fat plain yogurt
1 egg
1/2 cup dried fruit (apricots, currants, cherries, raisins, or apples)
Dash of ground cinnamon

Preheat the oven to 375 degrees. In a large bowl, mix together the first 4 ingredients. Cut in the butter. Stir in the brown sugar. Make a well in the center of the bowl and add the yogurt, egg, fruit, and cinnamon; mix just until moistened. Using a 1/4-cup measure, drop the batter onto a greased or parchment-lined baking sheet. Bake for 12 to 15 minutes. Makes about 18 scones.

CATHIE CAMERON
FIRST UNITED METHODIST CHURCH
BELLEVILLE, MICHIGAN

SEAFOOD

We thank you Lord, for this our food,
For rest and home and all things good.
For wind and rain and sun above
And most of all, for those we love.

FIRST UNITED METHODIST CHURCH,
BELLEVILLE, MICHIGAN

MERRY'S FARM-RAISED CATFISH FRY

6 (3/4 to 1 pound) farm-raised catfish fillets
*   or whole catfish*
1 cup buttermilk
1 1/2 to 2 tablespoons broil steak seasoning
1 1/2 cups plain yellow cornmeal
1/2 cup all-purpose flour
1 1/2 to 2 quarts peanut oil

Make shallow diagonal cuts 2 inches apart in the thickest portion of the sides of the fish. Place in a large shallow dish. In a bowl, combine the buttermilk and broil steak seasoning and pour the mixture over the fish. Cover and refrigerate overnight, turning the fish occasionally. Remove the fish from the marinade, discarding the marinade. In a medium bowl, combine the cornmeal and flour. Dredge the fillets in this mixture, coating them completely. Pour peanut oil to a depth of 1 1/2 inches into a large deep skillet; heat the oil to 370 degrees. Fry the fish for about 6 minutes, or until golden brown. Drain well on paper towels. Serve immediately.

MERRY R. JONES
GRIFFIN CHAPEL UNITED METHODIST CHURCH
STARKVILLE, MISSISSIPPI

CLAMS CASINO

3 cans minced clams
1 small green pepper (lemon size)
1 small to medium onion, minced
4 tablespoons Italian bread crumbs
3 tablespoons Parmesan cheese
2 tablespoons oil
Pinch of pepper
2 tablespoons parsley
Bacon
Paprika

Preheat the oven to 350 degrees. Drain the clams, reserving the juice. Mix all the ingredients in a bowl. Fill each shell with about 1 teaspoon of the mixture. Drizzle each clam with 1/2 teaspoon of the clam juice. Cover with 1-inch squares of bacon. Sprinkle with a few bread crumbs and paprika. Bake for 20 to 25 minutes until the bacon browns. Makes about 90 small shells (2 cookie sheets).

MARTHA FENOGLIO
TRINITY PRESBYTERIAN CHURCH
WILMINGTON, DELAWARE

CRAB CAKES

2 slices bread (crusts removed)
4 teaspoons milk
1 tablespoon mayonnaise
1 tablespoon Worcestershire sauce
1 tablespoon parsley flakes
1 tablespoon baking powder
3 teaspoons Old Bay seasoning
1 egg, beaten
1 teaspoon fresh lemon juice
1 pound lump crabmeat
Vegetable oil

Break the bread into small pieces and moisten with the milk. Combine the bread and the remaining ingredients in a small glass bowl and mix well. Shape into cakes. Fry or broil until golden brown.

MRS. TRINA MORRIS DICKERSON
BETHEL AME CHURCH
AUGUSTA, GEORGIA

BROILED CRAB CAKES

2 tablespoons butter
2 tablespoons all-purpose flour
1 cup milk
1 egg
1 teaspoon Old Bay seasoning
1 teaspoon Grey Poupon mustard
1 teaspoon mayonnaise
1 pound crabmeat

In a large skillet, melt the butter and add the flour. Stir until smooth and add the milk, stirring until the mixture thickens. Set aside to cool. Combine the remaining ingredients and add 2 tablespoons of the flour sauce to the mixture. Add the crabmeat and mix well. Form into 4-ounce crab cakes. Broil or bake at 350 degrees for 30 minutes.

WINIFRED KUNKEL
TRINITY UNITED METHODIST CHURCH
YORK, PENNSYLVANIA

CRAB IMPERIAL

4 tablespoons margarine
2 tablespoons all-purpose flour
1 pound crabmeat
1/2 cup milk
1 egg, beaten
1 hard-boiled egg, chopped
6 drops Worcestershire sauce
1 tablespoon mayonnaise
1/4 teaspoon Old Bay seasoning
1/4 teaspoon black pepper
1/2 cup bread crumbs

In a large saucepan, melt 2 tablespoons of the margarine; add the flour and stir to form a paste. Stir in the milk and cook until the mixture thickens to make a white sauce. Reserving 6 tablespoons of white sauce, add the rest to the crabmeat along with the raw egg, hard-boiled egg, Worcestershire sauce, mayonnaise, Old Bay, and pepper. Mix and pour into a casserole dish, topping with the reserved white sauce. Combine the remaining 2 tablespoons of melted margarine with the bread crumbs and sprinkle over the casserole. Bake at 350 degrees for 15 to 20 minutes, or until brown on top.

SUE MCCARTY
TRINITY UNITED METHODIST CHURCH
YORK, PENNSYLVANIA

CRAWFISH ÉTOUFFÉE

1 pound crawfish
Peanut oil
1/2 cup all-purpose flour
1/2 stick butter
1 Creole or white onion
1 bell pepper
2 garlic cloves
3 branches parsley
1 tablespoon Worcestershire sauce
2 bay leaves
1 (10-ounce) can tomato sauce
1 small can tomato paste
Dash of sugar
Tony's seasoning
1/2 can cream of mushroom soup
1 can sliced mushrooms

Rinse the crawfish once under cold water. Leave some fat, but not much. Cover the bottom of a large saucepan with the peanut oil. Brown the flour in the oil until it's golden brown. Add the butter. Then add the onion, pepper, garlic, and parsley. Cook down. Add the next 8 ingredients and simmer for 2 hours. Add the crawfish and simmer for another 30 minutes. Serve over rice.

JACK DUET
OAKMONT CHURCH OF GOD
SHREVEPORT, LOUISIANA

BROILED FLOUNDER WITH HERB BUTTER

2 tablespoons butter, softened
2 teaspoons reduced-fat cream cheese
1 tablespoon dill weed
1 teaspoon scallion tops
1 teaspoon drained horseradish
2 tablespoons plus 1/2 teaspoon lemon juice
4 flounder fillets
Salt to taste

In a medium bowl, beat the butter and cream cheese together until well combined. Stir in the dill, scallion greens, horseradish, and 1/2 teaspoon lemon juice; set aside. Sprinkle the flounder with 2 tablespoons lemon juice and salt. Broil 6 inches from the heat until the flounder is cooked through. Serve the flounder topped with the herb butter.

JUNE PAIGE
TRINITY UNITED METHODIST CHURCH
YORK, PENNSYLVANIA

FLOUNDER ROLL-UPS

6 bacon strips
1 (8-ounce) package herb stuffing
Melted butter or margarine
2 tablespoons minced parsley
1/4 cup minced onion
6 thin flounder fillets

In a skillet, fry the bacon until crisp; drain. Reserve the drippings. Prepare the stuffing mix according to the package directions, adding enough melted butter to the drippings to equal the amount of fat called for. Stir in crumbled bacon, parsley, and onion. Mix well. Spread equal amounts of stuffing on each fillet. Roll up and secure with toothpicks.

Place each roll-up in well-greased muffin cups or use cupcake papers. Brush with additional butter. Bake at 357 degrees for 30 minutes. Place the roll-ups under the broiler to brown lightly. Serve with Mushroom-Caper Sauce.

MUSHROOM-CAPER SAUCE:
1 (3-ounce) can sliced mushrooms
Milk or cream
1 (10 3/4-ounce) can cream of mushroom soup
2 tablespoons capers, drained

Drain the mushrooms, reserving the liquid. Measure the liquid and add enough milk to yield 1/3 cup. In a saucepan, blend this mixture with the soup. Add the mushrooms and capers and warm over low heat. Serve over roll-ups.

SALLY BISHOP
ST. PAUL CHURCH
WATERFORD, CONNECTICUT

BAKED HADDOCK WITH TARRAGON AND SOUR CREAM

2 pounds haddock fillets
2 scallions with tops, minced
2 tablespoons butter
1 cup dry white wine
Salt and pepper to taste
1 cup sour cream
1 teaspoon tarragon
Paprika

Preheat the oven to 425 degrees. Place the haddock in a buttered shallow baking dish. In a saucepan, sauté the scallions in butter until tender. Add the wine. Pour the scallions, butter, and wine over the fish. Season with salt and pepper. Bake until the fish flakes apart (20 minutes). In a small saucepan on low heat, warm the sour cream with the tarragon and pour the mixture over the fish. Sprinkle with paprika and serve. Makes 4 servings.

SEARSPORT SAILOR, JANE P.
FOREST AVENUE CONGREGATIONAL CHURCH
BANGOR, MAINE

BAKED HADDOCK OR COD IN SOUR CREAM AND DILL

2 pounds fish fillets
2 cups sour cream
1/2 cup mayonnaise
1 teaspoon celery salt
1/2 teaspoon black pepper
1/4 teaspoon thyme
1/2 teaspoon paprika
2 tablespoons diced pimientos
Sprigs of fresh dill
Sprigs of parsley, for garnish
Lemon wedges, for garnish

Preheat the oven to 350 degrees. Place the fish in a greased shallow baking dish. In a medium bowl, combine the sour cream and mayonnaise with the herbs. Pour over the fish and cover with the fresh dill. Bake for 40 minutes. Garnish with lemon wedges and parsley sprigs.

LOIS MURRAY
MATTAPOISETT CONGREGATIONAL CHURCH
MATTAPOISETT, MASSACHUSETTS

MACADAMIA-CRUSTED MAHI MAHI

6 ounces fresh mahi mahi
1 tablespoon olive oil
Salt and pepper to taste
1 ounce macadamia nuts
1 ounce panko (Japanese bread crumbs)
Asparagus spears, for garnish

Coat the mahi mahi steaks with oil and season with salt and pepper. Combine the nuts and the panko; dredge the steaks in the mixture. Heat a cast-iron skillet or nonstick pan and sear the mahi mahi over medium heat for 3 minutes on each side for medium rare. Garnish with the asparagus.

CHEF DAVID TARRIN OF ROY'S
NORTHBROOK UNITED METHODIST CHURCH
ROSWELL, GEORGIA

HERBED SCALLOPED OYSTERS

MIX NUMBER 1:
1 cup fresh bread crumbs
1 cup fresh cracker crumbs
1 stick butter, melted
1/4 cup minced fresh parsley
1/4 cup snipped fresh dill weed
48 oysters (about 3 cans)

Combine the first 5 ingredients in a bowl and mix. Place half of the mixture on the bottom of a 9 x 13-inch baking pan. Arrange the oysters on top of the crumb mix.

MIX NUMBER 2:
3 tablespoons liquor from oysters
1 1/2 tablespoons cream
Dash of Tabasco sauce
Dash each of salt and pepper

Mix all the ingredients and dribble over the oysters. Top the oysters with the remaining portion of Mix Number 1. Bake at 425 degrees for 20 to 25 minutes.

MATTAPOISETT CONGREGATIONAL CHURCH
MATTAPOISETT, MASSACHUSETTS

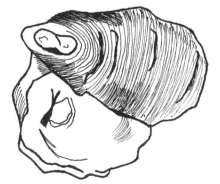

BAKED RED SNAPPER

2 pounds whole red snapper, cleaned
1 teaspoon sea salt
Juice of 1 lemon
3 tablespoons fresh oregano, chopped,
    plus more for garnish
Black pepper to taste
2 tablespoons olive oil
Lemon slices, for garnish

Preheat the oven to 350 degrees. Sprinkle the fish with sea salt. Score the fish by making 3 diagonal cuts about 1 inch apart and 1/2-inch deep into the thickest part. Combine the lemon juice, oregano, and pepper in a small bowl. Press the mixture into the slits. Brush each side of the fish with 1 tablespoon olive oil and lay in a baking dish big enough to hold the fish. Bake the fish for about 15 minutes or grill on medium heat for 10 minutes for every inch of thickness. Remove from the heat and serve garnished with lemon slices and sprigs of oregano.

Note: This recipe is low-cal, low-fat, and good enough for company when you're in a hurry.

LINDA HART
NORTHBROOK UNITED METHODIST CHURCH
ROSWELL, GEORGIA

RED SNAPPER ORLEANS

1 cup fine julienne-cut carrots
1 cup fine julienne-cut onions
1 cup fine julienne-cut celery
2 garlic cloves, minced
1/2 pound unsalted butter (2 sticks)
6 red snapper fillets (about 4 ounces per
    fillet)
Salt and freshly ground pepper to taste
1 cup chopped white portion of leeks
1/2 cup port wine
1/2 cup sherry
Watercress, for garnish

Preheat oven to 350 degrees. Sauté carrots, onions, celery and garlic in half the butter until tender. Season fish fillets with salt and pepper, slice each in half lengthwise to create a "pocket," and fill each with the cooked vegetables. Arrange fillets on a bed of chopped leeks in a baking pan. Add port and sherry, cover with aluminum foil, and bake for 20 minutes.

When fish is cooked, transfer it to a warm platter and keep warm. Cook the liquid remaining in the pan over direct heat until reduced by one-quarter. Strain sauce into a saucepan, then gradually whisk in remaining butter. Season with salt and pepper to taste. Ladle sauce onto a warm plate. Place stuffed fillets on top of the sauce and garnish with watercress.

MARY SMITH
BETHEL AME CHURCH
AUGUSTA, GEORGIA

BROILED SALMON WITH HERBS

1 1/2 pounds salmon steaks (about 3/4-inch thick)
1 tablespoon grated onion
6 tablespoons margarine, melted
1 teaspoon salt
1/4 teaspoon black pepper
1/2 teaspoon marjoram
2 tablespoons minced parsley
Juice of 1 lemon

Set the oven on Broil. Wipe the salmon steaks with a damp cloth or paper towel and arrange them on a greased broiler rack. In a small bowl, mix the remaining ingredients together and pour half of it over the steaks. Broil for about 6 minutes under medium heat, turn, and pour the remaining sauce over the fish. Broil for 5 to 6 minutes longer until the fish flakes easily. Transfer the steaks to a hot platter and garnish with additional parsley.

ANN JONES
UNITED BAPTIST CHURCH OF POULTNEY
EAST POULTNEY, VERMONT

HONEY-GINGER GRILLED SALMON

1 teaspoon ground ginger
1 teaspoon garlic powder
1/3 cup soy sauce
1/3 cup orange juice
1/4 cup honey
1 scallion, chopped
1 1/2 pounds salmon fillets

Combine the first 6 ingredients in a plastic bag and mix well. Add the salmon and seal. Turn the bag to distribute the marinade. Refrigerate for 15 to 30 minutes, turning the bag occasionally. Grill the fish on medium heat for 12 to 15 minutes per inch of thickness. Makes 4 servings.

SARAH MOKMA
FIRST UNITED METHODIST CHURCH
BELLEVILLE, MICHIGAN

Roasted Salmon with Honey-Mustard Sauce

6 tablespoons honey mustard
1 tablespoon balsamic vinegar
1 1/2 tablespoons soy sauce
1 garlic clove, finely chopped
4 (7-ounce) salmon fillets (each 1 1/4-inch
    thick at thickest part)
Salt and pepper to taste

Preheat the oven to 425 degrees. Place the mustard in a small bowl and whisk in the vinegar, soy sauce, and garlic. Set the sauce aside. Lightly oil the bottom of a baking pan large enough to hold all the fillets comfortably. Place the fillets in the pan and season with salt and pepper. Spoon 1 tablespoon of sauce over the top of each fillet. Bake until the sides of the fillets are slightly springy when pressed, 10 to 12 minutes until they are slightly underdone. Bake for another minute or 2 if you prefer the fish well done. To serve, place the fillets on warm plates. Spoon a little more sauce over each fillet. Makes 4 servings.

Barbara K. Klein
Mattapoisett Congregational Church
Mattapoisett, Massachusetts

BBQ Roasted Salmon

1/2 cup pineapple juice
2 tablespoons fresh lemon juice
4 (6-ounce) salmon fillets
2 tablespoons brown sugar
4 teaspoons chili powder
2 teaspoons grated lemon rind
3/4 teaspoon ground cumin
1/2 teaspoon salt
1/4 teaspoon ground cinnamon
Cooking spray
Lemon wedges, for garnish

Combine the first 3 ingredients in a zip lock bag; seal and marinate in the refrigerator for at least 1 hour, turning occasionally. Preheat the oven to 400 degrees. Remove the fish from the bag and discard the marinade. Combine the sugar and the next 5 ingredients in a bowl. Rub the mixture over the fish. Place the fish in an 11 x 7-inch baking dish coated with cooking spray. Bake for 12 minutes, or until the fish flakes easily. Serve with lemon wedges. Makes 4 servings.

Cathy Jobe
Northbrook United Methodist Church
Roswell, Georgia

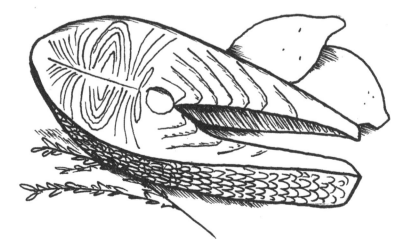

SALMON SALSA TOPPER

1 garlic clove, minced
1 tablespoon olive oil
1/4 cup dry white wine
1 tomato, chopped
2 tablespoons fresh chives, chopped
2 tablespoons lemon juice
4 salmon fillets (1-inch thick)

In a large saucepan, sauté the garlic in oil. Add the wine and cook until the liquid is reduced by half. Stir in the tomato, chives, and lemon juice. Set aside. Preheat the grill or broiler. Cook the salmon fillets 5 inches from medium-high heat for 10 minutes, or until the fish flakes easily. Turn once. Serve the warm salsa over the salmon. Makes 4 servings.

Note: This is what I like to call Cal-Mex. It combines the taste of my home state of California with the influence of Old Mexico.

LINDA HART
NORTHBROOK UNITED METHODIST CHURCH
ROSWELL, GEORGIA

SALMON AND PASTA

3 cups uncooked elbow pasta twists
6 tablespoons butter or margarine
4 tablespoons all-purpose flour
2 cups milk
2 ounces shredded Swiss cheese (1/2 cup)
2 ounces shredded Cheddar cheese
1/4 cup grated Parmesan
1 medium onion, chopped
1 tablespoon salad oil
3 medium zucchini, cut in half lengthwise
    and sliced
1/2 cup grated carrot
1 (15 1/2-ounce) can salmon, drained and
    flaked

TOPPING:
1 tablespoon grated Parmesan
1 tablespoon dry bread crumbs
1 tablespoon chopped fresh parsley

Cook elbow twists according to the package directions and set aside. In a medium saucepan, over medium heat, melt the butter. Stir in the flour, gradually add the milk, and cook, stirring until the mixture thickens. Add the cheeses and set aside.

In a large skillet over medium-high heat, sauté the onion in the oil for about 5 minutes. Add the zucchini and cook for 5 minutes, stirring often.

Preheat the oven to 375 degrees. In a large bowl, combine the twists, cheese sauce, onion mixture, carrot, and salmon; mix well. Pour into a 3-quart casserole. Make the topping.

Combine the topping ingredients in a small bowl and spread over the casserole. Bake for 25 minutes until the mixture is hot and the crumbs are lightly browned. Makes 8 servings.

GRACE DELORENZO
PRINCE OF PEACE CHURCH
GRANTSVILLE, WEST VIRGINIA

Easy Salmon Loaf

1/3 cup milk
1 cup soft bread crumbs
1 (15 1/2-ounce) can salmon
2 eggs, separated
Juice of 1 lemon
1/2 teaspoon salt
1/4 teaspoon onion salt
1/8 teaspoon black pepper

Medium White Sauce:

2 tablespoons butter or margarine
2 tablespoons all-purpose flour
1 cup milk
Salt and pepper to taste

In a medium bowl, combine the milk and bread crumbs; set aside. Drain the salmon and remove the skin and bones. Place the salmon in a large bowl; flake with a fork. In a separate bowl, beat the egg yolks until they're thick. Stir the bread crumb mixture, add the egg yolks, lemon juice, and seasonings into the salmon. Beat the egg whites until they're stiff but not dry. Fold into the salmon mixture. Spoon into a 7 1/2 x 3 x 2-inch greased loaf pan. Bake for 35 minutes at 400 degrees. Serve with sauce.

Medium White Sauce: Melt the butter in a heavy saucepan over low heat. Add the flour, stirring until smooth. Cook for 1 minute, stirring constantly. Gradually add the milk. Cook the sauce until it's thick and bubbly. Add salt and pepper.

Maxine Wills
Prince of Peace Church
Grantsville, West Virginia

Salmon Puff

2 eggs
2/3 cup milk
1/2 cup sour cream
3/4 cup dry bread crumbs
1 teaspoon seafood seasoning
1/2 teaspoon lemon pepper seasoning
1/4 teaspoon dill weed
3 cups cooked salmon flaked
3 tablespoons chopped celery
2 tablespoons chopped onion
4 1/2 teaspoons lemon juice

Topping:

1 1/3 cups mayonnaise
1 tablespoon prepared mustard
1 egg white
2 tablespoons minced parsley

In a bowl, combine the eggs, milk, and sour cream and stir until smooth. Add the bread crumbs, seafood seasoning, lemon pepper, and dill. Add the salmon, celery, onion, and lemon juice; mix well. Pour the mixture into a greased 11 x 17-inch baking dish. Bake at 350 degrees for 25 to 30 minutes, or until a knife inserted near the center comes out clean. Meanwhile prepare the topping by combining the mayonnaise and mustard in a bowl. In a separate bowl, beat the egg white until stiff peaks form; fold it into the mayonnaise mixture. Spread the topping over the salmon mixture and return to the oven for 10 to 15 minutes longer, or until lightly browned. Sprinkle with parsley.

Beatrice Walker
Cavendish Baptist Church
Cavendish, Vermont

DISHWASHER SALMON

Salmon fillet (size to fit number of
  servings needed)
Your choice of seasoning
Lemon juice to taste
Butter to taste

You will need dirty dishes.

Load the dishwasher with your dirty dishes, leaving enough room on the top rack for the salmon. Lay the salmon out on aluminum foil and season to taste. Wrap the salmon well in the aluminum foil, making sure all edges are sealed as tightly as possible. Place the salmon package on the top rack of the dishwasher and set it to its normal cycle. The heat and steam of the dishwasher will cook the salmon nicely. When the cycle is finished, unload the dishwasher and set the table. Unwrap the salmon and serve.

REV. WOODY WEILAGE
BUCKINGHAM UNITED METHODIST CHURCH
GARLAND, TEXAS

SALMON CAESAR

4 eggs
2 cups milk
1 (10 3/4-ounce) can cream of
  mushroom soup
6-ounce package Caesar croutons
1 pound canned salmon, flaked
1/2 cup chopped green pepper
1/4 cup chopped onion
2 tablespoons grated Parmesan cheese

In a medium bowl, beat together the eggs, milk, and soup. Stir in the croutons, flaked salmon, green pepper, and onion. Pour the mixture into a buttered 11 3/4 x 7 1/2 x 1 3/4-inch baking dish. Sprinkle Parmesan cheese over the top. Bake at 350 degrees for 45 minutes, or until the casserole is set in the center.

GRIFFIN CHAPEL UNITED METHODIST CHURCH
STARKVILLE, MISSISSIPPI

CHRISTMAS RECIPE FOR SALMON

2 cups fresh cranberries
1/4 cup water
2 cups diced fennel
1/4 teaspoon ground allspice
1/2 cup white wine
1 tablespoon onion, diced
Juice of 1 lime
1/2 teaspoon jalapeño or green pepper,
   chopped
1 tablespoon chopped cilantro
Salt and pepper to taste
4 salmon fillets, boneless and skinless
   (8 ounces each)
A basic court bouillon, white wine,
   or beer for poaching

Cook the cranberries in the water until the berries pop and the mixture thickens. Set aside to cool. Dice the fennel, removing the outer layers first. In a bowl, combine the cranberries, fennel, allspice, wine, onion, lime juice, jalapeño pepper, and cilantro. Season with salt and pepper and refrigerate for at least 4 hours to allow the flavors to blend.

Poach the salmon fillets in a basic court bouillon, white wine, or beer, allowing 8 minutes for each inch of thickness. To serve, place the cranberry relish on individual plates, top with a salmon fillet, and circle with accompanying vegetables of your choice.

CHURCH OF HOLY APOSTLES
VIRGINIA BEACH, VIRGINIA

CUCUMBER SAUCE

1 unpeeled cucumber
1/2 cup sour cream
1/4 cup mayonnaise
1 tablespoon minced parsley
2 teaspoons grated onion
2 teaspoons cider vinegar
1/4 teaspoon salt
Black pepper to taste

In a large bowl, grate enough cucumber to make 1 cup. Do not drain. Add the remaining ingredients and stir well. Chill. Serve with salmon.

PAM WILDES
BUCKINGHAM UNITED METHODIST CHURCH
GARLAND, TEXAS

DELECTABLE BAY SCALLOPS

1/4 stick butter
2 cups all-purpose flour
1 teaspoon salt
1/8 teaspoon black pepper
1 pound bay scallops
1/4 cup sherry

Preheat the oven to 425 degrees. Melt the butter in a baking dish. Combine the flour, salt, and pepper in a plastic bag with the scallops and shake. Place the floured scallops in the baking dish and bake for 10 minutes. Stir or turn the scallops and bake for another 6 minutes. Remove the dish from the oven, sprinkle with the sherry, and place under the broiler until golden brown.

NANCY EISENBISE
TRINITY PRESBYTERIAN CHURCH
WILMINGTON, DELAWARE

PEPPERED SHRIMP

1/2 stick butter
1 pound shrimp
1/4 teaspoon salt
1 teaspoon garlic
1 teaspoon black pepper

Preheat the oven to 350 degrees. In a glass baking dish, melt the butter in the oven. Remove the dish from the oven and add the salt, garlic, and black pepper. Meanwhile, wash the shrimp, leaving the shells on. Add the shrimp to the butter mixture and stir well to coat. Bake for 15 to 18 minutes.

Note: The original recipe calls for 2 tablespoons of black pepper. Adjust the pepper to your taste.

PINEMOUNT BAPTIST CHURCH
MCALPIN, FLORIDA

Baked Shrimp

5 pounds jumbo shrimp in shells
3 to 4 tablespoons black pepper
Juice of 2 large lemons
1 (16-ounce) bottle Wish-Bone Italian
    dressing
1 pound butter

Preheat the oven to 400 degrees. Place the shrimp in a shallow roasting pan. Combine the other ingredients in a bowl and pour the mixture over the shrimp. Bake for 10 to 15 minutes, or until the shrimp begins to separate from the shells. Stir several times.

KATHY MYATT
OAKMONT CHURCH OF GOD
SHREVEPORT, LOUISIANA

Fabulous Fast Shrimp

1 tablespoon butter or margarine
2 celery stalks, chopped
1/4 cup chopped green pepper
1/4 cup sliced scallions
1 pound large fresh shrimp, shelled and
    deveined
1 can Campbell's cream of chicken or other
    cream soup
1/2 cup water
Dash of cayenne pepper
Hot cooked rice
Paprika

Heat the butter in a large saucepan. Add the celery, green pepper, and scallions and cook until tender. Add the shrimp and cook for 3 to 5 minutes or until done. Add the soup, water, and cayenne pepper (for a thicker sauce, omit the water) and heat through. Sprinkle with paprika. Serve over rice. Makes 4 servings.

SHERRY BECKEMEYER
NORTHBROOK UNITED METHODIST CHURCH
ROSWELL, GEORGIA

SHRIMP SCAMPI

2 pounds jumbo shrimp
1 1/2 sticks butter
1/4 cup chopped onion
3 tablespoons chopped garlic
1 teaspoon salt
1/8 teaspoon black pepper
2 tablespoons lemon juice
1/4 cup chopped parsley

Shell and devein the shrimp. In a large saucepan, sauté the shrimp in butter with the onion and garlic for about 5 minutes; turn the shrimp once. Transfer the shrimp to a hot serving dish; set aside. Add the seasonings and lemon juice to the pan and heat. Pour the mixture over the shrimp and sprinkle with the chopped parsley. Serve.

KASI WALKER
CAVENDISH BAPTIST CHURCH
CAVENDISH, VERMONT

EASY SHRIMP CREOLE

2 tablespoons olive oil
1 onion, chopped
4 garlic cloves, minced
1/2 cup green pepper, chopped
1/2 cup celery, chopped
2 cans tomato sauce with tomato bits
1 can tomato soup
3 tablespoons Worcestershire sauce
1 or 2 pounds shrimp, shelled and deveined

In a large saucepan, sauté the onion, garlic, pepper, and celery in the olive oil until almost tender. Add the other ingredients, omitting the shrimp. Simmer for 45 minutes. Add the raw shrimp and cook 10 to 15 minutes longer, depending on the size of the shrimp. Serve over rice.

Note: You can add cooked shrimp and just heat them in the sauce.

MRS. R. A. FOSTER
HIGHLAND HEIGHTS PRESBYTERIAN CHURCH
CORDOVA, TENNESSEE

Shrimp with Mushrooms

2 tablespoons olive oil
1 teaspoon salt
Dash of pepper
1 pound raw shrimp
1/2 pound mushrooms
1/2 cup chicken bouillon
2 tablespoons cornstarch
2 tablespoons soy sauce
1/4 cup water

In a preheated heavy 10-inch skillet, place the oil, salt, and pepper. Shell and devein the shrimp. Cut each shrimp into 3 pieces and add to the skillet, cooking over moderate heat, and stirring constantly, for 5 minutes. Slice and add the mushrooms and the chicken bouillon. Cover the skillet tightly and cook over low heat for 5 minutes. Blend the cornstarch, soy sauce, and water and add the mixture to the skillet. Cook for a few minutes more, stirring constantly, until the juice thickens and the mixture is very hot. Serve immediately with hot boiled rice. Makes 4 servings.

MADELYN FOGLER
MATTAPOISETT CONGREGATIONAL CHURCH
MATTAPOISETT, MASSACHUSETTS

Shrimp and Cheese Casserole

3 eggs, beaten
1 can Cheddar cheese soup
1 1/2 cans milk
6 slices buttered bread
8 ounces sharp cheese, sliced
2 (5-ounce) cans medium shrimp
Salt and pepper to taste

In a large bowl, mix together the eggs, soup, and milk. Place 2 buttered slices of bread on the bottom of a buttered 2-quart casserole. Lay a slice of cheese on each, then half of the shrimp. Add a dash of salt and pepper. Make another similar layer, ending with bread and cheese. Pour the soup mixture over everything. Bake at 350 degrees for about 40 minutes until brown and puffy.

Note: Tuna or chicken can be used for the shrimp.

GRIFFIN CHAPEL UNITED METHODIST CHURCH
STARKVILLE, MISSISSIPPI

SHRIMP PAELLA

1 tablespoon olive or salad oil
1/2 pound Spanish or Polish sausage, thinly
   sliced
1/2 cup chopped onion
1 medium garlic clove, minced
1 (10 3/4-ounce) can condensed chicken
   broth
1 (8-ounce) can chopped tomatoes, including
   liquid
1/2 teaspoon cinnamon
1/4 teaspoon saffron
1 1/2 cups long-grain rice
1 (8-ounce) package frozen shrimp, thawed
   (or 1/2 pound fresh, shelled and deveined)
1 cup frozen peas

In a large saucepan over medium heat, cook the sausage, onion, and garlic in the oil until the sausage is tender (about 5 minutes). Add the broth, tomatoes with liquid, cinnamon, saffron, and rice. Bring to a boil. Cover and simmer for 15 minutes. Add the shrimp and peas; simmer for another 5 minutes.

Note: This recipe is another favorite from Philip's sister, Rebecca, who is a talented amateur gourmet chef.

CONNIE CHEEK
NORTHBROOK UNITED METHODIST CHURCH
ROSWELL, GEORGIA

SHRIMP ARNAUD

3 pounds fresh shrimp, shelled and deveined
   and boiled with Zatarain's shrimp and
   crab boil seasoning
4 tablespoons olive oil
Salt and pepper to taste
2 scallions, minced (including tops)
1/4 cup chopped celery
2 tablespoons vinegar
1 tablespoon mustard

In a large bowl, combine all the ingredients thoroughly and mix well. Refrigerate for 2 hours or more. Serve on slices of fresh tomatoes surrounded with crisp lettuce.

SARA COOPER
BUCKINGHAM UNITED METHODIST CHURCH
GARLAND, TEXAS

MANDARIN SHRIMP AND VEGETABLE STIR-FRY

1 cup orange marmalade
3 tablespoons soy sauce
2 tablespoons white vinegar
2 teaspoons Tabasco sauce
1 1/2 tablespoons cornstarch
2 tablespoons vegetable oil
1 tablespoon chopped fresh ginger
1 tablespoon chopped fresh garlic
24 fresh jumbo shrimp, peeled and deveined
1 red pepper, chopped
3 cups broccoli florets
1/2 cup water
Salt and pepper to taste
1 bunch scallions, chopped

In a small bowl, combine the first 5 ingredients. Stir to dissolve the cornstarch and set aside. Place a large skillet over high heat. Heat the pan for 1 minute. Add the oil, heating it for 30 seconds. Add the ginger, garlic, and shrimp. Stir-fry for 2 to 3 minutes until the shrimp begins to turn pink. Remove the shrimp from the heat and set aside. Add the pepper and broccoli to the pan and cook over high heat for 1 minute. Add the water, cover the pan and reduce the heat to medium. Cook the vegetables for 4 to 5 minutes until tender. Uncover the pan. Return the heat to high. Add the shrimp and marmalade mixture. Cook the shrimp for another 2 minutes until the sauce thickens and the shrimp is cooked. Season with salt and pepper as needed. Stir in the scallions and serve with boiled rice. Makes 4 to 6 servings.

GAILA CONWAY
MATTAPOISETT CONGREGATIONAL CHURCH
MATTAPOISETT, MASSACHUSETTS

LEMONY DILL SWORDFISH

2 teaspoons lemon juice
4 to 5 ounces swordfish
2 teaspoons nonfat creamy salad dressing
Pinch of dried dill weed

For each serving, sprinkle lemon juice on the swordfish steak and place it in a baking dish lined with foil. Sprinkle with the salad dressing and dill weed. Broil for 10 minutes per inch of thickness at the thickest part of the fish.

CHARLOTTE SNYDER
CAVENDISH BAPTIST CHURCH
CAVENDISH, VERMONT

Pecan-Crusted Swordfish

Swordfish steaks (as needed; about 1-inch
  thick)
1 teaspoon seasoning salt
1 cup pecans, finely chopped
Melted margarine

Lightly season both sides of the swordfish with the seasoning salt. Place the fish in a mixing bowl and add the pecans. Push the pecans into the fish for full coverage, including the sides. In a large skillet, sauté the fish in margarine for 7 minutes on one side, then flip over. Cook for an additional 5 to 7 minutes until the fish is cooked through and is no longer translucent in the middle. Serve with mashed potatoes and broccoli.

PAUL CASTRO AND GEOFF KOKOZSKA OF STONEY RIVER
NORTHBROOK UNITED METHODIST CHURCH
ROSWELL, GEORGIA

Broiled Brook Trout

Trout
Melted butter
Salt and pepper to taste

STUFFING (ALTERNATIVE
PREPARATION):
1/4 cup milk
2 cups soft bread crumbs
2 tablespoons butter
1 onion, minced
1 celery stalk, finely chopped
1 egg, well beaten
1/2 teaspoon sage
Salt and pepper to taste

Clean the trout and dry with paper towels. Rub each with melted butter. Place on a broiler and cook. Turn and repeat until golden brown. Season with salt and pepper. Serve.

Stuffing: Pour the milk over the bread crumbs and let stand. Melt the butter. Add the onion and brown. Add the onion to the bread mixture. Stir in the celery, egg, and seasonings. Mix well. Fill the fish with the stuffing and cook.

NEW ENGLAND FAVORITE OF SUN RISE BREAKFAST
FOREST AVENUE CONGREGATIONAL CHURCH
BANGOR, MAINE

TROUT AMANDINE

6 to 8 trout fillets (skinless)
2 eggs, beaten
Salt and pepper to taste
1 cup all-purpose flour
Shredded almonds
1 1/2 cups vegetable oil

SAUCE:
1/4 pound butter or margarine, melted
1/4 teaspoon salt
1/4 teaspoon pepper
2 tablespoons chopped parsley
1 tablespoon lemon juice

Dip the trout fillets in well-beaten eggs seasoned with salt and pepper. Dredge the trout in the flour. Fry in hot oil until browned, turning only once. Drain on paper towels. Place the trout on a hot platter and sprinkle with almonds. Serve hot with the sauce.

Sauce: Combine all the ingredients and mix well.

SARA COOPER
BUCKINGHAM UNITED METHODIST CHURCH
GARLAND, TEXAS

TUNA WITH LIME SOY MARINADE

1 1/2 pounds tuna steak
1/2 cup soy sauce
1/4 cup vegetable oil
1/4 cup sesame oil
1/4 cup fresh lime juice
2 teaspoons lime zest
2 tablespoons dry sherry
2 teaspoons minced ginger

Cut the tuna steaks into serving portions. In a small bowl, combine the soy sauce, oil, lime juice and zest, sherry, and ginger. Mix well. Place the steaks in a shallow pan and pour the mixture over and under the fish. Marinate the fish for about 2 hours, turning occasionally. Place the steaks on a lightly oiled or nonstick grill. Grill on high to sear—about 6 minutes for each 1/2-inch thickness of fish, or until the fish flakes easily. Baste frequently with the reserved marinade while grilling. Do not overcook—tuna dries out easily. Serve with your favorite side dishes and condiments, such as fried rice and fruit relish. Makes 4 servings.

Note: Swordfish can be substituted for the tuna.

CHEF DARRELL TOBIN
COUNTRY CLUB OF YORK
TRINITY UNITED METHODIST CHURCH
YORK, PENNSYLVANIA

Molded Tuna Loaf

3 (7-ounce) cans tuna, flaked
4 or 5 hard-boiled eggs, chopped
1 1/4 cups stuffed olives, chopped
1 pound onions, minced
1 cup diced celery
2 envelopes unflavored gelatin
1/2 cup cold water
3 cups mayonnaise
Lettuce leaves

In a large bowl or mold, combine the first 5 ingredients. In a separate bowl, sprinkle the gelatin over the cold water and set the bowl over a container of hot water. Stir the gelatin until it dissolves. Stir the mayonnaise into the gelatin and add the mixture to the other ingredients. Refrigerate until firm. Unmold and serve on lettuce leaves. Makes 20 servings.

MRS. LYLE MCALLISTER
MOSCA UNITED METHODIST CHURCH
MOSCA, COLORADO

Asian Tuna Steaks

1/4 cup reduced-sodium soy sauce
2 tablespoons dry sherry
2 teaspoons dark sesame oil or vegetable oil
1 teaspoon gingerroot, peeled and minced
1/2 teaspoon dried crushed red pepper flakes
1/2 teaspoon garlic, minced
4 (4-ounce) tuna steaks
Vegetable cooking spray

Combine the first 6 ingredients in a large zip lock bag. Add the fish. Shake gently until the fish is well coated. Marinate in the refrigerator for 10 minutes. Remove the fish from the marinade and reserve the marinade.

Coat a grill rack with cooking spray; place the rack over medium-hot coals (350 to 400 degrees). Place the fish on the rack; grill, covered, for 4 minutes on each side, or until the fish flakes easily.

Place the reserved marinade in a small saucepan. Bring to a boil, reduce the heat, and simmer, uncovered, for 1 minute. Drizzle the marinade evenly over the fish. (Freshly grated gingerroot tastes hot, while ground ginger gives a sweet but peppery flavor, so don't try substituting one for the other. If you don't have gingerroot, increase the red pepper flakes to 3/4 teaspoon.) Makes 4 servings.

DEBBIE COLLINS
CROSS IN THE DESERT UNITED METHODIST CHURCH
PHOENIX, ARIZONA

Tuna Soufflé

1 cup scalded milk
1 cup soft bread crumbs
1/2 cup grated cheese
1 cup canned tuna
1 tablespoon lemon juice
1/2 teaspoon salt
3 eggs, separated

Preheat the oven to 325 degrees. To scald the milk, place it in a small saucepan and bring to just under a boil. Combine the scalded milk with the bread crumbs and grated cheese. Flake the tuna and add it to the milk mixture, then add the lemon juice, salt, and well-beaten egg yolks. In a separate bowl, beat the egg whites until stiff and fold into the milk mixture. Turn into a buttered casserole dish and set the dish in a pan containing about a half inch of water. Bake for 40 minutes, or until golden brown.

CORRY MINTHORN
UNITED BAPTIST CHURCH OF POULTNEY
EAST POULTNEY, VERMONT

Oven-Fried Fish

1/4 cup milk
1/2 teaspoon Worcestershire sauce
1 teaspoon minced onion
1 teaspoon salt
1/2 teaspoon paprika
Dash of barbecue sauce
1/2 cup finely crushed cornflakes
1 pound fish fillets
1/4 cup melted butter or margarine

Preheat the oven to 500 degrees. In a medium bowl, combine the milk, Worcestershire sauce, onion, and salt. In a separate bowl, combine the paprika, barbecue sauce, and cornflakes. Dip the fish in the milk mixture and then roll in the cornflakes. Place the fillets in a shallow baking dish and pour the melted butter over them. Bake for 20 minutes. Serve with tartar or cucumber sauce. Makes 4 servings.

PETE STEINMETZ
HUNGARIAN PRESBYTERIAN CHURCH
ALBANY, LOUISIANA

ALISON'S BAKED FISH

1 pound white fish (add some scallops,
  shrimp, or a mix, if desired)
1 stick margarine, melted
12 crushed Ritz crackers (1/2 cup)
1/4 cup bread crumbs
1/2 teaspoon lemon juice
Oregano, white pepper, and Parmesan
  cheese to taste

Preheat the oven to 450 degrees. Cut the fish into bite-size pieces and layer into a casserole dish. In a large bowl, combine all the other ingredients with the melted margarine and spread over the fish. Bake for 20 minutes.

HELEN ELLIS AND GERTRUDE SOARES
MATTAPOISETT CONGREGATIONAL CHURCH
MATTAPOISETT, MASSACHUSETTS

BAKED FISH WITH TOMATOES

1 pound fish fillets, fresh or frozen
1/2 pound ripe tomatoes, chopped
1/2 teaspoon onion powder
3/4 teaspoon salt
1/2 teaspoon fresh thyme leaves, crushed
1/8 teaspoon ground black pepper
3/4 cup soft bread crumbs
2 tablespoons melted butter

Preheat the oven to 350 degrees. Place the fish in a large baking dish. In a bowl, combine the tomatoes, onion powder, salt, thyme, and black pepper. Spoon the mixture over the fish. Combine the bread crumbs and butter. Sprinkle this over the fish and tomatoes. Bake the mixture for 20 minutes, or until the fish flakes when tested with a fork. Turn the fillets over to broil, placing the broiling pan 4 inches from the heat and broiling until the top of the fish is browned, about 1 minute.

Serve piping hot.

A FISH-LOVING FRIEND
MIRACLE DELIVERANCE HOLINESS CHURCH
COLUMBIA, SOUTH CAROLINA

Lime Poached Fish

1/2 cup chicken broth
1/3 cup lime juice
2 tablespoons butter or margarine
1 medium onion, thinly sliced
1 pound fish fillets
1 generous teaspoon chicken bouillon
1 generous tablespoon dried dill weed

In a large saucepan, combine the chicken broth, lime juice, butter, and onion. Add the fish fillets and baste well with the liquid. Sprinkle the chicken bouillon and dill weed on top of the fillets. Spoon the onion rings on top of the fish, cover, and cook on low heat for 6 to 10 minutes, depending on the thickness of the fillets. About halfway through cooking, carefully baste the fillets.

Nancy Eisenbise
Trinity Presbyterian Church
Wilmington, Delaware

Seafood au Gratin

1 1/2 pounds shrimp
1/4 cup plus 1 tablespoon butter
2 teaspoons minced garlic
1 pound fresh crabmeat
1 cup grated Cheddar cheese
1 cup sour cream
1 can cream of mushroom soup
1/2 cup diced celery
1/4 cup chopped bell pepper
1/4 cup chopped onion
Cracker crumbs

Preheat the oven to 350 degrees. Shell and devein the shrimp. Sauté in 1 tablespoon butter and garlic. Combine the remaining ingredients in a large bowl, omitting the cracker crumbs and 1/4 cup butter. Pour the mixture into a lightly greased 9 x 12-inch casserole. Top with the cracker crumbs and pour the melted butter over all. Bake for 30 minutes. Makes 6 servings.

Annie R. Latson
Bethel AME Church
Augusta, Georgia

GARLIC SHRIMP AND SCALLOPS

1 teaspoon olive oil
2 tablespoons slivered garlic
1/2 teaspoon crushed red pepper flakes
1/2 pound large shrimp, shelled and
    deveined
1/2 pound bay scallops
1/2 teaspoon paprika
4 tablespoons chicken broth
1 teaspoon fresh lime juice
1/2 cup finely chopped fresh parsley
Salt and pepper to taste

In a large heavy skillet, heat the oil over medium heat. Add the garlic and sauté until it begins to brown. Remove the garlic with a slotted spoon and set aside. Add the pepper flakes to the skillet and increase the heat to medium high. Add the garlic, shrimp, scallops, and paprika. Sauté for 1 to 2 minutes, stirring constantly. Add the chicken broth and cook for 1 minute. Remove the shrimp and scallops with a slotted spoon and place on a platter; set aside and keep warm. Add the lime juice, parsley, and salt and pepper to the pan and just heat through. Pour the sauce over the shrimp and scallops. Serve immediately. Makes 4 servings.

CROSS IN THE DESERT UNITED METHODIST CHURCH
PHOENIX, ARIZONA

SEAFOOD CASSEROLE

1 cup dry white wine
1 teaspoon butter
1 teaspoon chopped fresh parsley
1 teaspoon salt
1 medium onion, chopped
1 pound bay scallops
1 pound medium shrimp, shelled and
    deveined
3 tablespoons butter
3 tablespoons all-purpose flour
1 cup half-and-half
1/2 cup shredded Swiss cheese
2 teaspoons lemon juice
1/8 teaspoon pepper
1/2 pound seafood mix
1 (4-ounce) can sliced mushrooms, drained
1 cup soft bread crumbs
1/2 cup grated Parmesan cheese
Chopped parsley
Paprika or Old Bay seasoning
3 whole cooked shrimp, peeled and deveined
    (optional)

Combine the first 5 ingredients in a large saucepan; bring to a boil. Add the scallops and shrimp and cook for 3 to 5 minutes; drain, reserving 2/3 cup of the liquid. Melt the butter in a Dutch oven over low heat; add the flour, stirring until smooth. Cook for 1 minute, stirring constantly. Gradually add the half-and-half; cook over medium heat, stirring constantly, until the mixture is thick and bubbly. Add the Swiss cheese, stirring until the cheese melts. Gradually stir in reserved liquid, lemon juice, and pepper; add the scallop mixture, seafood mix, and mushrooms. Spoon the mixture into a lightly greased 12 x 8 x 2-inch baking dish. Cover and refrigerate for 8 hours or overnight. Remove the baking dish from the refrigerator and let stand for 30 minutes at room temperature. Bake, covered, at 350 degrees for 40 minutes. Combine the bread crumbs and Parmesan cheese; sprinkle evenly over the seafood mixture and bake for an additional 5 minutes. Sprinkle with parsley and Old Bay; let stand for 10 minutes before serving. Garnish with whole shrimp, if desired. Makes 8 servings.

JANET NORTHBROOK
UNITED METHODIST CHURCH
ROSWELL, GEORGIA

Seafood Gumbo

1 cup vegetable oil
1 cup all-purpose flour
2 large onions, chopped
2 celery stalks, chopped
1 large green pepper, chopped
6 garlic cloves, minced
1 gallon seafood or chicken stock
4 cups sliced okra
1 (22-ounce) can peeled, crushed tomatoes
1 (8-ounce) can tomato sauce
1 (10-ounce) can Ro-Tel tomatoes
1 teaspoon red pepper
1 tablespoon Worcestershire sauce
Salt, pepper and Tabasco sauce to taste
2 pounds shrimp, shelled (preferably small to medium)
1 pint oysters (optional)
1 pound crabmeat (optional)
1/2 cup chopped parsley
1/2 cup chopped scallions

Make a roux by combining the oil and flour in a cast-iron skillet over medium heat. Cook, stirring constantly, until the roux is medium to dark brown in color (20 to 30 minutes). Be careful not to burn the roux! Add the onions, celery, green pepper, and garlic to the roux and sauté until the vegetables are soft. Transfer the roux to a large stock pot and add the stock slowly. Add the okra and all the tomatoes to the pot. Season with red pepper, Worcestershire sauce, salt and pepper, and Tabasco sauce. Cook over medium heat for about 2 to 3 hours, stirring occasionally. Add the seafood, parsley, and scallions. Simmer for 10 to 15 minutes until the shrimp are cooked. Serve over hot rice with crusty French bread.

Note: This is a favorite dish from my hometown of Gulfport, Mississippi. Make sure you don't use large shrimp, because you want them to fit on the spoon.

Susan Jones
Northbrook United Methodist Church
Roswell, Georgia

POULTRY

Accept our gratitude dear Lord
For all the blessing that you give.
Direct and guide our daily paths
And teach us how to live.

FIRST UNITED METHODIST CHURCH,
BELLEVILLE, MICHIGAN

LAZY FRIED CHICKEN

1/2 cup butter or margarine
1 tablespoon lemon juice
1 large chicken, cut up
2 cups cornflake crumbs
1 teaspoon garlic salt
1/2 teaspoon onion salt

Preheat the oven to 350 degrees. Melt the butter in a large saucepan. Add the lemon juice and dip the chicken in the mixture. Combine the dry ingredients on a large plate and roll the chicken pieces in the mixture. Place the chicken on a buttered cookie sheet and bake for 1 hour. Makes 6 to 8 servings.

FLO WYLES
HOLUM BAPTIST CHURCH
GRAYSON, LOUISIANA

CRISPY FRIED CHICKEN

1 1/2 cups all-purpose flour
1/2 cup cornmeal
1/4 cup cornstarch
1 tablespoon salt
2 teaspoons paprika
1 teaspoon dried oregano
1 teaspoon rubbed sage
1 teaspoon black pepper
2 eggs
1/4 cup water
2 broiler-fryer chickens (3 to 4 pounds each),
    cut up
Vegetable oil for frying

In a large resealable plastic bag, combine the flour, cornmeal, cornstarch, salt, paprika, oregano, sage, and pepper. In a shallow bowl, beat the eggs and water. Dip the chicken in the egg mixture; place in the bag, a few pieces at a time, and shake until coated. In an electric skillet, heat 1 inch of oil to 375 degrees. Fry the chicken, a few pieces at a time, for 3 to 5 minutes on each side or until golden and crispy. Place the chicken in 2 ungreased 15 x 10 x 1-inch baking dishes. Bake, uncovered, at 350 degrees for 25 to 30 minutes, or until the chicken is tender and the juices run clear. Makes 12 servings.

PINEMOUNT BAPTIST CHURCH
MCALPIN, FLORIDA

CRISPY BAKED CHICKEN

3 to 4 pounds chicken pieces
1 cup buttermilk
1/2 cup finely ground cornmeal
1/2 cup all-purpose flour
1 1/2 teaspoons salt
1 1/2 teaspoons chili powder
1/2 teaspoon dried oregano
1/4 teaspoon black pepper
1/3 cup butter, melted

Place the chicken in a large plastic resealable bag and add the buttermilk. Remove the air from the bag and seal. Refrigerate overnight to marinate. Preheat the oven to 375 degrees. Combine the next 6 ingredients to form a dry coating mix. Remove the chicken pieces from the bag and roll them in the dry mixture. Place in a greased 13 x 9-inch baking dish and drizzle with the melted butter. Bake, uncovered, for 50 to 55 minutes, or until the juices run clear.

PINEMOUNT BAPTIST CHURCH
MCALPIN, FLORIDA

Buttermilk Fried Chicken with Gravy

1 broiler-fryer chicken (2-3 pounds, cut up)
1 cup buttermilk
1 cup all-purpose flour
1 1/2 teaspoons salt
1/2 teaspoon pepper
Cooking oil for frying

Gravy:
3 tablespoons all-purpose flour
1 cup milk
1 1/2 to 2 cups water
Salt and pepper to taste

Place the chicken pieces in a large, flat dish. Pour the buttermilk over, cover and refrigerate for one hour. Combine the flour, salt and pepper in a double-strength paper bag. Drain the chicken pieces and toss them, one at a time, in the flour mixture. Shake off any excess flour and place the pieces on waxed paper to dry. Heat 1/8 to 1/4-inch of oil in a large skillet, then fry the chicken pieces until browned on all sides. Cover and simmer, turning occasionally, for 40-45 minutes, or until the juices run clear and the chicken is tender. Uncover and cook 5 minutes longer. Remove the chicken from the pan and keep warm. Drain all but 1/4 cup of the drippings from the skillet. Sprinkle in the flour and stir until bubbly. Add milk and 1 1/2 cups of water. Cook until thickened and bubbling, then cook one minute more. Add the remaining 1/4 cup of water if the gravy is too thick. Season with salt and pepper. Serve with the chicken. Makes 4 to 6 servings.

Betty Caton
Wellington Village Assembly of God
Little Rock, Arkansas

Rice Krispie Chicken

6 boneless chicken breasts
2 cups Rice Krispies, crushed
1 cup butter or margarine, melted

Dip chicken pieces in melted butter, then in cereal to coat. Place on foil lined baking sheet. Season with salt and pepper. Pour remaining butter over chicken. Bake in preheated 350 degrees oven 45 to 60 minutes or until chicken is tender and golden brown.

Note: If you're in a hurry, cut chicken into smaller pieces and it will bake faster. Also, add any seasoning you would like to the cereal (onion powder, garlic, chili powder, etc.).

Amy Binns
North Monroe Street Church of God
Monroe, Michigan

GARLICKY BAKED CHICKEN

1 whole chicken, cut up
2 large heads garlic, separated into cloves
3 celery ribs, cut into 1-inch pieces
3/4 cup dry white wine
1/4 cup olive oil
3 tablespoons fresh lemon juice
2 tablespoons chopped parsley
2 tablespoons chopped fresh basil, or 3/4
　　teaspoon dried
1/4 teaspoon freshly ground pepper
1/4 teaspoon crushed red pepper flakes
1/2 teaspoon grated lemon rind

Preheat the oven to 375 degrees. Arrange the chicken in a 13 x 9 x 2-inch baking dish, skin side up. Sprinkle the garlic cloves and celery over the chicken. Combine the wine, olive oil, lemon juice, parsley, basil, salt, black pepper, and pepper flakes. Pour the mixture over the chicken. Sprinkle lemon rind on top. Bake, covered, for 40 minutes. Uncover and bake for 15 minutes longer, until the chicken is tender. Makes 4 to 6 servings.

JUDY LOVE
BETHEL AME CHURCH
AUGUSTA, GEORGIA

GEORGIA BAR-B-Q CHICKEN

1/4 cup vinegar
1/2 cup water
3 tablespoons brown sugar
1 tablespoon white sugar
1 1/2 teaspoons salt
1/2 teaspoon black pepper
1/4 teaspoon cayenne pepper
1/2 teaspoon garlic powder
Juice of 1 lemon
1 large onion, thinly sliced
1/4 cup butter
3/4 cup ketchup
2 tablespoons Worcestershire sauce
1 1/2 teaspoons liquid smoke (substitutes:
　　hickory-smoked salt, or charcoal
　　seasoning, eliminating the salt in the
　　recipe)
Chicken pieces (about 1 chicken)

Preheat the oven to 350 degrees. In a medium saucepan, combine the first 11 ingredients. Bring to a boil and simmer, uncovered, for 20 minutes. Add the ketchup, Worcestershire sauce, and liquid smoke. Place the chicken in a shallow backing dish and pour the barbecue sauce over it. The sauce should just cover the pieces (this recipe is about enough to do one chicken). Lightly cover the dish with aluminum foil. Bake for 1 1/2 to 2 hours.

NANCY EISENBISE
TRINITY PRESBYTERIAN CHURCH
WILMINGTON, DELAWARE

HONEY-BARBECUE CHICKEN

1 (2 1/2- to 3-pound) broiler-fryer chicken, split
3/4 cup butter or margarine, melted
1/3 cup white vinegar
1/4 cup honey
2 garlic cloves, minced
2 teaspoons salt
1/2 teaspoon dry mustard
Dash of pepper

Place the chicken in a large shallow container. In a small bowl, combine the melted butter and the remaining ingredients, stirring well. Grill the chicken, skin side up, over hot coals for 30 to 35 minutes, or until done. Turn and baste frequently with the sauce mixture.

MERRY R. JONES
GRIFFIN CHAPEL UNITED METHODIST CHURCH
STARKVILLE, MISSISSIPPI

INDONESIAN BARBECUED CHICKEN

1 chicken
2 shallots, sliced
3 garlic cloves, sliced
1 teaspoon crushed ginger
1 teaspoon black pepper
1 teaspoon cumin seed
1/2 teaspoon turmeric
1 teaspoon lemon juice
1 1/2 cups shredded coconut
2 cups water
1 sprig of basil
Salt

Split the chicken in half down the breastbone. Pound together the shallots, garlic, and ginger, then mix in the pepper, cumin, turmeric, and lemon juice. Roll the chicken in this mixture and leave to marinate for 1 hour or so. Place the coconut in a container, pour in the water, and let the mixture stand for 10 minutes, then strain and squeeze through a piece of cheesecloth (or substitute a 2-ounce package of creamed coconut mixed with 2 cups of hot water). Place the chicken in a saucepan and add the basil, salt, and coconut milk. Bring slowly to simmering point and cook until tender, but before the flesh begins to loosen from the bones. Carefully lift out the chicken and broil over a charcoal fire until it is a rich brown, basting occasionally with the coconut milk.

SARAH
FOREST AVENUE CONGREGATIONAL CHURCH
BANGOR, MAINE

DIANNE'S QUICK AND EASY CHICKEN BREAST

Cooking spray
4 frozen skinless, boneless chicken breasts
1/2 cup Italian dressing
2 tablespoons teriyaki
1 teaspoon salt
2 tablespoons honey
1/2 teaspoon black pepper
1 teaspoon garlic

Spray a large skillet with cooking spray and arrange the frozen chicken breasts in it. Combine the remaining ingredients and mix well. Pour the mixture over the chicken and cover. Cook over medium heat for 10 minutes; turn the chicken breasts, and cook for an additional 10 minutes. Remove the lid and continue cooking until the chicken is golden.

PINEMOUNT BAPTIST CHURCH
MCALPIN, FLORIDA

CHICKEN TARRAGON

1/2 pound fresh mushrooms
4 tablespoons butter
6 large chicken breasts, boned
2 teaspoons seasoned salt
1/2 teaspoon leaf tarragon, crumbled
1 cup dry white wine
1 cup sour cream
1/2 cup chopped chives

Cut the mushrooms in half. In a large skillet, sauté the mushrooms in 2 tablespoons of the butter for 8 minutes. Remove the mushrooms. Add the remaining butter and the chicken. Season the chicken with salt and brown it completely. Return the mushrooms to the skillet. Add the tarragon and wine; simmer for 45 minutes. Transfer the chicken to a platter. Stir in the sour cream to combine with the pan juices. Pour the mixture over the chicken and garnish with chives.

NANCY SHERLIN
BUCKINGHAM UNITED METHODIST CHURCH
GARLAND, TEXAS

CHICKEN WITH DRESSING

4 chicken breast halves
4 slices Swiss cheese
1 can cream of chicken soup
1/2 cup sherry or milk
2 cups herb stuffing
1 stick butter melted

Preheat the oven to 350 degrees. Place the chicken in a casserole dish and cover with the Swiss cheese. Dilute the soup with the sherry and pour over the chicken. Top with the stuffing and drizzle with the butter. Bake for 1 to 1 1/2 hours.

DOROTHY SANDERS
CROSS IN THE DESERT UNITED METHODIST CHURCH
PHOENIX, ARIZONA

DRUNK CHICKEN

4 packages skinless, boneless chicken breasts
2 1/2 cups wine (white or Rhine)
4 tablespoons melted butter
2 tablespoons dried parsley
2 tablespoons dried onion
Lawry's seasoned salt
2 cups uncooked rice

Preheat the oven to 450 degrees. Place the chicken in a 13 x 9-inch baking dish. In a bowl, combine the next 3 ingredients. Pour the mixture over the chicken. Sprinkle with Lawry's salt. Bake for 35 minutes, then turn the chicken over. Add the rice and more wine if necessary. Continue cooking 20 minutes longer, or until the rice is tender. Makes 2 to 4 servings.

Note: You can cook the rice separately and pour the wine sauce over it.

SHELLEE STEWART
UNITED METHODIST CHURCH
ESTÂNCIA, NEW MEXICO

Pan-Glazed Chicken with Basil

4 (4-ounce) skinless, boneless chicken breast
    halves
1/2 teaspoon salt
1/4 teaspoon black pepper
2 tablespoons olive oil
2 tablespoons balsamic vinegar
1 tablespoon honey
2 tablespoons chopped fresh basil, (optional)

Season both sides of the chicken with salt and pepper. Heat the olive oil in a large nonstick skillet over medium-high heat. Add the chicken and cook for 5 minutes, or until lightly browned. Turn the chicken over and cook for 6 minutes more until done. Stir in the vinegar, honey, and basil, if desired. Cook 1 minute longer. Makes 4 servings.

Ruthann Herkimer
First United Methodist Church
Belleville, Michigan

Lemon-Garlic Chicken

5 garlic cloves, chopped
3/4 cup lemon juice
1 tablespoon salt
1/2 tablespoon black pepper
1 tablespoon oregano
1/4 to 1/2 cup oil
8 to 10 pieces chicken

In a large bowl, combine the first 6 ingredients. Pour the mixture over the chicken and marinate overnight (or all day). Cook the chicken on a grill, basting with the marinade. (You can also broil or bake the chicken in the oven at 400 degrees for 30 to 40 minutes. Baste as desired.)

Ester Brown
Griffin Chapel United Methodist Church
Starkville, Mississippi

CHICKEN PICCATA

4 skinless, boneless chicken breasts
All-purpose flour
1/4 teaspoon garlic powder
1/4 teaspoon garlic salt
1/4 teaspoon black pepper
1/4 teaspoon paprika
Margarine
1 can chicken broth
1 small jar capers, drained
Juice of 1 lemon
1/4 teaspoon dehydrated garlic, ground (optional)

Preheat the oven to 350 degrees. Pound the chicken breasts slightly. Dredge in a mixture of flour, garlic powder, garlic salt, pepper, and paprika. Brown in the margarine. Arrange the chicken in a baking dish. Combine the broth, capers, and lemon juice and pour the mixture over the chicken. Sprinkle with ground garlic or more garlic powder and cover with foil. Bake for 1 hour. Remove the foil for the last 15 minutes.

Note: The recipe can be made ahead of time and refrigerated.

DEAN MIESEN
HIGHLAND HEIGHTS PRESBYTERIAN CHURCH
CORDOVA, TENNESSEE

NEWLYWED LEMON CHICKEN

3 or 4 cans golden mushroom soup
2 teaspoons paprika
1/2 teaspoon salt
1/2 teaspoon lemon pepper
3/4 teaspoon tarragon, crushed between fingers
6 tablespoons lemon juice (less for less tangy and tart sauce)
2 pounds chicken pieces (fillets or nugget-size pieces work well)
Lemon slices

Preheat the oven to 350 degrees. In a large bowl, combine the soup, paprika, salt, lemon pepper, tarragon, and lemon juice. Spread a small amount of the mixture on the bottom of a casserole dish to prevent the chicken from sticking. Arrange the chicken pieces in the casserole. Pour the remaining mixture over the chicken. Cover with a lid or foil. Bake for 1 hour. Before serving, cut the lemon into 1/4-inch slices; make a cut halfway through lemon circle. Twist in opposite directions at the slit (180 degrees). Garnish.

Note: My husband and I ate this once a week for the first year of our marriage, because I knew how to make it! The recipe works great in a Crock-Pot. Cook for 4 to 6 hours on the high setting or for 8 to 10 hours on the low setting. Serve over rice.

JILL COOK
BUCKINGHAM UNITED METHODIST CHURCH
GARLAND, TEXAS

Hawaiian Chicken

4 chicken breasts, split
1 egg, slightly beaten
1 cup finely grated breadcrumbs
1 teaspoon salt
Oil for frying
1 cup pineapple juice
2 tablespoons lemon juice
1 tablespoon cornstarch
1 tablespoon sugar
1/4 teaspoon curry powder

Dip each split breast in egg, then roll into breadcrumbs. Season with salt. Pan fry in 1/4-inch hot oil in a heavy skillet until brown. Combine the juices, cornstarch, curry powder and sugar. Pour over the chicken. Cover skillet and cook slowly over low heat for 25 minutes. Serves 4.

MaryAnn Zehner
Prince of Peace Church
Grantsville, West Virginia

PARMESAN CHICKEN

1/2 cup butter or margarine, melted
2 teaspoons Dijon mustard
1 teaspoon Worcestershire sauce
1/2 teaspoon salt
1 cup dry bread crumbs
1/2 cup grated Parmesan cheese
6 to 8 skinless, boneless chicken breast halves

In a shallow bowl, combine the butter, mustard, Worcestershire sauce, and salt. In a plastic bag, combine the bread crumbs and cheese. Dip the chicken breasts in the butter mixture, then add them to the plastic bag and shake to coat. Place the chicken on an ungreased 9 x 13-inch baking pan. Drizzle with the remaining butter mixture. Bake at 350 degrees for 45 minutes, or until done.

CHRISTINE WALKER
CAVENDISH BAPTIST CHURCH
CAVENDISH, VERMONT

CHICKEN RUBY

1/3 cup all-purpose flour
1 teaspoon salt
2 1/2 to 3 pounds chicken, cut in pieces
4 tablespoons butter or margarine, melted
1 1/2 cups fresh cranberries
3/4 cup sugar
1/4 cup chopped onion
1 teaspoon orange peel
3/4 cup orange juice
1/4 teaspoon ground cinnamon
1/4 teaspoon ground ginger

Combine the flour and salt on a plate and dredge the chicken pieces in the mixture. In a skillet over medium heat, brown the chicken in melted butter, turning the pieces once. Combine the remaining ingredients in a saucepan; bring to a boil and pour the mixture over the chicken. Cover and simmer for 35 to 40 minutes, or until the chicken is tender. Makes 4 servings.

CINDY JOHNSON AND JEAN WEST
MATTAPOISETT CONGREGATIONAL CHURCH
MATTAPOISETT, MASSACHUSETTS

CHICKEN AND MUSHROOMS IN RED WINE SAUCE

3 strips bacon
1 package boneless chicken breasts, cubed
1 onion, sliced
1/2 pound fresh mushrooms, quartered
2 tablespoons all-purpose flour
Salt and pepper to taste
1/2 teaspoon thyme
1/2 cup chicken broth
1 cup red wine or cooking sherry

In a large skillet, fry the bacon until crisp. Remove the bacon from the skillet. Sauté the chicken in the bacon drippings until browned. Add the onion and sauté for 5 minutes. Add the mushrooms and sauté for 1 minute. Sprinkle the flour in the skillet and toss lightly. Crumble the bacon and add it to the skillet. Add the remaining ingredients. Cover and simmer for 30 minutes, or until the chicken is tender. If the gravy thickens too much, add water. Serve with rice or noodles. Makes 4 servings.

TONI WARE
HIGHLAND HEIGHTS PRESBYTERIAN CHURCH
CORDOVA, TENNESSEE

CHICKEN DIJON

3 tablespoons butter
4 skinless, boneless chicken breasts
2 tablespoons all-purpose flour
1 cup chicken broth
1/2 cup light cream
2 tablespoons Dijon mustard
2 tomatoes, cut into wedges
2 tablespoons minced parsley

Melt the butter in a large skillet. Add the chicken breasts and cook until lightly browned, about 20 minutes. Remove the chicken to a warm serving platter. Stir the flour into the drippings in the skillet and cook for 1 minute. Add the chicken broth and light cream. Stir and cook until the sauce thickens and bubbles. Stir in the mustard. Return the chicken to the skillet, cover, and heat for 10 minutes. Garnish with the tomatoes and sprinkle with the parsley. Makes 4 servings.

MARTHA BULKELEY
CROSS IN THE DESERT UNITED METHODIST CHURCH
PHOENIX, ARIZONA

SOUR CREAM CHICKEN

2 cups sour cream
1/4 cup lemon juice
4 teaspoons Worcestershire sauce
4 teaspoons salt
2 teaspoons paprika
1/2 teaspoon black pepper
Dash of garlic powder
10 to 12 boneless chicken breasts
Unflavored bread crumbs
3 tablespoons butter

Combine the sour cream, lemon juice, Worcestershire sauce, salt, paprika, pepper, and garlic powder in a container. Place the chicken in a baking dish, pour the mixture over the chicken, and marinate overnight. Just before cooking, roll the chicken pieces in the bread crumbs and return to the marinade. Dot with butter and bake at 350 degrees for 1 hour.

PAM HUNTER
UNITED BAPTIST CHURCH OF POULTNEY
EAST POULTNEY, VERMONT

CHICKEN KIEV

2/3 cup butter
1/2 cup dry bread crumbs
2 tablespoons grated Parmesan cheese
1 teaspoon basil
1/2 teaspoon garlic salt
2 chicken breasts, split
1/4 cup dry white wine or apple juice
1/4 cup chopped scallion
1/4 cup chopped parsley

Preheat oven to 375 degrees. In a 2-quart saucepan, melt butter. On a piece of wax paper, combine bread crumbs, cheese, basil and garlic salt. Dip chicken breasts in melted butter, then roll in bread crumbs to coat. Place skin side up in ungreased 9-inch square baking dish. Bake in 375 degree oven for 50 to 60 minutes. While chicken is baking, add the wine, onion and parsley to remaining melted butter. When chicken is golden brown, pour butter sauce over and around. Return to oven for 3 to 5 minutes more or just until sauce is hot. Serve with sauce spooned over. Good with wild rice as an accompaniment.

JENNY KOTTENBROOK
GRIFFIN CHAPEL UNITED METHODIST CHURCH
STARKVILLE, MISSISSIPPI

CHICKEN MOZZARELLA

4 skinless, boneless chicken breast halves
1/2 cup Progresso plain bread crumbs
1/4 cup grated Parmesan cheese
1/4 cup chopped fresh parsley
1 egg, beaten
2 tablespoons olive or vegetable oil
1/2 cup shredded mozzarella cheese
Spaghetti sauce

Pound the chicken with the flat side of a meat mallet until it's about 1/4-inch thick. In a bowl, combine the bread crumbs, Parmesan cheese, and parsley; mix well. Dip the chicken in the egg, then press into the bread-crumb mixture to coat. In a nonstick skillet, heat the oil until it's hot. Add the chicken and cook until done, turning once. Sprinkle the chicken with the cheese and cover to allow the cheese to melt. Transfer the chicken to a serving platter. Spoon heated spaghetti sauce over each chicken breast. Serve with angel hair pasta or thin spaghetti.

CHRISTIAN MILLHOUSE
BUCKINGHAM UNITED METHODIST CHURCH
GARLAND, TEXAS

ROLLED CHICKEN WASHINGTON

1/2 cup fresh mushrooms, finely chopped
2 tablespoons butter or margarine
2 tablespoons all-purpose flour
1/2 cup light cream
1/4 teaspoon salt, plus additional
Dash of cayenne pepper
5 ounces sharp natural Cheddar cheese,
    shredded (1 1/4 cups)
6 whole chicken breasts, boned
2 eggs, slightly beaten
3/4 cup fine dry bread crumbs
Oil, for frying

In a small skillet, cook the mushrooms in the butter for 5 minutes. Blend in the 2 tablespoons of flour. Stir in the cream. Add the salt and cayenne pepper. Cook, stirring, until the mixture is very thick. Add the cheese and simmer, stirring until the cheese melts. Turn the mixture into a pie plate. Cover and chill for 1 hour. Cut into 6 pieces, shaping into short sticks.

Remove the skin from the chicken breasts. Place each piece of chicken between plastic wrap and pound out with a wooden mallet to form cutlets not quite 1/4-inch thick. Peel off the wrap. Sprinkle the chicken with more salt. Place a cheese stick on each piece, tucking in the sides. Roll as you would if you were making a jelly roll. Press to seal well. Dust the rolls with flour. Dip the rolls in the egg, then in the bread crumbs. Cover and chill thoroughly for at least 1 hour.

An hour before serving, preheat the oven to 350 degrees. Fry the rolls in a little oil to brown. Transfer to a baking dish and bake for 30 to 45 minutes.

MARCIA B. RUSSELL
HIGHLAND HEIGHTS PRESBYTERIAN CHURCH
CORDOVA, TENNESSEE

SANTA FE CHICKEN

2 whole skinless, boneless chicken breasts
1/4 cup white wine

MARINADE:
Juice of 3 limes
1/4 cup soy sauce
1 1/2 teaspoons olive oil
1 1/2 teaspoons chili powder
1 1/2 teaspoons cumin seed
1 1/2 teaspoons ground coriander
6 garlic cloves, minced
1 1/2 teaspoons honey
3 tablespoons chopped cilantro leaves

GARNISH:
Mock or reduced-fat sour cream
1 lime, sliced into 6 thin slices
1/4 cup fresh salsa or papaya salsa

In a bowl, combine the marinade ingredients, stirring thoroughly. Pour the mixture into a shallow baking dish and lay the chicken breasts on top. Cover and refrigerate for 1 hour.

Preheat the broiler. After 1 hour, when the chicken has absorbed all the flavors of the marinade, pour in the white wine. Broil the chicken under a medium flame for 8 to 10 minutes, basting it with the juices to keep it moist. Transfer the chicken to a platter and slice it at an angle. Garnish each piece with a little of the pan juices, a dollop of sour cream, and slices of lime, as well as a dollop of salsa. Makes 4 servings.

CROSS IN THE DESERT UNITED METHODIST CHURCH
PHOENIX, ARIZONA

CHICKEN MOLE

2 1/2 to 3 pounds chicken breasts and/or
    thighs
2 teaspoons salt
2 tablespoons salad oil
1 cup onion, chopped
1/2 cup tomato sauce
1/4 cup creamy peanut butter
1 square (1 ounce) unsweetened chocolate,
    finely chopped or grated
1/4 cup dry bread crumbs
1/4 cup chili powder
1 1/2 teaspoons sugar
1/4 teaspoon ground cinnamon
1/4 teaspoon ground cumin
1/4 teaspoon cloves
1 garlic clove, crushed

Place the chicken pieces in a large saucepan with 1 teaspoon of the salt and 6 cups of water. Cover. Boil gently until tender, about 20 to 30 minutes. Remove the chicken and set it aside. Strain the broth, reserving 2 cups for the sauce. Return the chicken to the saucepan and keep warm.

In a large skillet, heat the oil. Add the onion and sauté until tender. Place the onions in a blender with the remaining ingredients, the other teaspoon of salt, and the 2 cups of broth. Cover and blend at high speed, stopping occasionally to scrape down the sides with a rubber spatula. Pour the sauce over the chicken. Cover the saucepan and cook slowly until heated through, about 5 to 10 minutes. Uncover and simmer until the sauce thickens, about 5 minutes. Makes 6 to 8 servings.

ANNE RHODES
HIGHLAND HEIGHTS PRESBYTERIAN CHURCH
CORDOVA, TENNESSEE

CHICKEN MARENGO

4 to 5 pounds cut-up chicken
1/3 cup olive oil
Salt and pepper to taste
1 large onion, chopped
2 garlic cloves, crushed
1/2 pound mushrooms, sliced
1/2 cup dry white wine
1 cup chopped tomatoes

In a large, deep skillet, heat the olive oil and add the chicken; brown lightly on all sides. Season with salt and pepper and remove the chicken to another container. Add the onion and garlic to the skillet and cook until soft. Return the chicken to the skillet and add the mushrooms, wine, and tomatoes. Cover and simmer for 30 to 40 minutes.

Note: This recipe is also excellent when veal stew meat is used instead of chicken. I use about 2 pounds of stew veal.

RONNY WILLIAMS
UNITED BAPTIST CHURCH OF POULTNEY
EAST POULTNEY, VERMONT

CHICKEN SALSA

1 1/2 cups salsa
3 tablespoons brown sugar
1 tablespoon Dijon mustard
1 tablespoon cornstarch
4 to 6 chicken breasts

Combine the salsa, sugar, mustard, and cornstarch in a small bowl and pour the mixture over the chicken breasts. Bake for 20 to 30 minutes at 400 degrees, or until done.

NANCY MCDONALD
TOWER HILL UNITED METHODIST CHURCH
TOWER HILL, ILLINOIS

CHICKEN ENCHILADAS

1 can cream of chicken soup
4 ounces chopped green chilies (optional)
2 cups Cheddar cheese
1/4 to 1/2 cup butter, melted
2 cups cooked chicken, cut into bite-size
*   pieces (2 or 3 breasts)*
8 small flour tortillas
2 cups Monterey Jack cheese

In a large bowl, combine the soup, chilies (if desired), and Cheddar cheese; stir. Add the chicken. Melt the butter in a 9 x 13-inch baking dish (just put it in a warm oven). Dip both sides of the tortillas in the butter. Add a spoonful of chicken mixture to each tortilla, roll them up, and place them in the baking dish. Sprinkle the Monterey Jack over the top. Cover with foil and bake for 30 minutes at 350 degrees.

MARSHA BERRYHILL
MEMORIAL BAPTIST CHURCH
TULSA, OKLAHOMA

Chicken Fajitas

1/4 cup soy sauce
2 tablespoons sugar
2 tablespoons lemon juice
1 tablespoon cornstarch
8 (8-inch) flour tortillas
1 tablespoon cooking oil (add more during cooking if necessary)
3 garlic cloves, minced
3 cups thinly sliced sweet peppers (any combination of red, green, yellow or orange)
1/2 cup thinly sliced onion
12 ounces skinless, boneless chicken, cut into thin strips

In a small bowl, stir together the soy sauce, sugar, lemon juice, and cornstarch; set aside. Wrap the tortillas in foil and stack them. Heat in a 350 degree oven for 10 minutes, or until warm.

Pour the oil into a wok or large skillet and preheat it over medium-high heat. Stir-fry the garlic for 15 seconds. Add the sweet peppers and onion; stir-fry for 2 to 3 minutes, or until crisp-tender. Remove the vegetables from the wok. Add more oil if necessary; add the chicken to the hot wok. Stir-fry for 4 to 5 minutes, or until the chicken is no longer pink. Push the chicken away from the center of the wok.

Stir the sauce and pour it into the center of the wok. Cook, stirring, until it thickens and bubbles. Return the cooked vegetables to the wok. Stir all the ingredients together, coating them well with the sauce. Cook for about 1 minute longer, or until heated through. Spoon the mixture onto the warm tortillas and roll up. Serve immediately. Makes 2 servings of 2 tortillas each.

Note: You can substitute 12 ounces of turkey-breast tenderloin steaks or 12 ounces of lean beef cubes for the chicken. Any of the three choices are very tasty and colorful.

BARBARA SNYDER
CAVENDISH BAPTIST CHURCH
CAVENDISH, VERMONT

Teriyaki Chicken

1/2 cup soy sauce
1 1/2 teaspoons red wine vinegar or cider vinegar
2 teaspoons vegetable oil
1 teaspoon garlic powder
1/2 cup sugar
3/4 teaspoon ground ginger
1 pound chicken breasts, boned and skinned

In a small bowl, combine the first 6 ingredients and pour over the chicken. (The recipe can be frozen at this point for later use. Thaw before cooking.) Bake for 35 minutes at 350 degrees, or until done. *Note:* This marinade can also be used with beef or pork or with stir-fry. Makes 4 servings.

CAROLYN CRUTCHER
TOWER HILL UNITED METHODIST CHURCH
TOWER HILL, ILLINOIS

CHICKEN WITH SUN-DRIED TOMATO CREAM

4 skinless, boneless chicken breasts
Salt and pepper to taste
2 tablespoons olive oil
5 garlic cloves, thinly sliced
1/2 cup white wine
1 cup heavy cream
1/4 cup sun-dried tomatoes, drained and
    chopped
3 tablespoons thinly sliced fresh basil

Season the chicken with salt and pepper. In a large skillet, sauté the chicken in olive oil until browned (about 4 to 5 minutes on each side). Add the garlic and sauté until fragrant (about 30 seconds). Add the wine, cream, and tomatoes and bring to a boil. Cover and reduce the heat. Simmer for another 2 to 3 minutes. Remove the chicken from the skillet and add the basil to the sauce. Increase the heat and boil until it thickens (about 2 minutes). Spoon the sauce over the chicken and serve.

Note: I adapted this recipe from Epicurious.com. It can be made in just 20 minutes or so.

SUSAN JONES
NORTHBROOK UNITED METHODIST CHURCH
ROSWELL, GEORGIA

SESAME CHICKEN AND SNOW PEAS IN APRICOT SAUCE

2 teaspoons dark sesame oil
3 garlic cloves, minced
1 pound skinless, boneless chicken breasts,
    cut into thin strips
1/3 cup (2 ounces) sliced dried apricots
1/2 cup water
1/2 cup (5 ounces) apricot preserves
1 tablespoon reduced-sodium soy sauce
1 tablespoon Dijon-style mustard
1/2 teaspoon grated fresh ginger
1/2 pound snow peas, ends trimmed
1 tablespoon sesame seeds

In a large nonstick skillet over medium heat, heat the sesame oil. Add the garlic, and sauté for 1 minute. Add the chicken and sauté until it is browned and no longer pink in the center, about 5 minutes. Add the apricots, water, apricot preserves, soy sauce, mustard, and ginger; bring to a boil. Reduce the heat to low and simmer for 5 minutes. Add the snow peas and simmer until crisp-tender, about 5 minutes longer. Sprinkle with the sesame seeds. Makes 4 servings.

CHARLOTTE SNYDER
CAVENDISH BAPTIST CHURCH
CAVENDISH, VERMONT

CHICKEN FLORENTINE

3 (10-ounce) packages frozen chopped
   spinach
2 eggs, beaten
1/2 cup grated Parmesan cheese, divided
1 1/2 cups Italian-style bread crumbs
4 whole chicken breasts, split, boned, and
   skinned
Salt and pepper to taste
5 tablespoons butter or margarine, melted

Cook the spinach according to the package directions, drain well, and allow to cool. In a large bowl, combine the spinach, eggs, and 2 tablespoons of Parmesan cheese; set aside. Combine the bread crumbs and the remaining Parmesan cheese in a shallow pan; set aside. Season the chicken breasts with salt and pepper; roll each in the bread-crumb mixture. Place in a greased 9 x 13-inch baking dish. Divide the spinach mixture evenly and spread on each chicken breast to form a 1/2-inch-thick layer. Sprinkle with the remaining bread-crumb mixture and drizzle with the butter. Bake at 350 degrees for 35 to 40 minutes. Makes 8 servings.

CHARLIE TILL
TRINITY PRESBYTERIAN CHURCH
WILMINGTON, DELAWARE

CHICKEN MARSALA

1 egg, beaten
1/4 cup skim or 2% milk
1/2 cup all-purpose flour
Salt and pepper to taste
16 ounces (3 packages) chicken breasts
3 tablespoons butter
3 tablespoons olive oil
1 to 2 garlic cloves
1 medium onion, diced
1 medium green pepper, diced
1 small red pepper, diced
1/2 pound mushrooms, sliced
1 cup Marsala wine
1 envelope instant chicken stock

Combine the egg and milk in a shallow bowl. On a plate, combine the flour and the salt and pepper. Dip the chicken in the egg mixture, then coat both sides with the flour mixture. Refrigerate for 2 to 2 1/2 hours. In a large skillet, heat the butter and olive oil. Brown the chicken and remove it from the skillet. Add the remaining ingredients. Simmer for 10 to 12 minutes to reduce the liquid. Place the chicken back in the skillet and reheat.

JERRY WALKER
FIRST UNITED METHODIST CHURCH
BELLEVILLE, MICHIGAN

PECAN CHICKEN WITH HONEY-MUSTARD SAUCE

4 boneless, skinless chicken breast halves
1/4 cup all-purpose flour
1 cup Honey Mustard Salad Dressing
1 cup finely chopped pecans
1/4 cup butter
2/3 cup sour cream

Pound each chicken breast as follows: Place between 2 pieces of waxed paper, boned side up, and pound gently with a rolling pin until the chicken is about 1/4-inch thick. Place the flour, 2/3 cup salad dressing, and pecans in three separate dishes. Coat the chicken with flour, then dressing, then pecans, pressing to coat well. Melt the butter in heavy nonstick skillet and cook the chicken for 2 to 3 minutes on each side until it's thoroughly cooked. Watch carefully, as the pecans can burn easily. Remove the pieces from the skillet as they are done and cover to keep warm. To the drippings in the skillet, add the remaining 1/4 cup of salad dressing and the sour cream and heat until the mixture begins to boil. Pour over the chicken and serve.

PINEMOUNT BAPTIST CHURCH
MCALPIN, FLORIDA

CHICKEN AND BROCCOLI STIR-FRY

1 tablespoon vegetable oil (add more if
    necessary during cooking)
1 pound skinless, boneless chicken breasts,
    cut into strips
2 cups broccoli florets
1 medium red pepper, cut into thin strips
1/2 cup thinly sliced onion
1 1/2 cups chicken broth
2 tablespoons soy sauce
2 tablespoons cornstarch
1 teaspoon garlic powder
1 teaspoon ground ginger
2 cups hot cooked rice

Heat the oil in a wok or large skillet over medium-high heat. Add the chicken; cook, stirring, for 4 to 5 minutes, or until no pink remains. Add the broccoli, pepper, and onion; cook, stirring, until the vegetables are crisp-tender and the broccoli turns bright green.

In a large bowl, combine the broth, soy sauce, cornstarch, garlic powder, and ginger until well blended. Stir into the center of the chicken mixture. Bring to a boil; cook, stirring, for 1 minute until the mixture thickens. Serve over hot rice. Makes 4 servings.

BARBARA SNYDER
CAVENDISH BAPTIST CHURCH
CAVENDISH, VERMONT

Easy Chicken Divan

2 (10-ounce) packages frozen broccoli
2 cups sliced cooked chicken or 3 breasts,
    cooked and boned
3/4 cup mayonnaise
1 teaspoon lemon juice
2 (10 1/2-ounce) cans condensed cream of
    chicken or mushroom soup
1/2 cup American or Muenster cheese,
    shredded
1 cup soft bread crumbs
1 teaspoon melted butter

Preheat the oven to 350 degrees. Cook the broccoli until it's tender; drain. Arrange the broccoli in a greased 12 x 7 1/2 x 2-inch baking dish. Lay the chicken on top. Combine the next 3 ingredients and pour the mixture over the chicken. Sprinkle with cheese. Combine the bread crumbs and butter; sprinkle over the chicken. Bake for about 35 minutes until heated. Makes 6 to 8 servings.

LOISTINE MCSHEPARD GRADY
GRIFFIN CHAPEL UNITED METHODIST CHURCH
STARKVILLE, MISSISSIPPI

Onion and Cheese Chicken Bake

2 tablespoons butter or margarine
1/2 teaspoon salt
1/2 teaspoon black pepper
3 whole chicken breasts, skinned
8 ounces fresh mushrooms, sliced
1 (3-ounce) can onion rings
1/2 cup Monterey Jack cheese, grated

In a small microwave-safe bowl, melt the butter on high for 1 to 1 1/2 minutes. Stir in the salt and pepper. Arrange the chicken in an 8 x 12-inch baking dish, with meatiest portion toward the outside of the dish. Cover with waxed paper. Microwave on high for 4 or 5 minutes. Top with the mushrooms. Cover with waxed paper; microwave on high until the chicken is no longer pink. Top with the onion rings and cheese. Microwave on high for 1 to 2 minutes, or until the cheese melts.

BARBARA HARVISON
BUCKINGHAM UNITED METHODIST CHURCH
GARLAND, TEXAS

Chicken Tetrazzini

6 to 8 cups cooked chicken, boiled
2 cans mushrooms
12 ounce shredded sharp cheese
1 green pepper (optional)
1 small can French fried onion rings
5 cans mushroom soup
1 can water chestnuts
1 jar pimientos
8 to 10 ounce spaghetti

Boil chicken and debone; save broth. Boil spaghetti in chicken broth until done. Combine all other ingredients with cooked spaghetti. Sprinkle onion rings on top. Bake in greased baking dish 30 to 60 minutes at 350 degrees.

This recipe is large enough to make 2 casseroles. Good to freeze.

DIANE CARLETON
MEMORIAL BAPTIST CHURCH
TULSA, OKLAHOMA

Chicken Almond Stir-Fry

2 tablespoons sesame or vegetable oil
4 skinless, boneless chicken breast halves
1 (2 1/4-ounce) package sliced almonds
1 (16-ounce) package frozen broccoli,
  carrots, and water chestnuts
1 tablespoon cornstarch
1 tablespoon brown sugar
1/2 teaspoon ground ginger
1/2 cup soy sauce
1/3 cup pineapple juice
Hot cooked rice

Pour the oil into a preheated wok or large nonstick skillet, coating the sides. Heat briefly at medium high. Cut the chicken into thin strips. Add the chicken and almonds to the wok and cook for 2 minutes, stirring constantly. Add the frozen vegetables. Cover and cook for 4 minutes, stirring once. Combine the cornstarch and the next 4 ingredients and add to the wok. Cook, stirring constantly, for 2 or 3 minutes, or until the mixture thickens. Serve over rice.

G. W. WIMSATT
ZION LUTHERAN CHURCH
ESTÂNCIA, NEW MEXICO

GOOD AND EASY CHICKEN POT PIE

2 1/2 to 3 pounds chicken cooked, skinned,
    and boned
1 cup chicken broth
1 cup milk
1 (8-ounce) package frozen mixed
    vegetables
1 cup frozen peas
2 medium potatoes, peeled and diced
1 (10-1/2-ounce) can cream of celery soup

CRUST
1-1/2 cups Bisquick
1 cup milk
1/3 cup margarine or butter, melted

Preheat the oven to 350 degrees. In a mixing bowl, break the cooked chicken into small pieces. Stir in the broth, milk, frozen vegetables, frozen peas, potatoes and soup. Mix well with a large slotted spoon. Spread the mixture into a 9 x 13-inch buttered baking pan.

Crust: In a small mixing bowl, mix together the Bisquick, milk and melted margarine or butter. Spread over the top of the chicken mixture. Bake for one hour. Let cool for 10-15 minutes. Serve warm. Makes 8 to 10 servings.

MAXINE HENDERSON
FIRST UNITED METHODIST CHURCH
BELLEVILLE, MICHIGAN

CHICKEN SPECTACULAR

3 cups cooked chicken, diced
1 can French green beans, drained
1 package wild rice, cooked
1 can cream of celery soup
1/2 cup mayonnaise
1/2 cup water chestnuts, sliced
2 tablespoons pimientos, chopped
1 medium onion, chopped
1 1/2 cups Cheddar cheese, shredded
Salt and pepper to taste
Paprika

Preheat the oven to 350 degrees. Combine all the ingredients except the paprika. Place in a 3-quart buttered casserole. Sprinkle the paprika on top. Bake for 45 minutes to 1 hour until the top is slightly browned.

CATHY JOBE
NORTHBROOK UNITED METHODIST CHURCH
ROSWELL, GEORGIA

Orange-Dijon Chicken Saltimbocca

4 boneless chicken breast halves
4 thin slices prosciutto
4 slices mozzarella (or provolone) cheese
1 tablespoon olive oil
1 can Campbell's Cream of Chicken Dijon
    Soup (or a cream soup of your choice)
3/4 cup orange juice
1 tablespoon chopped fresh sage, or 1
    teaspoon rubbed sage
1/2 cup drained mandarin orange segments

Cut a lengthwise pocket in each chicken breast. Stuff each with 1 slice of prosciutto and 1 slice of cheese. Heat the olive oil in a large skillet. Add the chicken and cook until browned on both sides. Add the soup, orange juice, and sage. Bring to a boil. Cover and simmer for 5 minutes, or until done. Add the mandarin orange segments and heat through. Makes 4 servings.

Sherry Beckemeyer
Northbrook United Methodist Church
Roswell, Georgia

Chicken Cordon Bleu

2 whole chicken breasts, skinned and boned
4 thin slices boiled ham (about 3 inches
    square)
4 thin slices Swiss cheese (3 inches square)
4 tablespoons (1/2 stick) butter or
    margarine, melted
1/2 cup fine, dry bread crumbs
1/2 teaspoon salt
1/8 teaspoon paprika

Halve the chicken breasts. Fold each slice of ham around each slice of cheese, roll up, and tuck inside a pocket of the chicken breast. Dip into the melted butter and then into a mixture of the remaining ingredients. Place in a single layer in a greased baking dish. Bake at 400 degrees for 40 minutes, or until golden brown.

Ruth Chubb
Trinity Presbyterian Church
Wilmington, Delaware

Addie's Chicken and Dumplings

1 broiler or fryer, cut up
salt and pepper, to taste
chicken broth
dumplings

Cook broiler in chicken broth until done. Season with salt and pepper. Make sure that you have plenty of liquid to add dumplings later.

After making dumplings drop the cooked chicken pieces into boiling broth. Drip 1/3 of dumplings into broth. Then add the next 1/3 dumplings. Finally add the remaining 1/3 dumplings and salt and pepper to taste. Cover and cook until done.

DUMPLINGS:
2 cups self-rising flour
1 egg
1 tablespoon shortening
1/8 cup chicken broth
1/8 cup water
1/4 cup milk
1/4 cup Pet condensed milk

Cut shortening into flour, add egg, broth, water and milk. Mix well. Turn dough onto floured board or surface. Knead dough real tight. Roll thin with rolling pin. Cut into strips about 1 1/2 x 2 inches.

ADDIE B. JONES
GRIFFIN CHAPEL UNITED METHODIST CHURCH
STARKVILLE, MISSISSIPPI

Chicken Gumbo

2 1/2 pounds skinned chicken, cut up
8 cups water
1/8 teaspoon chili powder
1/8 teaspoon pepper
1/4 cup diced onions
1/2 cup brown rice
1/4 cup chopped diced dried parsley
10 ounces frozen okra
2 diced celery stalks
3 diced carrots
1/2 diced green bell pepper
10 ounces frozen corn
1 pound tomatoes, chopped

Cover chicken with water and simmer for 20 minutes. Turn off heat. Remove chicken pieces from stock. Remove meat from bones and dice. Skim fat from broth. Add chicken and remaining ingredients to broth and simmer until rice is cooked and vegetables are tender (about 1 hour). If thicker broth is desired, blend 2-4 tablespoon water with 1-2 tablespoon cornstarch and mix into broth, heating until thickened.

GERALDINE HICKMAN
GRIFFIN CHAPEL UNITED METHODIST CHURCH
STARKVILLE, MISSISSIPPI

CHICKEN RATATOUILLE

1 tablespoon vegetable oil
4 medium chicken breast halves, skinned
   and cut into 1-inch pieces
1 zucchini (about 7-inches long; unpeeled),
   thinly sliced
1 small eggplant, peeled and cut into 1-inch
   cubes
1 medium onion, thinly sliced
1 medium green pepper, cut into 1-inch
   pieces
1/2 pound fresh mushrooms, sliced
1 (16 ounce) can whole tomatoes, cut up
1 clove garlic, minced
1 1/2 teaspoons dried basil, crushed
1 tablespoon fresh parsley, minced
black pepper to taste

Heat oil in large nonstick skillet. Add chicken and sauté about 3 minutes or until lightly browned. Add zucchini, eggplant, onion, green pepper and mushrooms. Cook about 15 minutes, stirring occasionally. Add tomatoes, garlic, basil, parsley and pepper; stir and continue cooking about 5 minutes or until chicken is tender.

MARY WHITE
OAKMONT CHURCH OF GOD
SHREVEPORT, LOUISIANA

ROASTED GAME HENS

6 game hens
Salt and pepper to taste
6 garlic cloves
6 bay leaves
6 sprigs of fresh thyme
6 sprigs of fresh rosemary
6 pats of butter

Prepare the hens by removing anything packed in the cavity and rinsing in water, then patting dry. Place the hens in a glass baking dish, lined with aluminum foil for easy cleanup. Fill each cavity with salt and pepper, garlic, bay leaf, thyme, and rosemary. Put one pat of butter on top of each hen. Refrigerate until your guests arrive. Preheat the oven to 425 degrees. Place the hens in the oven. After 30 minutes, reduce the heat to 325 to 350 degrees. Cook for another 30 minutes.

Note: Enjoy the fellowship of your friends! The game hens should be browned on top. If necessary, turn the oven up at the end to brown them.

JULIE PEACOCK
NORTHBROOK UNITED METHODIST CHURCH
ROSWELL, GEORGIA

CRISPY ROAST DUCK WITH ORANGE SAUCE

ROAST DUCK:
2 whole ducks (5 pounds each), rinsed and
  patted dry
1 teaspoon thyme
1/2 teaspoon paprika
1 tablespoon salt
Freshly ground black pepper
Orange, sliced for garnish

Preheat the oven to 450 degrees. Line a roasting pan large enough to hold the ducks with foil; set aside.

In a small dish, combine the thyme, paprika, salt, and pepper. Season the cavity and surface of the ducks with the mixture. Place the ducks, breast side up, in the prepared pan. Roast, discarding any fat midway through roasting, until just lightly browned (about 1 hour and 20 minutes).

Cool on a rack; pour the pan juices into a gravy separator or measuring cup. With kitchen shears, cut each duck into four pieces—2 breasts and 2 legs. Discard the backbone and remove any visible fat. (The recipe can be made up to this point a day ahead and refrigerated.) Discard any fat that floats on the surface of the juices; refrigerate the pan juices for the sauce.

To serve: Heat a cast-iron skillet or heavy roasting pan in the oven at 450 degrees until hot, about 10 minutes. Add the duck pieces to the skillet, meaty side down. Do not crowd. Sear until the skin is dark brown, about 15 minutes. Turn the pieces and roast until crispy, about 5 to 10 minutes longer. To serve, use tongs to transfer the duck to a warm platter. Brush lightly with Tangy Orange Sauce (below). Serve hot, garnished with orange slices. Pass the remaining sauce separately.

TANGY ORANGE SAUCE:
3 tablespoons butter
3 large shallots, minced
1 garlic clove, minced
1 1/2 tablespoons fresh ginger
2 1/4 cups chicken broth
3/4 cup orange juice concentrate
1/2 cup orange marmalade
3 tablespoons balsamic vinegar
Dash of salt, pepper, and ground red pepper
2 1/2 teaspoons cornstarch (blended with 5
  tablespoons chicken broth)
Skimmed duck juices

Melt the butter in a large nonstick skillet. When hot, add the shallots, garlic, and ginger. Cook until the shallots soften, about 4 minutes. Add the broth, orange juice, orange marmalade, balsamic vinegar, and seasonings. Bring to a boil. Whisk in the cornstarch mixture. Return to a boil and simmer until the mixture thickens, about 3 minutes. Strain through a fine sieve. (The recipe can be made a day ahead and refrigerated.)

ARLENE GLICK
TOWER HILL UNITED METHODIST CHURCH
TOWER HILL, ILLINOIS

Herb-Roasted Turkey

1 (22-pound) turkey (use giblets for stock)
Salt and pepper to taste
12 cups Sausage and Leek Stuffing (p.178)
1 tablespoon chopped fresh sage
1 tablespoon chopped fresh thyme
1/4 cup butter (1/2 stick)
8 cups canned reduced-sodium chicken broth
1 (18 x 16-inch) double-layered cheesecloth

Rinse the inside of the turkey and pat dry with paper towels. Season the cavity with salt and pepper. Stuff the main and neck cavities loosely with the stuffing. Sprinkle the herbs over the turkey; truss the turkey. Melt the butter and dip the cheesecloth in it; place the cheesecloth over the turkey. Pour 1 cup of broth over the turkey, basting with a cup of broth after 1 hour. Roast for 1 1/2 hours at 375 degrees, then reduce the heat to 350 degrees. Continue cooking for about 3 more hours, basting every half hour. Cook until the interior of the turkey registers 180 degrees on a meat thermometer. Remove the turkey from the oven and pour another cup of broth over the cheesecloth. Remove the cheesecloth and tent the turkey with foil to keep it warm.

Dorothy Ross
Mattapoisett Congregational Church
Mattapoisett, Massachusetts

Turkey Breast Satay with Peanut Sauce

1 pound skinless, boneless turkey breasts
3 tablespoons milk
1 teaspoon soy sauce
1 tablespoon chopped onion
1/2 teaspoon lemon zest
1/2 teaspoon crushed red pepper flakes
1/2 teaspoon gingerroot, minced
1/2 teaspoon coconut extract
1 tablespoon olive oil
Bamboo skewers soaked in water

PEANUT SAUCE:
1 garlic clove, minced
1 tablespoon chopped onion
1 1/2 teaspoons fresh lemon juice
1/4 teaspoon soy sauce
1/4 cup smooth peanut butter
1/8 teaspoon cayenne pepper
Dash of coconut extract
1/4 cup milk

Cut the turkey breasts in half lengthwise and place them between waxed paper; pound flat and cut into 1-inch-wide strips.

Marinade: In a bowl, combine the milk, soy sauce, onion, lemon zest, pepper flakes, gingerroot, and extract. Pour the marinade over the turkey strips and refrigerate for 4 hours. Weave the marinated turkey strips on skewers. Coat a grill with the olive oil, preheat the grill, and grill the turkey over direct heat for 2 to 3 minutes on each side, or until the turkey is no longer pink in the center.

Peanut Sauce: In a food processor, combine the garlic and onion for 10 seconds. Add the lemon juice, soy sauce, peanut butter, cayenne, and coconut extract and process until blended, about 20 seconds. With the food processor running slowly, add the milk and process until blended. Heat the mixture in a microwave on high for 20 to 30 seconds until it thickens. Serve the turkey strips with the sauce.

Note: This Indonesian dish can be served as a snack, an appetizer, or a main dish.

MARK CALDWELL
FIRST UNITED METHODIST CHURCH
BELLEVILLE, MICHIGAN

SAUSAGE AND LEEK STUFFING

2 (1 pound) loaves egg bread, crusts
   trimmed, cut into 3/4-inch cubes
1/4 cup melted butter
4 large leeks sliced, using both white and
   pale green parts (about 5 cups)
2 cups chopped onion
1 tablespoon dried thyme (2 tablespoons
   fresh)
2 pounds bulk pork sausage
2 cups chopped celery
1 tablespoon dried sage
2 cups canned, low-salt chicken broth

Preheat oven to 250 degrees. Arrange the bread on 2 large cookie sheets and bake until dry, about 20 minutes. Put into a large bowl and add the melted butter. Cook the sausage in a heavy skillet until brown, crumbling with a fork, about 10 minutes. Drain and transfer to the bowl with the bread mixture. Add the leeks, onions, and celery to the skillet and sauté to soften, about 8 minutes. Mix in the herbs, add the vegetable mixture to the bread and toss it all. This can be prepared a day ahead, just cover and chill. When you are ready to stuff the turkey, transfer 12 cups of stuffing to a medium-size bowl and add 1/4 to 1/2 cup of the broth. Stuff the turkey loosely. To bake the leftover stuffing: Preheat the oven to 350 degrees. To the leftover stuffing add 1 1/4 to 2 cups of broth and place in a 13 x 9 x 2-inch greased baking dish. Cover the dish with foil and bake for 40 minutes. Remove the foil, and bake for 5 minutes more.

DOROTHY ROSS
MATTAPOISETT CONGREGATIONAL CHURCH
MATTAPOISETT, MASSACHUSETTS

CROCK-POT STUFFING

1 pound pork sausage
1 1/2 cups chopped onion
1 1/2 teaspoons salt
2 teaspoons dried leaf sage
1/2 teaspoon pepper
1 teaspoon rosemary or poultry seasoning
1 teaspoon thyme
8 cups cornbread
16 pieces stale white bread
2 1/2 cups chicken broth
2 eggs
1/3 cup butter or margarine

In a large bowl, combine all the ingredients and pour into a Crock-Pot. Cook on low for 3 hours. It's a cinch.

LORETTA GIBERSON
PRAIRIE CHAPEL UNITED METHODIST CHURCH
MISSOURI

OLD-FASHIONED CORNBREAD

3 cups chopped celery
2 cups chopped onion
1 stick margarine
6 cups cornbread, crumbled fine in a food
    processor
3 cups white bread crumbs (leave out a few
    days before crumbling)
1 tablespoon poultry seasoning
1 tablespoon celery seed
3 tablespoons sage
1 tablespoon salt
1 teaspoon black pepper
4 eggs, well beaten
3 cups chicken broth
1 can cream of chicken soup
1 can cream of mushroom soup

Prcheat the oven to 350 degrees. In a large saucepan, sauté the celery and onion in the margarine. Pour the mixture over the cornbread, white bread, and the other dry ingredients. Add the eggs and mix well. Heat the chicken broth and pour over the bread mixture; blend well. Add the soups, undiluted and one at a time, checking that the consistency is not too moist. Mix well again. Pour into a casserole dish. Bake for 40 to 60 minutes until the cornbread is light brown and a knife inserted into the center comes out clean.

FRANCES CHAMBLEE
CROSS IN THE DESERT UNITED METHODIST CHURCH
PHOENIX, ARIZONA

MEAT

For these and all Thy gifts of love,
We give Thee thanks and praise.
Look down dear Father from above,
And bless us all our days.

FIRST UNITED METHODIST CHURCH,
BELLEVILLE, MICHIGAN

STANDING RIB ROAST

1 tablespoon lemon pepper
1 tablespoon paprika
1 1/2 teaspoons garlic salt
1 teaspoon rosemary, crushed
1/2 teaspoon cayenne pepper
1 (6- to 7-pound) standing rib roast
1 teaspoon instant beef bouillon

Preheat the oven to 325 degrees. Combine the spices in a small bowl and rub over the roast. Place the roast fat side up in a roasting pan. Bake the roast, uncovered, and let it stand for 15 minutes before carving. To make the gravy, prepare the bouillon according to the instructions and mix with the pan drippings. Heat briefly in a small saucepan on a low flame.

Roasting times:

Rare 20–25 minutes per pound, 140 degrees.
Medium rare 23–25 minutes per pound, 160 degrees.
Well done 27–30 minutes per pound, 170 degrees.

Makes 10 to 12 servings.

RHEA FEATHERINGILL
FIRST UNITED METHODIST CHURCH
BELLEVILLE, MICHIGAN

LUCILLE ARMSTRONG'S ROAST BEEF

2 garlic cloves
1 (4-pound) rump or sirloin tip roast
Black pepper (optional)
1 package dry onion soup mix **or** *1 to 2 cans cream of mushroom soup (undiluted)*

Preheat the oven to 350 degrees. Peel and slice the garlic. Cut slits (4 to 6) in the roast and insert the strips of garlic deeply. Season the roast with pepper to taste. Do *not* add salt, as the soup provides plenty. Trim the fat from the roast (you may brown each side using cooking spray in the pot or leave unbrowned as desired). Place the roast in a baking pan and bake, uncovered, for 1 hour. Remove the roasting pan from the oven and add either the dry onion soup mix or the cream of mushroom soup. Use 2 cans of soup if you want a lot of gravy. Cover the pan and return it to the oven for 2 hours.

This recipe produces a well-done, moist, tender roast with gravy. Test the roast for tenderness and cook longer if necessary.

SARA COOPER
BUCKINGHAM UNITED METHODIST CHURCH
GARLAND, TEXAS

MARINATED EYE OF ROUND

1 (5-pound) eye of round roast

MARINADE:
1/4 cup salad oil
2 tablespoons lemon pepper
1/2 cup red wine vinegar
1/2 cup lemon juice
1/2 cup soy sauce
1/2 cup Worcestershire sauce

Preheat the oven to 300 degrees. Wash the roast and sprinkle it with unseasoned meat tenderizer while preparing the marinade. In a large bowl, combine all the ingredients for the marinade and let marinate in the refrigerator for 1 to 3 days, turning at least once a day. In a Dutch oven, cook the roast, uncovered, with the marinade for 3 hours. Refrigerate overnight. Slice thin, heat with the marinade, and serve. Makes 16 servings.

VERA CLARK
GRIFFIN CHAPEL UNITED METHODIST CHURCH
STARKVILLE, MISSISSIPPI

SUNDAY POT ROAST

1 (3- to 4-pound) boneless beef chuck roast
1 tablespoon extra-virgin olive oil
3 teaspoons Worcestershire sauce
1/4 cup red cooking wine
1 package Good Seasons dry Italian
    dressing mix
4 dried red pepper pods
1 bell pepper, thinly sliced
1 small onion, thinly sliced
2 bay leaves
2 to 3 cups potatoes, cut into chunks

Preheat the oven to 325 degrees. Place the roast in a roasting pan. In a small bowl, combine the olive oil, Worcestershire sauce, and cooking wine. Pour the mixture over the roast, making sure every side is coated. Pour the dry Italian dressing mix into your hand and rub the mix onto every surface of the roast. Allow the roast to marinate for 1 to 2 hours in the refrigerator. Place the remaining ingredients in the roasting pan with the roast. Bake for 2 1/2 to 3 hours.

MRS. TRINA MORRIS DICKERSON
BETHEL AME CHURCH
AUGUSTA, GEORGIA

POT ROAST

1 (3- to 4-pound) lean chuck or rump roast
2 teaspoons salt
1/4 teaspoon pepper
2 teaspoons Wesson oil
1/2 cup water
1 (4-ounce) can mushrooms, drained
8 whole small onions
10 carrots, whole or cut
1 (8-ounce) can chili sauce
1 celery stalk, chopped
1 cup sour cream

Season the meat with the salt and pepper. In a large saucepan, brown the meat in hot Wesson oil. Add the water, cover, and simmer for 1 1/2 to 2 hours, or until the meat is tender. Sprinkle the mushrooms, onions, and carrots over and around the meat. Pour in the chili sauce and add the celery. Cover and simmer for 1 hour, or until the vegetables are done. Just before serving, remove the pan from the heat and gradually stir in the sour cream.

MRS. RAE POE
MOSCA UNITED METHODIST CHURCH
MOSCA, COLORADO

Slow Cooker Chuck Roast

1 (3- to 4-pound) boneless chuck roast,
    trimmed
1 (8-ounce) can tomato sauce
1 medium onion, chopped
1/4 cup water
1/4 cup cider vinegar
1/4 cup ketchup
1 teaspoon paprika
1/4 teaspoon beef bouillon granules
1/8 teaspoon garlic powder
2 teaspoons Worcestershire sauce
1 teaspoon prepared mustard

Place roast in a 6-quart Crock-Pot. In a bowl, combine the tomato sauce and the remaining ingredients. Pour the mixture over the roast. Cover. Cook on high for 5 to 6 hours or on low for 10 to 12 hours until the roast is tender. Skim the fat and discard from the sauce. Serve the roast with gravy. Makes 6 servings.

MADLYN ROSEL
HIGHLAND HEIGHTS PRESBYTERIAN CHURCH
CORDOVA, TENNESSEE

Tender Oven Brisket

1/3 cup white vinegar
1/2 cup undiluted tomato soup
1/3 cup Figaro hickory liquid smoke
    marinade
1 medium brisket

The night before cooking: In a large cooking bag mix the vinegar, soup, and liquid smoke marinade. Place the brisket in the bag and turn to coat with the marinade. Secure the bag, place it in a baking dish and refrigerate overnight. Remove the dish from the refrigerator about 1 hour before cooking. Preheat the oven to 375 degrees. Puncture the top of the baking bag but leave it in the dish. Bake for approximately 2 to 2 1/2 hours. This slices nicely when cooled. Save the marinade to mix with prepared barbecued sauce or to use when warming leftover brisket the next day.

MILDRED BAILEY
BUCKINGHAM UNITED METHODIST CHURCH
GARLAND, TEXAS

Flank Steak

3 1/2 to 4 pounds flank steak
1 cup teriyaki marinade
1/2 cup honey
1 tablespoon dark sesame oil
1/3 cup orange juice
1/2 cup chopped onion
1 tablespoon fresh rosemary, chopped
1 garlic clove, chopped

In a large resealable plastic bag, combine all the ingredients. Add the meat to the bag and marinate in the refrigerator for at least 1 hour. Grill or broil the meat to the desired doneness.

BEATRICE WALKER
CAVENDISH BAPTIST CHURCH
CAVENDISH, VERMONT

Peppered London Broil

1 (2- to 3-pound) London broil
1/4 cup olive oil
1 tablespoon black pepper
3 garlic cloves, minced
1 teaspoon cayenne pepper
1 tablespoon parsley
1 tablespoon thyme
1 teaspoon salt

Brush the steak with the olive oil. In a small bowl, combine the remaining ingredients and rub on both sides of the steak. Chill until you're ready to cook. Grill on a medium flame until done. Slice the meat into thin strips and serve with the juices from the meat.

Note: You can leave the steak to marinate overnight for extra flavor.

SOUTHERN GENTLEMAN, REX
FOREST AVENUE CONGREGATIONAL CHURCH
BANGOR, MAINE

Beef Jerky

2 tablespoons soy sauce
2 tablespoons Worcestershire sauce
2 tablespoons liquid smoke
1 (4- to 5-pound) beef brisket
Sugar
Black pepper
Smoked salt
Garlic powder
Seasoned salt

In a small bowl, combine the soy sauce, Worcestershire sauce, and liquid smoke and mix well. Pour the mixture over the brisket and marinate for 5 hours. Just before cooking, sprinkle the brisket with the sugar, black pepper, smoked salt, garlic powder, and seasoned salt. Bake in the oven at 140 degrees for 6 to 12 hours.

DELORES ELLIOTT, ABILENE, TEXAS
SUBMITTED BY BILLY RUTH ELLIOTT
HOLUM BAPTIST CHURCH
GRAYSON, LOUISIANA

GREEK MARINADE

2/3 cup olive oil
Juice of 1 lemon
1 onion, thinly sliced
Salt and pepper to taste

You can steep both meat and vegetables in this marinade.

SARAH
FOREST AVENUE CONGREGATIONAL CHURCH
BANGOR, MAINE

BASIC COOKED MARINADE

1 1/3 cups red wine or grape juice
2 carrots, sliced
2 shallots, sliced
3 garlic cloves, bruised
1 teaspoon salt
1 teaspoon black pepper

Simmer all the ingredients in a medium saucepan for 15 minutes and allow the mixture to cool before using it.

For lamb, rosemary leaves should be added.
For game, you can use port wine and add juniper berries.
For fish, bruise fennel or celery seeds and use white wine.

SARAH
FOREST AVENUE CONGREGATIONAL CHURCH
BANGOR, MAINE

CHINESE MARINADE

1/2 cup soy sauce
1 garlic clove, chopped
1 teaspoon sugar

Steep very thin slices of meat in this marinade for 1 hour and then cook in hot olive oil.

SARAH
FOREST AVENUE CONGREGATIONAL CHURCH
BANGOR, MAINE

INDIAN MARINADE

1 1/2 cups plain yogurt
1 garlic clove, crushed
1 teaspoon crushed aniseed
6 peppercorns, crushed
1 cardamom pod, peeled and crushed
Salt

Combine all the ingredients in a large container and allow the meat to marinate for 1 hour.

SARAH
FOREST AVENUE CONGREGATIONAL CHURCH
BANGOR, MAINE

Marinade for Grilling Meats

1 1/2 cup salad oil
3/4 cup soy sauce
1/4 cup Worcestershire sauce
2 tablespoons dry mustard
2 1/4 teaspoons salt
1 tablespoon pepper
1/2 cup wine vinegar
1 1/2 teaspoons parsley
2 garlic cloves, crushed
1/3 cup lemon juice

Mix all ingredients together and marinate meats 5 to 6 hours.

Note: Good for all meats.

Buckingham United Methodist Church
Garland, Texas

Moroccan Marinade

6 tablespoons lemon or lime juice
Handful of coriander leaves
1 garlic clove, crushed
1/2 teaspoon cumin seeds
1/2 teaspoon paprika
Salt

Combine all the ingredients and mix well. Use this marinade especially for marinating meat before outdoor cooking.

Sarah
Forest Avenue Congregational Church
Bangor, Maine

German Marinade

1 1/2 cups buttermilk
2 shallots, thinly sliced
5 peppercorns, crushed
1 bay leaf
1 sprig of thyme
2 cloves
Pinch of grated mustard

Combine all the ingredients and mix. This marinade makes for a rich addition to stews.

Sarah
Forest Avenue Congregational Church
Bangor, Maine

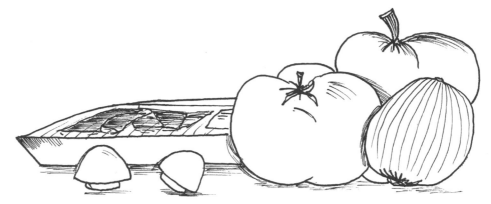

Steak Bake

1 1/2 pounds cube or sirloin steak, cut into
    narrow strips
1 teaspoon salt
1/4 teaspoon pepper
1/3 cup all-purpose flour
1 onion, sliced
1 green pepper, sliced
1 (16-ounce) can tomatoes
1 (4-ounce) can mushroom stems and pieces,
    drained
3 tablespoons molasses
3 tablespoons soy sauce
1 (10-ounce) package frozen French-cut
    beans, thawed and drained, or use 1
    (16-ounce) can French-cut green beans,
    drained

Preheat the oven to 400 degrees. Season the meat with the salt and pepper and coat with the flour. Brown in oil in a large skillet. While the meat is browning, slice the onion and green pepper into a large bowl; add the remaining ingredients and mix well. Pour into a 9 x 12-inch pan and bake, uncovered, for 40 minutes. Makes 6 to 8 servings.

Evelyn Overman
Prince of Peace Church
Grantsville, West Virginia

Green Pepper Steak

1 pound beef chuck or round, fat trimmed
1/4 cup soy sauce
1 garlic clove
1 1/2 teaspoons grated fresh ginger or 1/2
    teaspoon ground
Vegetable oil
1 cup green thinly sliced onions
1 cup red or green peppers, cut into 1-inch
    squares
2 celery stalks, thinly sliced
2 tablespoons cornstarch
1 cup water
2 tomatoes, cut into wedges

With a very sharp knife, cut the beef across the grain into thin slices, about 1/8-inch thick. In a large bowl, combine the soy sauce, garlic, and ginger; add the beef. Toss and set aside while you prepare the vegetables.

In a large frying pan or wok, heat enough oil to cover the bottom of the pan. Add the beef and toss over high heat until browned. Taste the meat. If it is not tender, cover and simmer for 30 to 40 minutes over low heat. Turn the heat up and add the vegetables. Toss until the vegetables are crisp-tender, about 10 minutes. Mix the cornstarch and water. Add to the pan; stir and cook until the sauce thickens. Add the tomatoes and heat through.

Virginia Calkins
Prince of Peace Church
Grantsville, West Virginia

Steak Cantonese

1 1/2 pounds boneless round steak
2 tablespoons vegetable oil
2 large tomatoes, coarsely chopped
2 medium green peppers, cut into strips
1/4 cup soy sauce
1/2 teaspoon garlic salt
1/4 teaspoon black pepper
1/4 teaspoon ginger
Water chestnuts (optional)
Bean sprouts (optional)
1 tablespoon cornstarch
1/4 cup water
1 beef bouillon cube
3 cups cooked rice

Slice the meat into thin strips, cutting diagonally across the grain. In a large skillet, brown the steak in oil on all sides over high heat. Reduce the heat and stir in the tomatoes, green peppers, soy sauce, seasonings, water chestnuts, and bean sprouts. Cover and simmer for 10 minutes. Combine the cornstarch and water; stir into the meat mixture. Add the bouillon cube. Cook, stirring, until the mixture thickens and the bouillon cube dissolves. Cover and simmer for 10 minutes. Serve over rice. Makes 4 to 6 servings.

JOAN GEROW
TRINITY PRESBYTERIAN CHURCH
WILMINGTON, DELAWARE

Steak with Honeyed Onions

1/3 cup red wine vinegar
2 tablespoons honey
1/2 teaspoon dried thyme, crushed
1 large red (or Vidalia) onion, thinly sliced
1 pound beef top loin or tenderloin steaks
1/2 teaspoon cracked pepper
2 tablespoons fresh parsley (optional)

In a medium bowl, combine the vinegar, honey, thyme, and onion. Stir. Trim the fat from the beef and cut into four 1-inch-thick serving pieces. Sprinkle with the cracked pepper, pressing the pepper into the surface of the meat. Cook the meat in a large nonstick skillet for 10 minutes over medium-high heat.

Remove the steaks from the skillet and add the onion mixture to the pan drippings. Cook over medium heat for 3 to 4 minutes, or until the onion is just crisp-tender, stirring occasionally. Return the steaks and any accumulated juices to the skillet. Reduce the heat to medium low. Cook, uncovered, for 3 to 4 minutes or until the steak is the desired doneness and the liquid is slightly reduced, occasionally spooning the cooking liquid over the steaks. Transfer the steaks to serving plates. Stir snipped parsley into the onion mixture, if desired, and spoon over the steaks. Garnish with flat-leaf parsley, if desired.

CHARLOTTE SNYDER
CAVENDISH BAPTIST CHURCH
CAVENDISH, VERMONT

GARLIC SWISS STEAK

1 1/2 pounds round steak
1/3 cup all-purpose flour
1 teaspoon salt
1/2 teaspoon black pepper
2 tablespoons vegetable oil
1 (14-ounce) can stewed tomatoes
1 small onion, chopped
1/2 medium green pepper, chopped
2 garlic cloves, minced

Preheat the oven to 350 degrees. Cut the steak into serving-size pieces, discarding the bone. Combine the flour, salt, and pepper; sprinkle over the steak and pound into both sides. In a large skillet over medium heat, brown the steak in the oil on both sides. Transfer to a greased 13 x 9 x 2-inch baking dish. Combine the tomatoes, onion, green pepper, and garlic and pour over the steak. Cover and bake for 1 to 1 1/2 hours, or until tender. Makes 6 servings.

MARTHA YEARY
NORTH MONROE STREET CHURCH OF GOD
MONROE, MICHIGAN

WHOLESOME JOES

3/4 pound ground beef
1/2 cup onion
1 clove garlic, minced
1 (8 oz.) can tomato sauce
1/2 cup uncooked lentils
2/3 cup water
1/4 cup ketchup
1 teaspoon vinegar
1/2 teaspoon celery salt
1/2 teaspoon dry mustard
1/4 teaspoon pepper
6 whole wheat sandwich buns

In a large skillet over medium-high heat, brown the beef with the onion and garlic. Drain well. Stir in remaining ingredients, except sandwich buns. Bring to a boil. Reduce heat; cover and simmer for 40 minutes or until lentils are tender. Spoon 1/2 cup of the mixture into each bun. Makes 6 servings.

KELLY HERTZINGER
BETHEL AME CHURCH
AUGUSTA, GEORGIA

SALISBURY STEAK

1 pound ground beef
2 eggs, beaten
1/2 cup chopped onion
1 teaspoon salt
1/4 teaspoon black pepper
1 cup soft bread crumbs or oatmeal
1/2 cup milk
1/4 cup chopped parsley (optional)

SAUCE:
2 cans cream of mushroom soup
1/2 cup milk

Preheat the oven to 350 degrees. In a large bowl, combine the beef, eggs, onion, salt, pepper, bread crumbs, and parsley. Stir in the milk and form into patties. In a large skillet with a small amount of oil, brown the patties on both sides. Place the patties in a casserole dish and cover with sauce. Bake for 45 minutes.

Sauce: Mix the ingredients until well blended.

SANDY TOLER
BUCKINGHAM UNITED METHODIST CHURCH
GARLAND, TEXAS

SPICY TENDERLOIN (COMPANY ENTRÉE)

3/4 cup unsweetened pineapple juice
1/2 cup steak sauce
1/3 cup Worcestershire sauce
1/3 cup port wine
1/4 cup lemon juice
2 teaspoons seasoned salt
1 teaspoon black pepper
1 teaspoon lemon pepper
1 teaspoon dry mustard
1 (3- to 4-pound) beef tenderloin
2 teaspoons cracked pepper
3 to 4 bacon slices
1/3 cup chutney

For the marinade, in a large bowl, combine the pineapple juice, steak sauce, Worcestershire sauce, wine, lemon juice, seasoned salt, pepper, lemon pepper, and dry mustard; mix well. Place the meat in a large plastic bag set in a baking dish. Pour the marinade over the meat and close the bag. Refrigerate for several hours or overnight, turning the meat occasionally to distribute the marinade. Drain, reserving the marinade.

Preheat the oven to 425 degrees. Remove the beef from the plastic bag and rub it with the cracked pepper. Place the meat on a rack in a shallow roasting pan. Arrange the bacon slices over the tenderloin. Roast, uncovered, for 30 to 45 minutes, or until a meat thermometer registers 135 degrees. Baste the tenderloin twice during roasting with the reserved marinade.

Spoon the chutney evenly over the tenderloin. Bake for 5 to 10 minutes longer, or until the thermometer registers 140 degrees. Transfer the tenderloin to a serving platter. Let stand for about 15 minutes before slicing. Makes 12 to 16 servings (plan on 4 servings per pound).

CROSS IN THE DESERT UNITED METHODIST CHURCH
PHOENIX, ARIZONA

TERIYAKI STEAK

1/4 cup honey
1/2 cup chicken stock or consommé
1/4 cup soy sauce
2 tablespoons ketchup
1/8 teaspoon ginger
1/2 garlic clove, crushed
6 medium steaks (about 1 pound each)

In a large saucepan, combine the honey, chicken stock, soy sauce, ketchup, ginger, and garlic. Cook slowly for 4 to 5 minutes. Cool. Place the steaks in a glass casserole and pour the sauce over them. Refrigerate for at least 6 hours. Broil.

For cocktails, place small pieces of steak on bamboo sticks; broil over a small hibachi as needed. Makes 6 servings.

HELEN STOWERS
BUCKINGHAM UNITED METHODIST CHURCH
GARLAND, TEXAS

BULGOKI (KOREAN STEAK)

5 pounds beef
1/2 cup sugar
1/2 cup plus 3 tablespoons soy sauce
1/4 cup sesame seed oil or corn oil
3 tablespoons ground sesame seed
1 cup onion, chopped
1 tablespoon garlic powder
1 teaspoon black pepper

Cut the beef into thin slices, then into 3-inch squares. In a large bowl, combine the sugar, soy sauce, and remaining ingredients. Mix well. Add the beef and let marinate for at least 20 minutes.

Broil on a gas or charcoal grill or fry in small amount of sesame seed oil until tender. Serve with rice and flamed seaweed.

VICKIE MOLLBERG
PITT COMMUNITY CHURCH
BAUDETTE, MINNESOTA

SAUERBRATEN

3 pounds beef shoulder
Garlic
2 teaspoons salt
Black pepper
2 cups vinegar
2 cups water
1/2 cup sliced onion
2 bay leaves
1 teaspoon peppercorns
1/4 cup sugar
Fat
All-purpose flour
1 cup sweet or sour cream

Rub the meat with the garlic, salt, and pepper and place in a bowl. In a large saucepan, heat the vinegar, water, onion, bay leaves, peppercorns, and sugar together, but do not boil. Pour the hot mixture over the meat, cover the bowl, and let it stand in a cool place for 4 to 8 days, turning the meat each day. Drain, saving vinegar mixture. Brown the meat in fat, add half of the vinegar mixture, cover the pan, and simmer until tender (2 to 3 hours), adding more vinegar as required to keep the liquid about 1/2-inch deep in the pan. Strain the liquid and thicken it with 2 tablespoons of flour for each cup of liquid. Cook until the mixture thickens, then add the cream.

Note: This recipe is from Frank's grandmother.

DEBBIE BURBACH
NORTHBROOK UNITED METHODIST CHURCH
ROSWELL, GEORGIA

Easy Goulash

1 pound ground beef
1 onion, chopped
1 garlic clove, minced
1 can tomatoes
1 can mushrooms
1 teaspoon salt
1 tablespoon Cavender's seasoning
1 tablespoon Worcestershire sauce
1 tablespoon red cooking wine
1 cup water
1 cup macaroni

Brown the beef in a large skillet. Add the onion and garlic, sauté until tender. Add the tomatoes, mushrooms, and seasonings. Simmer for 15 minutes. Add the wine, water, and macaroni and stir. Cover and simmer another 10 to 12 minutes, stirring occasionally. Makes 4 servings.

Brandy Steele
Holum Baptist Church
Grayson, Louisiana

Beef Stroganoff

1 1/2 pounds top round steak, 1/2-inch thick
5 tablespoons all-purpose flour
3 tablespoons oil or shortening
1 medium onion, thinly sliced
1 1/2 cups sliced mushrooms
1 cup bouillon or consommé
1 teaspoon lemon juice or white wine
1/2 teaspoon salt
1/4 teaspoon black pepper
1/8 teaspoon dry mustard
1 cup sour cream
Hot noodles or rice

Cut the meat into 1 x 2-inch strips and dredge in 3 tablespoons of the flour. In a large skillet brown the meat in the oil. Push the meat to one side of the pan and add the onion; cook until soft. Add the mushrooms, 1/2 cup of the bouillon, the lemon juice, salt, pepper, and mustard to the meat. Cover the pan; cook over low heat for 45 to 50 minutes, or until the meat is tender. Blend the remaining flour with the remaining bouillon and add this to the hot mixture; cook over low heat until the sauce is smooth and thick, stirring constantly. Blend in the sour cream and heat. Do not allow the sauce to boil. Serve over hot noodles or rice. Makes 6 servings.

Cross in the Desert United Methodist Church
Phoenix, Arizona

Best Meat Loaf

2 slices toasted bread, crumbled
1 cup milk
1 pound lean ground beef
1 egg, slightly beaten
1/4 cup grated onion
1 teaspoon salt
1 teaspoon black pepper
1 teaspoon basil
1 teaspoon garlic salt

Most Delicious Sauce:
6 tablespoons brown sugar
1/2 teaspoon nutmeg
1/2 cup ketchup
2 teaspoons dry mustard

Preheat the oven to 350 degrees. In a large bowl, soak the bread crumbs in the milk. Add the meat, egg, and seasonings. Mix well and place in a loaf pan (sprayed with Pam). Cover with Most Delicious Sauce. Bake for 1 hour.

For the sauce, combine all the ingredients in a small bowl and mix well.

Note: If you have any leftovers, this recipe makes great sandwiches.

Patricia McCormick
Northbrook United Methodist Church
Roswell, Georgia

Today's Meat Loaf

3/4 cup whole wheat bread crumbs
1/3 cup nonfat milk
1 teaspoon butter or margarine
1 small onion, finely chopped
1/2 green pepper, finely chopped
1 tablespoon water
1 1/2 pounds lean round steak, ground
2 tablespoons minced fresh parsley
1/4 teaspoon dried thyme
1/4 teaspoon dried sage
1/4 teaspoon black pepper
2 egg whites
2 bay leaves

Preheat the oven to 350 degrees. In a large bowl, soak the bread crumbs in the milk. Add the meat. In a large skillet, melt the butter and sauté the onion and green pepper. Add the water. Cover and steam-cook for about 5 minutes until softened. Add the meat mixture to the skillet, along with the parsley, thyme, sage, salt, pepper, and egg whites. Mix well until thoroughly combined. Shape into a loaf, about 4 x 9 inches long. Press the bay leaves onto top and place the meat loaf on a rack in a shallow pan. Bake for 1 hour and 15 minutes. Remove bay leaves. Serve.

Freida Warren
Northbrook United Methodist Church
Roswell, Georgia

Meat Loaf

2 tablespoons butter
1 medium onion, finely chopped
1/2 red pepper, finely chopped
1 celery stalk, finely chopped
1 garlic clove, minced
1 1/2 pounds ground beef
1 egg
3/4 cup plain bread crumbs
2/3 cup milk (at room temperature)
1 (8-ounce) can tomato sauce
1/2 teaspoon salt
Pepper to taste

Glaze:
1/2 cup ketchup
3 tablespoons brown sugar
1/4 teaspoon mustard

In a large skillet, melt the butter and sauté the onion, pepper, celery, and garlic for 2 minutes. Pour the vegetables into a large bowl and add the meat and egg. In a separate bowl, combine the bread crumbs and milk, adding this to the meat mixture. Add the tomato sauce, and the salt and pepper. Mix thoroughly, shaping the ingredients into a loaf. Place the meat loaf in a baking pan lightly coated with Crisco. Let stand in the refrigerator for 4 hours.

Preheat the oven to 350 degrees. Combine the ingredients for the glaze and pour the mixture over the meat loaf. Bake for 1 hour.

Sally Goodavage
Prince of Peace Church
Grantsville, West Virginia

FOR A NEW MOTHER

Dear New Mother:
When your help has gone home
And you're left on your own
With a new baby
To diaper and feed.

There's bound to be times
When things don't go fine
And cooking a meal
Is a chore you don't need.

When you're feeling unable
To get a meal on the table
Here's a meat loaf
To help you a bit.

When it's near time to eat
Just thaw it and heat
Then round up something
To serve with it.

Make up your favorite meat loaf. Wrap it in foil and freeze. As a gift to a friend, type up the above "ingredients" message and present it with your favorite meat loaf.

CROSS IN THE DESERT UNITED METHODIST CHURCH
PHOENIX, ARIZONA

LEMON BARBECUED BEEF LOAVES

1 1/2 pounds ground beef
1/4 cup lemon juice
1/2 cup water
1 egg, slightly beaten
4 slices day-old bread, finely diced
1/4 cup finely chopped onion
2 teaspoons seasoned salt
1/2 cup ketchup
1/3 cup brown sugar
1 teaspoon dry mustard
1/4 teaspoon ground cloves
1/4 teaspoon ground allspice
6 thin lemon slices

Preheat the oven to 350 degrees. In a large bowl, combine the beef, lemon juice, water, egg, bread, onion, and seasoned salt. Mix well and shape into 6 individual loaves. Place the loaves in a rectangular baking dish and bake for 15 minutes.

Meanwhile, mix together the ketchup, brown sugar, mustard, cloves, and allspice. Pour the mixture over the partially baked loaves. Top each loaf with a lemon slice and continue baking for 30 minutes. Baste occasionally with sauce from the pan. Makes 6 servings.

LIBBY HULSE
MEMORIAL BAPTIST CHURCH
TULSA, OKLAHOMA

MEAT LOAF IN AN ONION

1 pound lean ground beef
1 egg
1/4 cup cracker crumbs
1/4 cup tomato sauce
1/2 teaspoon salt
1/8 teaspoon pepper
1/2 teaspoon dry mustard
4 large onions, peeled and halved
18-inch heavy-duty aluminum foil

In a 1-gallon plastic self-sealing bag, combine the beef, egg, cracker crumbs, tomato sauce, salt, pepper, and dry mustard. Mix by squeezing the bag and set it aside. Cut off the root ends on the onions to ease removal of the center, leaving a 3/4-inch-thick shell. Divide the meat mixture into four portions and roll them into balls. Place the balls in the center of four onion halves. Put the onions back together. Wrap each onion in foil and fold down the foil at the top and on the sides to make a packet. Cook over hot coals for 15 to 20 minutes on each side.

PINEMOUNT BAPTIST CHURCH
MCALPIN, FLORIDA

Jeanne's Easy Cheesy Meat Loaf

1 1/2 pounds ground beef
1 (8-ounce) can tomato sauce
3/4 cup quick-cooking oats
1/4 cup chopped onion
1 egg
1 tablespoon Worcestershire sauce
1 1/2 teaspoons salt
1/2 teaspoon oregano
1/2 teaspoon garlic powder
1/4 teaspoon pepper
1 (6-ounce) package mozzarella or Cheddar
    cheese

Preheat the oven to 350 degrees. In a large bowl, combine all the ingredients except the cheese and mix well. Divide the mixture into thirds. Pat a third into the bottom of a 9 x 5-inch loaf pan. Cover with half of the cheese. Repeat layers, ending with the meat mixture. Bake for 1 hour. Makes 4 to 6 servings.

VICKIE MOLLBERG
PITT COMMUNITY CHURCH
BAUDETTE, MINNESOTA

Beef Roll-Ups

1/2 cup chopped onions
2 tablespoons butter or margarine
1 cup finely diced carrots
1 cup finely diced potatoes
1 can mushroom soup
2 tablespoons chopped fresh parsley
1/2 teaspoon dill weed
4 cube steaks or 1 1/2 pounds round steak,
    1/8-inch thick
Salt and pepper to taste
2 tablespoons shortening
1 medium-sized can tomatoes, cut up
1/2 glass white wine (optional)

In a large saucepan, sauté the onions in the butter. Add the carrots, potatoes, half of the soup, parsley, and 1/4 teaspoon of the dill weed. Cook until partially tender. Season the meat with salt and pepper. If you're using round steak, cut it into 4 or 5 pieces and flatten. Place the stuffing in the center of the meat. Roll up, tuck in the ends, and skewer with toothpicks. Melt the shortening in a skillet and brown roll-ups on all sides. Remove the excess fat. Stir in the remaining soup, the rest of the dill weed, tomatoes, and the remaining stuffing. Simmer for about 1 hour, but stir frequently. Add the wine and simmer for 15 minutes longer.

BUDDY CASWELL
WESTSIDE BAPTIST CHURCH
ANTLERS, OKLAHOMA

THREE-PEPPER BEEF KABOBS

1 tablespoon vegetable oil
2 teaspoons Dijon-style mustard
1 tablespoon fresh lemon juice
1 tablespoon water
1 teaspoon honey
1/2 teaspoon oregano
1/4 teaspoon black pepper
1 pound boneless sirloin steak,
  cut into 1-inch pieces
1 medium green, red, and yellow bell
  pepper, cut into 1-inch pieces
8 large mushrooms (or more)

In a large bowl, whisk together the oil, mustard, lemon juice, water, honey, oregano, and black pepper. Add the cut-up beef, bell peppers, and mushrooms, stirring to coat. Allow the mixture to marinate for a little while. When you're ready to broil, alternately thread pieces of beef, bell pepper, and mushrooms on skewers. Heat the oven to broil. Place the kabobs on a rack in a broiler pan and broil 3 to 4 inches from the heat. Broil 9 to 12 minutes for rare to medium, turning once.

DEBRA GALLO
UNITED BAPTIST CHURCH OF POULTNEY
EAST POULTNEY, VERMONT

SNOW-TIME BEEF CASSEROLE

1 pound ground beef
2 (8-ounce) cans tomato sauce
1/4 cup chopped onion
1 tablespoon dried parsley flakes
1/2 teaspoon crushed oregano
1 teaspoon crushed basil
1 teaspoon salt
1/4 teaspoon pepper
2 (10-ounce) packages frozen chopped
  spinach, cooked and drained
1 pint cottage cheese
1 (8-ounce) package mozzarella cheese,
  sliced

Preheat the oven to 375 degrees. Brown the meat in a large skillet and pour off the fat. Stir in the tomato sauce, onion, parsley, oregano, basil, 3/4 teaspoon of the salt, and the pepper. Simmer, uncovered, for about 10 minutes, stirring occasionally. Combine the cooked spinach with the cottage cheese, adding the remaining 1/4 teaspoon salt. Spoon the spinach mixture around the edge of a 9 x 13-inch baking dish. Pour the meat mixture into the center. Cut the mozzarella cheese into lengthwise strips and arrange in a lattice pattern over the meat. Bake for about 20 minutes.

MABEL WESCOTT
UNITED BAPTIST CHURCH OF POULTNEY
EAST POULTNEY, VERMONT

PEGGY'S BEST BARBECUE

1/3 cup oil
1 cup onion, chopped fine
1 cup celery, chopped fine
2 pounds ground beef
2 (8-ounce) cans tomato sauce
1 tablespoon dry mustard
2 tablespoons vinegar
2 tablespoons Worcestershire sauce
1/2 cup prepared chili sauce
1 tablespoon sugar

Heat the oil in medium saucepan. Add the onion, celery, and beef, cooking until the onion and celery are translucent and the beef is browned. Add the remaining ingredients and bring to a boil; simmer, uncovered, for 1 1/2 hours. Add water if the mixture becomes too thick. Serve on hamburger buns.

Note: The recipe is easily doubled for a crowd.

JAN WICKLIFFE
CROSS IN THE DESERT UNITED METHODIST CHURCH
PHOENIX, ARIZONA

Oven-Barbecued Short Ribs

4 to 5 pounds beef short ribs (lean)
1 very large onion, finely chopped
1 teaspoon celery seeds
1 teaspoon salt
1/4 cup vinegar
1/4 cup Worcestershire sauce
1 cup ketchup
1/4 cup brown sugar
2 cups water

Preheat the oven to 350 degrees. Have the ribs cut into serving-size pieces. In a shallow roasting pan, place the meat fat side down and salt lightly. Bake, uncovered, for 35 to 40 minutes. Drain off any fat. In a large saucepan, combine the remaining ingredients and bring to a boil. Pour the hot sauce over the meat. Reduce the oven to 300 degrees and cook for 1 1/2 to 2 hours or until done. Baste frequently. Makes 6 to 8 servings.

Karen Hasser
Handsprings Ranch
McClave United Methodist Church
McClave, Colorado

Oven-Barbecued Beef

3 pounds beef cubes
1/2 cup chopped onion
1 tablespoon brown sugar
3/4 cup ketchup
3/4 cup water (or more)
1 tablespoon prepared mustard
1 tablespoon Worcestershire sauce
1/2 teaspoon salt
1/2 teaspoon pepper

Preheat the oven to 350 degrees. Place the meat in a casserole dish. In a large bowl, combine the remaining ingredients and pour over the beef. If you wish, whole potatoes and carrots can be placed on top. Cover tightly and bake for 2 hours.

June Damery
Mattapoisett Congregational Church
Mattapoisett, Massachusetts

Really Good Meatballs

1 pound ground beef
1/2 cup rolled oats
2/3 cup milk
2 teaspoons minced onion
1 teaspoon salt
1/2 teaspoon black pepper
2 tablespoons oil

Sauce:
1 1/2 tablespoons sugar
2/3 cup ketchup
1/2 cup water (more if desired)
1 1/2 tablespoons Worcestershire sauce
2 tablespoons vinegar
4 tablespoons minced onion

In a large bowl, combine the first 6 ingredients and mix well. Form the mixture into balls, roll in a little flour, and brown lightly in the 2 tablespoons of oil.

Preheat the oven to 350 degrees. In a saucepan, combine all the ingredients for the sauce and boil for 1 minute. Pour over the meatballs. Bake for 30 to 40 minutes.

Note: This recipe was given to me by Maxine Peterson in about 1967 or 1968.

Ellen Hodges
Tower Hill United Methodist Church
Tower Hill, Illinois

ITALIAN MEATBALLS

1 pound ground chuck
1/2 pound ground pork
1/2 pound ground veal
2 eggs, slightly beaten
1/2 cup Italian flavored bread crumbs
1/2 cup Parmesan cheese
4 large garlic cloves, minced
1/4 cup fresh parsley, chopped
1 teaspoon salt
1/2 teaspoon black pepper
Spaghetti sauce

In a large bowl, combine all the ingredients except the spaghetti sauce and mix well. Form 1 tablespoon of the meat mixture into balls by rolling it between your hands. Do not roll too long. Refrigerate for 1 hour; brown and add to spaghetti sauce. Heat and serve.

WILL GOODAVAGE
PRINCE OF PEACE CHURCH
GRANTSVILLE, WEST VIRGINIA

BARBECUED MEATBALLS

MEATBALLS:
3 pounds ground beef
1 (12-ounce) can evaporated milk
1 cup oatmeal
1 cup cracker crumbs
2 eggs
1/2 cup chopped onion
1/2 teaspoon garlic powder
2 teaspoons salt
1/2 teaspoon black pepper
2 teaspoons chili powder

To make the meatballs, combine all the ingredients (mixture will be soft) and shape into walnut-size balls. Place the meatballs in a single layer on a cookie sheet lined with waxed paper. Freeze until solid. Store the frozen meatballs in freezer bags until you're ready to cook. Makes 80 meatballs.

SAUCE:
2 cups ketchup
1 cup brown sugar
1/2 teaspoon liquid smoke (or to taste)
1/2 teaspoon garlic powder
1/4 cup chopped onion

Preheat the oven to 350 degrees. To make the sauce, combine all the ingredients and stir until the sugar dissolves. Place the frozen meatballs in a 9 x 13 x 2-inch baking pan. Pour the sauce over the meatballs. Bake for 1 hour.

KARMETTA RUPPEL
CALVARY UNITED METHODIST CHURCH
TAYLOR, NEBRASKA

Sweetbriar Sweet-and-Sour Meatballs

1 pound beef
1/2 cup bread crumbs
1/2 teaspoon salt
1/2 teaspoon black pepper
1/2 teaspoon garlic powder
1 tablespoon minced onion
1 (15-ounce) can tomato sauce (use 1/3 of the can)
1 egg, beaten

Sauce:
2/3 (remaining) can tomato sauce
2 tablespoons brown sugar
1/4 cup sugar
1 tablespoon vinegar
1 teaspoon mustard

Preheat the oven to 375 degrees. Combine all the ingredients in a Dutch oven or big roasting pan. Form into meatballs (small meatballs cook in 20 minutes). Bake for 45 minutes. Drain off any excess fat or juice.

In a medium saucepan, combine all the ingredients and boil for 3 minutes. Pour the hot sauce over the meatballs. Bake uncovered, for an additional 15 minutes.

Note: For later use, freeze the meatballs uncooked. Freeze the sauce in muffin tins, then put the tins in Ziploc bags. Thaw the meatballs and cook. Drain. Thaw the sauce, pour it over the meatballs, and bake as directed.

Cathey Goddard
Memorial Baptist Church
Tulsa, Oklahoma

Beef Stew

3 tablespoons all-purpose flour
1 1/2 pounds beef chuck, cut into 3/4-inch cubes
1 1/2 cups sliced carrots (1/4-inch slices)
1 large onion, thinly sliced
1 cup beer
1 (8-ounce) can tomato sauce
1 tablespoon instant beef bouillon granules
2 teaspoons packed brown sugar
1 1/2 teaspoons Worcestershire sauce
1 teaspoon salt
1 garlic clove, minced
1/8 teaspoon black pepper
1 cup frozen peas (optional)

In this recipe, the beer is used to tenderize the meat, not to flavor it. To prepare beef bourguignonne, substitute dry red wine for the beer; omit the brown sugar and add a can of sliced mushrooms with the peas.

For stew or bourguignonne, place the ingredients in a Crock-Pot and cook until done.

Griffin Chapel United Methodist Church
Starkville, Mississippi

BEEF BURGUNDY

3 to 4 pounds beef chuck, left whole
4 to 6 onions, sliced
2 cups water, more as needed
Salt and pepper to taste
Seasoning of choice (garlic, thyme, bay leaf, etc)
1 cup Burgundy wine
1 large can sliced mushrooms

In a large skillet, brown the beef well in a small amount of oil. Add the onions and cook until transparent. Add the water and simmer for 2 to 4 hours, or until the meat is tender and the water has evaporated. Remove the meat from the pan; add salt and pepper, other seasonings of choice, wine, and a little more water; thicken to a light sauce. Return the meat to the pan. Add the mushrooms and cook until the sauce thickens.

Note: The recipe is best if it is prepared a day before serving and reheated.

VERONICA (RONNY) WILLIAMS
UNITED BAPTIST CHURCH OF POULTNEY
EAST POULTNEY, VERMONT

ELEPHANT STEW

1 elephant
Brown gravy
Salt and pepper to taste
2 rabbits (optional)

Cut the elephant into bite-size pieces. Cover with the gravy. Cook over low heat for about 4 weeks. This will serve 4,200 people. If more are expected, the 2 rabbits may be added, but do this only if necessary, as most people do not like to find hare in their stew.

AGATHA GARRISON
UNITED METHODIST CHURCH
ESTÂNCIA, NEW MEXICO

Sweet-Sour Beef Stew

2 tablespoons vegetable oil
1 1/2 pounds beef stew meat, cut into 1-inch
    cubes
1 cup chopped carrot
1 cup sliced onion
1 (8-ounce) can tomato sauce
1/4 cup brown sugar
1/4 cup vinegar
1 tablespoon Worcestershire sauce
1/2 cup water
1 teaspoon salt
4 tablespoons cornstarch
1/4 cup cold water
Hot cooked noodles

In a large skillet, heat the oil and brown the meat in the hot oil. Add the next 6 ingredients, 1/2 cup of water and the salt. Cover and cook over low heat until the meat is tender, about 2 hours. Combine the cornstarch and the 1/4 cup cold water; add to the beef mixture. Cook, stirring, until the sauce is thick and bubbly. Serve over noodles. Garnish with carrot curls and parsley, if desired. Makes 4 servings.

Lee Till
Trinity Presbyterian Church
Wilmington, Delaware

Western-Style Beef and Beans

3 pounds ground beef
2 medium onions, chopped
2 celery stalks, chopped
2 teaspoons beef bouillon granules
2/3 cup boiling water
2 (28-ounce) cans baked beans with
    molasses
1 1/2 cups ketchup
1/4 cup prepared mustard
3 garlic cloves, minced
1 1/2 teaspoons salt
1/2 teaspoon black pepper
1/2 pound sliced bacon, cooked and
    crumbled

Preheat the oven to 375 degrees. In a Dutch oven over medium heat, cook the beef, onions, and celery until the meat is no longer pink and the vegetables are tender; drain. Dissolve the bouillon in the water; stir into the beef mixture. Add the beans, ketchup, mustard, garlic, salt, and pepper; mix well. Cover and bake for 60 to 70 minutes, or until bubbly; stir. Top with the bacon. Makes 12 servings.

Carol Hays
Memorial Baptist Church
Tulsa, Oklahoma

Best Corned Beef

Corned Beef:
1 (3- to 4-pound) corned brisket of beef
Vegetables, such as potatoes, carrots,
   cabbage, onions, or turnips
Glaze (below)

Glaze:
1 cup brown sugar
2 tablespoons mustard
1 tablespoon currant jelly

Preheat the oven to 350 degrees. Place the corned beef on a rack in a baking pan with enough water to just touch the meat. Cover tightly with aluminum foil and bake for 1 hour. After that time, open the foil and add desired vegetables. Cover and continue cooking until the meat is tender, about 2 to 3 hours. Open the foil and pour the glaze over the beef. Cook, uncovered, for 10 minutes longer.

In a small bowl, combine all the ingredients for the glaze. Pour the mixture over the beef during the last 10 minutes of cooking.

Cindy Wagner
United Baptist Church of Poultney
East Poultney, Vermont

Saucy Beef and Vegetable Stir-Fry

1 (1-pound) beef flank steak,
   cut into 1/4-inch strips
1 teaspoon minced fresh gingerroot
2 tablespoons vegetable oil
1 1/2 cups broccoli florets
1 cup julienned zucchini
1 cup sliced fresh mushrooms
1/2 cup red or green bell pepper chunks
1 (12-ounce) jar Heinz home-style brown
   gravy with onion
2 tablespoons soy sauce
Chow mein noodles or hot cooked rice
Sesame seeds, for garnish

In a large preheated skillet or wok, stir-fry the steak and gingerroot in the oil; remove from the skillet. Stir-fry the broccoli, zucchini, mushrooms, and bell pepper for 2 to 3 minutes, or until crisp-tender, adding more oil if necessary. Stir in the gravy and soy sauce. Return the steak to the skillet; heat for 1 to 2 minutes, or until hot. Serve with chow mein noodles or hot cooked rice. Garnish with sesame seeds, if desired. Makes 4 servings (about 4 1/2 cups).

Tara Satkowski
North Monroe Street Church of God
Monroe, Michigan

Seasoned Liver and Onions

1 pound calves' liver
2 tablespoons all-purpose flour
2 tablespoons brown sugar
1 teaspoon dry mustard
Salt and pepper to taste
3 tablespoons oil
2/3 cup water
1 bunch scallions sliced, or 1 slice onion

In a large bowl, combine the flour, sugar, mustard, salt and pepper, and mix. Coat the liver with the mixture and brown quickly in the oil. Add the water and onion. Simmer for 20 minutes.

Sybil Foust
Memorial Baptist Church
Tulsa, Oklahoma

Veal Steak Paprikas (Paprikas Borjuszelet)

1 tablespoon shortening
1 1/2 pounds veal steak
Salt and pepper to taste
1 small green pepper, chopped
1 tomato, chopped
2 onions, chopped
1/2 cup water
1/2 teaspoon paprika

In a large skillet, melt the shortening and brown the meat on both sides; season with salt and pepper. Add pepper, tomato, and onions; add the water and paprika and cover. Cook until the meat is tender.

Prince of Peace Church
Grantsville, West Virginia

STUFFED VEAL (TOLTOTT BORJU)

3 rolls
1 tablespoon butter
1 onion, chopped
1 tablespoon fresh parsley
Salt and pepper to taste
Dash of paprika
3 eggs
1 (4-pound) breast of veal with pocket
1 tablespoon shortening
1 cup water

Soak the rolls in water and squeeze out. Place on a board and chop with a large knife. In a large skillet, melt the butter and brown the onion; add the parsley, salt and pepper, and paprika. Mix well and add the rolls. Remove from the heat and cool for a few minutes. Add the eggs; mix well and cool for a few minutes. Spoon the stuffing into the washed and salted veal pocket. Sew the pocket and place it in a roaster with 1 tablespoon of shortening. Pour 1 cup of water over it and roast for 1 1/2 hours, or until the meat is tender.

PRINCE OF PEACE CHURCH
GRANTSVILLE, WEST VIRGINIA

GRILLED MARINATED LAMB

1 (3- to 5-pound) boned leg of lamb
3/4 cup sherry wine
Juice of 1/2 lemon
1/4 cup olive oil
1 teaspoon oregano
1 rounded teaspoon fresh or dried parsley
1 rounded teaspoon grated onion or onion flakes
1 tablespoon crushed rosemary leaves
Salt and pepper to taste

In a large bowl, combine the wine, juice, olive oil, and spices. Marinate the lamb in the mixture for 24 hours. Grill the meat for about 45 minutes. Turn meat once during grilling, and baste often with the marinade.

BOB FAST
UNITED BAPTIST CHURCH OF POULTNEY
EAST POULTNEY, VERMONT

LEMON LEG OF LAMB

1 tablespoon grated lemon zest
1 tablespoon oregano
1 tablespoon rosemary
3 garlic cloves, minced
1/3 cup all-purpose flour
6 tablespoons lemon juice
Salt and pepper to taste
1 (7- to 8-pound) leg of lamb

Add 1/4 cup of water to a roasting pan. Make a paste of the first 7 ingredients. Rub the mixture into the leg of lamb. Bake at 350 degrees until done.

ARLENE GLICK
TOWER HILL UNITED METHODIST CHURCH
TOWER HILL, ILLINOIS

GRILLED BUTTERFLIED LEG OF LAMB

1 (7- to 8-pound) leg of lamb, trimmed of
    all fat, boned, and butterflied by butcher
    (4 to 4 1/2 pounds boneless)
1 lemon

HERB RUB:
8 garlic cloves
3 tablespoons chopped fresh thyme
2 tablespoons chopped fresh rosemary
2 tablespoons chopped fresh parsley
1/2 teaspoon freshly ground black pepper
1 tablespoon coarse salt
3 tablespoons olive oil paste

Butterflied leg of lamb can sometimes get a little unwieldy. To secure loose flaps of meat, run 2 long metal skewers lengthwise and 2 skewers crosswise through the lamb, bunching the meat together. Securing the lamb this way will also help it cook more evenly.

For the herb rub, finely chop the garlic and in a small bowl stir it together with the remaining herb-rub ingredients. Place the lamb in a large dish and, with the tip of a small sharp knife held at a 45-degree angle, cut 1/2-inch-deep slits all over the meat, rubbing the herb mixture into the slits and all over the lamb. Marinate the lamb at room temperature for 1 hour.

Prepare the grill.

Lightly pat the lamb dry. On a lightly oiled rack, set 5 to 6 inches over glowing coals, grill the lamb for about 10 minutes on each side, or until an instant-read thermometer horizontally inserted into the thickest part of the meat registers 125 degrees for medium rare. (Alternatively, roast the lamb in a roasting pan in the middle of a 425 degree oven for about 25 minutes, or until an instant-read thermometer horizontally inserted into the meat registers 125 for medium rare.) Transfer the lamb to a cutting board. Halve and seed the lemon. Squeeze the juice over the lamb and let it stand, loosely covered with foil, for 15 minutes. Cut the lamb into slices and serve with any juices that have accumulated on the cutting board. Makes 8 servings.

LIZ HAY
CROSS IN THE DESERT UNITED METHODIST CHURCH
PHOENIX, ARIZONA

LAMB WITH GREEN BEANS
(BARANYHUS ZOLDBABBAL)

4 slices bacon, diced
1/2 cup chopped onion
2 pounds boneless lamb shoulder, cut into
   1-inch cubes
2 teaspoons salt
1 teaspoon caraway seeds
1 teaspoon paprika
2 cups meat broth
1 pound green beans
1/4 cup all-purpose flour
1/2 cup thick sour cream

Place bacon into the skillet; cook slowly until bacon is lightly browned. Remove bacon and set aside. Add chopped onion to the bacon fat. Cook slowly until onion is transparent. Remove onion to dish containing the bacon and set aside. Cut lamb and add to the bacon fat. Brown slowly on all sides and sprinkle salt, caraway seeds and paprika over the meat. Remove skillet from heat and slowly pour in meat broth. Return bacon and onion to skillet. Cover and simmer 1 1/2 to 2 hours or until meat is tender.

About an hour before meat is tender, cut into 1-inch pieces and cook the green beans until just tender. Drain beans and set aside. Cool the cooking liquid. Mix 1/2 cup liquid (reserved bean cooking liquid) and flour. Bring contents of skillet to boiling; add the four mixture into skillet. Bring this gravy to boiling; cook 3 to 5 minutes. Remove from heat and stir about 1/2 cup of the gravy, 1 tablespoon at a time, into the sour cream. Pour the mixture gradually into the skillet. Gently mix in the green beans. Cook over low heat 3 to 5 minutes, until heated thoroughly; do not boil.

PRINCE OF PEACE CHURCH
GRANTSVILLE, WEST VIRGINIA

Lamb Chops with Dill Sauce
(Becsi Baranykottlet Kapormartassal)

3 tablespoons fat
1/2 cup onion
4 lamb shoulder chops, cut 1/2-inch thick
2 tablespoons water
1 tablespoon vinegar
1 teaspoon salt
1/4 teaspoon black pepper
1 bay leaf

Sauce:
2 tablespoons butter or margarine
2 tablespoons all-purpose flour
1/4 teaspoon salt
Dash of pepper
1/2 cup beef broth
1 tablespoon chopped fresh dill weed
1/2 cup dry white wine (such as Chablis or Sauternes)
2 tablespoons vinegar

In a large skillet, melt the fat and add the onion. Cook until transparent and remove from the skillet; set aside. Slowly brown the lamb chops on both sides. Combine the remaining ingredients in a small bowl and add to the browned lamb. Return the onion to the skillet; cover the skillet and simmer for 25 to 30 minutes, or until the lamb is tender.

Melt the butter in a small skillet over low heat. Blend the flour, salt, and pepper into the butter until is smooth. Heat the mixture until it bubbles and is lightly browned. Remove the skillet from the heat. Gradually add the broth and dill. Bring to a boil and cook for 1 to 2 minutes. Remove the sauce from the heat and add the wine and vinegar. Serve the sauce over the lamb chops.

Prince of Peace Church
Grantsville, West Virginia

BAKED HAM

1 (15- to 20-pound) large ham (uncooked)
1 large onion
3 garlic cloves

Place the ham in a large kettle and cover with water. Add the onion and garlic and allow to come to a boil. Simmer or boil slowly for about 6 hours, or until tender. Let stand in the water overnight. In the morning, remove from the water and let stand on a rack. Remove the bone and tie the ham. When the ham is cold, it is ready to slice.

PRINCE OF PEACE CHURCH
GRANTSVILLE, WEST VIRGINIA

HAM AND SCALLOPED POTATOES

4 slices cheese
2 1/2 cups milk
1/8 cup all-purpose flour
1/4 cup butter
1 tablespoon salt
2 teaspoons pepper
2 cups boiled ham, cut into chunks
5 cups potatoes, cut into chunks

Preheat oven to 350 degrees. Mix milk, flour, salt and pepper. Place ham and potatoes in a 9 x 13 inch pan. Pour milk mixture over ham and potatoes (you may need to add more milk). Place butter on top in slices. Bake for 2 hours. After it's done, lay cheese on top to melt.

PINEMOUNT BAPTIST CHURCH
MCALPIN, FLORIDA

Ham and Pork Loaf

1 pound smoked ham
2 pounds fresh lean pork
1/2 cup milk
1 cup bread crumbs
2 eggs, beaten
1 cup tomato soup
1 small onion, grated

Sauce:
1 tablespoon butter
1 tablespoon all-purpose flour
1/4 cup sugar
1 teaspoon dry mustard
1/4 cup vinegar
1 1/2 cups tomato juice
1 egg, beaten

Grind meat 3 times. Add remaining ingredients; stir well. Fill a well-greased loaf pan with mixture. Bake for 2 hours at 375 degrees and serve with sauce.

Sauce: Melt butter. Add flour and stir well. Add rest of ingredients and cook, stirring until thick. Serves 8.

DIANE
FOREST AVENUE CONGREGATIONAL CHURCH
BANGOR, MAINE

Polynesian Ham

1 (10-ounce) can pineapple chunks
2 tablespoons butter
3 tablespoons all-purpose flour
2 tablespoons brown sugar
2 teaspoons prepared mustard
1/2 teaspoon salt
3/4 cup water
1 tablespoon vinegar
2 cups cooked ham
1/2 cup coarsely chopped celery
1/2 green pepper, sliced
1 small can bean sprouts (optional)
1 small can sliced mushrooms (optional)

Drain the pineapple, reserving the juice; set aside. In a saucepan over medium-high heat, melt the butter; blend in the flour, sugar, mustard, and salt. Gradually stir in the reserved pineapple juice, water, and vinegar. Cook, stirring constantly, until the mixture thickens. Add the drained pineapple, ham, celery, and green pepper. Bring to a boil, cover, reduce the heat, and simmer for 10 minutes, or until the vegetables are tender. If desired, add bean sprouts or mushrooms, drained. Serve with rice.

PINEMOUNT BAPTIST CHURCH
MCALPIN, FLORIDA

Roast Pork

1/2 cup dry white wine
1/4 cup olive oil
6 tablespoons Dijon mustard
2 tablespoons soy sauce
2 tablespoons fresh lemon juice
2 tablespoons melted butter
2 tablespoons minced onion
1/2 cup fresh mushrooms, chopped
1/4 teaspoon freshly ground black pepper
1 (5-pound) boneless pork loin roast

In a bowl, combine the wine, olive oil, mustard, soy sauce, lemon juice, butter, onion, mushrooms, and pepper and mix well. Pour the mixture over the pork roast and marinate, covered, for 24 hours, turning occasionally. Drain and save the marinade. Place the pork in a roasting pan. Cook at 350 degrees for 2 1/2 hours, or until a meat thermometer measures 155 to 160 degrees. During the last 30 minutes, baste frequently with the reserved marinade. Makes 8 to 10 servings.

Note: This recipe is wonderfully different and always a hit!

Justine McDonald
Northbrook United Methodist Church
Roswell, Georgia

Tender Pork Tenderloin

1 (2-pound) pork tenderloin
1 garlic clove, cut into slivers
Salt and pepper to taste
1/2 teaspoon ground cumin
2 tablespoons extra-virgin olive oil
1/2 cup chicken broth
1/2 cup dry white wine

Preheat the oven to 400 degrees. With the tip of a sharp knife, make small deep slits all over the tenderloin and insert the garlic slivers. Season with salt, pepper, and cumin. Place the oil in an ovenproof skillet and sear the tenderloin well on medium-high heat for about 10 minutes, turning the meat over as it browns. Add the chicken broth and white wine to the pan and return it to the oven for 10 minutes longer. Let the tenderloin rest for 10 to 12 minutes before carving. It will continue to cook as it sits. Slice and serve immediately. Makes 2 servings.

Cross in the Desert United Methodist Church
Phoenix, Arizona

SLOW-COOKED BARBECUE PORK ROAST

1 cup frozen small whole onions
3 pounds boneless pork loin roast
3/4 cup barbecue sauce
2 tablespoons honey
1/2 teaspoon mustard powder
8 ounces medium egg noodles
1 tablespoon cornstarch
1 tablespoon chopped fresh parsley, for
   garnish

Place the onions on the bottom of a Crock-Pot. Top with the roast. Combine 1/4 cup of the barbecue sauce, honey, and mustard; pour over the roast. Cover and cook on low until tender, about 8 hours. Cook the noodles according to the package directions; drain. Transfer to a serving platter. Place the pork on the platter beside the noodles. Transfer the liquid and onions to a saucepan, stir in the cornstarch and remaining barbecue sauce, and add to the pot. Cook until the sauce thickens. Pour the sauce and onions over the pork and noodles. Garnish with the parsley.

PINEMOUNT BAPTIST CHURCH
MCALPIN, FLORIDA

HONEY AND HERB GRILLED PORK

3 pounds boneless pork roast
1 cup beer or ginger ale
1/2 cup honey
1/2 cup Dijon mustard
1/4 cup vegetable oil
2 tablespoons onion powder
1 1/2 teaspoons fresh rosemary, crushed
1 teaspoon salt
1 teaspoon garlic powder
1/4 teaspoon black pepper

Place the pork in a heavy resealable plastic bag. Combine the remaining ingredients in a bowl and pour the mixture over the pork. Seal the bag. Marinate in the refrigerator for 1 hour. Remove the pork from the marinade. Place over a drip pan, filled with a pinch of water, on the grill. Grill, covered, or bake at 350 degrees for 30 minutes per pound, or until a meat thermometer registers 160 degrees. Baste with the marinade occasionally. Simmer any leftover marinade for 5 minutes. Serve with the roast. Makes 8 to 10 servings.

KARIN VOELKER
ST. PAUL CHURCH
WATERFORD, CONNECTICUT

PORK CHOPS AND SAUERKRAUT

1/4 cup tart apples, chopped
2 tablespoons butter
2 pounds loin pork chops
1 (16-ounce) package sauerkraut, drained
3 tablespoons brown sugar
1 onion, thinly sliced
1/2 teaspoon caraway seeds
2 bay leaves
1 can onion soup

Preheat the oven to 350 degrees. In a large skillet, lightly sauté the apples in the butter. Brown the chops in this mixture. Place the chops in a baking dish and pour the apple and butter mixture on top. Place the sauerkraut over the chops. Add the onion, caraway seeds, bay leaves, and onion soup. Cover and bake for 1 hour.

JOAN DREGER
ST. PAUL CHURCH
WATERFORD, CONNECTICUT

BAKED PORK CHOPS

6 lean center-cut pork chops (1/2-inch thick)
1 egg white
1 cup evaporated skim milk
1/4 cup cornflake crumbs
1/4 cup fine dry bread crumbs
4 teaspoons paprika
2 teaspoons oregano
1/4 teaspoon chili powder
1/2 teaspoon garlic powder
1/2 teaspoon black pepper
1/8 teaspoon cayenne pepper
1/8 teaspoon dry mustard
1/2 teaspoon salt
Nonstick cooking spray (as needed)

Preheat the oven to 375 degrees. Trim all the fat from the chops. Beat the egg white with the evaporated milk. Place the chops in the milk mixture and let stand for 5 minutes, turning the chops once.

Meanwhile, in a small bowl combine the cornflake crumbs, bread crumbs, spices, and salt. Spray a 9 x 13-inch baking pan with nonstick cooking spray. Remove the chops from the milk mixture and coat thoroughly with the crumb mixture. Place the chops in a pan and bake for 20 minutes. Turn the chops and bake for 15 minutes longer, or until no pink remains.

Note: You can substitute skinless, boneless chicken, turkey parts, or fish for the pork chops and bake for 20 minutes.

EVELYN WOLFE
OAKMONT CHURCH OF GOD
SHREVEPORT, LOUISIANA

Sesame Pork Chops

1/4 cup bottled barbecue sauce
2 tablespoons apricot preserves
1 tablespoon sesame seeds, toasted
4 pork loins, cut 3/4-inch thick (1 1/2 to 1 3/4 pounds)
Salt and pepper to taste

For the sauce, in a small saucepan combine the barbecue sauce and apricot preserves and stir. Cook over low heat just until the preserves dissolve. Stir in the sesame seeds. Remove the mixture from the heat. Trim any fat from the pork chops and season with salt and pepper. Place the chops on an unheated rack in a broiler pan. Broil 3 to 4 inches from the heat for 10 minutes. Brush the chops with sauce and turn over. Broil for 10 to 15 minutes longer, until the meat is no longer pink. Brush with sauce during the last 5 minutes.

Jeff Keller
Trinity United Methodist Church
York, Pennsylvania

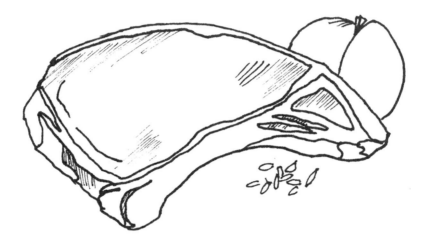

Glazed Pork Chops with Corn Stuffing

1 can chicken broth (1 3/4 cups)
1/8 teaspoon ground red pepper
1 cup corn kernels
1 celery stalk, chopped
1 onion, chopped
4 cups corn bread stuffing
Nonstick cooking spray
6 pork chops (boneless)
2 tablespoons brown sugar
2 teaspoons spicy brown mustard

In a large saucepan, combine the broth, pepper, corn, celery, and onion and bring to a boil. Remove from the heat. Add the stuffing and mix lightly. Spray a 3-quart shallow baking dish with nonstick cooking spray. Spoon the stuffing into the dish. Top with the chops. In a small bowl, combine the sugar and mustard and spread the mixture over the chops. Bake for 30 minutes, or until done. Makes 6 servings.

Vicki
Forest Avenue Congregational Church
Bangor, Maine

Dianne's Pork Chops Over Rice

4 pork chops
Salt and pepper
1 cup all-purpose flour
1 cup diced tomatoes
1 teaspoon onion powder
1 tablespoon sugar
1 cup water
Cooking spray
1 cup rice, uncooked
1/2 teaspoon garlic powder
1 teaspoon salt
1 small onion, sliced
1/2 cup grated Parmesan cheese

Preheat the oven to 350 degrees. Season the pork chops with salt and pepper to taste, dredge in the flour, and brown in a large skillet. Drain the oil from the pan (leaving the pan drippings). Add the tomatoes, onion powder, sugar, and water to the skillet and stir until the mixture simmers. Remove from the heat. Spray a baking dish with cooking spray, sprinkle the rice evenly over the bottom. Add the garlic powder and salt to the rice. Place the pork chops on top of the rice and pour the tomato mixture over the pork chops. Top off with onion slices and cheese. Bake, uncovered, for 35 minutes.

PINEMOUNT BAPTIST CHURCH
MCALPIN, FLORIDA

Sweet-and-Sour Pork

1 pound pork
1 egg
1 teaspoon salt
1/4 cup cornstarch
1/4 cup all-purpose flour
1/4 cup chicken stock
3 cups peanut oil

SAUCE:
1 tablespoon peanut oil
1 teaspoon chopped garlic
1 large green pepper, cut into 1/2-inch strips
1 medium carrot, cut into 1/2-inch strips
1/2 cup chicken stock
4 tablespoons sugar
4 tablespoons red wine vinegar
1 teaspoon soy sauce
1 tablespoon cornstarch, dissolved in 2 tablespoons cold water

Trim the pork of fat and cut into 1-inch cubes; set aside. In a bowl, combine the egg, salt, cornstarch, flour, and chicken stock; set aside. Add the pork cubes to the egg and flour mixture and stir until the meat is well coated.

Preheat the oven to 250 degrees. Pour the 3 cups of peanut oil into a wok and set it over high heat. When the oil begins to smoke (375 degrees), drop in the pork cubes, one by one. Fry for 5 to 6 minutes. Remove and keep warm in the oven.

To prepare the sauce, pour off the cooking oil and add the 1 tablespoon peanut oil. Add the garlic, green pepper, and carrot; stir-fry for 2 to 3 minutes. Pour in the chicken stock, sugar, vinegar, and soy sauce. Boil for 1 minute. Add cornstarch mixture. When the mixture thickens, pour it over the pork and serve.

CRYSTAL HULKEWICZ
BUCKINGHAM UNITED METHODIST CHURCH
GARLAND, TEXAS

PORK SPARERIBS

4 pounds pork spareribs, cut up
3 tablespoons butter
1 large onion, minced
1 garlic clove, crushed
2 tablespoons cider vinegar
2 tablespoons orange juice
6 tablespoons brown sugar
3 teaspoons salt
1 tablespoon mustard
1 teaspoon cinnamon
4 tablespoons Worcestershire sauce
2 cups ketchup
1 1/2 cups diced celery
1 (8-ounce) can crushed pineapple

Preheat the oven to 350 degrees. In a large saucepan, cover the ribs with water and boil for 15 minutes; drain. In a separate saucepan, melt the butter and simmer the onion and garlic until tender. Add the remaining ingredients and cook for 5 to 10 minutes. Add the ribs and cook gently. Pour the entire mixture into a baking dish and bake in the oven for about 30 minutes, or until the meat is tender.

Note: This recipe freezes well.

PINEMOUNT BAPTIST CHURCH
MCALPIN, FLORIDA

BARBECUED RIBS (CROCK-POT RECIPE)

2 teaspoons instant minced onion
1/2 teaspoon crushed red pepper flakes
1/2 teaspoon ground cinnamon
1/2 teaspoon garlic powder
3 pounds pork loin back ribs, cut into
    serving-size pieces
1 medium onion, sliced
1/2 cup water
1 cup of your favorite bottled barbecue sauce

In a small bowl, combine the onion, red pepper flakes, cinnamon, and garlic powder and mix well. Rub the mixture into the ribs. Layer the ribs and onion in a Crock-Pot. Pour the water around the ribs. Cover. Cook on low 8 to 9 hours. Remove the ribs from the Crock-Pot. Drain and discard the liquid and onions. Return the ribs to the Crock-Pot. Brush the ribs on both sides with the barbecue sauce and pour any remaining sauce over the meat. Cover and cook on low for 1 hour.

Note: We love tender ribs, and these fall right off the bone.

VALERIE NORRIS
NORTHBROOK UNITED METHODIST CHURCH
ROSWELL, GEORGIA

Sweet-Sour Pork Sausage Balls

MEATBALLS:
1 pound bulk pork sausage
1 egg, slightly beaten
1/3 cup fine bread crumbs
1/2 teaspoon sage

SAUCE:
1/2 cup ketchup
2 tablespoons brown sugar
1 tablespoon vinegar
1 tablespoon soy sauce

In a large bowl, combine the sausage, egg, bread crumbs, and sage and mix well. Shape into about 2 dozen 1 1/2-inch meatballs. In an ungreased skillet, brown the meatballs slowly on all sides, about 15 minutes. Pour off the grease. Combine the sauce ingredients and pour the mixture over the meat. Cover and simmer for 30 minutes, stirring occasionally to coat the meatballs. Serve over rice as a main dish.

Note: The dish can also be served as an appetizer if the meatballs are made smaller.

DARLA VOLENTINE
HOLUM BAPTIST CHURCH
GRAYSON, LOUISIANA

Venison Roast

1 (4- to 6-pound) venison roast
2 garlic cloves, minced
1/2 cup chopped onion
Salt and pepper to taste
4 bacon strips
Italian salad dressing
1 cup water
1 tablespoon cooking oil

With a sharp knife, make deep holes across the grain of the meat. In a small bowl, combine the garlic, onion, salt and pepper, and insert into the holes. Top with pieces of bacon. Marinate the meat overnight in the Italian dressing. In a large saucepan, combine the water and oil and add the roast. Bring to a boil, uncovered. Put the lid on the pot and cook on low heat for 4 to 6 hours. If gravy is desired, thicken the juices with cornstarch.

ANNA ARCENNEAUX
HUNGARIAN PRESBYTERIAN CHURCH
ALBANY, LOUISIANA

ONE-DISH MEALS

Thank you God for the food before us,
The friends beside us
And the love between us.

Breakfast Casserole

1/2 stick margarine
6 slices white bread, with crust removed
1 pound bulk sausage
1 1/2 cups grated cheese
5 eggs
2 cups cream (or combine 1 small can evaporated milk with whole milk)
1 teaspoon dry mustard
1 teaspoon salt

Preheat the oven to 300 degrees. Melt the margarine in a 9 x 13-inch dish. Cut the bread into small pieces and scatter them on the bottom of the dish. Cook and drain the sausage and spread it over the bread. Spread the cheese over the sausage. In an electric mixer, combine the eggs, milk, and seasonings and blend; pour the mixture evenly over the bread and sausage. (You may prepare the recipe in advance and refrigerate overnight.) Bake for 45 minutes to 1 hour.

JENNY KOTTENBROOK
GRIFFIN CHAPEL UNITED METHODIST CHURCH
STARKVILLE, MISSISSIPPI

Holiday Brunch Casserole

4 cups cubed day-old bread
2 cups sharp Cheddar cheese, shredded
10 eggs
4 cups milk
1 teaspoon dry mustard
1 teaspoon salt
1/4 teaspoon onion powder
Freshly ground black pepper to taste
1 package sausage, cooked, drained, and crumbled
1/2 cup chopped, peeled tomatoes
1/2 cup chopped mushrooms

Preheat the oven to 325 degrees. Place the bread in a well-buttered 9 x 13-inch baking dish. Sprinkle with cheese. In a large bowl, combine the eggs, milk, mustard, salt, onion powder, and pepper and mix well. Pour the mixture evenly over the bread and cheese. Sprinkle with the sausage, tomatoes, and mushrooms. Cover and chill overnight. Bake, uncovered, for 1 hour. Tent with foil if the top begins to brown too quickly. Makes 6 servings.

REBECCA JEHS
MEMORIAL BAPTIST CHURCH
TULSA, OKLAHOMA

EGGS HUSSARDE

2 large thin slices ham, grilled
2 Holland rusks or biscuits
1/4 cup Marchande de Vin Sauce
1 slices tomato, grilled
2 eggs, soft poached
3/4 cup Hollandaise sauce
Paprika

MERCHAND DE VIN SAUCE:

3/4 cup butter
1/3 cup finely chopped mushrooms 1/3 cup
    minced ham
1/2 cup finely chopped shallots
1/2 cup finely chopped onions
2 tablespoons garlic, minced
2 tablespoons all-purpose flour
1/2 teaspoon salt
1/2 teaspoon pepper
Dash cayenne
3/4 cup beef stock
1/2 cup red wine

Lay a large slice of ham across each rusk and cover with Marchand de Vin Sauce. Cover next with tomato and then egg. Top with Hollandaise Sauce. Garnish with sprinkling of paprika.

To make Marchand de Vin Sauce: In a 9-inch skillet met butter and lightly sauté the mushrooms, ham, shallots, onion and garlic. When the onion is golden brown, add the flour, salt, pepper and cayenne. Brown well, about 7 to 10 minutes. Blend in the stock and the wine and simmer over low heat for 35 to 45 minutes.

CLIFF HARWICK
NORTHBROOK UNITED METHODIST CHURCH
ROSWELL, GEORGIA

QUICHE LORRAINE

1 tablespoon butter or margarine
9-inch unbaked pastry shell
6 slices lean bacon, cut into 1/4-inch pieces
    (or 1/2 cup chopped ham)
4 eggs
1 1/2 cups heavy cream
1/2 teaspoon salt
Pinch of black pepper
3/4 cup grated Swiss cheese (or Parmesan
    and Swiss)

Spread the butter over the bottom of the pastry shell. Cook the bacon until crisp and scatter it over the bottom of the pastry shell. In a bowl, beat the eggs and stir in the cream and seasonings. Stir in the cheese. Gently ladle the egg-cheese custard into the pastry shell. Bake at 425 degrees for 10 minutes. Reduce the heat to 325 degrees and bake for 35 to 40 minutes longer, or until a knife inserted into the center comes out clean.

CLEONE STETLER
TRINITY UNITED METHODIST CHURCH
YORK, PENNSYLVANIA

ZUCCHINI QUICHE

2 tablespoons butter
3 cloves garlic, chopped
1 onion, chopped
1/2 green pepper, chopped
2 medium zucchini, sliced 1/4-inch thick
1 tomato, chopped
2 teaspoons dried basil
1 teaspoon dried oregano
1 teaspoon salt
1/8 to 1/4 teaspoon pepper
8 ounces shredded mozzarella cheese
3 or 4 large eggs, beaten with wire whisk
1 cup milk
1/4 cup sour cream
3/4 cup Bisquick

Preheat the oven to 375 degrees. Heat the butter in a nonstick skillet over medium heat. Add the garlic, onion and green pepper. Saute until softened, then add the zucchini, tomato, basil, oregano, salt, and pepper.(You can substitute 2 tablespoons of your favorite Italian seasoning for the basil and oregano, if you like). Cook, covered, for about 10 minutes, stirring often. Combine the mozzarella, eggs, milk, sour cream, and Bisquick and add to the zucchini mixture. Pour into a greased 10-inch pie plate. Bake for 25 minutes or until the center is set. Let stand 10 minutes before serving.

LaVerne White
Memorial Baptist Church
Tulsa, Oklahoma

SWISS MUSHROOM QUICHE

1 9-inch unbaked pastry shell
3 tablespoons butter
8 ounces (about 2 cups) fresh mushrooms, chopped
1/4 cup chopped scallions
4 eggs
2 tablespoons all-purpose flour
1 cup plain yogurt (not vanilla)
1 cup shredded Swiss cheese
1/2 cup milk
1/2 teaspoon salt

Preheat the oven to 400 degrees. Bake the pastry shell for 8 minutes. Remove from the oven and reduce the temperature to 350 degrees. In a medium skillet, melt the butter and sauté the mushrooms and scallions until the mushrooms are golden. Spoon into the cooled pastry shell. In a large bowl, beat the eggs, gradually adding the flour. Stir in the yogurt, cheese, milk, and salt. Pour the mixture over the mushrooms. Bake for 35 to 40 minutes, or until set and the top is golden. Let the quiche stand for at least 10 minutes before serving. Makes 4 to 8 servings.

Karen Wagner
Trinity United Methodist Church
York, Pennsylvania

MUSHROOM SOUFFLÉ

1 pound fresh mushrooms, sliced
4 tablespoons margarine
1/2 cup chopped scallions
1/2 cup sliced celery
1/2 cup chopped green pepper
1 teaspoon salt
1/2 teaspoon black pepper
4 tablespoons chopped fresh parsley
1/2 teaspoon Accent
1/2 cup mayonnaise
6 to 8 slices firm white bread
3 eggs
2 cups milk
1/4 cup grated Parmesan cheese

Preheat the oven to 325 degrees. In a large skillet, sauté the mushrooms in the margarine for 5 minutes. Add the scallions, celery, green pepper, salt, and pepper. Sprinkle with the parsley and Accent. Cook for 3 minutes longer and add the mayonnaise. Remove the crust from the bread and cut the bread into 1-inch squares. Put half the bread into a greased casserole dish. Spoon the mushroom mixture over the bread mixture and cover with the remaining bread. Beat the eggs until frothy and add the milk; pour over the bread, cover, and refrigerate for 1 hour or overnight. Bake for 50 minutes. Sprinkle with the cheese and bake for 10 minutes longer, or until golden.

DOROTHY ROSS
MATTAPOISETT CONGREGATIONAL CHURCH
MATTAPOISETT, MASSACHUSETTS

GREEK SPINACH CHEESE PIE

1 package frozen spinach, chopped
3 eggs
1 pound small-curd cottage cheese
3 to 4 tablespoons all-purpose flour
1/2 stick butter, melted
1/4 pound Brick or Monterey Jack cheese
1/4 pound American cheese

Preheat the oven to 350 degrees. In a large saucepan, boil the spinach until thawed; drain well. In a large bowl, combine the spinach, eggs, cottage cheese, flour, and butter. Cube the Brick and American cheeses and add to the mixture. Stir well and pour into a buttered baking dish (I use a round white soufflé dish). Bake for 1 hour.

MARCIA B. RUSSELL
HIGHLAND HEIGHTS PRESBYTERIAN CHURCH
CORDOVA, TENNESSEE

BAKED CHEESE FONDUE

6 slices white bread
2 tablespoons butter or margarine, softened
6 slices American cheese
2 eggs
1/2 cup beer
1/2 cup milk
1/2 teaspoon salt
1/2 teaspoon dry mustard
1 teaspoon Worcestershire sauce
1/4 teaspoon black pepper
6 cooked strips bacon, for garnish

Preheat the oven to 350 degrees. Remove the crust from the bread and spread with the butter. Arrange the bread and cheese in a 1-quart casserole dish. (To make individual casseroles, quarter the bread and cheese slices.) In a bowl, beat the eggs well with a rotary beater and stir in the beer, milk, and seasonings. Pour the mixture over the bread and cheese. Bake for 40 minutes, or until brown. Roll the hot bacon strips into curls and place them on top of the finished fondue.

VELMA REED
UNITED BAPTIST CHURCH OF POULTNEY
EAST POULTNEY, VERMONT

PIZZA CRUST

2 1/2 to 3 cups all-purpose flour
1 1/2 teaspoons sugar
2 teaspoons salt
1 package active dry yeast
1 cup hot water
2 tablespoons oil

In a large bowl, combine 1 cup of the flour, the sugar, salt, and undissolved yeast. Gradually add the hot water and oil to the dry ingredients, beat for 1 minute at low speed, and stir into flour to make a soft dough. Turn out onto a lightly floured board. Knead for 8 to 10 minutes. Place the dough in a greased bowl, turning it to the top. Cover and let rise in a warm place until doubled in size (about 45 minutes). Punch the dough down and press it into a large baking pan.

LYNETT BARRINGER
TOWER HILL UNITED METHODIST CHURCH
TOWER HILL, ILLINOIS

SEAFOOD PIE

6 ounces frozen crabmeat, shrimp, or tuna
1 cup sharp American cheese
3 ounces cream cheese (cut into 1/4-inch cubes)
1/4 cup thinly sliced scallions
2 cups milk
1 cup Bisquick
4 eggs
3/4 teaspoon salt
Dash of nutmeg

Thaw, rinse well, and drain the seafood. Preheat the oven to 400 degrees and grease a 10-inch pie plate. In a large bowl, combine the seafood, cheeses and onion. Spoon the mixture into the pie plate. In a blender set on high, beat the remaining ingredients until smooth, about 15 seconds. Pour over the ingredients in the pie plate. Bake until golden brown, 35 to 40 minutes. Let stand for 5 minutes before cutting.

BAR HARBOR SPECIAL
FOREST AVENUE CONGREGATIONAL CHURCH
BANGOR, MAINE

SWISS AND CRAB QUICHE

4 ounces Swiss cheese, shredded (1 cup)
1 (9-inch) unbaked pastry shell
1 (7 1/2-ounce) can crabmeat, drained, flaked, and cartilage removed
2 scallions, sliced (with tops)
3 eggs, beaten
1 cup light cream
1/2 teaspoon salt
1/2 teaspoon grated lemon peel
1/4 teaspoon dry mustard
Dash of ground mace
1/4 cup sliced almonds

Preheat the oven to 325 degrees. Sprinkle the cheese evenly over the bottom of the pastry shell. Top with the crabmeat and sprinkle with the scallions. In a bowl, combine the eggs, cream, salt, lemon peel, mustard, and mace. Pour the mixture evenly over the crabmeat. Top with the almonds. Bake for about 45 minutes, or until set. Remove the quiche from the oven and let it stand for 10 minutes before serving. Makes 6 servings.

FATHER ROUGHAN
ST. PAUL CHURCH
WATERFORD, CONNECTICUT

SALMON QUICHE

CRUST:
1 cup whole wheat flour
2/3 cup shredded sharp Cheddar (3 ounces)
1/4 cup chopped almonds
1/2 teaspoon salt
1/4 teaspoon paprika
6 tablespoons vegetable oil

FILL:
2 cans skinless, boneless salmon
3 eggs, beaten
1 cup sour cream
1/4 cup mayonnaise
1/2 cup shredded sharp Cheddar cheese
    (2 ounces)
1/4 teaspoon dried dill weed
3 drops Tabasco sauce (optional)
1 tablespoon grated onion

Make the crust: In a large bowl, combine the flour, cheese, almonds, salt, and paprika. Stir in the oil and set aside 1/4 cup of the mixture for topping. Press the remainder into a deep 9-inch pie plate. Bake at 400 degrees for 10 minutes. Remove from the oven and reduce the heat to 350 degrees.

Drain the salmon. In a large bowl, combine the eggs, sour cream, and mayonnaise and mix well. Stir in the remaining ingredients. Spoon the mixture into the pie plate. Sprinkle the reserved crust mixture on top. Bake for 45 minutes, or until the quiche is firm in the center.

SHERRY WAGNER
BUCKINGHAM UNITED METHODIST CHURCH
GARLAND, TEXAS

Shrimp Stuffed Peppers

4 large green peppers
2 cups boiling water
2 cups cooked shrimp, cut up
1/2 cup minced onion
2 tablespoons butter
1 teaspoon Worcestershire sauce
Salt and pepper to taste
1 1/2 cups cooked rice
1 cup tomato puree
2/3 cup buttered crumbs

Preheat the oven to 375 degrees. Cut the tops from the peppers and remove the seeds. Serve whole or cut in half lengthwise. Simmer the peppers in the boiling water for 5 minutes, then drain. In a large bowl, combine the next 8 ingredients and fill the peppers. Top with the crumbs and bake in a casserole dish with 1/2 cup water for 25 to 30 minutes.

Note: A deep muffin pan is good for baking the whole peppers, and it makes a pretty serving platter. If you cut the peppers in half, prepare more buttered crumbs.

Esther Dillon
Trinity United Methodist Church
York, Pennsylvania

Harborside Fish Hash

4 bacon slices
1 small onion, chopped
2 cups cooked, flaked fish
2 cups cooked, peeled, and diced potatoes
1 to 2 tablespoons fresh chopped parsley
3/4 teaspoon finely chopped fresh thyme, or
   1/4 teaspoon dried
3/4 teaspoon finely chopped rosemary, or
   1/4 teaspoon dried
1/2 teaspoon Worcestershire sauce
Salt and pepper to taste
Fresh Mexican salsa, ketchup, or chili sauce

In a large skillet, cook the bacon until crisp; drain on paper towels. With 3 tablespoons of bacon drippings, sauté the onion until it's soft and transparent. Add the fish, potatoes, parsley, thyme, rosemary, and Worcestershire sauce. Season with salt and pepper. Stirring constantly, cook over medium-high heat until the mixture starts to brown. Serve from the skillet or place in a bowl. Crumble bacon; scatter over hash. Serve hot with salsa.

Janell Morgan
Buckingham United Methodist Church
Garland, Texas

CLASSIC BAKED MACARONI AND CHEESE

2 tablespoons cornstarch
1 teaspoon salt
1/2 teaspoon dry mustard (optional)
1/4 teaspoon black pepper
2 1/2 cups milk
2 tablespoons butter or margarine
2 cups American or Cheddar cheese
8 ounces elbow macaroni (about 1 3/4 cups),
    cooked and drained

In a medium saucepan combine the first 4 ingredients; stir in the milk. Add the butter, stirring constantly, and bring to a boil over medium-high heat; boil for 1 minute. Remove from the heat. Stir in 1 3/4 cups of the cheese until melted. Add the macaroni. Pour the mixture into a greased 2-quart casserole. Sprinkle with the reserved cheese. Bake, uncovered, for 25 minutes, or until lightly browned. Makes 4 to 6 servings.

Note: Add 1 cup diced ham before baking.

MERRY R. JONES
GRIFFIN CHAPEL UNITED METHODIST CHURCH
STARKVILLE, MISSISSIPPI

MACARONI AND CHEESE SOUPERB

6 quarts boiling water
1 teaspoon salt
2 cups elbow macaroni
1/4 cup butter or margarine
1/2 cup chopped onion
1 can cream of celery soup
1 can cream of mushroom soup
1 1/2 cups milk
2 cups shredded Cheddar cheese
2 tablespoons dry bread crumbs

Preheat the oven to 350 degrees. Add the salt to the boiling water. Gradually add the macaroni. Cook, uncovered, stirring often for 6 to 8 minutes, or until just tender; drain. In a large saucepan, melt the butter and cook the onion until crisp-tender. Stir in the soups, milk, and 1 1/2 cups of the cheese. Heat, stirring often, until the cheese melts. Add the macaroni and pour the mixture into a greased 3-quart casserole dish. Sprinkle the top with the bread crumbs and the remaining cheese. Bake for 30 minutes, or until browned and bubbly. Makes 8 servings.

BARBARA SNYDER
CAVENDISH BAPTIST CHURCH
CAVENDISH, VERMONT

CROCK-POT MACARONI 'N' CHEESE

1 (8-ounce) box macaroni
1 (12-ounce) can evaporated milk
1 1/2 cups milk
2 eggs, beaten
1/4 cup melted butter
1 teaspoon salt
3 cups sharp cheese

Cook and drain the macaroni. Grease the Crock-Pot. Combine all the ingredients in the Crock-Pot, reserving some of the cheese for topping when you've finished cooking. Cook on low for 3 to 4 hours.

Note: This is a great comfort food. It can be prepared the night before, then all you have to do is plug it in.

MALINDA JERNIGAN
NORTHBROOK UNITED METHODIST CHURCH
ROSWELL, GEORGIA

TUNA NOODLE CASSEROLE

1 (16-ounce) package egg noodles, cooked and drained
1 or 2 cans light tuna, drained
1 can cream of mushroom soup
1 soup can of milk
1/2 package frozen peas, cooked and drained
Salt and pepper to taste
2 teaspoons celery salt
Potato chips

Preheat the oven to 350 degrees. In a large bowl, combine all the ingredients and mix well. Pour the mixture into a greased casserole dish. Bake for 45 minutes. I top my casserole with crushed potato chips before baking.

CHRISTINE WALKER
CAVENDISH BAPTIST CHURCH
CAVENDISH, VERMONT

OLD-TIME TUNA BAKE

7 ounces uncooked egg noodles (4 cups)
1 (12-ounce) can evaporated milk
1 tablespoon instant minced onion
2 teaspoons seasoned salt
2 (6 1/2-ounce) cans tuna, drained
1 (9-ounce) package frozen peas, thawed
   and drained
Shredded Cheddar cheese

Preheat the oven to 350 degrees. Cook the noodles to the desired doneness according to the package directions. Drain and rinse with hot water. In an ungreased 3-quart casserole dish, combine the evaporated milk, onion, and seasoned salt. Add the cooked egg noodles, tuna, and peas, mixing well. Cover and bake for 30 minutes. Remove from the oven and mix well. Sprinkle with the Cheddar cheese and bake for 5 minutes longer.

CHRISTIE QUELLETTE
WESTSIDE BAPTIST CHURCH
ANTLERS, OKLAHOMA

FRIENDSHIP CASSEROLE

Sorrow
Love
Smiles
Laughter
Kindness
Forgiveness

Fold 2 hands together and express a dash of sorrow. Marinate it overnight and work on it tomorrow. Chop one grudge into tiny pieces. Add several cups of love. Dredge with a large smile. Mix the above ingredients. Dissolve the hate within you by doing a good deed: cut in and help a friend in need. Stir in laughter and kindness from the heart. Toss with forgiveness and give neighbor some. The number of people served will depend on you. It can serve the whole wide world if you want it to.

SHARON
FOREST AVENUE CONGREGATIONAL CHURCH
BANGOR, MAINE

Aunt Mosy's Pastitsio

1 1/2 pounds macaroni
2 pounds ground beef
1/2 stick margarine
1 onion, chopped
1/2 can tomato paste
Grated mozzarella or other cheese, for
    topping

Crust:
3 tablespoons cornstarch or all-purpose flour
4 medium or 2 large eggs, beaten
1/2 cup sugar
1 1/2 quarts hot milk
Cinnamon

Cook the macaroni, drain, and set aside. In a large saucepan, melt the margarine and add the beef, onion, and tomato paste. Scramble the ingredients as you cook. In a 13 x 9 pan arrange alternate layers of macaroni and the beef mixtures, ending with macaroni. Top with cheese.

Preheat the oven to 350 degrees. In a large bowl, dissolve the cornstarch in a little cold water. Add the eggs, sugar, and hot milk. In a small saucepan, cook the mixture until it becomes soft like custard. Spread over the macaroni and sprinkle with cinnamon. Bake for about 40 to 45 minutes.

Alex
Forest Avenue Congregational Church
Bangor, Maine

Lasagna

3 tablespoons olive oil
1 cup finely chopped onions
1 garlic clove, crushed
1 pound ground beef
2 teaspoons salt
1 (14-ounce) can tomatoes
1 (8-ounce) can tomato sauce
1 (6-ounce) can tomato paste
3/4 cup water
1/2 teaspoon dried basil
1/2 teaspoon dried oregano
1 teaspoon sugar
1 tablespoon parsley flakes
1 (16-ounce) package lasagna noodles
1 pound ricotta cheese
1 egg
1 pound mozzarella cheese, thinly sliced
1 cup grated Parmesan cheese

In a Dutch oven or large heavy saucepan, heat 2 tablespoons of the olive oil and sauté the onions and garlic for 5 minutes. Stir in the beef and cook over medium heat until browned. Drain off the fat. Add the salt, tomatoes, tomato sauce, tomato paste, water, basil, oregano, sugar, and parsley flakes. Bring the sauce to a boil, then simmer for 15 minutes. Meanwhile, cook the lasagna according to the package directions. Add the remaining oil to the noodles while cooking to prevent them from sticking. Drain, rinse, and cool. In a bowl, blend the ricotta cheese and egg. Preheat the oven to 375 degrees. Grease a 13 x 9 x 2-inch baking pan and arrange alternate layers of sauce, lasagna, ricotta cheese, and mozzarella cheese, finishing with sauce. Sprinkle with Parmesan cheese. Bake for 35 minutes. Let stand for 10 minutes before serving.

Betsy Guerin
Northbrook United Methodist Church
Roswell, Georgia

AMERICAN LASAGNA

1 large package egg noodles or linguine,
    cooked
1 to 2 pounds ground beef
1 onion, chopped
3 small cans tomato sauce
1/2 teaspoon dried oregano
1 tablespoon garlic powder
Salt and pepper to taste
1 (8-ounce) cream cheese
1 small carton cottage cheese
1 small carton sour cream
6 scallions, sliced
Bread crumbs or Cheddar cheese

Preheat the oven to 350 degrees. In a large saucepan, brown the ground beef and sauté the onion in a little oil. In a bowl, combine the cream cheese, cottage cheese, and sour cream. Add the scallions, including the tops. Mix well. In a casserole dish, arrange alternate layers of noodles, meat, and the cheese mixture. Cover with the bread crumbs and bake for 30 or 40 minutes.

SUE HUGHES
UNITED METHODIST CHURCH
ESTANCIA, NEW MEXICO

MOCK LASAGNA (CROCK-POT RECIPE)

3 tablespoons olive oil
1 pound ground beef
1/2 pound Italian sausage
1 (12-ounce) tomato paste
1/2 cup water
1 garlic clove, minced
1 teaspoon dried basil
1 1/2 tablespoons dried parsley flakes
1/2 teaspoon black pepper
1 1/2 teaspoons salt
12 ounces mozzarella cheese, shredded
12 ounces cottage cheese
10 ounces broad lasagna noodles

In a large skillet, heat 1 tablespoon of the olive oil and brown the beef and sausage; drain. Place in a lightly greased Crock-Pot. Add the tomato paste, water, and seasonings and mix well. Add the mozzarella and cottage cheese. Break the noodles into bite-size pieces and cook. Drain and toss in the remaining oil. Pour the mixture into the Crock-Pot and cook on low for 7 to 8 hours or on high for 3 to 4 hours.

JOAN O'BRYAN
CROSS IN THE DESERT UNITED METHODIST CHURCH
PHOENIX, ARIZONA

Mexican Lasagna

1 pound lean ground beef
1 garlic clove, minced
2 teaspoon chili powder
1 tablespoon. sugar
1/2 teaspoon salt
1 (14 -1/2-ounce) can cut tomatoes
1 (6-ounce) can tomato paste
1 (4-ounce) can diced green chilies
2 tablespoons water
1 egg, beaten
1 1/2 cups low-fat cottage cheese
1/4 cup grated Parmesan cheese
1 teaspoon dried oregano or 1 tablespoon
  fresh oregano, chopped
3 wheat tortillas
Non-stick cooking spray
1 1/4 cups shredded mozzarella

Preheat the oven to 375 degrees. Brown beef in non-stick skillet. Drain. Stir in the garlic, chili powder, sugar, salt, tomatoes, tomato paste, chilies and water. Bring to a boil, stirring occasionally. Reduce the heat and simmer uncovered for 15 minutes. Combine the egg, cottage and Parmesan cheeses and oregano. Spray the baking pan or casserole with cooking spray. Preheat the oven to 375 degrees. Place one tortilla in bottom of the pan. Top with half of the cheese mixture, half of the meat sauce and one-third of the mozzarella. Repeat with the second tortilla, layering on the rest of the cheese mixture, and half of the remaining meat sauce and mozzarella. Top with the remaining tortilla, meat sauce, and mozzarella cheese. Bake uncovered until hot and bubbly, about 30 minutes. Let stand 15 minutes before serving. Serves 4.

JAN WICKLIFFE
CROSS IN THE DESERT UNITED METHODIST CHURCH
PHOENIX, ARIZONA

Fettuccine Alfredo

1/2 pound fettuccine pasta
4 tablespoons unsalted butter
2 cups heavy cream
1 cup grated Parmesan cheese
Salt and pepper to taste

Cook the pasta according to the package directions. Drain. In a large sacuepan, heat the butter and cream. Add the pasta and heat thoroughly. Add the Parmesan and toss gently. Be careful not to break the pasta. Season with salt and pepper. Makes 4 to 6 servings.

SYMPHONY OF KANSAS CITY
FOREST AVENUE CONGREGATIONAL CHURCH
BANGOR, MAINE

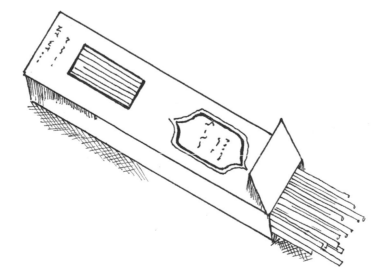

CARBONARA

1 pound cooked ham, finely chopped
    (1/2- to 3/4-inch strips)
4 tablespoons corn margarine or butter
1 cup lightly packed fresh minced parsley
1 pound hot cooked spaghetti and fettuccine,
    drained
5 eggs, beaten
1 cup grated or shredded Parmesan cheese,
    plus additional
Freshly ground black pepper

In a heavy skillet or wok over medium heat, cook the ham until it's lightly browned. Remove the pan from the heat. Have ready, in separate containers, the butter or margarine, parsley, eggs, and 1 cup Parmesan, as well as the pepper. Add the hot spaghetti, butter, and parsley to the ham. Mix quickly to blend. Pour in the eggs and continue to blend, quickly lifting and mixing the paste to coat well with the egg. Stir in the cheese and a dash of pepper; mix well again. Serve with additional cheese.

GAMILIE ISRAEL
TRINITY UNITED METHODIST CHURCH
YORK, PENNSYLVANIA

PASTA PRIMAVERA

1 pound spaghetti
1/3 cup olive or corn oil
3 tablespoons tarragon vinegar
1 tablespoon Dijon mustard
1 teaspoon salt
1/2 teaspoon freshly ground black pepper
1/4 teaspoon cayenne pepper
1/2 cup snipped fresh basil, tarragon, chives,
    and/or parsley
6 scallions, sliced diagonally
2 bell peppers (red or green or mixed)
2 small firm zucchini, sliced
1 cup cherry tomatoes
1 1/2 cups broccoli florets, blanched
1/2 cup frozen peas, thawed and blanched
Zest of 1 lemon (optional)

Cook the spaghetti according to the package directions. Rinse with cold water, drain, and toss with 1 tablespoon of the oil; set aside. Prepare the dressing by combining the remaining oil, vinegar, mustard, salt, black pepper, and cayenne pepper. Place the remaining ingredients in a large bowl. Add the cooled pasta and dressing and toss gently.

GAMILIE ISRAEL
TRINITY UNITED METHODIST CHURCH
YORK, PENNSYLVANIA

SEAFOOD BY THE BAY

9 ounces linguine
2 cups broccoli florets
1–2 tablespoons olive oil
1/3 cup chopped onion
1/3 cup chopped sweet red pepper
1/3 cup thin sliced leek
3 cloves minced garlic
2 tablespoons butter
1/4 cup dry white wine
1 tablespoon fresh snipped parsley
1 tablespoon lemon juice
1/4 teaspoon salt
1/4 teaspoon pepper
1 cup heavy cream
8 ounces medium shrimp peeled and
    deveined
4 ounces bay scallops, cut into 1 inch pieces
1–8 ounces lobster tail (1 to 1 1/2 cups)
    cooked, cut in chunks
2–3 tablespoons fresh snipped dill weed
1/4 cups grated Parmesan cheese

Cook linguini according to package directions, adding broccoli the last 2 minutes of cooking. Drain and add 1 to 2 tablespoons olive oil; mix lightly, cover and set aside. Meanwhile; cook onion, sweet pepper, leek and garlic in melted butter in a large saucepan until tender. Add wine, parsley, lemon juice, salt, pepper and cook uncovered for 2 minutes. Add cream, bring to a boil, then simmer gently, uncovered, for about 7 minutes or until thickened. Add shrimp and scallops to cream sauce and return to a boil. Reduce heat and cook uncovered about 2 minutes or until shrimp and scallops are opaque. Stir in lobster and dill weed, cook and stir until heated through. Toss with hot pasta mixture, top with Parmesan cheese and serve.

I like to serve this with baked stuffed tomatoes and mesclun salad greens, mixed with mandarin orange slices, sliced water chestnut, sliced almonds and raspberry vinaigrette dressing.

Serves 6.

DOROTHY ROSS
MATTAPOISETT CONGREGATIONAL CHURCH
MATTAPOISETT, MASSACHUSETTS

STUFFED SHELLS

25 jumbo shells
2 cups ricotta cheese
8 ounces mozzarella cheese
1/2 cup Parmesan cheese
2 eggs, slightly beaten
1 teaspoon salt
1/8 teaspoon black pepper
1 teaspoon dried parsley
1/2 teaspoon dried oregano
1/2 pound ground beef
1 (28-ounce) jar spaghetti sauce

Cook the shells according to the package directions; drain. In a large bowl, combine the cheeses, eggs, salt, pepper, parsley, and oregano. Preheat the oven to 350 degrees. Fill each shell with 2 tablespoons of the mixture. In a large skillet, brown the beef and mix with the spaghetti sauce. Spread a thin layer of sauce in 3-quart rectangular baking dish. Place the shells 1 deep in the dish and cover with sauce. Sprinkle with Parmesan cheese. Bake for 35 minutes. Makes 6 servings.

NANCY E. RUPP
TRINITY UNITED METHODIST CHURCH
YORK, PENNSYLVANIA

BAKED ZITI

1 carrot, grated
1 onion, diced
2 tablespoons margarine
1 can plum tomatoes
1 can tomato sauce
1 can tomato paste
1 teaspoon salt
ground black pepper to taste
1/2 teaspoon garlic powder
1 teaspoon sugar
2 teaspoons basil
2 bay leaves
1 pound lean ground beef
1 teaspoon oregano
1/4 cup dry white wine or white cooking
   wine
1 pound-package ziti (No. 2)
1 pound shredded mozzarella cheese
1/3 cup grated Parmesan cheese

Preheat oven at 350 degress. In a Dutch oven, sauté carrots and onions in margarine. Remove tomatoes from can, tear into pieces, and put into pot with sautéed vegetables. Reserve liquid from tomatoes to dilute the sauce if made a day ahead. Add tomato sauce, tomato paste, salt, pepper, garlic powder, sugar, basil and bay leaves. Bring to a boil, reduce heat, cover and simmer for a half hour. Stir and separate beef in frying pan until pink is gone. Add beef, oregano and white wine; continue to cook another hour.

Meanwhile, cook ziti as directed. Drain and mix with sauce in a 13 x 9 x 2-inch roasting pan. Top with mozzarella and Parmesan cheese. Bake uncovered for 25 to 30 minutes.

ROSALYN C. SMITH
PRINCE OF PEACE CHURCH
GRANTSVILLE, WEST VIRGINIA

MANICOTTI

1 tablespoon olive oil
1 1/2 pounds ground chuck
1 garlic clove, crushed
1 pound mozzarella, shredded
2 cups cottage cheese
1 cup mayonnaise
1 jar spaghetti sauce
Parmesan cheese
1 box jumbo shells, cooked

Preheat the oven to 350 degrees. In a large skillet, heat the tablespoon of oil and brown the beef with the garlic; drain and cool. In a large bowl, combine the mozzarella, cottage cheese, and mayonnaise. When the beef is cool, add it to the cheese mixture and mix well. Stuff the meat mixture into the cooked shells and arrange them in a large baking dish. Pour the spaghetti sauce over the shells; sprinkle Parmesan over the top. Cover the dish with foil and bake for 25 minutes. Remove the foil and bake for 20 to 25 minutes longer, or until bubbly.

TAMMY HAMMITTE
NORTH MONROE STREET CHURCH OF GOD
MONROE, MICHIGAN

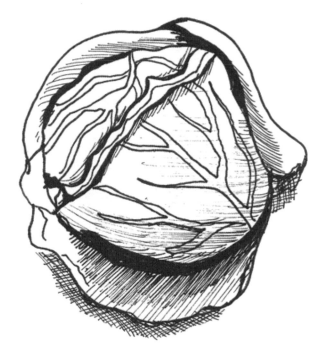

Cabbage Rolls

1 1/2 pound hamburger meat
1 onion, chopped
2 stalks celery, chopped
1 cup uncooked rice
2 unbeaten eggs
1 can tomato paste
3 cloves garlic
Salt and pepper
1 head cabbage

In a large bowl, combine hamburger, onion, celery, rice, eggs, tomato paste, 1 crushed clove of garlic, salt, and pepper. Separate cabbage leaves after wilting, by placing in boiling water for a few minutes. Drain leaves thoroughly. Place 1/2 cup mixture on each leaf and roll up securely. Place rolls in Dutch oven. Place rest of crushed garlic over rolls. Cover pot and cook on top of stove over medium/medium-low heat for 2 hours or until done. Shake pot occasionally to prevent sticking.

MIKE AND WANDA GRIFFIN
BUCKINGHAM UNITED METHODIST CHURCH
GARLAND, TEXAS

Fancy Brown Rice

2 cups chicken broth
1 1/2 cups brown rice
3 tablespoons vegetable oil
1 medium onion, chopped
2 large celery stalks, thinly sliced
1 small green bell pepper
1 small red bell pepper
1 small yellow bell pepper
1/2 teaspoon salt
1 cup slivered blanched almonds (toasted)
1/4 cup fresh parsley, coarsely chopped
Water chestnuts (optional)

In a 4-quart saucepan, combine 4 cups of water with the broth and bring to a boil. Add the rice and reduce the heat to low and simmer for 40 to 45 minutes, or until the rice is tender and the liquid is absorbed. In a 12-inch skillet over medium heat, heat the oil. Add the onion and cook until crisp-tender. Add the celery, bell peppers, and salt, cooking until crisp-tender. Stir frequently. Gently stir the rice into the vegetables. Stir in the almonds, parsley, and water chestnuts (if desired) and serve hot. (The dish can be refrigerated at this point and served cold later).

CAROLYN CRUTCHER
TOWER HILL UNITED METHODIST CHURCH
TOWER HILL, ILLINOIS

SPANISH RICE

2 tablespoons vegetable oil
1/2 medium onion, chopped
2 tablespoons chopped bell pepper
1/2 to 3/4 pound ground beef
Salt and pepper to taste
2 teaspoons chili powder
1/2 cup uncooked rice
1 (8-ounce) can tomato sauce
   (or you can use fresh tomatoes)
2 (8-ounce) cans of water

In a large skillet, heat 1 tablespoon of the oil and brown the onion and bell pepper. Add the beef, salt and pepper, and chili powder and continue to brown. In another pan, brown the rice in the remaining tablespoon of oil. Add the rice to the meat mixture. Stir in the tomato sauce and water. Simmer for 1 to 1 1/2 hours.

MARGARET BRIDGEWAWTER/MAY SEITZ
CROSS IN THE DESERT UNITED METHODIST CHURCH
PHOENIX, ARIZONA

CAJUN RED BEANS AND RICE

1 pound dried red beans
1 meaty ham bone
3 scallions, sliced
1 large onion, chopped
1 large garlic clove, minced
1 celery stalk, chopped
1 bay leaf
1 tablespoon chopped parsley
Salt and pepper to taste
1 pound Creole or Polish sausage
1 quart or more cold water
   (much less if you use canned beans)
Cooked rice

Wash the beans. Place them in a large saucepan and cover with water. Bring to a boil and boil rapidly for 2 minutes. Turn off the heat and let the beans sit, covered, for 1 hour. Bring the beans to a boil again and lower the heat. Add the ham bone, scallions, onion, garlic, celery, bay leaf, parsley, and salt and pepper. Cook slowly for 2 to 3 hours. Add the sausage during the last hour or so. Add about a cup of water toward the end of the cooking if the mixture becomes too dry. Stir frequently and scrape down the sides and bottom of the pan with a wooden spoon to prevent scorching. Stir the entire contents about every 30 minutes. Serve over cooked rice.

TERRY HALFORD
HIGHLAND HEIGHTS PRESBYTERIAN CHURCH
CORDOVA, TENNESSEE

Curried Chicken and Rice

1 (10-ounce) package frozen broccoli
3 cups cooked white rice
2 chicken breasts, cooked and chopped
1 can cream of mushroom soup
1/2 cup Miracle Whip
1 teaspoon lemon juice
1 1/2 teaspoons curry powder
1 1/2 cups grated sharp Cheddar cheese
1 cup bread crumbs
2 tablespoons melted butter or margarine

Thaw the broccoli. Place the rice in the bottom of a casserole dish. Layer first the chicken and then the broccoli over the rice. In a small bowl, combine the soup, Miracle Whip, lemon juice, and curry powder. Sprinkle 1 cup of the cheese over the broccoli and cover with the soup mixture. Combine the bread crumbs and butter and spread this over the soup as evenly as possible. Sprinkle with the remaining cheese. Microwave for about 7 minutes or bake at 350 degrees for 30 minutes.

Note: Curry has a very strong flavor; you can get by with less if you aren't a big fan of curry. You can also use a milder Cheddar.

SUSI HANSON
BUCKINGHAM UNITED METHODIST CHURCH
GARLAND, TEXAS

Chicken à la King

1/4 cup margarine
1 (2-ounce) can mushrooms, drained
1/4 cup chopped green pepper
1/4 cup all-purpose flour
1/2 teaspoon salt
1/8 teaspoon black pepper
1 cup chicken broth (can be bouillon)
1 cup cream (nondairy creamer like Coffee Mate)
1 cup diced cooked chicken
1/4 cup chopped pimiento (optional)

In a large saucepan, melt the margarine and sauté the mushrooms and green pepper. Blend in the flour and seasonings. Cook over low heat, stirring until the mixture is smooth and bubbly. Remove from the heat. Slowly stir in the broth and cream. Bring to a boil over low heat, stirring constantly. Boil for 1 minute. Add the chicken and pimiento, if desired. Heat through. Serve over toast points, biscuits, or chow mein noodles.

KATY EVANS
HIGHLAND HEIGHTS PRESBYTERIAN CHURCH
CORDOVA, TENNESSEE

CHICKEN BISCUIT STEW

4 tablespoons margarine
5 tablespoons all-purpose flour
1/4 teaspoon salt
1/4 teaspoon black pepper
1/2 cup skim milk
1 (10 1/2-ounce) can reduced-sodium
    chicken broth
1 1/2 cups diced cooked chicken breasts
1/3 cup chopped onion
1 (8 1/2-ounce) can green peas, drained
1 (8 1/4-ounce) can sliced carrots, drained
1 small can biscuits

Preheat the oven to 375 degrees. In a large skillet, melt the margarine and stir in the flour, salt, and pepper. Gradually add the milk and broth, stirring with a wire whisk. Cook for 4 minutes, or until the mixture is thick and bubbly, stirring constantly. Add the chicken, onion, peas, and carrots. Cool for 1 minute, then remove from the heat. Split the biscuits in half horizontally and place them over the chicken mixture. Bake for 20 minutes, or until the biscuits are brown.

DOROTHY ARCHER
HIGHLAND HEIGHTS PRESBYTERIAN CHURCH
CORDOVA, TENNESSEE

EASY CHICKEN POT PIE

1 2/3 cups frozen mixed vegetables, thawed
1 cup diced cooked chicken
1 (10 3/4-ounce) can condensed cream of
    chicken soup
1 cup Bisquick original baking mix
1/2 cup milk
1 egg

Preheat the oven to 400 degrees. In a large bowl, combine the vegetables, chicken, and soup and mix well. Pour the mixture into an ungreased 9-inch pie plate. Combine the remaining ingredients and stir with a fork until blended. Pour into the pie plate. Bake for 30 minutes, or until golden brown. Makes 6 servings.

Note: Beef or turkey can be substituted for the chicken. The recipe reheats well in the microwave.

ISLA EMERTON
CALVARY UNITED METHODIST CHURCH
TAYLOR, NEBRASKA

Ruidoso Winner

1 (8-ounce) package green spinach noodles
1/4 cup butter
1/4 cup all-purpose flour
1 cup milk
1 cup chicken stock
1 pint sour cream
1/3 to 1/2 cup lemon juice
1 (6-ounce) can mushrooms
2 teaspoons seasoned salt
1 teaspoon MSG
1/2 teaspoon nutmeg
1 teaspoon paprika
2 teaspoons black pepper
1/2 teaspoon cayenne pepper
1 tablespoon parsley flakes
4 cups coarsely cut cooked chicken
1/2 cup toasted bread crumbs
Parmesan cheese

Preheat the oven to 325 degrees. Cook the noodles according to the package directions and drain. In a large saucepan, melt the butter and stir in the flour. Add the milk and chicken stock. Cook over low heat, stirring constantly, until the sauce thickens. Add the sour cream, lemon juice, mushrooms, seasoned salt, MSG, nutmeg, paprika, peppers, and parsley flakes. Mix well. Butter a 3-quart casserole dish and place the noodles in it. Add a layer of chicken. Pour some of the sauce over the chicken. Sprinkle with half of the bread crumbs and cheese. Repeat, ending with the cheese. Bake until bubbly, about 25 minutes.

Note: This dish can be made the night before and refrigerated. Bake at 325 degrees for 1 hour.

BRYAN MCKINNEY FAMILY
BUCKINGHAM UNITED METHODIST CHURCH
GARLAND, TEXAS

Chicken Enchiladas

2 (16-ounce) cans chicken
1 onion, chopped
10 ounces cheese, grated
1 (10-ounce) package medium corn tortillas

SAUCE:
2 cans cream of mushroom soup
1 (8-ounce) container sour cream
1 (4-ounce) can green chilies

Preheat the oven to 350 degrees. In a bowl, combine the chicken, onion, and half of the cheese. Spread on the tortillas and roll up. Place in a casserole dish.

For the sauce, combine all the ingredients and mix well. Pour the mixture over the tortillas. Sprinkle the remaining cheese over the top. Bake for 30 minutes.

VANESSA KEY
HOLUM BAPTIST CHURCH
GRAYSON, LOUISIANA

CHICKEN DIABOLO

2 boxes Uncle Ben's wild rice, or 1 box and
   1 cup cooked rice
2 (8-ounce) packages cream cheese, softened
2 tablespoons mustard
1 large jar sliced mushrooms, drained
2 tablespoons parsley flakes
1 can cream of mushroom soup
1/2 cup chicken broth
4 chicken breasts, baked, boiled, or sautéed,
   cut up

TOPPING:
1/2 cup melted butter
1 cup brown sugar
1/2 cup chopped walnuts or pecans

Preheat the oven to 350 degrees. Cook the rice. In a large bowl, combine the cream cheese, mustard, mushrooms, parsley, soup, and broth. Add the chicken. You can either layer the rice in a greased casserole dish followed by the chicken mixture or you can combine the rice and chicken. Sprinkle with the topping and bake for 30 to 45 minutes.

ANITA OLIVER
NORTHBROOK UNITED METHODIST CHURCH
ROSWELL, GEORGIA

WHITE CHICKEN CHILI

1 tablespoon olive oil
1 pound boneless, skinless chicken breasts,
   cut into 1/2-inch cubes
1/4 cup chopped onion
1 cup chicken broth
1 (4.5-ounce) can green chilies, chopped and
   undrained
4 teaspoons garlic powder
1/2 teaspoon ground cumin
1/2 teaspoon dried oregano
1/2 teaspoon dried parsley
Salt and pepper to taste
1 (19-ounce) can white kidney beans or
   Northern beans
Shredded cheese (optional)
Sour cream (optional)
Scallions (optional)

In a 3-quart saucepan over medium to high heat, heat the olive oil and add the chicken. Cook for 45 minutes. Remove from the pan and set aside. Add the onion to the saucepan and cook for 2 minutes. Stir in the chicken broth, chilies, seasonings, and beans and cook for about 20 minutes on low heat. Add the chicken and simmer for 10 minutes. Top with shredded cheese, sour cream, or scallions if desired.

LORETTA RUSSELL
NORTH MONROE STREET CHURCH OF GOD
MONROE, MICHIGAN

KING RANCH CASSEROLE

3 to 4 pounds chicken breasts
1 dozen corn tortillas
1 can cream of mushroom soup
1 can cream of chicken soup
1 cup chopped green peppers
1 cup chopped onions
1 tablespoon chili powder
1 can Ro-Tel tomatoes
3/4 pound grated Cheddar cheese

Preheat the oven to 350 degrees. Boil the chicken breasts until tender. Dice the chicken and reserve the stock. Line the bottom and sides of a greased 3-quart casserole dish with half of the tortillas. Sprinkle with 4 to 6 tablespoons of the chicken stock. Add the cream of mushroom soup, undiluted. Make alternate layers with half of the chicken and half of the remaining ingredients. Top this with stock and the cream of chicken soup, undiluted. Make another layer with the remaining ingredients. Cover with foil and bake for 1 hour. Makes 8 to 10 servings.

PATRICIA LOW
BUCKINGHAM UNITED METHODIST CHURCH
GARLAND, TEXAS

HONOLULU CHICKEN

1/4 cup all-purpose flour
1/4 teaspoon salt
Dash of black pepper
1 broiler chicken, cut up
Oil
1 (10-ounce) jar peach preserves
1/2 cup barbecue sauce
1/2 cup chopped onion
2 tablespoons soy sauce
1 large can water chestnuts, drained and
    sliced
1 green pepper, cut into strips
Hot cooked rice

In a large bowl, combine the flour, salt, and pepper. Coat the chicken with the seasoned flour. In a large skillet, brown the chicken in a small amount of oil; drain. In a separate bowl, combine the preserves, barbecue sauce, onion, and soy sauce and pour the mixture over the chicken. Cover and simmer for 40 minutes, or until the chicken is tender. Add the water chestnuts and green pepper during the last 10 minutes of cooking. Serve with rice.

CHARLOTTE JACOBSON
FIRST UNITED METHODIST CHURCH
BELLEVILLE, MICHIGAN

Hot Chicken Salad

6 cups diced cooked chicken
3 cups chopped celery
2 to 3 teaspoons grated onion
3 to 4 tablespoons lemon juice
Dash of Tabasco sauce
1/2 to 1 cup slivered almonds
2 tablespoons chicken stock
1 1/3 cups crushed potato chips
1 cup grated Cheddar cheese
2 cups mayonnaise

Preheat the oven to 375 degrees. In a large bowl, combine the chicken and celery. Add the seasonings, then the mayonnaise, almonds, and stock. Pour the mixture into a 3-quart shallow casserole dish. Combine the potato chips and cheese; spread over the top of the salad. Bake for 20 minutes—do not overbake.

FREDA B. ZAHN
TRINITY UNITED METHODIST CHURCH
YORK, PENNSYLVANIA

Turkey Tetrazzini

4 1/2 ounces uncooked spaghetti
1/4 cup reduced-calorie margarine
1 minced garlic clove
1/4 cup finely chopped onion
3 tablespoons cornstarch
1 1/2 cups chicken broth
1 1/2 cups evaporated skim milk
1/2 teaspoon seasoned salt
Dash of white pepper
16 ounces turkey, cooked and cubed
1 (4-ounce) can mushrooms, drained
1 1/2 ounces grated Parmesan cheese
Paprika

Preheat the oven to 350 degrees. Cook the spaghetti in boiling water and drain. In a large saucepan, melt the margarine over medium heat. Add the garlic and onion and sauté until the onion is transparent. In a small bowl, dissolve the cornstarch in the broth and whisk into the margarine mixture, stirring constantly, until the mixture boils and thickens. Add the milk, blending well, and cook for 5 minutes. Stir in the salt, pepper, turkey, mushrooms, and cooked spaghetti. Mix well. Spray a 13 x 9-inch pan with nonstick cooking spray. Spread the mixture evenly in the pan. Sprinkle with the Parmesan cheese and paprika. Bake for 25 to 30 minutes.

SHIRLEY SMITH
TRINITY UNITED METHODIST CHURCH
YORK, PENNSYLVANIA

Chipped Beef Casserole

1 can cream of mushroom soup
2 cups cooked macaroni
2 to 3 hard-boiled eggs, chopped
1 cup milk
3 tablespoons chopped onion
1 (4-ounce) package chipped beef
7 ounces grated sharp cheese

In a large bowl, combine all the ingredients and pour the mixture into a casserole dish. Refrigerate for about 2 hours. Bake at 350 degrees for 1 hour with the lid on; remove the lid and continue baking for 10 minutes longer. Serve with a salad and crusty bread.

MAXINE WILLS
PRINCE OF PEACE CHURCH
GRANTSVILLE, WEST VIRGINIA

CORNED BEEF CASSEROLE

1 (8-ounce) package egg noodles
1 can corned beef, crumbled
1/4 pound cheese slices
1 can cream of chicken soup
1 cup milk
1/4 cup chopped onion
Potato chips, crushed (optional)

Cook the noodles and drain. In a casserole dish, arrange alternate layers of noodles, corned beef, and cheese. Preheat the oven to 350 degrees. In a small saucepan, combine the soup and milk and heat, but do not boil. Pour the soup mixture over the layers and top with the crushed potato chips. Bake for 45 minutes, or until slightly browned.

VICKIE MOLLBERG
PITT COMMUNITY CHURCH
BAUDETTE, MINNESOTA

REUBEN CASSEROLE

28-ounce can sauerkraut
2 cup Swiss cheese, shredded
1/2 pound corned beef, chopped
1/2 cup thousand island dressing
1/4 cup mayonnaise
Party rye bread

Preheat the oven to 400 degrees. Rinse and drain sauerkraut. Place in the bottom of a greased 1 1/2 quart casserole. Mix together dressing and mayonnaise. Top the sauerkraut with half of the cheese, then half of the dressing, all of the corned beef, then the remaining cheese, and remaining dressing.

Bake until it starts to bubble. Top with rye slices, brushed with melted butter and bake 10 minutes more.

Yield: 4 servings.

Good spooned onto rye slices as an open faced sandwich.

LUANNE GENGA
FIRST UNITED METHODIST CHURCH
BELLEVILLE, MICHIGAN

BEEF QUESADILLAS

3/4 pound ground beef
1/2 cup refried beans
1 (4-ounce) can chopped green chilies,
   drained
1/2 teaspoon dried oregano
1/2 teaspoon ground cumin
1/4 teaspoon salt
4 (8-inch) flour tortillas
2 tablespoons melted butter or margarine
1 1/3 cups shredded taco cheese
Paprika

Preheat the oven to 475 degrees. In a large skillet, cook the beef over medium heat until no pink remains; drain. Stir in the beans, chilies, oregano, cumin, and salt. Cook over medium-low heat for 3 to 4 minutes, or until heated through. Brush one side of each tortilla with butter. Spoon 1/2 cup of the meat mixture over the unbuttered side of each tortilla. Top each tortilla with 1/3 cup of cheese and fold it in half. Place the tortillas on a lightly greased baking sheet and sprinkle with paprika. Bake for 10 minutes, or until crisp and golden brown. Cut into wedges. Makes 4 servings.

FOREST AVENUE CONGREGATIONAL CHURCH
BANGOR, MAINE

TACO PIE

1 envelope taco seasoning
1 pound ground beef
1 can diced green chilies
Minced onions to taste
Half of an 8-ounce package of corn chips
1 cup shredded Cheddar cheese
8 ounces sour cream
1 (8-ounce) jar mild taco sauce

Preheat the oven to 350 degrees. In a 10-inch skillet, prepare the taco seasoning mix according to the package directions. Add the beef, chilies, and minced onion. Line a 9-inch pie plate with the corn chips. Spoon the beef mixture into the pie plate and sprinkle with the cheese. Spread the sour cream over the cheese. Bake for 20 minutes. In a small saucepan, heat the taco sauce until it's hot. Spoon the sauce around the edges of the pie. Makes 4 main-dish servings.

KAREN SCHUMAN
CROSS IN THE DESERT UNITED METHODIST CHURCH
PHOENIX, ARIZONA

TACO BATTER

1/2 cup cornmeal
1 cup all-purpose flour
1/4 teaspoon salt
1 1/2 cups water
1 egg

Beat together. Pour onto a hot griddle, and spread out with a fork, making each the size of a pancake. Fry until lightly brown. Fill with your taco meat, etc.

Recipe comes from Mom Hodges sister. Her daughter and family lived in Mexico for years.

ELLEN HODGES
TOWER HILL UNITED METHODIST CHURCH
TOWER HILL, ILLINOIS

Beef Jambalaya

3 tablespoons bacon drippings
1 garlic clove, minced
2 green peppers, chopped
2 cups chopped onions
1 pound ground beef
2 1/2 cups tomatoes
1/4 teaspoon paprika
1/4 teaspoon chili powder
1/2 teaspoon Worcestershire sauce
1 1/2 teaspoons salt
1/4 teaspoon black pepper
1 bay leaf
1 tablespoon chopped parsley
3/4 cup uncooked rice

In a Dutch oven, heat the drippings and brown the garlic for 5 minutes. Remove the garlic and discard. Brown the green peppers and onions until soft. Add the meat and brown. Add the next 8 ingredients. Cover and simmer for 30 minutes. Add the rice and continue cooking for 15 or 20 minutes longer.

BILLY RUTH ELLIOTT
HOLUM BAPTIST CHURCH
GRAYSON, LOUISIANA

Dianne's Eggplant Parmesan

1 pound eggplant
1/2 teaspoon black pepper
1/2 pound ground chuck
1/2 cup diced onion
1/2 cup diced bell pepper
1 cup shredded Parmesan cheese
1/2 cup ground Parmesan cheese
1 teaspoon salt
1 medium jar Prego traditional spaghetti
   sauce
2 tablespoons brown sugar

Peel and thinly slice the eggplant lengthwise. Sprinkle with 1/2 teaspoon of the salt. Place a colander in a shallow pan. Place the eggplant slices in the colander and place a similar sized and shaped bowl on top of the slices to press. Allow the slices to drain for 45 to 60 minutes. Meanwhile, in a large skillet over medium heat, cook the meat until it's no longer pink. (Drain fat if necessary.) Add the onion, bell pepper, 1/2 teaspoon salt, and black pepper; stir and continue to cook until the onion and pepper are tender. Add the spaghetti sauce and brown sugar. Reduce the heat, cover, and simmer for 30 minutes. Preheat the oven to 375 degrees. Coat a glass baking dish with cooking spray. Spread about 1/2 cup of the meat sauce on the bottom of the dish. Layer eggplant on top of the sauce and sprinkle with both cheeses. Repeat until all the sauce and eggplant have been used, ending with a layer of sauce. Sprinkle the top layer generously with the remaining cheese. Loosely cover the dish with aluminum foil and bake for 30 minutes. Remove the foil and bake for 10 to 12 minutes longer, or until the cheese is golden brown.

PINEMOUNT BAPTIST CHURCH
MCALPIN, FLORIDA

Texas Hash

1 pound ground beef
1 medium onion, sliced
1 bell pepper, cut into 1/2-inch pieces
1 (16-ounce) can tomatoes
1 (8-ounce) can tomato sauce
1/3 cup rice
1 cup water
1/2 teaspoon chili powder
1/2 teaspoon dried basil
1/2 teaspoon dried oregano
Pinch of black pepper
2 garlic cloves, sliced
1/4 cup grated cheese

In a large saucepan, cook the beef, onion, bell pepper until the beef is browned. Add the tomatoes, tomato sauce, rice, water, and seasonings. Bring to a boil. Simmer for 20 to 30 minutes until the rice is done. Add the cheese and cook until it melts. Serve with garlic bread and a green salad. Makes 4 servings.

Note: Add mushrooms and green beans, if desired.

MARILYN SEDDON
UNITED METHODIST CHURCH
ESTÂNCIA, NEW MEXICO

Super Sloppy Joes

2 pounds ground beef
1/2 cup chopped onion
2 celery stalks, chopped
1/4 cup chopped green pepper
1 2/3 cups crushed tomatoes
1/4 cup ketchup
2 tablespoons brown sugar
1 tablespoon Worcestershire sauce
1 tablespoon steak sauce
1/2 teaspoon garlic salt
1/4 teaspoon ground mustard
1/4 teaspoon paprika
8 to 10 hamburger buns, split

In a large saucepan, brown the beef and cook over medium heat with the vegetables until the meat is no longer pink and the vegetables are tender. Drain the pan and add the crushed tomatoes, ketchup and remaining seasonings. Simmer, uncovered, for 35 to 40 minutes, stirring occasionally. Spoon into the buns. Makes 8 to 10 servings.

MARG MUMFORD
FIRST UNITED METHODIST CHURCH
BELLEVILLE, MICHIGAN

MOM'S POT ROAST

1/3 cup salad oil
1 (3- to 4-pound) beef chuck blade roast
10 small unpeeled new potatoes, diced
4 to 6 carrots, peeled and coarsely chopped
1/4 cup Worcestershire sauce
2 tablespoons parsley flakes
1 teaspoon Lawry's lemon pepper
1 teaspoon dried thyme
2 cups fresh green beans, rinsed and sliced
1/2 pound fresh mushrooms, rinsed and cut
    in half
1 medium onion, cut into large wedges
1/2 cup dry red wine
1 (1 5/8-ounce) package beef stew seasoning
    (not pot roast seasoning)
1 teaspoon Knorr Swiss Aromat seasoning
    for meat
1 teaspoon garlic salt
2 cups water

Preheat the oven to 350 degrees. In a large baking dish (use a Dutch oven if you have one), add the oil and put it in the oven for 10 minutes or until the oil is hot. Place the roast in the hot oil and let it cook for 5 minutes on each side. Remove from the oven. Put all the remaining ingredients on top of the roast, adding the water last to make sure the seasonings are wet. Cook, uncovered, for 1 hour, then cover and cook for 2 hours longer.

NANCY SHERLIN
BUCKINGHAM UNITED METHODIST CHURCH
GARLAND, TEXAS

NEW ENGLAND BOILED DINNER

4 pounds corned beef brisket
1 head cabbage
6 turnips
8 beets
6 carrots, sliced
6 onions, chopped
8 potatoes, diced

In a large saucepan with a lid, cover the meat with water and simmer for 3 hours. Cut the cabbage into eighths and the turnips into quarters and add to the meat. Cook the beets separately in boiling water. Add the remaining vegetables to the meat and cook until tender. Spoon the meat mixture onto a platter. Drain and slice the beets and serve with the meat and the other vegetables.

FAVORITES OF FOREST AVENUE CONGREGATIONAL CHURCH SUPPERS
FOREST AVENUE CONGREGATIONAL CHURCH
BANGOR, MAINE

St. Patrick's Day: Corned Beef and Cabbage

Menu

4:30: Veggies and dip, cheese and crackers, Brie with almonds and bread, wine or juice.

5:00: Corned beef and cabbage and root vegetables with 3 mustard choices and homemade bread. Oven-baked chicken for non-corned beef/cabbage lovers. Asparagus with hollandaise sauce (packet). Juices, lemon water, or milk. Apple Crisp with ice cream.

Morning Preparation:

Parsnips, rutabaga, turnips, carrots, and onions, peeled and kept in water
Green peppers, carrots, mushrooms, broccoli, radishes, grape tomatoes, etc.

Wash and cut up the vegetables for the corned beef and veggie tray.

Other:
Prepare the bread in the bread machine.
Clean and skin the chicken pieces.
Prepare the cheeses for the cheese and cracker tray.
Set up the coffee.
Set the table.
Chill the lemon water.

Corned Beef:

12:45: In a large saucepan, bring the corned beef and salt pork to a boil, then lower the heat and simmer.

4:00: Remove the corned beef and salt pork; add the vegetables, omitting the cabbage, and cook for 15 minutes.

4:15: Add the cabbage and cook for 15 to 20 minutes longer.

5:00 Feast

Other:

2:00: Prepare the Apple Crisp.

2:30 Start the chicken: coat and brown.

3:00: Bake the chicken at 300 degrees for 1 hour.

4:00: Remove the chicken and set the oven to 425 degrees. Bake the bread.

4:20: Put out the veggies and cheese tray. Reduce the oven to 300 degrees. Spread the bread with Brie and sprinkle with almond slivers; warm in the oven.

4:45: Prepare the hollandaise sauce, following the package directions. Sauté the asparagus in butter, then steam for 2 minutes. Turn on the coffee.

Denise Stinn
Prince of Peace Church
Grantsville, West Virginia

Beef Stew with Vegetables

2 pounds beef chuck, cut into 1-inch pieces
3 tablespoons vegetable oil
2 medium onions, cut into 3/4-inch pieces
1/4 cup all-purpose flour
3 cups boiling water
3 beef bouillon cubes
2 bay leaves
1/2 teaspoon dried thyme
2 (16-ounce) cans whole tomatoes, cut into
    bite-size pieces
Salt and pepper to taste
8 carrots, cut into 1/2-inch pieces
5 medium potatoes, cut into 1-inch chunks

In a large saucepan, sauté the meat in the oil until it turns light brown. Sprinkle the onions over the meat and mix well; sauté for 5 minutes longer, or until the meat is browned and the onions are translucent. Sprinkle the flour over the meat and mix well. Dissolve the bouillon in the boiling water. Add the broth, bay leaves, thyme, and tomatoes, stirring well. Season to taste with salt and pepper. Bring to a boil, then simmer slowly for 2 hours. Remove the bay leaves. (The recipe can be cooled and frozen at this point for later use.) Add the carrots and potatoes and simmer until the vegetables are tender. Makes 8 servings.

Note: If you are using the frozen stew base, cook the carrots and potatoes separately until tender and add to the heated stew base. Simmer for 10 minutes.

Jan Wickliffe
Cross in the Desert United Methodist Church
Phoenix, Arizona

Easy Beef Stew

2 pounds beef stew meat
4 carrots, sliced
4 medium potatoes, cubed
1 cup sliced celery
1 medium onion, cubed
1/2 teaspoon salt
1/8 teaspoon black pepper
1/2 teaspoon onion salt
1/2 teaspoon garlic salt, or a fresh garlic
    clove
1 bay leaf
1 tablespoon sugar
2 tablespoons instant tapioca
1/8 teaspoon allspice
2 cups tomato juice
Parsley (optional)
Sour cream (optional)

Preheat the oven to 250 degrees. In a large bowl, combine all the ingredients and mix well. Pour the mixture into a 3- or 4-quart casserole dish. Cover tightly with foil or a tight lid. Bake for 4 hours. Garnish with parsley and sour cream, if desired.

Note: The dish can also be prepared in a Crock-Pot set on high for 4 hours or on medium for 8 hours.

Laurie Petrey
Buckingham United Methodist Church
Garland, Texas

SHEPHERD'S PIE

1 pound ground beef
Salt, pepper, and garlic to taste
1 onion, chopped
1 (10 1/2-ounce) can cream of mushroom
    soup
1 (15 1/4-ounce) can corn, drained
1 (15-ounce) can beans, drained
Medium pan mashed potatoes with butter
Cheddar cheese to taste

Preheat the oven to 350 degrees. In a large saucepan, brown the beef with the salt, pepper, garlic, and onion. Drain the fat. Spread the mixture over the bottom of a 9 x 13-inch baking dish. Spread the soup over the meat. Add the corn and beans. Top with the mashed potatoes, spreading it across the dish so that it forms a seal for the ingredients underneath. Top with the cheese. Cover with aluminum foil and bake for approximately 45 minutes, removing the foil for the last 15 minutes or when the cheese is bubbly.

Note: This is a good dish to make ahead and keep in the fridge until you're ready to bake.

LARRY STINNETT
BUCKINGHAM UNITED METHODIST CHURCH
GARLAND, TEXAS

BEST EVER CHILI

4 tablespoons vegetable oil
2 pounds ground sirloin
2 small onions, chopped
4 garlic cloves, chopped
1 small green pepper, chopped
4 celery stalks, sliced
1 (16-ounce) can chopped tomatoes
1 (16-ounce) can kidney beans
1 (16-ounce) can tomato sauce
1 (8-ounce) can tomato sauce
1 teaspoon salt
2 bay leaves
1 teaspoon garlic powder
2 teaspoons chili powder
2 dashes hot sauce (optional)

In a large skillet, heat the oil and brown the meat with the onions and garlic. Add the green pepper, celery, tomatoes, beans, and tomato sauce. Stir in the remaining ingredients. Simmer for 5 hours, checking occasionally to make sure nothing is sticking to the bottom of the skillet. Adjust the seasonings, adding a little sugar if necessary.

JOHN DAWE
FIRST UNITED METHODIST CHURCH
BELLEVILLE, MICHIGAN

Home-Style Chili

1/4 cup olive oil
2 large onions, chopped
1 1/2 pounds lean ground beef
1 1/2 pounds ground pork
4 cups tomato juice
1 (28-ounce) can tomatoes in sauce
3 cups beef broth
1 1/2 teaspoons cayenne pepper (or less)
2 teaspoons salt
1/3 cup chili powder
8 garlic cloves, chopped
2 tablespoons dried oregano
3 tablespoons yellow cornmeal
2 tablespoons cinnamon
3 tablespoons unsweetened cocoa
Pinch of sugar
2 (15-ounce) cans kidney beans, drained
   and rinsed

In a large saucepan, heat the olive oil and sauté the onions and meat until the meat is browned. Add all of the remaining ingredients except the kidney beans. Heat thoroughly and simmer on low heat for about 3 hours, stirring often. Add the kidney beans and cook for 30 minutes longer.

JEAN O'BRIEN
UNITED BAPTIST CHURCH OF POULTNEY
EAST POULTNEY, VERMONT

Tamale Pie

2 tablespoons lard
1/2 cup chopped onion
1 pound ground beef
1 teaspoon salt
1 can whole-kernel corn
1 can tomatoes
1 teaspoon chili powder
1/2 cup cornmeal
1/2 cup all-purpose flour
1 tablespoon sugar
1 teaspoon baking powder
1 cup milk
1 egg

In a large skillet, heat the lard and brown the onion. Add the beef and brown well. Stir in 1/2 teaspoon of the salt, the corn, tomatoes, and chili powder. Cook for 15 minutes. Preheat the oven to 425 degrees. Pour the mixture into a baking dish. In a large bowl, combine the cornmeal, flour, sugar, baking powder, remaining salt, milk, and egg. Mix well. Pour this over the beef mixture. Bake for 25 to 30 minutes.

BETTY FUSSELL
HOLUM BAPTIST CHURCH
GRAYSON, LOUISIANA

CHIMICHANGAS

1/4 cup bacon grease
2 cups shredded cooked chicken, beef or pork
1 medium onion, diced
2 garlic cloves, minced
2 medium tomatoes, chopped
2 (4 ounce) cans green chilies, chopped
1 large peeled potato, boiled and diced
Salt to taste
1 1/2 teaspoons dried oregano
1 to 2 teaspoons chili powder (to taste)
2 tablespoons fresh cilantro
12 large tortilla shells, warmed
Vegetable oil

TOPPINGS:
Shredded Cheddar cheese
Sour cream
Salsa
Shredded lettuce
Chopped tomatoes
Sliced ripe olives

In a skillet, melt bacon grease over medium heat. Saute meat, onion, garlic, tomatoes, chilies, and potato until onion softens. Add salt, oregano, chili powder, and cilantro. Simmer 2 to 3 minutes.

Place a scant 1/2 cup meat filling on each tortilla. Fold envelope-style, like a burrito. Fry, seam side down, in 1/2 inch oil at 360 to 375 degrees until crispy and browned. Turn and brown other side. Drain briefly on paper towel.

Place on serving plate and top with your favorite toppings: shredded cheddar cheese, sour cream, salsa, shredded lettuce, chopped tomatoes, sliced ripe olives.

Serve immediately. Serves 12.

DOREEN VAN DIEST
CALVARY UNITED METHODIST CHURCH
TAYLOR, NEBRASKA

YANKEE RED-FLANNEL HASH

1 1/2 cups cooked corned beef, finely chopped
3 cups potatoes, finely chopped
1 1/2 cups cooked or canned beets, finely chopped
1/3 cup onion, finely chopped
1/3 cup milk
1 teaspoon salt
A few drops of Tabasco sauce
3–4 tablespoons fat

Lightly toss together corned beef, potatoes, beets, onion and milk. Season mixture to taste with salt and Tabasco sauce. Melt the fat in a large skillet and spread the meat mixture evenly over the bottom. Cook over medium heat until the underside is browned and crusty.

BEVERLY BLAIR
UNITED BAPTIST CHURCH OF POULTNEY
EAST POULTNEY, VERMONT

MEXICAN FRITTATA

2 pounds lean bulk sausage
8 eggs, beaten
2 tablespoons all-purpose flour
1/2 teaspoon garlic powder
1/2 teaspoon salt
1/2 teaspoon ground cumin
1 1/3 cups heavy cream or evaporated milk
1 (4-ounce) can diced green chilies, drained
1 cup grated Cheddar cheese
1 cup grated Swiss cheese

Preheat the oven to 350 degrees. In a large heavy skillet, sauté the sausage until browned. Pour off the grease and cool the sausage. In a large bowl, combine the remaining ingredients. Fold in the sausage and pour the mixture into a lightly greased 13 x 9-inch baking dish. Bake for 1 hour, or until the center is firm. Cut into squares to serve. Makes 10 to 12 servings.

GAMILIE ISRAEL
TRINITY UNITED METHODIST CHURCH
YORK, PENNSYLVANIA

SAUSAGE AND PEPPERS

1 pound (or more) sweet sausage
3 potatoes
1 red bell pepper
1 yellow bell pepper
1 green bell pepper
3 small onions
1 package dry onion soup mix
1 cup water

Spray a large skillet with cooking spray and brown the sausage. Drain the fat. Cut the potatoes, bell peppers, and onions into small pieces and add to the sausage. In a small bowl, mix the onion soup mix with the water. Pour over the sausage mixture. Bring to a boil. Cover and simmer for 30 minutes.

JANE WALTER LOUCKS
TRINITY UNITED METHODIST CHURCH
YORK, PENNSYLVANIA

Jambalaya

2 tablespoons vegetable oil
3/4 cup smoked ham, diced
1 smoked sausage, sliced 1/2-inch thick
1 pound boneless chicken, cubed
1 1/2 cups chopped onion
1 cup chopped celery
1 green pepper, chopped
2 garlic cloves, minced
2 bay leaves
1 1/2 teaspoons dried oregano
1 teaspoon dried thyme
1 1/2 teaspoons salt
1 teaspoon white pepper
1/2 teaspoon black pepper
1 (8-ounce) can tomato sauce
1 (14.5-ounce) can chicken broth
2 cups rice
4 medium potatoes, peeled and chopped

Preheat the oven to 350 degrees. In a large Dutch oven, heat the oil over medium heat. Stir in the ham, sausage, and chicken. Sauté until lightly browned, stirring frequently, 4 to 8 minutes. Stir in the onion, celery, and green pepper. Sauté until crisp-tender, about 5 minutes. Stir in the garlic, bay leaves, oregano, thyme, salt, pepper, and white pepper. Cook over medium heat, stirring constantly and scraping the pan, for 5 minutes. Add the tomato sauce and chicken broth. Bring to a boil. Stir in rice and potatoes. Cover. Bake for 20 to 25 minutes or until the rice is tender. Remove the bay leaves. Serve hot. Makes 10 servings.

DAWNA MASON JACOB
MEMORIAL BAPTIST CHURCH
TULSA, OKLAHOMA

Favorite Quick Supper

Measure 3 cups flour into a large bowl. Answer telephone. Take large bowl off baby's head; sweep the floor. Measure 3 more cups flour into bowl. Measure 1/4 cup shortening. Answer doorbell. Wash shortening from baby's face and head. Add 1/4 cup shortening to flour. Mix well, rock crying baby 10 minutes. Answer telephone. Put child in bathtub and scrub well. Scrape flour and shortening from floor. Mixing enough tears to relieve tension, open 1 can of beans and serve with remaining strength.

NELL HAMMETT
WELLINGTON VILLAGE ASSEMBLY OF GOD
LITTLE ROCK, ARKANSAS

June Meyer's Authentic Hungarian Sauerkraut and Pork (Szekely Gulyás)

Long ago, people had to lay away food to see them through the winter. Every house in the "old country" had a root cellar in which people stored their winter supply of onions, apples, squash, potatoes, carrots, parsley roots, and cabbage heads. In the fall you could smell the shredded cabbage fermenting in several large 30-gallon stoneware containers. I remember my father and mother bending over a wooden board that was made to shred cabbage heads. After the cabbage was shredded, it was packed in layers with salt and stored in large stoneware containers. It was hard work, but that sauerkraut was eaten with gusto and left you with a sense of well-being.

Sauerkraut was not only cheap and plentiful but full of vitamins that helped to ward off illness. It was a mainstay of Austrian-Hungarian winter cuisine. This dish is an unusual blend of sauerkraut, tomato, pork, onion, and sour cream, along with that ever present Hungarian sweet paprika.

Regards,

June Meyer

2 tablespoons oil or lard (if meat is very lean)
2 pounds pork, cubed
2 white onions, chopped
2 tablespoons Hungarian sweet paprika (no generic, please)
1 1/2 pounds sauerkraut, rinsed and drained
1 large can crushed tomatoes; or fresh tomatoes, peeled and crushed
1 tablespoon sugar
2 bay leaves
1 cup water
Salt and pepper to taste
1/2 pint sour cream

In a large saucepan with a lid, brown the meat and onions in the oil. Add the paprika to the meat and onion mixture; stir to mix, being careful not to burn. Stir in the drained sauerkraut, crushed tomatoes, sugar, bay leaves, water, and salt and pepper; mix. Cover the pot and cook slowly for about 1 hour, or until the meat is tender. Add the sour cream and stir. Makes 4 servings.

PRINCE OF PEACE CHURCH
GRANTSVILLE, WEST VIRGINIA

Szechwan Pork with Peppers

3 tablespoons hoisin sauce
1 tablespoon soy sauce
1 teaspoon sugar
1 tablespoon vegetable oil
4 garlic cloves, thinly sliced
2 cups red bell peppers, cut into 1-inch squares
2 cups green bell peppers, cut into 1-inch squares
12 ounces lean boneless pork, cut into bite-size strips
1 teaspoon ground ginger
2 cups hot cooked noodles or rice

In a small bowl, stir together the hoisin sauce, soy sauce, and sugar; set aside. Heat the oil in a wok or large skillet over medium-high heat. (Add more oil as necessary during cooking.) Stir-fry the garlic in the hot oil for 15 seconds. Add the bell peppers and ground ginger. Stir-fry for 3 to 4 minutes, or until crisp-tender. Remove the pepper mixture from the wok.

Add the pork to the hot wok. Stir-fry for 3 to 4 minutes, or until no pink remains; push the pork away from the center of the wok. Pour the sauce into the center of the wok. Cook, stirring until bubbly. Return the pepper mixture to the wok. Stir all the ingredients together until they are well coated with sauce. Cook and stir for 1 minute longer, or until heated through. Serve immediately over hot cooked noodles or rice. Makes 4 servings.

BARBARA SNYDER
CAVENDISH BAPTIST CHURCH
CAVENDISH, VERMONT

Party Ham Casserole

1 (4-ounce) package noodles
1 can cream of mushroom soup
1/2 cup milk
1 teaspoon instant minced onion
2 teaspoons mustard
1 cup sour cream
2 cups cooked ham, cut into 1-inch slivers
1/4 cup dry bread crumbs
1 1/2 tablespoons melted butter
1 tablespoon grated Parmesan cheese

Preheat the oven to 325 degrees. Cook the noodles according to the package directions. In a large bowl, combine the soup and milk. Add the onion, mustard, sour cream, and ham; blend well. Stir in the well-drained noodles. Pour the mixture into a greased 1 1/2-quart casserole dish. In a small bowl, combine the bread crumbs, butter, and cheese. Top the casserole with this mixture. Bake, uncovered, for 25 minutes. Makes 4 to 6 servings.

MEMORIAL BAPTIST CHURCH
TULSA, OKLAHOMA

HOPPIN JOHN

1 pound dried black-eyed peas
1 1/2 pounds smoked ham hocks
1 slice onion
1 whole cayenne pepper
1 teaspoon salt
1 cup cooked rice

Place all ingredients in a pot of water. Bring to a boil. Reduce heat. Cover and simmer for 1 1/2 hours until peas and meat are tender. Remove the pepper and ham hock. Cut the meat off the bone and add back into the pot. Add the cooked rice and heat for 5 minutes.

SISTER JOAN DUNBAR
MIRACLE DELIVERANCE HOLINESS CHURCH
COLUMBIA, SOUTH CAROLINA

7-BEAN CASSEROLE

1 pound ground beef, browned and drained
1 pound bacon, browned and drained
1 can red kidney beans
1 can butter beans
1 can navy beans
1 can great Northern beans
1 can chili beans
1 can pork and beans
1 can B&M baked beans
1/2 cup brown sugar
1 tablespoon dry mustard
1 tablespoon vinegar
1/2 cup ketchup

Preheat the oven to 200 degrees. In a large bowl, combine all the ingredients and pour into a baking dish. Bake for 1 1/2 hours. You can also combine the ingredients the night before and heat the casserole on the stove the next day, then transfer to a Crock-Pot and cook for 1 hour on low. Alternatively, combine the ingredients and cook in a Crock-Pot for 3 to 6 hours on low.

CHRISTY BROWN
ST. PAUL CHURCH
WATERFORD, CONNECTICUT

A Sad Recipe

I didn't have potatoes, so I substituted rice
I didn't have paprika, so I used another spice
I didn't have tomato sauce, so I used tomato paste
A whole can, not a half can, I don't believe in waste.
A friend gave me this recipe
She said you couldn't beat it.
There must be something wrong with her,
I couldn't even eat it.

ARLENE STROHL
CALVARY UNITED METHODIST CHURCH
TAYLOR, NEBRASKA

VEGETABLES

Come, Lord Jesus,
Be our guest
Let this food
To us be blest.

GRILLED ARTICHOKES

10 medium-sized artichokes (about 4 ounces each)
1/2 cup olive oil
4 garlic cloves, finely chopped
3 tablespoons finely chopped fresh parsley
Salt and pepper to taste
Juice of 1 lemon
1 teaspoon dried oregano

Preheat the grill for 15 minutes on medium low. Trim off the top inch of each artichoke. In a small bowl, whisk together the olive oil, garlic, parsley, and salt and pepper to taste. Spread the leaves of the artichoke apart with your fingers and pour the sauce over the top. Place the artichokes on the grill and cook, turning until the outside leaves are black, for about 45 minutes. Remove, drizzle with lemon juice mixed with oregano, and serve. Makes 10 servings.

Note: This recipe is a great mix of San Francisco and the influence of Old Sicily.

LINDA HART
NORTHBROOK UNITED METHODIST CHURCH
ROSWELL, GEORGIA

ARTICHOKE SQUARES

2 (6-ounce) jars marinated artichoke hearts
1 small onion, finely chopped
4 eggs
1/4 cup fine dry bread crumbs
1/4 teaspoon salt
1/8 teaspoon black pepper
2 tablespoons chopped fresh parsley
1/8 teaspoon dried oregano
1/8 teaspoon Tabasco sauce
2 cups grated Cheddar cheese

Preheat the oven to 325 degrees. Drain the artichokes, saving the marinade from 1 jar. In a small skillet, sauté the onion in the marinade; cut up the artichokes and add them to the skillet. In a large bowl, beat the eggs and add the bread crumbs and seasonings. Stir in the remaining ingredients and turn the mixture into a greased 7 x 11-inch pan. Bake for 30 minutes. Serve hot or cold.

LINDA JUERGENS
BUCKINGHAM UNITED METHODIST CHURCH
GARLAND, TEXAS

ROASTED ASPARAGUS

1 pound fresh asparagus
3 tablespoons butter
Parmesan cheese
Juice of 1 lemon

Preheat the oven to 500 degrees. Peel the bottoms of the asparagus spears. Immerse the asparagus in boiling water for 1 minute. Transfer the asparagus to a small baking pan and spread lightly with butter. Sprinkle with Parmesan cheese and roast for 8 minutes. Sprinkle with lemon juice and serve.

JOANNE BISHOP
ST. PAUL CHURCH
WATERFORD, CONNECTICUT

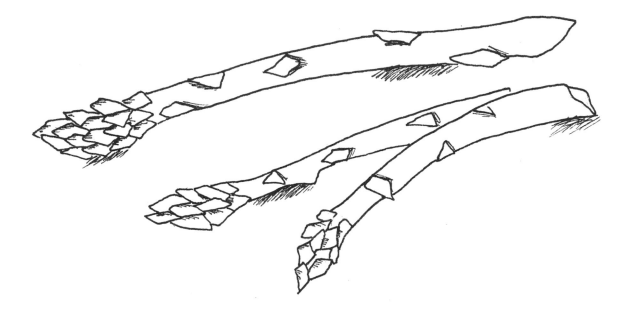

ASPARAGUS WITH MUSTARD SAUCE

1 pound fresh asparagus
3 tablespoons reduced-fat sour cream
2 tablespoons nonfat mayonnaise
1 teaspoon prepared mustard
1 teaspoon lemon juice
1/8 to 1/4 teaspoon hot sauce (optional)
Dash of paprika

Snap off the tough ends of the asparagus as close to the bottom as possible. Wash the asparagus, peeling the bottoms if the stalks are tough. Arrange the asparagus in a vegetable steamer over boiling water. Cover and steam for 6 to 8 minutes, or until crisp-tender. Transfer to a serving dish. Set aside and keep warm. In a small saucepan, combine the next 5 ingredients and cook over medium heat, stirring constantly. Let the mixture boil for 1 minute, stirring. Spoon over the asparagus and sprinkle with the paprika. Makes 4 servings.

CHARLOTTE SNYDER
CAVENDISH BAPTIST CHURCH
CAVENDISH , VERMONT

Vermont Maple Baked Beans

2 pounds yellow-eyed peas
1 cup maple syrup
1 tablespoon dry mustard
2 teaspoons ground ginger
1 teaspoon salt
1/4 teaspoon black pepper
1/2 pound ham or turkey ham, diced

Preheat the oven to 300 degrees. Soak the peas overnight in cold water. Rinse well, cover with cold water, and bring to a boil. Drain the peas and rinse well. Cover with fresh cold water, add the syrup and seasonings, and simmer until the peas are crisp-tender. Transfer to a baking dish and add the diced meat. Bake for 2 to 4 hours, adding more water if necessary to keep the peas moist.

RONNY WILLIAMS
UNITED BAPTIST CHURCH OF POULTNEY
EAST POULTNEY, VERMONT

Sweet-and-Sour Baked Beans

8 bacon slices, drained and crumbled
2 large onions, cut into rings
1/2 to 1 cup brown sugar
1 teaspoon dry mustard
1/2 teaspoon garlic powder
1 teaspoon salt
1/2 cup vinegar
1 can green beans, drained
1 (15-ounce) can green lima beans, drained
1 (15-ounce) can red kidney beans, drained
1 (15-ounce) can pork and beans, undrained

In a large skillet, cook the bacon and set it aside. Add the onions to the skillet, then the sugar, mustard, garlic powder, salt, and vinegar. Cook for 20 minutes, covered, on low heat. Add the next 4 ingredients to the onion mixture; add the crumbled bacon. Pour the mixture into a casserole dish or 9 x 13-pan and bake for 30 minutes. Serve hot or cold.

KATHRYN TOBIN
CROSS IN THE DESERT UNITED METHODIST CHURCH
PHOENIX, ARIZONA

Dad's Favorite Baked Beans

2 pounds dried great Northern beans
1 cup dark brown sugar, firmly packed
1/2 cup granulated sugar
1 tablespoon dry mustard
3/4 cup molasses
3 medium onions, chopped
3/4 cup ketchup
2 tablespoons cider vinegar
1 teaspoon salt
1/4 pound sliced bacon, cut into 1-inch
  squares
1/4 cup rum (optional)

Wash and pick over the beans. Place in a large bowl and cover with 2 inches of water. Let soak overnight. Or use the quick-cooking method: Place the beans in a large deep pot, add enough water to cover by 2 inches, and bring to a boil. Boil for 2 minutes, remove from the heat and let stand for 1 hour.

Drain the beans and place in a large pot. Add water to cover the beans by 2 inches and bring to a boil. Simmer, covered, for 1 to 1 1/2 hours until tender; add more water if necessary. Drain. Preheat the oven to 300 degrees. In a 4-quart casserole dish, combine the sugars, mustard, molasses, onions, ketchup, vinegar, and salt. Stir in the beans. Cook the bacon in a skillet until partially done; drain on paper towels. Stir into the beans. Cover and bake for 2 hours. Stir in the rum, if desired. Bake, uncovered, for 1 hour.

Note: I frequently substitute dried baby lima beans for the great Northern beans.

MARGARET SMITH
TRINITY UNITED METHODIST CHURCH
YORK, PENNSYLVANIA

Bacony Green Beans

3 lean slices bacon, diced
1/2 pound fresh string beans
Salt and freshly ground black pepper
1 tablespoon olive oil
1/4 cup chopped onion
3 garlic cloves

In a medium skillet, cook the bacon until crisp; drain on paper towels, reserving the pan drippings. Cut the beans into thirds and steam to cook. Pour the bacon drippings into a medium saucepan and add the beans, and salt and pepper; cook just until crisp-tender. In a clean skillet, heat the olive oil; add the onion and garlic and sauté until limp. Add the bacon and green beans and toss to coat evenly. Sauté until warmed through.

PINEMOUNT BAPTIST CHURCH
MCALPIN, FLORIDA

Green Beans Caesar

1 1/2 pounds fresh green beans, or 2 (16-
  ounce) cans
2 tablespoons vegetable oil
1 tablespoon vinegar
1/4 teaspoon salt
1/8 teaspoon black pepper
1 tablespoon butter or margarine, melted
1/2 small onion, sliced
1 garlic clove, crushed
2 tablespoons dry bread crumbs
2 tablespoons grated Parmesan cheese
Paprika to taste

Preheat the oven to 350 degrees. If you're using fresh beans, steam until tender. In a large bowl, combine oil, vinegar, salt, and pepper and toss the beans in the mixture. In a medium skillet, melt the butter and add the onion and garlic; cook until tender. Add the bread crumbs and cheese to the butter mixture; sprinkle over the green beans, adding the paprika (if desired). Pour the beans into a casserole dish and bake, uncovered, until heated through, 15 to 20 minutes.

FRANCIS SILVESTRI
ST. PAUL CHURCH
WATERFORD, CONNECTICUT

Szechuan Green Beans

1 pound green beans
1 tablespoon sesame oil
2 garlic cloves, minced
2 tablespoons chopped sweet onion
1 tablespoon minced ginger
2 tablespoons soy sauce
Salt and pepper to taste
Crispy rice noodles

Steam the green beans until crisp-tender. In a large skillet, heat the sesame oil and sauté the garlic, onion, and ginger for 2 to 3 minutes. Add the green beans, soy sauce, and salt and pepper. Cook for 2 to 3 minutes longer. Remove from the heat and sprinkle with the rice noodles.

DORRIS
FOREST AVENUE CONGREGATIONAL CHURCH
BANGOR, MAINE

Baked Lima Beans

1 pound dried lima beans
1 cup brown sugar
1/2 cup molasses
1 cup ketchup
Salt and pepper to taste
1 onion, chopped
1 tablespoon Worcestershire sauce
3 teaspoons sugar
1 teaspoon mustard
1/2 pound bacon

Wash the beans. In a large saucepan, cover the beans with salt water and cook slowly for 45 minutes. Drain and cover with hot water. Cook for another 45 minutes. (This method helps to keep the beans from popping their skins.) Preheat the oven to 350 degrees. In a large bowl, combine the remaining ingredients, omitting the bacon, and add cooked beans. Pour the mixture into a large casserole dish. Lay strips of bacon on top. Bake for at least 1 hour, until the bacon is browned and the beans are bubbly.

RUTH REED
TRINITY PRESBYTERIAN CHURCH
WILMINGTON, DELAWARE

Harvard Beets

1/2 cup sugar
1/2 tablespoon cornstarch
1/4 cup water
1/4 cup vinegar
1/8 teaspoon ground cloves
1/2 teaspoon grated orange rind, or orange extract
12 small beets, cubed
2 tablespoons butter or margarine

In a saucepan, combine the sugar and cornstarch. Add the water, vinegar, and flavorings. Bring to a boil and cook for 5 minutes. Add the beets, stir, remove from the heat, and let stand for 30 minutes. Add the butter before serving.

MARION HUGHES
UNITED BAPTIST CHURCH OF POULTNEY
EAST POULTNEY, VERMONT

BEETS WITH ORANGE SAUCE

1/3 cup sugar
3/4 teaspoon salt
2 tablespoons cornstarch
3/4 cup orange juice
1 tablespoon butter or margarine
3 cups cooked beets
2 tablespoons lemon juice

In a large saucepan, combine the sugar, salt, and cornstarch. Add the orange juice. Cook until thickened, stirring constantly. Remove from the heat. Add the butter and lemon juice. Add the beets and reheat.

MARGE MARTNER
UNITED METHODIST CHURCH
ESTÂNCIA, NEW MEXICO

PICKLED BEETS

3/4 cup sugar
3/4 cup vinegar
3/4 cup water
1 1/2 teaspoons salt
3/4 to 1 teaspoon pepper
1 large onion, thinly sliced
2 cans sliced beets (undrained)
sliced scallions (optional)

In a saucepan, combine the sugar, vinegar, water, salt, pepper and onion; bring to a boil. Reduce the heat; cover and simmer for 5 minutes. Remove from the heat; add the beets. Let stand at room temperature for 1 hour. Cover and chill 6 hours or overnight. Garnish with scallions if desired.

JOY STEWART
MEMORIAL BAPTIST CHURCH
TULSA, OKLAHOMA

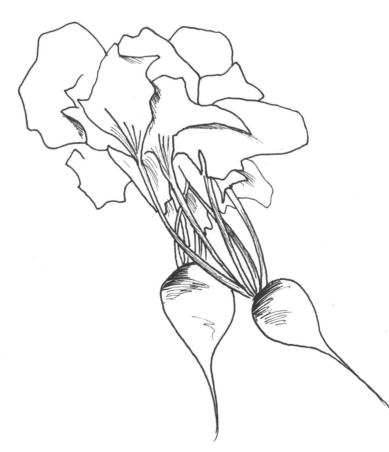

Sesame-Broccoli Stir-Fry

2 teaspoons tamari sauce
1 teaspoon sweet soy sauce or brown sugar
3 tablespoons cornstarch
1 cup water
2 teaspoons to 1 tablespoon sesame oil
4 to 6 garlic cloves, crushed
8 cups broccoli florets
1/2 cup chopped mushrooms (optional)
Black pepper
Sesame seeds
Cooked white or brown rice

In a small bowl, combine the first 4 ingredients. Blend until there are no lumps. Heat a large skillet or wok over medium-high heat. Add the sesame oil and heat for 15 seconds. Add the garlic to the hot oil and sauté for about 30 seconds. Add the broccoli, stirring to coat with oil and garlic. Add the mushrooms, if desired. Cover and let cook for 2 to 3 minutes, adding a little water, if necessary, to keep the broccoli from sticking. Add the tamari-cornstarch mixture and stir until thickened, about 30 seconds. Serve over rice and sprinkle with black pepper and sesame seeds. Makes 4 servings.

CHARLOTTE SNYDER
TRINITY PRESBYTERIAN CHURCH
WILMINGTON, DELAWARE

Broccoli Casserole

Butter for greasing casserole dish
2 (10-ounce) packages frozen broccoli
2 (10-ounce) cans cream of mushroom soup
2 cups shredded sharp cheese
1 (2-ounce) package slivered almonds (optional)
1 individual roll Ritz crackers, crushed into crumbs
1/4 cup margarine, melted

Preheat the oven to 350 degrees. Butter a 10 1/2-quart casserole dish and set aside. In a medium saucepan, over medium-high heat, boil the broccoli in water to cover for 4 to 5 minutes. Drain and pat dry. Place half the broccoli on the bottom of the prepared casserole dish. Top with 1 can of the soup, a third of the cheese and half of the almonds. Repeat layers of broccoli, the other can of soup, another third of the cheese and the remaining almonds. Cover with cracker crumbs. Drizzle margarine over the casserole and top with the remaining cheese. Place in the oven and bake until the cheese melts and the top bubbles, about 25 minutes.

GEORGIA HECKLER
NORTHBROOK UNITED METHODIST CHURCH
ROSWELL, GEORGIA

Lemon Broccoli Risotto

2 teaspoons olive oil
1 small onion, chopped
2 garlic cloves, minced
3 tablespoons lemon juice
2 teaspoons finely grated lemon zest
1 cup uncooked Arborio rice
2 1/2 cups vegetable stock or broth
2 cups broccoli florets
1 cup peas
1/3 cup grated Romano cheese
1/4 cup chopped fresh flat-leaf parsley
1/4 teaspoon ground black pepper

In a large nonstick skillet over medium heat, heat the olive oil. Add the onion and garlic and sauté until the onion is tender, about 2 minutes. Add the lemon juice, lemon zest, and rice and sauté, stirring frequently, until the rice is golden, about 2 minutes.

Add 1/2 cup vegetable stock; reduce the heat to low and simmer until the liquid is absorbed, about 5 minutes. Continue adding stock or broth 1/2 cup at a time, stirring constantly and waiting until each addition is absorbed before adding the next, about 5 minutes. With the last 1/2 cup of stock, add the broccoli and peas. Cook until the liquid is absorbed and the vegetables are tender, about 5 minutes. Remove from the heat; add the cheese, parsley, and pepper and stir until the cheese melts. Makes 4 servings.

CHARLOTTE SNYDER
TRINITY PRESBYTERIAN CHURCH
WILMINGTON, DELAWARE

Brussels Sprouts Toss

2 (10-ounce) packages frozen brussels
    sprouts, thawed
1 (16-ounce) package frozen pearl onions,
    thawed
1 medium butternut squash, peeled, seeded,
    and cut into 1 1/2-inch pieces
1 tablespoon olive oil
1 tablespoon chopped fresh marjoram, or 1
    teaspoon dried
Salt and pepper to taste

Preheat the oven to 400 degrees. Drain the brussels sprouts and onions on paper towels. In a bowl, toss together the butternut squash, olive oil, and marjoram to coat; season with salt and pepper. Spread on a baking sheet coated with cooking spray. Roast for 10 minutes on low heat. Add the brussels sprouts and onions. Toss well. Roast for 15 minutes longer, or until caramelized. Makes 8 servings.

LINDA COUTURE
NORTH MONROE STREET CHURCH OF GOD
MONROE, MICHIGAN

Country Cabbage

3 tablespoons butter
2 onions, chopped
1 cabbage, cut into wedges
2 tomatoes, chopped, or 1 can diced tomatoes
Salt and pepper to taste

Melt the butter in a large skillet and sauté the onions until tender. Add the cabbage and tomatoes and season with salt and pepper. Cover and cook over low heat for 20 to 30 minutes, or until the cabbage is tender. Makes 6 to 8 servings.

Cleo Williams
Memorial Baptist Church
Tulsa, Oklahoma

Red Cabbage

5 bacon slices, diced
1 medium onion, chopped
3 tablespoons sugar
6 to 8 cups red cabbage
1 apple, peeled and chopped
1/2 cup vinegar
1/2 cup water
5 peppercorns
4 whole cloves
1 teaspoon salt
1 bay leaf

In a large skillet, brown the bacon with the onion until the onion is soft. Stir in the sugar and cook for 1 minute. Add the cabbage, apple, and vinegar. Cook for 10 minutes, stirring occasionally. Add the water, peppercorns, cloves, salt, and bay leaf. Cover and simmer for 1 1/2 hours. Makes 6 to 8 servings.

Luanne Genga
First United Methodist Church
Belleville, Michigan

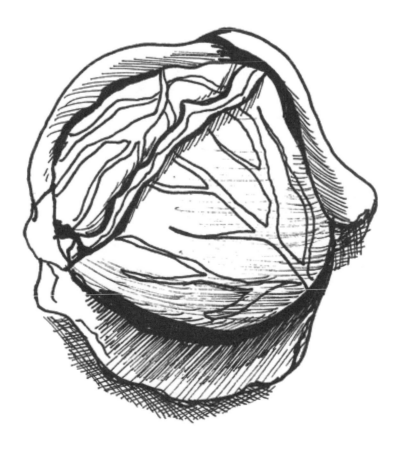

Carrots Almondine

1 pound carrots, peeled and thinly sliced
1/4 cup golden raisins
1/4 cup margarine
3 tablespoons honey
1 tablespoon lemon juice
1/4 teaspoon ground ginger
1/4 cup slivered or sliced almonds

Preheat the oven to 375 degrees. In a large saucepan, cook the carrots in a small amount of water for about 10 minutes. Drain. Spoon into a 1 1/2-quart baking dish and stir in the remaining ingredients. Bake for 35 to 45 minutes. Do not cover.

Joan H. Murray
Pitt Community Church
Baudette, Minnesota

Scalloped Carrots

4 cups sliced carrots
1 tablespoon butter
1 medium onion, chopped
1 can condensed cream of celery soup
1/8 teaspoon pepper
1/2 cup grated Cheddar cheese
3 cups herbed bread stuffing
1/3 cup melted margarine

Preheat the oven to 350 degrees. In a small saucepan, cover the carrots with water and cook until done; drain. In a large saucepan, melt the butter and cook the onion until soft. Stir in the soup, pepper, cheese, and carrots. Pour into a greased casserole dish. Toss the bread stuffing with the 1/3 cup margarine. Spoon the mixture over the carrots. Bake until thoroughly heated, about 20 minutes. Makes 6 servings.

Helen Spring
Trinity United Methodist Church
York, Pennsylvania

Carrots in Orange Sauce

1/4 cup chopped onion
1/3 cup butter
5 cups cooked carrots
4 teaspoons cornstarch
1 teaspoon salt
1 1/2 cups orange juice
2 tablespoons lemon juice
2 tablespoons sugar
2 tablespoons chopped fresh parsley

In a large skillet, melt the butter and sauté the onion until soft but not browned. Stir in the cornstarch and salt, then the orange juice. Heat to boiling, stirring constantly. Cook until the mixture becomes clear and thickens slightly. Stir in the lemon juice, sugar, and parsley. Pour over the drained carrots and mix lightly.

FREDA B. ZAHN
TRINITY UNITED METHODIST CHURCH
YORK, PENNSYLVANIA

Carrot Souffle

2 cups mashed cooked carrots
1/2 cup butter, softened
1 cup brown sugar
3 eggs
1 tablespoon all-purpose flour
1 teaspoon baking powder
1 cup milk
1/4 teaspoon cinnamon

Preheat the oven to 350 degrees. In a large bowl, combine the carrots, butter, sugar, eggs, flour, baking powder, milk, and cinnamon and mix well. Spoon into a 2-quart baking dish. Bake for 45 minutes. Makes about 8 servings.

Note: This is the only way I can get my husband and son to eat carrots.

JUSTINE MCDONALD
NORTHBROOK UNITED
METHODIST CHURCH
ROSWELL, GEORGIA

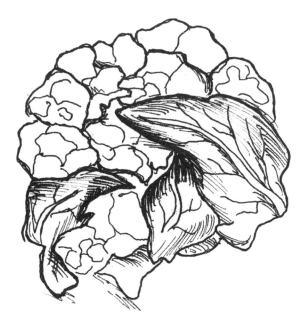

Cauliflower au Gratin

1 tablespoon butter
1 tablespoon all-purpose flour
1 cup milk
1/2 cup diced American cheese
Salt and pepper to taste
4 cups cauliflorets

Preheat the oven to 350 degrees. In a large skillet, melt the butter. Blend the flour into the milk and add the mixture to butter; cook over low heat until slightly thickened. Add the cheese and cook until the mixture is well blended. Season with salt and pepper. Place the cauliflower in a greased baking dish and cover with the cheese mixture. Bake for 20 minutes. Makes 8 servings.

Gussie Onsurez
Buckingham United Methodist Church
Garland, Texas

Celery Roast

1 cup bread crumbs (9 pieces of toast)
1/2 cup tomato soup
3/4 cup chopped walnuts
1 cup chopped celery
1 tablespoon butter or margarine
2 eggs, well beaten
2 tablespoons grated onion
1 package beef broth

Preheat the oven to 350 degrees. In a large bowl, combine all the ingredients and mix well. Pour the mixture into an oiled loaf pan or casserole dish and bake for 35 to 40 minutes.

Mrs. Lavonna Heide
Mosca United Methodist Church
Mosca, Colorado

COAT OF MANY COLLARDS

4 pounds collard greens, well rinsed with
  stems removed
4 tablespoons olive oil
6 garlic cloves, sliced
1 meaty ham bone
1 cup defatted chicken broth
Freshly ground black pepper to taste
Salt, if desired

Stack the collard greens in piles and roll them up from stem to tip. Cut the rolls crosswise into 1-inch strips and set aside. Heat the oil in a large, heavy saucepan over low heat. Add the garlic and cook, stirring, until it begins to color slightly, about 5 minutes. Add the collard greens and raise the heat to medium high, tossing lightly until they wilt, about 5 minutes. Add the ham bone and chicken broth. Stir, reduce the heat to medium, and cook until the greens are very tender. Remove the ham bone and set aside. Season with salt and pepper. When the ham bone cools, shred any meat from the bone and add it to the greens.

PINEMOUNT BAPTIST CHURCH
McALPIN, FLORIDA

IOWA CORN CASSEROLE

1 pound bacon, diced
2 cups bread crumbs
1/4 cup minced onion
1/2 cup chopped green pepper
2 (16.5-ounce) cans cream-style corn

Preheat the oven to 350 degrees. In a skillet, fry the bacon until lightly browned. Remove and set aside. Pour 1/8 to 1/4 cup of bacon drippings over the bread crumbs; set aside. Discard all but 2 tablespoons of the remaining drippings and sauté the onions and green pepper until tender. Stir in the corn and bacon. Spoon the mixture into a 1-quart casserole dish and sprinkle with the bread crumbs. Bake for 20 to 25 minutes, or until bubbly. Makes 6 to 8 servings.

ST. JAMES CATHOLIC CHURCH
CAMP DOUGLAS, WISCONSIN

FAVORITE CORN CASSEROLE

1 (15 1/4-ounce) can whole-kernel corn
1 (14 3/4-ounce) can cream-style corn
1/2 cup chopped onion
1 egg, beaten
1 cup cracker crumbs
1/2 cup chopped green pepper
1/3 cup milk
2 tablespoons sugar
1/4 cup margarine, melted
1 small jar pimientos, chopped
1 cup grated cheese

Preheat the oven to 350 degrees. Drain whole-kernel corn. In a large bowl, combine all the ingredients except the cheese and mix well. Pour into a casserole dish or loaf pan and bake for 45 to 60 minutes. Sprinkle the cheese on top and continue baking until the cheese melts and the top is slightly browned.

AMY COCHRAN
OAKMONT CHURCH OF GOD
SHREVEPORT, LOUISIANA

JALAPEÑO CORN CASSEROLE

1 can creamed corn
1 can whole-kernel corn
1/2 cup cornmeal
1 egg, beaten
1 stick butter, melted
1/2 cup sugar
2 garlic cloves, or garlic salt or powder
1 onion, finely chopped
1 to 4 jalapeño peppers, finely chopped

Preheat the oven to 350 degrees. In a large bowl, combine all the ingredients and mix well. Pour the mixture into a casserole dish and bake until set and slightly browned on top.

MACKEY CASSELS
HOLUM BAPTIST CHURCH
GRAYSON, LOUISIANA

Eggplant Tomato Casserole

1 large eggplant
1 1/2 teaspoons salt
2 eggs, beaten
2 tablespoons melted butter
Freshly ground black pepper
2 to 3 tablespoons chopped onion
1/2 teaspoon dried oregano
1 teaspoon dried basil
1/2 cup dry bread crumbs
2 large tomatoes, thinly sliced
2 ounces Cheddar cheese, grated
1/4 cup grated Parmesan cheese
Paprika

Preheat the oven to 375 degrees. Peel and slice the eggplant. Place the slices in a saucepan with the salt and 2 to 3 inches of boiling water; cover tightly. Cook for about 10 minutes and drain, removing all the water by mashing the eggplant. In a large bowl, combine the eggplant, eggs, butter, pepper, onion, oregano, basil, and bread crumbs. Butter a shallow 1 1/2-quart baking dish and cover the bottom with half the tomato slices. Spoon in all the eggplant mixture and spread evenly over the tomatoes. Arrange the rest of the tomato slices on top. In a separate bowl, combine the cheeses and sprinkle over the top layer of tomatoes. Add a sprinkle of paprika and bake for about 45 minutes. Makes 6 servings.

Note: I always look forward to picking ripe tomatoes from our summer garden for this dish.

MARY HANEY
NORTHBROOK UNITED METHODIST CHURCH
ROSWELL, GEORGIA

Garlic-Butter Mushrooms

2 dozen large mushrooms
1/2 cup butter, melted
2 garlic cloves, minced
2 shallots, minced
1/2 cup minced parsley
Juice of 1/2 lemon
1/2 teaspoon salt
1/4 teaspoon black pepper

Preheat the oven to 400 degrees. Clean the mushrooms, removing the stems. In a blender or food processor, combine the butter, garlic, shallots, and parsley. Blend. Add the lemon juice, salt, and pepper and blend briefly again. Place the mushrooms cap side up in a shallow baking dish. Fill each mushroom with a dollop of the garlic-butter mixture (about 1/2 to 1 teaspoon each). Bake for 10 to 12 minutes.

PINEMOUNT BAPTIST CHURCH
MCALPIN, FLORIDA

STUFFED MUSHROOMS

1 pound large fresh mushrooms
3/4 cup finely ground Italian seasoned
    bread crumbs
1/4 to 1/2 cup grated Parmesan or Romano
    cheese
Handful of finely chopped fresh parsley
Olive oil

Preheat the oven to 350 degrees. Clean the mushrooms, remove the stems, and place the mushroom cap cut side up in a baking dish. Chop the stems up fine and combine with the bread crumbs, cheese, and parsley. Fill each mushroom with the mixture and drizzle a drop or two of oil over each one. Add about 1/8 inch water to the bottom of the baking dish and cover with foil. Bake for about 25 minutes.

SUE CLAIRE CALLESIS
UNITED BAPTIST CHURCH OF POULTNEY
EAST POULTNEY, VERMONT

FRESH OKRA AND TOMATOES

2 tablespoons margarine
1 garlic clove, minced
1/2 cup chopped onion
1/2 cup chopped green pepper
3 cups sliced okra
1/4 teaspoon oregano
1/2 teaspoon black pepper
4 cups chopped tomatoes
1/4 cup tasso ham
1/2 teaspoon salt

In a large saucepan, melt the margarine and sauté the garlic, onion, and green pepper for about 10 minutes, or until tender. Add the remaining ingredients and cook for about 20 minutes, stirring often. Makes 6 to 8 servings.

MICHELLE FONTENOT
HOLUM BAPTIST CHURCH
GRAYSON, LOUISIANA

GRILLED VIDALIA ONIONS

4 large Vidalia onions
4 tablespoons butter
4 beef bouillon cubes
Salt and pepper to taste

Peel the onions, wash, and core. Place 1 tablespoon butter and 1 beef bouillon cube in the center of each onion and sprinkle with salt and pepper. Wrap each onion in a double thickness of heavy-duty aluminum foil. Cook on the grill for about 45 minutes or in the oven at 350 degrees for 45 minutes. To cook the onions in the microwave, wrap them in waxed paper and cook on high for 20 minutes.

ZAIDEE CLARK
NORTHBROOK UNITED METHODIST CHURCH
ROSWELL, GEORGIA

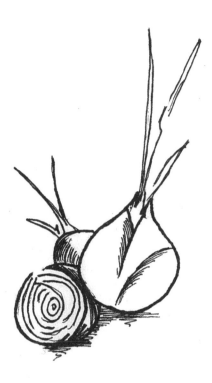

DIANNE'S VIDALIA ONION GRATIN

1 stick butter, divided
4 cups chopped Vidalia onions
4 large potatoes, cut into bite-size pieces
2 tablespoons self-rising flour
1 cup evaporated milk
1/2 cup sour cream
3/4 cup shredded Cheddar cheese
3/4 cup Parmesan cheese
1 1/2 teaspoons salt
1/2 teaspoon black pepper

In a saucepan over medium heat, melt half of the butter and add the onions. Cook until the onions are very soft but not browned. Meanwhile, boil the potatoes until tender. Drain and pour into a greased casserole dish. Preheat the oven to 350 degrees. Add the flour to the onions and stir until the mixture is well blended and starts bubbling. Remove from the heat. Add the milk, sour cream, the cheeses, salt, and pepper. Stir until well mixed and pour over the potatoes. Dot the top with the remaining butter and bake, uncovered, for 35 to 40 minutes, or until golden brown on top.

PINEMOUNT BAPTIST CHURCH
McALPIN, FLORIDA

ONION RINGS

2 large onions
1 cup thick buttermilk
1 teaspoon salt
Dash of pepper
1/2 cup all-purpose flour
Vegetable oil, for frying

Peel and slice the onions, separating the rings. In a small bowl, combine the next 4 ingredients and stir to make a batter. Dip the onion rings into the batter and, using a heavy skillet, deep-fry in hot oil.

KITTY SOLOMON
UNITED METHODIST CHURCH
ESTÂNCIA, NEW MEXICO

CAJUN BLACK-EYED PEAS

1 pound dried black-eyed peas
8 cups water
6 bacon slices
1 bunch scallions
1 large onion
1 green pepper
1 cup chopped fresh parsley
1 small jalapeño pepper, seeded and minced
3 garlic cloves, crushed
2 tablespoons Worcestershire sauce
1/4 teaspoon hot sauce
1 1/2 teaspoons salt
1 teaspoon pepper
1/4 teaspoon dried oregano
1/4 teaspoon dried thyme
1 pound smoked sausage, sliced
1 1/2 cups chopped smoked ham
1 (14 1/2-ounce) can Cajun-style tomatoes
   (undrained)

Place the peas in a large Dutch oven and add water to a depth of 2 inches above the peas. Cover and let stand for 8 hours or overnight. Drain the peas and return them to the Dutch oven. Add the water and bring to a boil. Cover, reduce the heat, and simmer for 30 minutes. Add the bacon and the next 12 ingredients. Return to a boil, cover, reduce the heat, and simmer for 30 minutes or until the peas are tender. Add the sausage, ham, and tomatoes. Return to a boil. Cover, reduce the heat, and simmer for 30 minutes. Remove the bacon, if desired.

BETTY FUSSELL
HOLUM BAPTIST CHURCH
GRAYSON, LOUISIANA

STUFFED GREEN PEPPERS

5 large or 6 medium bell peppers
1 1/2 pounds ground beef
1 small onion, chopped
1 1/2 cups cooked rice
1 teaspoon dried oregano
1 teaspoon garlic powder
1 egg
2 tablespoons grated Parmesan cheese
Salt and pepper to taste
1 quart spaghetti sauce

Preheat the oven to 350 degrees. Slice the tops off the peppers, seed, and rinse. Steam the peppers for about 5 minutes, or until they're a little soft. In a large bowl, combine the beef with the next 7 ingredients and mix well. Stuff the peppers, place them in a baking dish, and pour the spaghetti sauce over this. Bake for 45 minutes. Alternatively, you may cut the peppers in half, lay them in a baking dish, and fill with the beef mixture. During the last 5 minutes of baking, sprinkle with shredded mozzarella cheese and serve with a green salad and garlic bread.

PINEMOUNT BAPTIST CHURCH
MCALPIN, FLORIDA

CORNBREAD-STUFFED BELL PEPPERS

1 pound ground beef
2 tablespoons bacon drippings or margarine
1 medium onion, chopped
1/2 cup chopped scallions
1 rib celery stalk, chopped
1 teaspoon salt
1/2 teaspoon black pepper
3 cups cornbread, crumbled
1/2 cup grated Cheddar cheese (optional)
6 medium blanched bell peppers
1 egg, beaten
1 small can tomato sauce
1 sauce can water

Brown the meat in the bacon drippings. Add the onion, scallions, celery, salt, and pepper. Cook until done. Remove from the heat. Add the crumbled cornbread and cheese. Stir in the egg. Mix well. Fill the peppers with the stuffing. Place in a baking dish. Combine the tomato sauce and water and pour the mixture over the stuffed peppers. Bake, covered, until the peppers are done (about 1 hour covered and 15 minutes uncovered to brown).

HORTENSE COURTNEY
HOLUM BAPTIST CHURCH
GRAYSON, LOUISIANA

CHEESY NEW POTATOES

12 new potatoes, unpeeled and diced
Salt and pepper
16 bacon slices, fried crisp and crumbled
1/2 cup melted butter
3 scallions, chopped
2 cups grated Old English cheese

Boil the unpeeled diced potatoes until just tender. Drain and season with salt and pepper. Layer half of the potatoes, half of the bacon, half of the butter, half of the onions, and half of the cheese in a large casserole dish. Repeat layering with the remaining half of the ingredients. Cover and bake for 20 to 30 minutes at 350 degrees.

VERNA ACKERMAN
BUCKINGHAM UNITED METHODIST CHURCH
GARLAND, TEXAS

HASH BROWN CASSEROLE

30 ounces frozen country-style hash browns
2 cups shredded Cheddar cheese
1 stick butter or margarine
1 pint sour cream
1/2 cup chopped onion
1 teaspoon salt
1/4 teaspoon black pepper

Preheat the oven to 350 degrees. In a skillet, melt the butter over low heat. Add the cheese until melted. Remove from the heat. In a large bowl, combine the sour cream, onion, salt, and pepper. Add the butter and cheese mixture, then add the frozen hash browns. Spread the mixture in a large casserole dish. Dot the top with butter and bake for 30 minutes.

KAREN SCHUMAN
CROSS IN THE DESERT UNITED METHODIST CHURCH
PHOENIX, ARIZONA

GARLIC MASHED POTATOES

1 pound (about 2 large) potatoes, peeled and
  quartered
2 large garlic cloves, chopped
2 cups skim milk
1/2 teaspoon white pepper

Cook the potatoes, covered, in a small amount of boiling water for 20 to 25 minutes, or until tender. Remove from the heat. Drain and cover. In a small saucepan over low heat, cook the garlic in the milk until the garlic is soft, about 30 minutes. Add the milk-garlic mixture and white pepper to the potatoes. Beat with an electric mixer on low speed or mash with a potato masher until smooth.

Microwave directions: Scrub the potatoes, pat dry, and prick with a fork. Place the potatoes on a plate and cook, uncovered, on high until tender, about 12 minutes, turning the potatoes over once. Let stand for 5 minutes. Peel and quarter. Meanwhile, in a 4-cup glass measuring cup combine the milk and garlic. Cook, uncovered, on medium until the garlic is soft, about 4 minutes. Continue as directed.

EVELYN WOLFE
OAKMONT CHURCH OF GOD
SHREVEPORT, LOUISIANA

PARMESAN MASHED POTATOES

3 to 4 pounds red potatoes, washed and
  quartered
3 garlic cloves, minced
1/2 cup grated Parmesan cheese
1/4 cup butter
1/4 cup cream
Salt and pepper to taste

Cook the potatoes in salted water until tender. Drain. Add the garlic, cheese, butter, cream and salt and pepper. Mash the potatoes until smooth.

SOUTHERN GENTLEMAN, REX
FOREST AVENUE CONGREGATIONAL CHURCH
BANGOR, MAINE

PARMESAN POTATO STICKS

2 pounds potatoes
1/2 cup fine bread crumbs
1/2 cup Parmesan cheese
1/2 teaspoon salt
1/8 teaspoon garlic powder
1/8 teaspoon black pepper
1/2 cup margarine, melted

Preheat the oven to 400 degrees. Peel the potatoes, cut lengthwise into quarters, and cut each quarter into three strips. In a large bowl, combine the bread crumbs, cheese, and seasonings. Roll the potatoes in the margarine, then in the bread crumb mixture. Place in a single layer in a shallow dish. Pour any remaining margarine over the potatoes and bake for 30 to 35 minutes, or until the potatoes are tender.

MARION HUGHES
BUCKINGHAM UNITED METHODIST CHURCH
GARLAND, TEXAS

SCALLOPED POTATOES

1/2 cup finely chopped onion
2 tablespoons all-purpose flour
1 teaspoon salt
1/4 teaspoon black pepper
4 cups pared, thinly sliced potatoes
2 tablespoons butter or margarine, divided
2 cups milk
Paprika

Preheat the oven to 325 degrees. In a small bowl, combine the onion, flour, salt, and pepper. Spread half of the potatoes in the bottom of a greased 2-quart baking dish. Sprinkle with half the flour mixture and dot with 1 tablespoon of the butter. Repeat with the other half of the potatoes and the remaining flour mixture, dotting with the rest of the butter. Pour the milk over the potatoes and sprinkle with the paprika. Bake, covered, for 45 minutes. Uncover the dish and bake for 30 minutes longer, or until the potatoes are tender. Makes 6 to 8 servings.

MARGARET BRIDGEWATER/MAY SEITZ
CROSS IN THE DESERT UNITED METHODIST CHURCH
PHOENIX, ARIZONA

Parmesan Scalloped Potatoes

3/4 cup freshly grated Parmesan cheese, plus
    an extra 3 tablespoons
1 tablespoon dried marjoram, plus an
    additional 1 1/2 teaspoons
1 teaspoon salt
3/4 teaspoon garlic powder
1/4 teaspoon nutmeg
1/4 teaspoon black pepper
6 large baking potatoes, peeled and thinly
    sliced
2 cups whipping cream
1/2 cup water

Preheat the oven to 350 degrees. Combine the first 6 ingredients in a small bowl and set aside. Arrange a third of the potatoes in a lightly greased 9 x 13-inch pan. Sprinkle with half of the cheese mixture. Repeat layers with the remaining potatoes and cheese mixture, ending with the potatoes. Combine the whipping cream and water. Pour over the potatoes and sprinkle with the 3 tablespoons cheese and the 1 1/2 teaspoons marjoram. Cover and bake for 1 1/2 hours. Uncover and bake for 30 minutes longer. Let stand for 10 minutes before serving.

BECKY BLIZZARD
NORTHBROOK UNITED METHODIST CHURCH
ROSWELL, GEORGIA

Maple-Glazed Sweet Potatoes

2 1/2 pounds sweet potatoes
3 tablespoons butter or margarine
1/4 cup pancake syrup
2 tablespoons brown sugar
2 tablespoons flaked coconut (optional)
1/3 cup pecans, chopped
1 1/2 cups miniature marshmallows

Spray an 8 x 8 x 2-inch baking dish with cooking spray. In a 3-quart saucepan, place the sweet potatoes and enough water to cover. Heat to boiling. Reduce the heat, cover, and simmer for 25 to 30 minutes until tender. Drain the potatoes and cool slightly. Peel and cut into large chunks. Place in the prepared dish. Preheat the oven to 350 degrees. In a small saucepan, melt the butter and stir in the syrup, sugar, and coconut, if desired. Over low heat, cook, stirring, for 3 to 5 minutes until blended. Sprinkle the nuts over the sweet potatoes, then top with the syrup mixture. Bake for 25 minutes. Top with the marshmallows. Bake for 5 to 7 minutes until the marshmallows are lightly browned. Makes 6 to 8 servings.

Note: 1 (40-ounce) can of sweet potatoes, drained, may be substituted for the cooked sweet potatoes.

ETHEL FLOYD
UNITED METHODIST CHURCH
ESTÂNCIA, NEW MEXICO

SWEET POTATO–APPLE CASSEROLE

6 medium sweet potatoes
1 1/2 pounds cooking apples
2/3 cup light brown sugar
1 tablespoon lemon juice
6 tablespoons butter
1/2 cup apple cider or water
3 tablespoons maple syrup
1 teaspoon cinnamon
1/2 teaspoon ground ginger

Preheat the oven to 325 degrees. Cook the potatoes in the skin for about 30 minutes. Peel when cool. Cut into 1/2-inch slices. Slice the apples, sprinkle with the lemon juice, and set aside. Combine the remaining ingredients and cook at a slow boil for about 10 minutes. Pat the apples dry. In a buttered casserole dish, arrange alternate layers of sweet potatoes and apples. Cover with the sauce. Bake for 25 to 30 minutes. Baste occasionally. Makes 8 to 10 servings.

EMMA RULAPAUGH
CROSS IN THE DESERT UNITED METHODIST CHURCH
PHOENIX, ARIZONA

SWEET POTATO CASSEROLE WITH NUT TOPPING

2 eggs
3 1/4 cups mashed cooked sweet potatoes
1/4 cup butter or margarine, melted
1 cup sugar
1 teaspoon vanilla extract
1/4 cup milk

TOPPING:
1 cup light brown sugar
1/2 cup all-purpose flour
1/3 cup butter or margarine, softened
1 cup chopped pecans or other nuts

Preheat the oven to 350 degrees. In a large bowl, beat the eggs slightly. Add the sweet potatoes, butter, sugar, vanilla, and milk. Blend well. Pour into a lightly buttered 3-quart casserole or baking dish. In a separate bowl, combine the topping ingredients (below) and sprinkle on top of the casserole. Bake for 30 minutes. Makes 6 to 8 servings.

Note: This was once prepared with the topping ingredients, minus the butter and nuts, being added to the potato mixture. We mixed it well and still did the topping. It was really good!

VIRGINIA ROBERSON
HIGHLAND HEIGHTS PRESBYTERIAN CHURCH
CORDOVA, TENNESSEE

YAMS WITH CRANBERRIES

1/2 cup all-purpose flour
1/2 cup packed brown sugar
1/2 cup quick oats (uncooked)
1/3 cup butter
2 (17-ounce) cans yams, drained
2 cups cranberries
1 1/2 cups mini marshmallows

Preheat the oven to 350 degrees. In a large bowl, combine the flour, sugar, and oats. Work in the butter with your fingertips until the mixture resembles coarse crumbs. In a 1 1/2-quart casserole dish, combine the yams, cranberries, and 1 cup of the crumb mixture. Mix well. Top with the remaining crumb mixture and bake for 35 minutes. Sprinkle with the marshmallows and broil until lightly browned. Makes approximately 6 servings.

Note: This recipe is great served with turkey, ham, or roast pork.

SUSAN DAVIS
CAVENDISH BAPTIST CHURCH
CAVENDISH, VERMONT

CREOLE CANDIED YAMS

1 (30-ounce) can whole yams
Juice of 1 lemon
1 teaspoon cinnamon
1/2 cup dark brown sugar
1/2 cup granulated sugar
2 tablespoons butter, plus one tablespoon
1/4 cup seedless raisins
1 apple, cored and sliced
2 peaches, peeled and sliced

Preheat the oven to 400 degrees. Place the yams in a casserole dish, pouring the liquid into a bowl. Add the lemon juice, cinnamon, and sugars and mix until dissolved. Pour the mixture over the yams. In a separate bowl, combine the raisins, apple, and peaches; add to the yams. Dot with the butter. Bake for about 45 minutes, or until the syrup has thickened slightly and the yams look glazed.

PINEMOUNT BAPTIST CHURCH
MCALPIN, FLORIDA

POTATO SKINS

4 baking potatoes
1/2 cup shredded Cheddar cheese
8 slices bacon, cooked and drained
2 green chile peppers, cut into thin strips

Bake the potatoes at 350 degrees for 1 hour. Cut the potatoes in half and scoop out, leaving only the shell. Fill the shells with a mixture of the remaining ingredients. The filling will be very thin in the shells. Place under the broiler for 5 minutes.

MCCLAVE UNITED METHODIST CHURCH
MCCLAVE, COLORADO

BAKED PUMPKIN WEDGES

1 pumpkin
1/2 to 3/4 cup butter, melted
1/4 cup brown sugar or honey
1/4 teaspoon salt
1 teaspoon cinnamon
1/4 teaspoon mace

Preheat the oven to 350 degrees. Wash the pumpkin well and cut it into wedges, scraping out the strings and seeds. Place the wedges in an oiled glass baking dish and make several shallow cuts in each wedge. In a small saucepan, melt the butter over low heat and add the sugar, salt, and spices. Brush the mixture over the wedges. Bake for 45 minutes until tender.

THE GREAT PUMPKIN
BUCKINGHAM UNITED METHODIST CHURCH
GARLAND, TEXAS

EASY SPINACH

1 teaspoon sesame oil
1 teaspoon olive oil
1/4 teaspoon salt
1/4 teaspoon red pepper flakes
1 package fresh spinach
Lemon

In a large skillet, heat the first 4 ingredients over medium-high heat. Add the spinach and sauté gently. Drizzle with fresh lemon juice and serve.

JULIE PEACOCK
NORTHBROOK UNITED METHODIST CHURCH
ROSWELL, GEORGIA

SPINACH CASSEROLE

4 bacon slices
2 tablespoons minced onion
2 (10-ounce) packages frozen chopped
  spinach
1 egg
1/2 cup milk
1/2 teaspoon salt
1/2 cup bread crumbs
3/4 cup shredded sharp cheese
Paprika

Preheat the oven to 375 degrees. In a large skillet, cook the bacon until crisp. Remove from the skillet and drain off most of grease. Sauté the onion in a small amount of grease until transparent and drain on paper towels. In a saucepan, cook the spinach according to the package directions and drain thoroughly. In a large bowl, beat the egg with the milk. Add the salt, then stir in the spinach, crumbled bacon, bread crumbs, onion, and 1/2 cup of the cheese. Pour the mixture into a 1 1/2-quart casserole and sprinkle with the remaining cheese and paprika. Bake for 30 minutes.

ANN ODGEN
ST. PAUL CHURCH
WATERFORD, CONNECTICUT

Spinach Soufflé

3 1/2 to 4 tablespoons butter or margarine
3 eggs
1 cup all-purpose flour
1 cup milk
1 teaspoon salt
1 teaspoon baking powder
2 (10-ounce) packages frozen spinach
1 small onion, chopped
14 ounces Cheddar cheese, grated

Preheat the oven to 350 degrees. Thaw and drain the spinach well. Melt the butter in a 13 x 9 x 2-inch pan. In a large bowl, beat the eggs, flour, milk, salt, and baking powder; mix well. Then add the spinach, onion, and cheese. Spoon into the baking dish and level off. Bake for about 35 minutes. Let cool, then cut into squares. This recipe also freezes well: Place on a cookie sheet, freeze, and store in plastic bags. Heat in a hot oven for 5 minutes or so.

ANN CUPELLO
ST. PAUL CHURCH
WATERFORD, CONNECTICUT

Apple Baked Squash

1 medium butternut squash
1 medium apple, peeled and thinly sliced
1/4 cup light brown sugar
1 tablespoon softened margarine
3 tablespoons applesauce
1 1/4 teaspoons all-purpose flour
1/2 teaspoon salt
1/4 teaspoon ground cinnamon

Peel and cut squash into 1/2- inch pieces and arrange in a 12 x 8-inch baking dish. Place apples on top of squash. Combine remaining ingredients and blend well. Drop by spoonfuls over squash-apple mixture. Place in microwave and cook for 17 minutes at medium power. To bake in the oven: Preheat the oven to 350 degrees. Bake about 50 minutes or until squash is tender. Serves 4 with 4 grams of fat per serving.

ESTER ZEIMETZ
MATTAPOISETT CONGREGATIONAL CHURCH
MATTAPOISETT, MASSACHUSETTS

Summer Squash Casserole

1 stick margarine, melted
1 (8-ounce) package herb stuffing mix
2 pounds sliced squash
1 carrot, grated
1 medium onion, grated
1 cup sour cream
1 can cream of chicken soup

Preheat the oven to 350 degrees. In a large bowl, combine the margarine with the stuffing mix. In a saucepan, cook the squash, carrot, and onion until tender; drain. Add 2/3 cup of the stuffing mixture to the squash mixture. In a separate bowl, combine the sour cream and soup and add to the squash mixture. Pour into a greased casserole dish and top with the remaining stuffing mix. Bake for 30 minutes.

CHRISTINE WALKER
CAVENDISH BAPTIST CHURCH
CAVENDISH, VERMONT

BAKED SQUASH CASSEROLE

2 pounds zucchini or yellow summer squash
3 tablespoons chopped onion
3 eggs, beaten
1/2 teaspoon Tabasco sauce
2 teaspoons parsley flakes
Salt and pepper to taste
1/2 cup butter or margarine, melted
2 cups cracker crumbs

Preheat the oven to 350 degrees. Slice the squash into 1/2-inch-thick pieces. In a large saucepan, boil the squash for 3 minutes or until tender; drain. Add the onion, eggs, and seasonings. Mix until well blended and pour into a 1-quart buttered casserole. Combine the butter and the cracker crumbs; sprinkle over the squash. Bake for 35 to 40 minutes until browned. Makes 6 servings.

GERALDINE VOLENTINE
HOLUM BAPTIST CHURCH
GRAYSON, LOUISIANA

QUICK SQUASH AU GRATIN

3 medium yellow summer squash
1 small onion, peeled and sliced
1 teaspoon salt
1/4 cup water
1 slice white bread, cut into small cubes
2 tablespoons butter or margarine
1/2 cup grated Cheddar cheese

Wash the squash, trim the ends, then cut into 1/4-inch-thick slices. Place in medium skillet adding the onion, salt, and water. Cook, stirring once or twice, for 10 to 12 minutes or until tender. While the squash cooks, in another skillet sauté the bread cubes in butter just until toasty. Spoon the squash and onion into a heated serving bowl and sprinkle with the cheese and toasted bread cubes.

PEG OLNEY
MATTAPOISETT CONGREGATIONAL CHURCH
MATTAPOISETT, MASSACHUSETTS

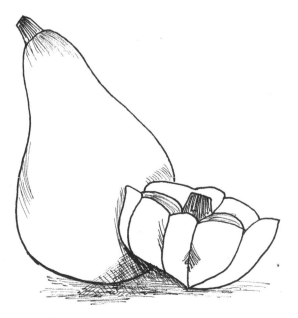

Butternut Squash

3 cups cooked, mashed butternut squash
1/2 cup sugar
1/4 teaspoon salt
1/4 cup butter
1 egg
1/2 cup milk
1/2 cup coconut
1/2 cup pecans

Preheat the oven to 350 degrees. In a large bowl, combine the squash, sugar, salt, butter, egg, milk, coconut, and pecans. Bake for 1 hour.

Kay Cargile
Memorial Baptist Church
Tulsa, Oklahoma

Stuffed Zucchini

4 to 6 large zucchini squash
1 cup Italian seasoned bread crumbs
1/4 cup chopped onion
3 tablespoons chopped fresh parsley
1 large tomato, chopped
Salt, pepper, and garlic powder to taste
1/2 cup grated Parmesan cheese

Preheat the oven to 350 degrees. Wash the squash, cut off the ends, and cook in boiling, salted water for 5 minutes. Drain. Cut in half lengthwise and remove the pulp with a spoon. Chop the pulp and combine it with the bread crumbs, onion, parsley, tomato, and seasonings in a large bowl. Arrange the shells of the squash in a large baking dish, fill with filling, and top with the cheese. Bake for 25 to 30 minutes.

Sue Callesis
United Baptist Church of Poultney
East Poultney, Vermont

Zucchini Pie

2 tablespoons butter or margarine
4 cups unpeeled sliced zucchini
1 small sliced onion, quartered or chopped
1/2 teaspoon garlic salt
1/2 teaspoon dried basil
1/2 teaspoon oregano
2 tablespoons fresh parsley
1 to 2 tablespoons mustard
Crescent rolls
2 to 3 eggs, beaten
8 ounces Mozzarella cheese, shredded
8 ounces Swiss cheese, shredded

Preheat the oven to 375 degrees. In a large skillet, melt the butter and sauté the zucchini, onion, garlic salt, basil, oregano, and parsley for about 15 minutes. Coat the bottom and sides of a baking pan with the mustard and press the crescent rolls into the pan. Pour the zucchini mixture into the prepared crescent rolls. Beat together the eggs and cheeses and pour over the crescent rolls. Bake 18 to 20 minutes, or until the top of pie is golden brown.

MARY SANCRAINTE
JUNE SHARPE
NORTH MONROE STREET CHURCH OF GOD
MONROE, MICHIGAN

Zucchini Casserole

Fresh sliced zucchini
Fresh tomatoes, sliced
1 onion, sliced
Grated cheese
Salt and pepper to taste
1 stick butter or margarine

Preheat the oven to 350 degrees. In a glass baking dish or your favorite casserole dish, arrange each ingredient in a layer in the order given, sprinkling with salt and pepper and dotting with butter. Cover and bake for 45 minutes. Uncover and bake for 15 minutes longer.

RHONDA FALKNOR
CROSS IN THE DESERT UNITED METHODIST CHURCH
PHOENIX, ARIZONA

VEGETABLE PANCAKES

1 cup grated carrots (about 2 whole carrots)
1/2 cup grated zucchini (1/2 zucchini)
2 scallions, chopped (or 1/4 cup chopped onion)
1/2 cup all-purpose flour
1/2 teaspoon baking powder
Salt and pepper to taste
1 egg
1/4 cup milk
2 tablespoons oil

Combine the dry ingredients. In a separate bowl, beat the egg, milk, carrot, zucchini, and scallions. Stir the wet ingredients into the dry ingredients just until combined. Heat 1 tablespoon of oil in a skillet over medium heat. Pour batter in by tablespoons, making a few pancakes at a time. Cook two minutes on each side until golden. Add oil to the skillet as needed. Serve hot. Makes about 18 pancakes.

KAY MOON
CALVARY UNITED METHODIST CHURCH
TAYLOR, NEBRASKA

FRIED GREEN TOMATOES

5 medium green tomatoes
1/2 cup cornmeal
1 teaspoon salt
1/2 teaspoon black pepper
1/2 cup shortening

Select tomatoes that have the whitish look they get just before turning pink. Cut the tomatoes crosswise into 1/2-inch thick slices. Heat the shortening in a skillet until it is sizzling hot. Put in the sliced tomatoes and cook quickly until they are browned on the underside. Turn the tomatoes over carefully, reduce heat and cook until thoroughly hot and soft through the center. Drain on paper towels. Do not stack the tomatoes on top of each other in the pan. Cook one batch at a time until finished. Yields 4 servings.

AMANDA NEWMAN
WELLINGTON VILLAGE ASSEMBLY OF GOD
LITTLE ROCK, ARKANSAS

GREEK TOMATOES

3 small plum tomatoes, cut in half
Vegetable cooking spray
1 tablespoon dry bread crumbs
2 tablespoons crumbled Feta cheese with
    basil and tomato
1/4 teaspoon dried oregano
1/8 teaspoon pepper

Preheat the oven (or toaster oven) to 350 degrees. Place the tomato halves on a baking sheet coated with the cooking spray. Sprinkle the tomatoes with the bread crumbs, then the cheese, and top with the oregano and pepper. Bake for 20 to 25 minutes. Serve warm.

CHARLOTTE SNYDER
CAVENDISH BAPTIST CHURCH
CAVENDISH, VERMONT

TOMATO PIE

1 Pillsbury pie shell
12 ounces mozzarella cheese
Pepper
Fresh basil, chopped
3 large tomatoes, sliced
1/4 cup olive oil

Preheat the oven to 375 degrees. Place the pie shell in a pie dish and sprinkle the cheese on the bottom. Sprinkle with the pepper and basil. Layer the sliced tomatoes next and sprinkle with more pepper. Pour the olive oil over the tomatoes and bake for 45 minutes.

PAT WEST
HIGHLAND HEIGHTS PRESBYTERIAN CHURCH
CORDOVA, TENNESSEE

PANZANELLA

6 medium tomatoes, cut into 1/2-inch-thick
   cubes
1/2 cup chopped onion
1/2 cup torn fresh basil leaves
1/4 cup extra-virgin olive oil
1 garlic clove, crushed
Salt and pepper to taste
4 (1/2-inch-thick) slices day old bread
   (wheat, sourdough, Italian)

In a large bowl, combine the tomatoes, onion, basil, oil, garlic, salt, and pepper. Cover and set aside at room temperature for at least 1 hour, but no more than 2. Grill, broil, or toast the bread. Cut into 1/2-inch cubes and add to the tomato mixture. Toss gently until well combined. Let stand for 15 minutes before serving so that the bread will absorb the juices. Taste. Add more oil, salt, or pepper if necessary.

LINDA JUERGENS
BUCKINGHAM UNITED METHODIST CHURCH
GARLAND, TEXAS

TOMATO-RICOTTA BAKE

2 cups Italian bread crumbs
1/4 cup olive oil, plus 1 tablespoon
1 cup whole-milk ricotta cheese
1/2 cup Parmesan cheese, grated
2 eggs
2 tablespoons fresh basil
1/2 teaspoon salt
1/2 teaspoon black pepper
1 1/2 pounds beefsteak tomatoes
1 tablespoon sugar

Preheat the oven to 400 degrees. In a 9-inch springform pan, toss the bread crumbs with 1/4 cup of the olive oil; press the bread crumbs evenly into the bottom of the pan. In a bowl, whisk together the ricotta, Parmesan, eggs, basil, and salt and pepper. Pour over the crust and arrange the sliced tomatoes on top. Sprinkle the sugar over the tomatoes and brush with the 1 tablespoon of olive oil. Bake until the tomatoes are almost dry (approximately 35 to 45 minutes); let cool. Remove from the pan. Serve warm or at room temperature.

PINEMOUNT BAPTIST CHURCH
MCALPIN, FLORIDA

Easy Garden Bake

1 cup sliced zucchini
1/4 cup sliced green pepper (optional)
1 large tomato, sliced into thin wedges
1/2 cup sliced onion
1/4 cup Parmesan cheese
1/4 cup grated Cheddar cheese
1 cup milk
1/2 cup Bisquick
4 eggs
Salt and pepper to taste

Preheat the oven to 350 degrees. Layer the first 4 ingredients in a greased 8 x 8-inch pan. Sprinkle with the cheeses. In a bowl, beat the milk, Bisquick, eggs, and salt and pepper in an electric mixer on high for 1 1/2 minutes. Pour the egg mixture into the pan. Bake for 1/2 hour, covered. Remove the cover and finish baking at 400 degrees, about 15 to 20 minutes until the top is browned.

BARB PREEDOM
CAVENDISH BAPTIST CHURCH
CAVENDISH, VERMONT

Greek Vegetables

1 zucchini, chopped
1 small eggplant, chopped
1 medium to large onion, chopped
1/2 cup olive oil
3 tablespoons butter
1 pound string beans, sliced
1 pound fresh peas or lima beans
1 pound tomatoes, chopped
Fresh dill weed to taste
Fresh mint to taste
1 teaspoon sugar
Salt and pepper to taste
Garlic powder to taste

In a large saucepan, sauté the zucchini, eggplant, and onion in the oil and butter. Add the remaining vegetables, dill weed, mint, sugar, and salt and pepper. Cover and cook on low until tender.

TOLLIE VOLENTINE
HOLUM BAPTIST CHURCH
GRAYSON, LOUISIANA

Calavacitas Con Chili Verde

Fresh corn from one cob
4 tablespoons bacon drippings
4 cups fresh green chilies, chopped
1 garlic clove, minced
1/2 cup onion, chopped
4 medium summer squash, diced
1/2 teaspoon salt
1/4 teaspoon black pepper
1 sprig of fresh coriander (optional)

Cut the corn from the cob. In a large skillet, fry the corn slowly in the bacon drippings. Add the chilies, garlic, and onion; cook until the onion is transparent. Add the squash, salt, pepper, and coriander. Cover and cook until the squash is tender. Serve.

Frances Q. Lopez
United Methodist Church
Estância, New Mexico

Stir-Fried Vegetables

1/4 pound green beans, sliced
2 carrots, sliced
1/4 small cauliflower, cut into 1-inch pieces
1 stalk broccoli, cut into 1-inch pieces
2 tablespoons olive oil
1 onion, sliced
2 garlic cloves, diced
1 small zucchini, sliced
2 tablespoons gingerroot, chopped
1/4 pound snow peas
1 tablespoon soy sauce
Salt and pepper to taste

In a large saucepan, blanch the green beans, carrots, cauliflower, and broccoli until just tender. Drain and cool under cold water. Drain thoroughly. Heat a small amount of the oil in a heavy skillet or wok over medium heat. Add the onion and 1/2 teaspoon of the garlic; stir-fry for 3 to 4 minutes. Add the zucchini, some ginger, and more garlic. Stir-fry for 3 minutes longer. If necessary, add more oil. When the pan becomes too crowded, transfer some of the cooked vegetables as they are done. Add more ginger, garlic, and oil as you go. Add the snow peas. Combine all the vegetables in a large bowl and toss with the soy sauce and salt and pepper to taste. Makes 8 servings.

Chin Lee
Forest Avenue Congregational Church
Bangor, Maine

OVEN-ROASTED VEGGIES

3 large onions, each cut into 12 wedges
2 pounds carrots, peeled and cut into 2 x 1-inch pieces
2 pounds parsnips, peeled and cut into 2 x 1-inch pieces
2 medium red peppers, cut into 1 1/2-inch pieces
1 whole head garlic, separated into cloves and peeled
3 tablespoons olive oil
2 teaspoons salt
1/4 teaspoon freshly ground black pepper

Preheat the oven to 475 degrees. In a large bowl, toss the vegetables with the oil, salt, and pepper until evenly coated. Divide the vegetable mixture between two shallow large roasting pans. Place the pans on 2 oven racks and roast the vegetables for 45 minutes or until tender and golden, rotating the pans between the upper and lower racks halfway through the cooking time and tossing the vegetables once. Makes about 13 cups, or 24 accompaniment servings.

Note: To save time, use bottled peeled garlic. When halving the recipe, use only one pan, lower the temperature to 375 degrees, and cook for only 30 minutes. It's easy, delicious, and healthful!

JEANIE DUBROUILLET
NORTHBROOK UNITED METHODIST CHURCH
ROSWELL, GEORGIA

ROASTED VEGETABLES

Cooking spray
2 red potatoes
1 sweet potato, peeled
1 red bell pepper
1 yellow bell pepper
1 medium zucchini
1 red onion
2 tablespoons balsamic vinegar
1 tablespoon honey
1 tablespoon olive oil
1 teaspoon pepper
4 garlic cloves, minced
1/4 cup fresh basil

Preheat the oven to 425 degrees. Spray a large shallow pan with nonstick cooking spray. Cut the potatoes into 1-inch chunks. Place them in a pan and bake for 15 minutes. Cut the bell peppers into 1-inch chunks. Slice the zucchini and cut the onion through core into 1/2-inch wedges. Add the vegetables to pan.

Combine the vinegar, honey, olive oil, pepper, and garlic. Remove the vegetables from the oven and toss with the vinegar mixture to coat. Return to the oven and bake for 45 minutes, or until the vegetables are brown and tender, stirring every 15 minutes. Toss the vegetables with the basil before serving. Makes 4 servings.

CLARA HOWARD
FOREST AVENUE CONGREGATIONAL CHURCH
BANGOR, MAINE

CAKES, PIES, & PUDDINGS

Lord, make me an instrument of your peace.
Where there is hatred, let me sow love;
Where there is injury, pardon;
Where there is doubt, faith;
Where there is despair, hope;
Where there is darkness, light;
Where there is sadness, joy.

PRAYER OF ST. FRANCIS

Yellow Layer Cake

2 cups sugar
2 sticks butter
6 medium eggs
2 cups all-purpose flour
1 cup milk
1 teaspoon vanilla extract

Preheat the oven to 350 degrees. In the bowl of an electric mixer, cream the sugar and butter for 12 minutes. Beat in the eggs, one at a time, then add the flour and milk alternately. Add the vanilla. Bake in layer pans for 20 to 35 minutes. Use an icing or filling of your choice.

Cynthia J. Knights
Bethel AME Church
Augusta, Georgia

Black Magic Cake

2 cups all-purpose flour
2 cups sugar
3/4 cup cocoa
2 teaspoons baking soda
1 teaspoon baking powder
1/2 teaspoon salt
2 eggs
1 cup brewed black coffee
1 cup milk
1/2 cup salad oil
2 teaspoons vanilla extract

Preheat the oven to 350 degrees. Sift all dry ingredients into a large bowl; add the eggs and remaining liquid ingredients. Stir until batter is smooth (it will be thin). Pour into a well-greased 9 x 13-inch pan. Bake for 35 minutes. Frost when cooled—buttercream icing goes well or use your own favorite!

Mary Lou Frey
Trinity United Methodist Church
York, Pennsylvania

Jill Biden's Chocolate Cake

1 (8-ounce) package cream cheese, at room
    temperature
2 (1-pound) boxes powdered sugar
1 teaspoon vanilla extract
1 stick butter, at room temperature
5 squares unsweetened chocolate, melted
1/2 cup milk, at room temperature
2 1/2 cups all-purpose flour
1/3 cup butter, softened
4 eggs
1 1/2 cups milk
Dash of salt
1 teaspoon baking powder
1 teaspoon baking soda

Preheat the oven to 350 degrees. In a large bowl, combine the first 6 ingredients and mix well. Divide the mixture in half, reserving one half for the icing. To the other half, add the next 7 ingredients and mix well. Grease 2 round 9-inch baking pans and divide the batter between the 2 pans. Bake for 30 to 40 minutes. Let the cake cool and ice with the reserved mixture.

THE HONORABLE THOMAS CARPER
GOVERNOR OF DELAWARE
TRINITY PRESBYTERIAN CHURCH
WILMINGTON, DELAWARE

Scripture Cake from the Bible

(Takes time, but worth it!)

1 cup Judges 5:25 (last clause - butter)
1 3/4 cups Jeremiah 6:20 (sugar)
1/4 cup Proverbs 24:13 (honey)
6 Job 39:14 (eggs)
3 3/4 cups 1 Kings 4:22
    (flour, reserve 1/2 cup)
1 teaspoon Leviticus 2:13 (salt)
3 teaspoons Amos 4:5 (baking powder)
1 1/2 teaspoons cinnamon
1/2 teaspoon cloves
1 teaspoon allspice
1 teaspoon nutmeg
1 cup Genesis 24:11 (buttermilk)
1 Kings 10:2 (spices)
1 teaspoon Amos 4:5 (raisins)
2 cups Revelations 6:13
    (cut-up figs or dates)
1 cup Numbers 17:8 (chopped almonds)

Preheat oven to 300 degrees. Heavily grease and flour 10-inch tube pan or Bundt pan or two 9 x 5 x 3-inch loaf pans. In a large bowl, with electric mixer, beat butter smooth. On low speed, add sugar gradually. Beat in well. Blend in honey. Add eggs, one at a time. Combine remaining dry ingredients alternately with buttermilk. Toss reserved 1/2 cup flour with raisins, figs and almonds. Pour batter into pan. Cut through batter to distribute evenly. Bake 1 1/2 hours or until tester in center comes out clean. Let cool in pan for 30 minutes.

DENNIS AND SHIRLEY STONESIFER
TRINITY UNITED METHODIST CHURCH
YORK, PENNSYLVANIA

MISSISSIPPI MUD CAKE

CAKE:
2 cups sugar
1 cup shortening or oil
4 eggs
3 teaspoons vanilla extract
1 1/2 cups self-rising flour
1/3 cup cocoa
1 teaspoon salt
1 cup chopped pecans
Miniature marshmallows

ICING:
1 1/2 sticks margarine, melted
1 (1-pound) box powdered sugar
1/3 cup cocoa
1/2 cup milk
1 tablespoon vanilla extract
1 cup chopped pecans

Preheat the oven to 325 degrees. In the bowl of an electric mixer, cream the sugar and shortening. Add the eggs and vanilla and beat well. In a separate bowl, sift together the flour, cocoa, and salt and add to the mixer, beating well. Stir in the nuts. Pour the batter into an oblong pan and bake for 40 minutes. Top with the miniature marshmallows and bake for 10 minutes longer. Let the cake cool for 20 minutes, then add the icing (recipe below).

In the bowl of an electric mixer, combine all the ingredients except the nuts and beat until the icing is smooth. Stir in the nuts.

HAZEL PECK
HIGHLAND HEIGHTS PRESBYTERIAN CHURCH
CORDOVA, TENNESSEE

HOT CHOCOLATE FUDGE SAUCE CAKE

1 cup all-purpose flour
3 tablespoons plus 1 1/2 teaspoons cocoa
3/4 cup granulated sugar
2 teaspoons baking powder
1/4 teaspoon salt
1/2 cup milk
1 teaspoon vanilla extract
2 tablespoons melted butter
1/2 cup brown sugar
1/2 cup chopped pecans
1 cup cold water

Preheat the oven to 350 degrees. In a large bowl, combine the flour, 1 1/2 teaspoons of the cocoa, 1/4 cup of the granulated sugar, the baking powder, and salt. Stir in the milk, vanilla, and butter and continue stirring until the batter is smooth. Pour into a greased 8 x 8-inch baking pan. In a separate bowl, combine the remaining 1/2 cup of the granulated sugar, brown sugar, 3 tablespoons of the cocoa, and the pecans. Sprinkle the mixture evenly over the batter in the baking pan. Pour the cold water over the top and bake for 45 minutes.

PINEMOUNT BAPTIST CHURCH
MCALPIN, FLORIDA

CHOCOLATE MAYONNAISE CAKE

1/2 cup mayonnaise
2 cups all-purpose flour
4 tablespoons cocoa
1 1/2 teaspoons baking soda
1 cup sugar
1 teaspoon vanilla extract
1 cup water (hot or cold)

Preheat the oven to 350 degrees. Sift the dry ingredients together. Add the vanilla and water and mix. Then stir in the mayonnaise. Bake in a greased pan for 30 to 35 minutes. Double the recipe for a two-layer cake.

SANDY PARTERIDGE
TRINITY UNITED METHODIST CHURCH
HUDSON, NEW YORK

GERMAN SWEET CHOCOLATE CAKE

1 (4-ounce) package Baker's German sweet
    chocolate
1/2 cup boiling water
2 sticks butter or margarine, softened
2 cups sugar
4 egg yolks
1 teaspoon vanilla extract
2 1/4 cups sifted all-purpose flour, or 2 1/2
    cups sifted cake flour
1 teaspoon baking soda
1/2 teaspoon salt
1 cup buttermilk
4 egg whites, stiffly beaten

Preheat the oven to 350 degrees. Melt the chocolate in the boiling water. In the bowl of an electric mixer, cream the butter and sugar until fluffy. Add the egg yolks, one at a time, beating well after each addition. Blend in the vanilla and chocolate. In a separate bowl, sift together the flour, baking soda, and salt. Add the flour mixture to the chocolate mixture alternately with the buttermilk, beating after each addition until smooth. Fold in the egg whites. Pour the batter into three 9-inch layer pans lined with waxed paper. Bake for 30 to 35 minutes. Cool the cakes and frost the tops only (frosting below).

CHOCOLATE-PECAN FROSTING:

1 cup evaporated milk
1 cup sugar
3 egg yolks, slightly beaten
1/2 cup butter or margarine
1 teaspoon vanilla extract
1 1/2 cups Baker's Angel Flake coconut
1 cup chopped pecans

In a large saucepan, combine the first 5 ingredients and cook, stirring, over medium heat until the mixture thickens (about 12 minutes). Add the coconut and pecans. Cool the frosting until it's thick enough to spread, beating occasionally. Makes 2 1/2 cups.

ELIZABETH C. GAINOUS
BETHEL AME CHURCH,
AUGUST, GEORGIA

MARBLE CAKE

1 square unsweetened chocolate
2 1/4 cups cake flour
3 1/2 teaspoons baking powder
1/2 teaspoon salt
1 1/2 cups sugar
1/4 cup shortening
1/4 cup butter, at room temperature
1 cup whole milk
1 teaspoon vanilla extract
4 large egg whites

Preheat the oven to 350 degrees. In a small saucepan, melt the chocolate. In the bowl of an electric mixer, sift together the flour, baking powder, salt, and sugar. Add the shortening, butter, 2/3 cup of the milk, and vanilla and beat on medium for 2 minutes. Add the remaining milk and egg whites and beat for 2 more minutes. Pour half of the batter into a greased and floured tube, Bundt, or 9 x 13-inch pan. Add the melted chocolate to the remaining batter and pour over the top of the white batter. Cut through with a knife to achieve a marbled effect. Bake for 50 to 55 minutes if you're using a tube or Bundt pan or for 30 to 35 minutes if you're using a 9 x 13-inch pan. Cool the cake for 10 minutes after removing it from the oven. Remove the cake from the pan to a cooling rack. Cool completely. Serve plain or frost with your favorite chocolate frosting.

JAN WICKLIFFE
CROSS IN THE DESERT UNITED METHODIST CHURCH
PHOENIX, ARIZONA

WALDORF RED VELVET CAKE

1 cup shortening
1 1/2 cups sugar
2 eggs
2 tablespoons cocoa
1/4 cup red food coloring
1 teaspoon salt
1 teaspoon vanilla
1 cup buttermilk
2 1/4 cups flour (cake flour is best)
1 tablespoon vinegar
1 teaspoon baking soda

Preheat oven to 350 degrees. Cream the sugar and shortening. Add the eggs. Beat the mixture until fluffy. Mix the cocoa and food coloring to form a smooth paste and add to the first mixture. Add the salt and vanilla to the buttermilk. Add about 1/3 of the buttermilk mixture to first mixture, then add about 1/3 of the flour. Mix. Alternate mixing in the flour and the buttermilk mixture until all is well blended. Mix vinegar with baking soda and stir into the batter. Bake at 350 degrees for 30 minutes in two 8 or 9-inch round cake pans. Bake until toothpick comes out clean or bounces back to touch. Don't overbake. Cover cooled layers with whipped cream icing.

BECKY GAYLOR
CROSS IN THE DESERT UNITED METHODIST CHURCH
PHOENIX, ARIZONA

Maple Layer Cake

8 tablespoons unsalted butter
2 cups maple syrup
3 large eggs
2 3/4 cups all-purpose flour
1 tablespoon baking powder
1/4 teaspoon salt
1 teaspoon ground ginger
1 cup milk
1 teaspoon vanilla extract
1 1/2 cups chopped walnuts

Preheat the oven to 350 degrees. Butter two 9-inch baking pans and dust with flour, tapping out the excess. In the bowl of an electric mixer, beat the butter until it's creamy. Add the maple syrup and beat until the mixture is combined. Add the eggs and beat until combined. In a separate bowl, sift together the flour, baking powder, salt, and ginger. Add the flour mixture to butter mixture and beat to combine. Beat in the milk and vanilla until combined. Stir in 3/4 cup of the walnuts. Divide the batter between the 2 pans and bake until done. Rotate the pans halfway through. Transfer to a rack until cool. Turn out the cakes. Spread 1 1/2 cups of Maple Buttercream Frosting (recipe below) on top of one cake and cover with the other. Spread the remaining 2 1/2 cups on the sides and top of the cake. Gently push the remaining walnuts onto the side of the cake.

GRAMMY
FOREST AVENUE CONGREGATIONAL CHURCH
BANGOR, MAINE

Maple Buttercream Frosting

6 large egg yolks
2 cups maple syrup
2 cups butter, cut into pieces

In the bowl of an electric mixer, beat the egg yolks on high until the mixture is light and fluffy, 3 to 5 minutes.

In a small saucepan, bring the syrup to a boil over medium heat for about 15 minutes. Remove the pan from the heat, and while mixer is turning, slowly pour the syrup down the side of the bowl. When the syrup is blended (about 1/2 minute), beat the mixture until the bowl is warm to the touch, 5 to 6 minutes. Add the butter, one piece at a time, until the frosting is fluffy (about 4 minutes). Frost the cake.

GRAMMY
FOREST AVENUE CONGREGATIONAL CHURCH
BANGOR, MAINE

MANDARIN CAKE

CAKE:
2 cups granulated sugar
2 eggs
2 cups all-purpose flour
2 teaspoons baking soda
1/2 teaspoon salt
2 (11 1/2-ounce) cans mandarin oranges

Preheat the oven to 350 degrees. In the bowl of an electric mixer, beat the eggs and sugar together. Add the flour, baking soda, salt, and oranges; beat well. Pour the batter into a greased 9 x 13 x 2-inch baking pan and bake for 30 to 35 minutes. Remove the pan from the oven and pour hot topping over the warm cake. Cool before serving. Serve the cake with whipped topping, too, if you like.

TOPPING:
3/4 cup packed brown sugar
3 tablespoons milk
3 tablespoons butter or margarine

Place all the ingredients in a small saucepan and bring to a slow boil. Pour the hot mixture over the warm cake.

PAT LECUIVE
UNITED BAPTIST CHURCH OF POULTNEY
EAST POULTNEY, VERMONT

LOVE'S WEDDING CAKE

Equal parts flower of love between two tender youths

Just enough Good Looks
Plenty of Dry wit
Heaping Measure of Common sense
A bit of self-forgetfulness
Season well with rippling, laughter and Joy
Just enough Sweet Temper
Pinch of friendly argument
Cup overflowing with forgiveness
A lot of Spiritual Guidance
Add salt of kindness and a dash of Good attitude

Mix the above ingredients and place in a modestly furnished house and let it bake gently forever and ever.
ENJOY! ENJOY!

BOBBYE C. KUDZMA
DAMASCUS UNITED METHODIST CHURCH
DAMASCUS, MARYLAND

CHARLOTTE SMITH'S LEMON BUTTER ICING

1 (1-pound) box powdered sugar
1 stick butter, softened
Zest of lemon
Juice of 1 lemon
Juice of 1/2 orange

In the bowl of an electric mixer, combine all the ingredients and beat until the mixture is spreadable and smooth. It's heavenly over angel food cake!

IN MEMORY OF CHARLOTTE SMITH
MEMORIAL BAPTIST CHURCH
TULSA, OKLAHOMA

TUTTI-FRUITCAKE

1 (6-ounce) container frozen orange juice
    concentrate, thawed
1/2 cup light molasses
3 cups raisins
2 cups mixed candied fruits and peels
1/2 cup butter
2/3 cup sugar
3 eggs
1 1/4 cups sifted all-purpose flour
1/4 teaspoon baking soda
1 teaspoon ground cinnamon
1/2 teaspoon ground nutmeg
1/4 teaspoon ground cloves
1/4 teaspoon ground allspice
1/2 cup chopped walnuts

Preheat the oven to 275 degrees. In a large saucepan, bring the orange juice concentrate, molasses, and raisins to a boil. Reduce the heat and simmer for 5 minutes. Stir in the candied fruits and set aside. In the bowl of an electric mixer, cream the butter and sugar, then beat in the eggs, one at a time. In a separate bowl, sift together the flour, baking soda, and spices; stir into the creamed mixture. Add the fruit mixture and nuts. Pour the batter into a greased and floured 8 1/2-inch fluted tube pan. Bake for 2 1/2 hours. Cool for 1/2 hour. Remove the cake from the pan. Wrap it in foil, and refrigerate.

ELFRIEDE M. BLACKBURN
MATTAPOISETT CONGREGATIONAL CHURCH
MATTAPOISETT, MASSACHUSETTS

EARTHQUAKE CAKE

1 cup chopped pecans
1 cup shredded coconut
1 package German chocolate cake mix
1 (1-pound) box powdered sugar
1 stick butter, softened
1 (8-ounce) package cream cheese
1 teaspoon vanilla extract

Preheat the oven to 350 degrees. Scatter the nuts and coconut over the bottom of a 9 x 13-inch baking pan. In a large bowl, mix the cake according to the package directions. Pour the mixture over the nuts and coconut. Do not stir. In a separate bowl, combine the powdered sugar, butter, cream cheese, and vanilla and drop by teaspoonfuls on top of the cake mix batter. Do not stir. Pour the batter into an aluminum baking pan. Bake for 45 to 50 minutes, or until cracks appear in the cake. There is no need to ice the cake.

Note: This is a big, larger than normal cake.

BOB McCLUSKEY
MEMORIAL BAPTIST CHURCH
TULSA, OKLAHOMA

PINEAPPLE SHEET CAKE

2 eggs, beaten
2 cups sugar
1/2 teaspoon salt
2 cups all-purpose flour
1/2 cup chopped nuts
1 teaspoon vanilla extract
2 teaspoons baking soda
1 (20-ounce) can crushed pineapple and
 juice

ICING:
1 (8-ounce) package cream cheese
1/2 stick margarine
1 teaspoon vanilla extract
1 3/4 cups powdered sugar
1/4 to 1/2 cup chopped nuts

Preheat the oven to 350 degrees. In a large bowl, combine all the ingredients and pour the batter into a greased 9 x 13-inch baking pan (larger for a thinner cake). Bake for 30 to 40 minutes.

In a large bowl, combine all the ingredients and spread on the warm or cooled cake.

HALLIE LACKEY
MEMORIAL BAPTIST CHURCH
TULSA, OKLAHOMA

STRAWBERRY CAKE

1 box white cake mix
1 box strawberry Jell-O
3 tablespoons flour (self-rising or all-purpose)
1/2 cup water
1 cup Wesson oil
4 eggs
1 teaspoon vanilla extract
1 cup frozen strawberries, thawed

ICING:
1/4 pound margarine or butter
1 (1-pound) box powdered sugar
1 cup frozen strawberries, thawed

Preheat the oven to 350 degrees. In the bowl of an electric mixer, combine the cake mix, flour, Jell-O, water, and oil. Beat well. Add the eggs, one at a time, beating well after each addition. Add the vanilla and strawberries. Divide the batter among 3 layer pans. Bake for 25 to 30 minutes.

In a large bowl, combine all the ingredients. Mix with a fork for best results. Spread the icing on the cake while the layers are warm.

TRACIE V. GALLOP
BETHEL AME CHURCH
AUGUSTA, GEORGIA

MARRIAGE CAKE

2 cups understanding, sifted 3 times
1 cup sense of humor
1 teaspoon teasing
2 teaspoons spunk
1 cup patience
1/2 cup sharing
2 tempers, separated

Sift understanding once through his love, once through hers, and once through the love of Christ. Add teasing and spunk; sift once more. Separate tempers. Beat his until tender, hers until light and frothy. To his, add patience and sharing. To her, add understanding to which has been added a sense of humor. Fold in hers with spice of your own choice. This can be varied from time to time, for variety is the spice of life. Handle all ingredients tenderly. Bake in for loving arms, well prepared with forgiveness, at a comfortable temperature. Put layers together with love and kisses. Slice in generous slices and serve often.

REV. JOHN E. LEHR
TRINITY UNITED METHODIST CHURCH
YORK, PENNSYLVANIA

MARTHA'S POUND CAKE

2 cups all-purpose flour
2 cups plus 2 tablespoons sugar
2 sticks butter, room temperature
6 eggs
1 tablespoon vanilla extract

Preheat the oven to 350 degrees. In the bowl of an electric mixer, combine the flour, sugar, and butter and beat well. Beat in the eggs, one at a time, and add the vanilla. Pour the batter into a Bundt pan coated with cooking spray. Bake for 50 minutes.

LAURIE PETREY
BUCKINGHAM UNITED METHODIST CHURCH
GARLAND, TEXAS

CHOCOLATE POUND CAKE

1 cup butter
4 ounces unsweetened chocolate
1 cup milk
3 teaspoons baking powder
2 cups sugar
1 1/2 cups all-purpose flour
4 eggs
2 teaspoons vanilla extract

Preheat the oven to 350 degrees. In a small saucepan, melt the butter and chocolate. Pour the mixture into the bowl of an electric mixer. Add the rest of the ingredients. Do not stir until all the ingredients are in, then beat on high speed until the batter is smooth. Pour into a greased tube pan and bake for 30 to 45 minutes. Remove the cake from the pan and cover immediately.

Note: Covering the cake immediately creates a moist glaze.

LINDA JUERGENS
BUCKINGHAM UNITED METHODIST CHURCH
GARLAND, TEXAS

Spice Cake

1 cup butter or margarine
2 cups sugar
5 eggs, beaten
3 cups sifted all-purpose flour
1/2 teaspoon ground nutmeg
1/2 teaspoon ground cinnamon
1/2 teaspoon ground cloves
1/2 teaspoon ground allspice
1 tablespoon baking powder
1 1/4 cups milk
1 teaspoon vanilla extract

Preheat the oven to 325 degrees. In the bowl of an electric mixer, cream the butter and sugar. Add the eggs, one at a time, beating well after each addition. In a separate bowl, combine the flour and the spices, then add the baking powder and mix well. Add the flour mixture to the creamed mixture alternately with the milk, beginning and ending with the flour. Stir in the vanilla. Divide the batter between 2 greased and floured 9-inch cake pans and bake for 25 minutes. Cool. Frost the cake with your favorite icing after it has cooled completely. Makes 1 (2 layer) cake.

ALICE FONTENOT
HOLUM BAPTIST CHURCH
GRAYSON, LOUISIANA

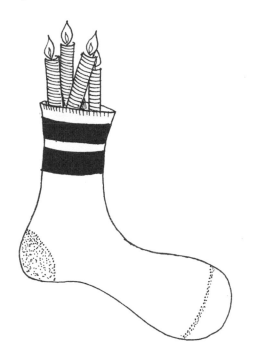

Sock It to Me Cake

1 package yellow cake mix
1 cup sour cream
1/3 cup salad oil
1/4 cup granulated sugar
1/4 cup water
4 eggs
1/2 cup chopped pecans
2 tablespoons brown sugar
2 tablespoons ground cinnamon
1 teaspoon melted butter
1 tablespoon milk
1/4 teaspoon vanilla extract

Preheat the oven to 350 degrees. In the bowl of an electric mixer, combine the cake mix, sour cream, oil, granulated sugar, water, and eggs. Beat until smooth and set aside. In a separate bowl, combine the pecans, brown sugar, cinnamon, melted butter, milk, and vanilla, mixing well. Spoon some of the batter into a greased and floured 9-inch tube pan. Cover with a layer of crumb mixture. Alternate the batter and crumbs until everything has been used. Bake for 45 to 55 minutes, or until done. Cool the cake in the pan.

A. ELAINE PATE
BETHEL AME CHURCH
AUGUSTA, GEORGIA

ASPIRIN CAKE

Light the oven. Get out bowl and spoon. Get all ingredients. Grease pan. Crack nuts. Put the cat outside. Remove books and baby doll from table. Measure 7 cups flour. Get baking powder. Remove Becky's hands from flour. Get pan and broom. Sweep up flour and broken bowl. Get another bowl. Answer phone. Remove Becky's hands from the broken eggs. Wash Becky. Get 2 more eggs. Answer the doorbell. Take 1/4 cup salt out of greased pan. Take shallow bowl. Empty out cracked nuts. Slap Becky's hands. Pick up broken measuring cup as Becky flees. Wash kitchen floor, table, walls and dishes. Call Bakery. Take an aspirin or two. Lie down.

FIRST UNITED METHODIST CHURCH
BELLEVILLE, MICHIGAN

GREAT GRANDMA'S GINGER CAKE

2 1/4 cups all-purpose flour
1 teaspoon baking soda
1 teaspoon ground ginger
1 teaspoon ground cinnamon
2 teaspoons salt
Dash of ground cloves
1/2 cup sugar
1/2 cup shortening
2/3 cup molasses
1 egg, beaten
3/4 cup boiling water
Whipped topping

Combine flour, baking soda, ginger, cinnamon, salt and cloves. Set aside. In a mixing bowl, cream sugar and shortening. Add molasses and egg. Mix well. Stir in the dry ingredients alternating with the water. Mix well. Pour in a greased 9-inch square baking pan. Bake at 350 degrees for 35 to 40 minutes. Cool completely and top with a drop of whipped cream after cutting in squares. Yields 9 servings.

BETTY CATON
WELLINGTON VILLAGE ASSEMBLY OF GOD
LITTLE ROCK, ARKANSAS

NEW YORK CHEESECAKE

1 1/4 cups graham cracker or vanilla wafer crumbs
4 tablespoons butter, softened
1/4 cup sugar (optional)
3 (8-ounce) packages cream cheese, at room temperature
5 eggs
1 1/2 cups sugar
3 teaspoons vanilla extract
1 1/2 pints sour cream

Preheat the oven to 300 degrees. Pack the first 3 ingredients into the bottom of a 9 x 13-inch baking pan. In the bowl of an electric mixer, cream the cheese and add the eggs, one at a time. Gradually add 1 cup of the sugar and stir in 1 1/2 teaspoons of the vanilla. Pour the cream cheese mixture over the crumb mixture and bake for 1 hour. Cool for 5 minutes. In another bowl, combine the sour cream, the remaining 1/2 cup of the sugar, and the remaining 1 1/2 teaspoons of vanilla. When the cake has cooled, top it with the sour cream mixture. Bake for 5 minutes longer. Refrigerate.

JENNY KOTTENBROOK
GRIFFIN CHAPEL UNITED METHODIST CHURCH
STARKVILLE, MISSISSIPPI

HEAVENLY CHOCOLATE CHEESECAKE

CRUST:
2 cups crushed vanilla wafers
1 cup ground toasted almonds
1/2 cup sugar
1/2 cup melted butter or margarine

FILLING:
2 cups Nestlé Toll House milk chocolate morsels
1 envelope flavored gelatin
1/2 cup milk
2 (8-ounce) packages cream cheese, at room temperature
1/2 cup sour cream
1/2 teaspoon almond extract
1/2 cup whipping cream, whipped

For the crust, in a medium bowl combine the vanilla wafer crumbs, almonds, sugar, and butter; mix well. Press firmly into bottom and 2 inches up the sides of a 9-inch spring-form pan.

For the filling, in a small heavy saucepan over low heat melt the chocolate, stirring frequently. In another small saucepan, sprinkle the gelatin over the milk and let the mixture stand for 1 minute. Warm over low heat, stirring frequently, until the gelatin dissolves. In the bowl of an electric mixer, beat the cream cheese, sour cream, and chocolate until fluffy. Beat in the gelatin mixture and almond extract. Fold in the whipped cream and pour the mixture into the crust. Chill for about 3 hours, or until firm. Run a knife around the edge of the cheesecake to remove the rim and garnish as desired. Makes 8 to 10 servings.

JOSEPHINE CHURCH
PRINCE OF PEACE CHURCH
GRANTSVILLE, WEST VIRGINIA

PUMPKIN CHEESECAKE

CRUST:
1 cup graham cracker crumbs
1 tablespoon sugar
2 tablespoons butter or margarine

FILLING:
3 (8-ounce) packages cream cheese, at room temperature
1 cup sugar
1 cup sour cream
1 teaspoon vanilla extract
1 tablespoon pumpkin pie spice
6 eggs
1 (15-ounce) can pumpkin

Preheat the oven to 375 degrees.

For the crust, combine the graham cracker crumbs, sugar, and butter; mix well. Spread evenly in a 9-inch pie plate and set aside.

For the filling, combine the cream cheese and sugar in the bowl of an electric mixer. Beat on medium speed until the mixture is light and creamy. Add the sour cream and mix for 1 minute. Add the vanilla and spice, mixing for 1 minute. Add the eggs, mixing for 1 minute. Add pumpkin and mix for 2 minutes. Pour the filling into the crust. Bake for 45 minutes, or until firm. Chill in the refrigerator overnight. Serve with cranberry sauce, if desired.

JOYCE BALDWIN
MEMORIAL BAPTIST CHURCH
TULSA, OKLAHOMA

BUTTERSCOTCH CHEESECAKE

1 1/2 cups graham cracker crumbs
3/4 cup sugar
6 tablespoons melted butter or margarine
1 package regular (not instant) butterscotch pudding mix
Milk according to the pudding directions
3 (8-ounce) packages cream cheese, at room temperature
3 eggs
1 teaspoon vanilla extract
1 cup sour cream
1/4 cup sifted powdered sugar
1 banana (optional)

In a large bowl, combine the graham cracker crumbs, 1/3 cup sugar, and butter; press into the bottom and 2 1/2 inches up the sides of a 9-inch spring-form pan.

In a small saucepan, combine the pudding mix and the remaining sugar; stir in the milk. Cook, stirring, until the mixture is thick and bubbly. Remove the pan from the heat and cover the surface with clear plastic wrap; cool.

Preheat the oven to 375 degrees. In the bowl of an electric mixer, beat the cream cheese until it's fluffy; add the eggs and beat until blended. Add the vanilla and cooled pudding, blending well. Pour the mixture into the crumb-lined spring-form pan. Bake for 50 minutes, or until a knife inserted just off center comes out clean. Combine the sour cream and powdered sugar; spread atop the cheesecake. Return the cheesecake to the oven for 2 minutes longer. Cool to room temperature and store in the refrigerator. Garnish with banana slices, if desired, and chocolate curls or chips. Makes 12 servings.

BECKY GAYLOR
CROSS IN THE DESERT UNITED METHODIST CHURCH
PHOENIX, ARIZONA

Mini Cheesecakes

12 vanilla wafers
2 (8-ounce) packages cream cheese, at room
    temperature
1/2 cup sugar
1 teaspoon vanilla extract
2 eggs

Preheat the oven to 325 degrees. Line a 12-cup muffin tin with paper cups. Place a wafer in each liner. In a large bowl, combine the remaining ingredients and mix well; pour over the wafers three-fourths full in each cup. Bake for 25 minutes. When the cheesecakes have cooled, top them with fruit preserves or nuts.

Kay Andrews
Pinemount Baptist Church
McAlpin, Florida

Spicy Cupcakes

5 cups all-purpose flour
1 teaspoon baking soda
1 1/2 tablespoons baking powder
2 teaspoons salt
2 teaspoons ground nutmeg
1 1/2 tablespoons ground cinnamon
2 1/2 cups brown sugar
1 1/2 cups shortening
8 eggs
3 cups milk
5 cups oats (uncooked)
1 cup chopped nuts
1 cup raisins

Preheat the oven to 375 degrees. In the bowl of an electric mixer, sift together the flour, baking soda, baking powder, salt, and spices. Add the sugar, shortening, eggs, and half of the milk. Beat until smooth. Fold in the remaining milk, the oats, nuts, and raisins. Fill baking cups or greased muffin pans about one-half full. Bake for 15 to 20 minutes. Makes 100 cupcakes.

Geraldine Volentine
Holum Baptist Church
Grayson, Louisiana

PASTRY FOR SINGLE-CRUST PIE

1 1/4 cups all-purpose flour
1/2 teaspoon salt
1/3 cup shortening
4 to 5 tablespoons cold water

In a bowl, combine the flour and salt; cut in the shortening until the mixture is crumbly. Gradually add the water, tossing with a fork until a ball forms. Turn the dough out onto a floured bread board and roll out pastry to fit a 9- or 10-inch pie plate. Transfer the pastry to the pie plate. Trim the pastry to 1/2 inch beyond the edge of the pie plate and flute the edges. Fill or bake the shell according to the recipe directions.

Note: When rolling out the pastry, mend any cracks by wetting your fingers and pressing the dough together.

FRIEDA WARREN
TOWER HILL UNITED METHODIST CHURCH
TOWER HILL, ILLINOIS

PASTRY FOR DOUBLE-CRUST PIE

2 cups all-purpose flour
3/4 teaspoon salt
2/3 cup shortening
6 to 7 tablespoons cold water

In a bowl, combine the flour and salt; cut in the shortening until the mixture is crumbly. Gradually add the water, tossing with a fork until the dough forms a ball. Divide the dough in half so that one ball is slightly larger than the other. Turn the dough out onto a floured bread board and roll out the larger ball to fit a 9- or 10-inch pie plate. Transfer the pastry to the pie plate. Trim the pastry even with the edge of the plate. Pour the desired filling into the crust. Roll out the second ball, cutting steam vents in the pastry. Position the pastry over the filling and trim it to 1 inch beyond the edge of the pie plate. Fold the top crust over the bottom crust and crimp together; flute the edges. Bake according to the recipe directions.

Note: This recipe is also used when preparing a lattice-topped pie.

FRIEDA WARREN
TOWER HILL UNITED METHODIST CHURCH
TOWER HILL, ILLINOIS

FLAKY PIE CRUST

2 cups all-purpose flour
1 1/2 tablespoons sugar
1/2 teaspoon salt
1/2 cup and 2 tablespoons butter
1 large egg
2 tablespoons ice water

Mix together the flour, sugar, and salt in a large bowl. Cut the butter into small pieces and begin working it into the flour with a pastry cutter. Work with the dough until each piece of butter is the size of a raisin. Make sure to do this quickly. Mix together the egg and water in a small bowl, then add it to the flour/butter mixture. Smear this mixture and knead through it with the heel of your hand until it barely holds together. Don't overwork the dough. Flatten the dough into a disc shape, wrap it in plastic, and chill it in refrigerator for at least 30 minutes. Roll out the dough for the pie shell and place in a 10-inch pie pan. Line the shell with parchment paper and place baking beans or weights over it. Preheat the oven to 350 degrees. Chill for 30 minutes, then bake for 15 minutes. Remove parchment and weights and continue to bake for an additional 12 minutes or until crust is light golden brown. Let cool.

PINEMOUNT BAPTIST CHURCH
MCALPIN, FLORIDA

TIPS FOR TOP-NOTCH CRUSTS

Use ice-cold water to make the pastry dough. Add only enough water, a tablespoon at a time, to moisten the flour mixture. The amount of water will vary according to weather conditions.

Avoid overmixing or excess handling once the water has been added to the flour mixture.

Roll out the pastry with as little additional flour as possible for more tender crusts. A pastry cloth and a rolling pin cover will make the job easier without the use of excess flour.

Ease the rolled pastry into the pie plate. Stretching it to fit will cause the bottom crust to shrink while the pie is baking. Select glass or dull-finished aluminum pie plates for crisp golden crusts.

To prevent excess browning, cover the edge of the crust with foil before placing the pie in the oven. Uncover after 20 minutes of baking.

FRIEDA
TOWER HILL UNITED METHODIST CHURCH
TOWER HILL, ILLINOIS

Pat in the Pan Crust

2 cups Gold Medal all-purpose flour
2/3 cup margarine or butter, softened
1/2 cup almonds, toasted and finely chopped
1/2 cup powdered sugar

Preheat the oven to 350 degrees. In a medium bowl, combine all the ingredients and stir with a fork until the mixture is crumbly; press it firmly and evenly into the bottom of an ungreased 13 x 9 x 2-inch rectangular pan. Bake until set, 15 to 20 minutes.

JOSEPHINE CHURCH
PRINCE OF PEACE CHURCH
GRANTSVILLE, WEST VIRGINIA

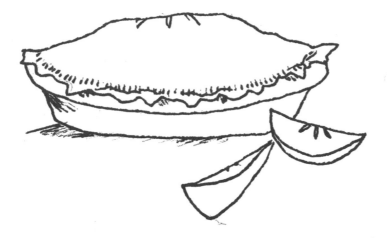

Apple Pie Contest Winner

CRUMB TOPPING:
1 cup packed brown sugar
1/2 cup all-purpose flour
1/2 cup quick-cooking oats
1/2 cup butter

PIE:
1 (9-inch) pastry crust for a deep-dish pie
   (homemade or store-bought)
3 tablespoons all-purpose flour
1/2 cup granulated sugar
1 teaspoon ground cinnamon
1/8 teaspoon salt
6 cups thinly sliced apples (Golden Delicious
   and Fuji, combined)
1/2 cup chopped pecans
1/4 cup caramel topping

For the Crumb Topping, in a large bowl stir together the brown sugar, flour, and oats. Cut in the butter until the mixture resembles crumbs.

Preheat the oven to 375 degrees. In a separate mixing bowl, stir together the flour, granulated sugar, cinnamon, and salt. Add the apple slices and toss gently until they're coated. Transfer the apple mixture to the pie shell. Sprinkle the Crumb Topping over the apples. Place the pie on a cookie sheet and cover the edge with aluminum foil. Bake for 25 minutes. Remove the foil and bake for 25 to 30 minutes longer. Remove the pie from the oven. Sprinkle with the pecans, then drizzle with caramel. Cool on a wire rack. Enjoy warm or at room temperature.

BARBARA HARVISON
MARSHA BROOKS, WINNER
BUCKINGHAM UNITED METHODIST CHURCH
GARLAND, TEXAS

APPLE, PEACH, OR PLUM KUCHEN

4 tablespoons soft margarine
1 cup sifted all-purpose flour
4 tablespoons sugar
1/2 teaspoon salt
1 1/2 teaspoons baking powder
1 egg, beaten
1/4 cup milk
Cinnamon-sugar mixture
Apples (peeled and sliced), peaches (unpeeled
    and sliced), plums (unpeeled and sliced)

Preheat the oven to 375 degrees. In a medium bowl, combine the margarine, flour, sugar, salt, and baking powder. Add the egg and milk and mix well. Spread the dough thinly in the bottom of two 8-inch greased cake pans. Place the sliced fruit of choice on top of the batter and sprinkle with the cinnamon-sugar mixture. Bake for 30 minutes, or until the dough browns.

IN MEMORY OF EDITH MOORE
UNITED BAPTIST CHURCH OF POULTNEY
EAST POULTNEY, VERMONT

SWEDISH APPLE PIE (SELF-CRUST PIE)

Apples, peeled and sliced (enough to fill a pie
    plate two-thirds full)
1 cup plus 1 tablespoon sugar
1 teaspoon ground cinnamon
1 cup all-purpose flour
1 egg
3/4 cup margarine
Pinch of salt
1/4 to 1/2 cup chopped nuts

Preheat the oven to 350 degrees. Fill an empty pie plate two-thirds full with the apples. Combine the tablespoon of sugar and the cinnamon and sprinkle over the apples. In a bowl, mix together the 1 cup of sugar, flour, egg, margarine, salt, and nuts; spread the mixture over the apples. Bake for 45 minutes.

PEGGY PARKER
UNITED BAPTIST CHURCH OF POULTNEY
EAST POULTNEY, VERMONT

DEEP DISH ALMOND-APPLE PIE

1 (15-ounce) package refrigerated pie crust
All-purpose flour for dusting
1/2 cup sugar
3/4 cup brown sugar
1/4 cup all-purpose flour
1 teaspoon ground cinnamon
1/4 teaspoon ground nutmeg
1/4 teaspoon salt
8 medium apples
2/3 cup sliced almonds
1/2 teaspoon almond extract
3 tablespoons butter

Preheat the oven to 375 degrees. Remove one crust from the package and sprinkle both sides with flour. Roll the crust out to 14 inches. Place in a deep dish pie plate; taking care not to stretch the dough. In a big mixing bowl, combine the sugar, brown sugar, flour, cinnamon, nutmeg and salt. Peel, core, and slice the apples. Gently toss the apple slices with the sugar mixture. Turn into the prepared crust.

Sprinkle the apples with the almonds and almond extract. Dot with small pieces of butter. Dust with flour the second crust and roll out to 13 inches. Place on top of apple mixture, seal and flute the edges of the pie crust.

Cut slits in several places on the surface of the pie. Bake for 50 to 55 minutes or until the filling bubbles and the apples are tender. Cover the edges of the crust with foil during the last 15 to 20 minutes if desired, to prevent over-browning. Yields 8 servings.

MELISSA CLARK
WELLINGTON VILLAGE ASSEMBLY OF GOD
LITTLE ROCK, ARKANSAS

APPLE-CRANBERRY CRISP

1/2 cup plus 2 tablespoons all-purpose flour
1/2 cup firmly packed light brown sugar
1/3 cup butter or margarine
3/4 cup old-fashioned or quick-cooking oats
3/4 cup chopped walnuts
4 medium Granny Smith apples
1 1/2 cups fresh or frozen cranberries
1/2 cup granulated sugar
1 teaspoon ground cinnamon
Vanilla ice cream

To make the topping, combine 1/2 cup of the flour and the brown sugar in a medium bowl. Mix well. With a pastry blender or two knives, cut in the butter until the mixture resembles coarse crumbs. Stir in the oats and nuts. Mix well and set aside.

Peel and core the apples, then cut them into 1/4-inch slices. In a shallow 2-quart microwave-safe dish, combine the apple slices, cranberries, granulated sugar, the 2 tablespoons of flour, and cinnamon. Mix well. Sprinkle the topping evenly over the apple mixture. Microwave on high for 12 to14 minutes, or until the apples are tender, rotating a quarter turn every 4 minutes. Serve warm with vanilla ice cream. Makes 6 servings.

Note: You can refrigerate the pie and reheat individual servings. It usually tastes better the next day.

VIRGINIA ROBERSON
HIGHLAND HEIGHTS PRESBYTERIAN CHURCH
CORDOVA, TENNESSEE

CINNAMON APPLE PUFFS

1 cup plus 2 tablespoons sugar
1 cup water
1/2 teaspoon red food coloring
4 to 5 apples, peeled and sliced
1/2 cup all-purpose flour
2 teaspoons baking powder
1/2 teaspoon salt
1/4 cup shortening
3/4 cup milk
2 tablespoons melted butter
1/2 teaspoon cinnamon

Preheat the oven to 450 degrees. In a small saucepan, boil the 1 cup sugar, water, and food coloring until it thickens to a syrup. Place the apples in a greased 8 x 12-inch pan. In a large bowl, sift together the dry ingredients and cut in the shortening. Add the milk, enough to make a soft dough. Drop the dough by spoonfuls on top of the apples and make a dent in the top of each mound. In a small bowl, combine the butter, 2 tablespoons sugar, and cinnamon. Place some cinnamon-sugar mixture in each dent. Bake for 25 to 30 minutes. Serve warm with cream or cold with whipped cream.

DELPHINE SINDELIR
PITT COMMUNITY CHURCH
BAUDETTE, MINNESOTA

Lemon Meringue Pie

3 tablespoons cornstarch
2 teaspoons lemon zest
1 cup sugar
1 1/4 cups warm water
Juice of 1 lemon
3 eggs, separated
1 teaspoon vanilla extract
1 (9-inch) pie shell (homemade or store-
   bought)

Preheat the oven to 350 degrees. In a medium saucepan, cook the first 5 ingredients and the egg yolks until the mixture thickens, stirring occasionally. Cool and pour into the cooked pie shell. In a small bowl, beat the egg whites, add the vanilla. Spread the egg white meringue evenly over the pie. Put in the oven to brown meringue, about 8 minutes.

PINEMOUNT BAPTIST CHURCH
MCALPIN, FLORIDA

Key Lime Pie

3 eggs, separated
1 can (14-ounce) condensed milk
1/2 cup lime juice, fresh or from concentrate
1 (9-inch) unbaked pastry shell (homemade
   or store-bought)
1/2 teaspoon cream of tartar
1/3 cup sugar

Preheat the oven to 325 degrees. In the bowl of an electric mixer, beat the egg yolks. Gradually beat in the condensed milk (*not* evaporated milk!) and lime juice. Pour the mixture into the pastry shell. Bake for 30 minutes and remove from the oven. Increase the oven temperature to 350 degrees. For the meringue, with a clean mixer, beat the egg whites and cream of tartar until soft peaks form. Gradually beat in the sugar, 1 tablespoon at a time. Beat for 4 minutes, or until stiff, glossy peaks form and the sugar dissolves. Immediately spread the meringue over the hot pie, carefully sealing to the edge of the crust to prevent the meringue from shrinking. Bake for 15 minutes. Cool the pie for 1 hour. Chill for at least 3 hours. Store, covered, in the refrigerator.

JEANNE TOOMEY
MATTAPOISETT CONGREGATIONAL CHURCH
MATTAPOISETT, MASSACHUSETTS

FRENCH STRAWBERRY PIE

1 package cream cheese
Whipping cream
1 9-inch pie shell, baked and cooled
1 quart fresh strawberries, hulled
1 cup sugar
3 tablespoons cornstarch
1 cup whipping cream

Mix cream cheese with enough cream to soften and spread over the bottom of a baked, cooled pie shell. Place half the strawberries in the cheese-coated pie shell. In a saucepan mash the remaining berries until the juice runs. Mix the sugar and cornstarch in a bowl. Bring to a boil and slowly stir in the sugar and cornstarch mixture. Cook slowly for about 10 minutes, stirring occasionally. Cool and pour over the uncooked berries in the pie shell. Serve with whipping cream.

ROBERTA MULLINIX
DAMASCUS UNITED METHODIST CHURCH
DAMASCUS, MARYLAND

BARBARA'S LEMON SPONGE PIE

1 unbaked (9-inch) pastry shell
  (homemade or store-bought)
3 tablespoons butter
1 cup sugar
2 eggs, separated
1 teaspoon grated lemon rind
1/4 cup lemon juice
3 tablespoons all-purpose flour
1/8 teaspoon salt
1 cup milk

Preheat the oven to 450 degrees. In the bowl of an electric mixer, cream the butter and sugar, blending well. Add the egg yolks, one at a time, beating after each addition. Add the lemon rind and juice, flour, and salt; mix well. Add the milk. In a separate bowl beat the egg whites until the mixture is stiff but not dry and fold this into the lemon mixture. Pour the filling into the pastry shell and bake for 10 minutes. Reduce the oven temperature to 350 degrees and bake for 35 minutes longer, or until a knife inserted into the center comes out clean.

Note: To make 2 pies, double the recipe.

RICHARD WATSON,
IN MEMORY OF HIS WIFE, BARBARA WATSON
TRINITY UNITED METHODIST CHURCH
YORK, PENNSYLVANIA

BLUEBERRY BUCKLE

1/4 cup shortening
3/4 cup sugar
1 egg
1/2 cup milk
2 cups sifted all-purpose flour
1/2 teaspoon salt
2 teaspoons baking powder
2 cups fresh or frozen blueberries

TOPPING:
1/2 cup sugar
1/3 cup all-purpose flour
1/2 teaspoon ground cinnamon
1/4 cup soft butter, softened

Preheat the oven to 375 degrees. In the bowl of an electric mixer, cream the shortening, adding the sugar and egg. Blend thoroughly. Add the milk, then the dry ingredients. Fold in the blueberries. Spread the batter in well-greased 9-inch square pan.

In a small bowl, combine all the ingredients and sprinkle over the cake. Bake for 45 to 50 minutes.

DELPHINE SINDELIR
PITT COMMUNITY CHURCH
BAUDETTE, MINNESOTA

FRESH RHUBARB-STRAWBERRY PIE

1 2/3 cup sugar
1/3 cup all-purpose flour
4 cups sliced fresh rhubarb
1/2 cup sliced strawberries
2 tablespoon butter or margarine
1 (9-inch) double pie shell (homemade or store-bought)

Preheat the oven to 400 degrees. In a large bowl, combine the sugar, flour, rhubarb, and strawberries. Let the mixture set for a while. Dot a pastry-lined pie plate with the butter. Pour in the rhubarb mixture and top with the second crust. Cut 5 or 6 steam vents in the crust, seal, and flute the edges. Sprinkle with a little sugar. Cover the edge with 2- or 3-inch strips of aluminum foil to prevent excessive browning. Remove the foil during the last 15 minutes of baking. Bake for 40 to 50 minutes, or until the crust is brown and the juice begins to bubble through the slits in the crust.

WANDA MORRIS
CHURCH OF CHRIST
ESTÂNCIA, NEW MEXICO

PERFECT PEACH COBBLER

3 cups sliced peaches
1 tablespoon lemon juice
1 cup sifted all-purpose flour
1 cup sugar
1/2 teaspoon salt
1/2 teaspoon ground cinnamon
1 egg beaten
6 tablespoons melted butter or margarine

Preheat the oven to 375 degrees. Place the peaches in a 10 x 6 x 1 1/2-inch pan. Sprinkle with the lemon juice. In a large bowl, sift together the dry ingredients. Add the egg and toss with a fork until the mixture is crumbly. Sprinkle the crumb mixture over the peaches and drizzle with the butter. Bake for 35 to 40 minutes. Serve warm with ice cream or whipped cream.

BECKY GAYLOR
CROSS IN THE DESERT UNITED METHODIST CHURCH
PHOENIX, ARIZONA

PEACH PIE

7 cups peaches, peeled, pitted, and sliced
1/2 cup granulated sugar
1/3 cup brown sugar
1 teaspoon ground cinnamon
Pinch of nutmeg
Pinch of salt
1 (9-inch) double pie shell (homemade or
    store-bought)
1/4 cup heavy cream
1/4 cup butter
1 egg white, beaten

Preheat the oven to 450 degrees. Place the peaches in a bowl with the sugars, spices, and salt. Pour in the cream and stir. Pour the mixture into a pastry-lined pie plate. Dot with butter. Top with the second crust and flute the edges. Cut several steam vents in the top. Brush with the egg white and bake for 10 minutes. Reduce the heat to 375 and bake for 40 to 45 minutes longer.

GRAMMY
FOREST AVENUE CONGREGATIONAL CHURCH
BANGOR, MAINE

ETERNAL CHERRY PIE

Pie pastry for double 2-crust pie
    (homemade or store-bought)
2 cans sour red cherries, or 4 cups pitted,
    fresh red cherries
1 tablespoon lemon juice
1 1/4 cups sugar
1/4 cup all-purpose flour
1/8 teaspoon salt
1/8 teaspoon ground cloves
1/4 teaspoon ground cinnamon
1 tablespoon butter

Preheat the oven to 400 degrees. In a large bowl, sprinkle the cherries with the lemon juice. In a separate bowl, combine the sugar, flour, salt, and spices; add to the cherries and mix gently but thoroughly. Pour the filling into an unbaked pastry crust and dot with butter. Top with the second crust and seal and crimp the edges; cut 5 or 6 steam vents in the crust. Bake for 35 to 40 minutes, or until the pie is nicely browned.

PINEMOUNT BAPTIST CHURCH
MCALPIN, FLORIDA

RAISIN PIE

1 unbaked double pie shell (homemade or
    store-bought)
2 cups raisins
1 1/2 cups water
1/2 cup sugar
2 tablespoons all-purpose flour
1/2 cup chopped walnuts
1 teaspoon grated lemon zest
3 tablespoons lemon juice

Preheat the oven to 425 degrees. Line a 9-inch pie plate with the pastry. In a medium saucepan, combine the raisins and water; cook, covered, for 10 minutes or until the raisins are plumped. In a bowl, combine the sugar and flour and stir into the raisins. Cook, stirring over low heat until the mixture thickens and bubbles. Cook for 1 minute longer. Remove the pan from the heat; stir in the nuts, lemon zest, and juice. Pour the hot raisin mixture into the pastry-lined pie plate. Top with the second crust; cut 5 to 6 slits to allow steam to escape. Seal and flute the edges. Bake for 30 to 40 minutes.

EVELYN SAYLOR
TRINITY UNITED METHODIST CHURCH
YORK, PENNSYLVANIA

No-Crust Cream Cheese Pie

2 (8-ounce) packages cream cheese
2/3 cup plus 3 tablespoons sugar
4 eggs
1 teaspoon vanilla extract
1 teaspoon cornstarch
1/2 pint sour cream
1 (20-ounce) can crushed pineapple, drained

Preheat the oven to 350 degrees. In the bowl of an electric mixer, cream together the cream cheese, 2/3 cup of the sugar, eggs, vanilla, and cornstarch. Pour the mixture into a lightly greased pie plate and bake for 25 minutes. Combine the sour cream, the remaining 3 tablespoons of the sugar, and pineapple. Pour on top of the baked pie and bake for 10 minutes longer.

Note: A fruit glaze can be substituted for the pineapple. Just spread this on after baking.

MARYSUE WALTER
TRINITY UNITED METHODIST CHURCH
YORK, PENNSYLVANIA

Cream Pie (Banana or Coconut)

1/3 cup all-purpose flour
2/3 cup plus 6 tablespoons sugar
1/4 teaspoon salt
2 cups scalded milk
3 eggs, separated
2 tablespoons butter
1/4 teaspoon vanilla extract
1 (9-inch) baked pie shell (homemade or
    store-bought)
1/8 teaspoon cream of tartar

In a medium saucepan, combine the flour, 2/3 cup of the sugar, and salt; gradually add the scalded milk. Cook over moderate heat, stirring briskly and constantly, until the mixture thickens and boils. Cook for 2 minutes and remove the pan from the heat. Beat the egg yolks and add a small amount of the milk mixture to the yolks. Stir the beaten yolks into the remaining milk mixture. Cook for 1 minute, stirring constantly. Add the butter and vanilla. Cool slightly and pour into the baked pie shell.

Preheat the oven to 375 degrees. In the bowl of an electric mixer, beat the egg whites on high speed. After they foam up, gradually add the cream of tartar and the remaining 6 tablespoons of sugar; continue beating until stiff peaks form. Gently pour the egg whites onto the pie and bake for 15 minutes.

Note: For a coconut pie, add 1 cup coconut to the filling.

For a banana pie, add 2 sliced bananas.

SARA COOPER
BUCKINGHAM UNITED METHODIST CHURCH
GARLAND, TEXAS

CHOCOLATE PEANUT BUTTER PIE

2 cups heavy whipping cream
9 ounces bittersweet chocolate, finely
    chopped
1 1/4 teaspoons vanilla extract
1 (9-inch) crumb crust
1 cup peanut butter
4 ounces cream cheese
1 cup powdered sugar

In a medium saucepan, bring 1 cup of the cream to a gentle boil over medium-low heat. Remove the pan from the heat and stir in the chocolate. Let the mixture stand for 1 to 2 minutes. Add 1/4 teaspoon of the vanilla and whisk until smooth. Pour the mixture into the pie shell and spread evenly. Refrigerate for 30 to 60 minutes, or until set.

In a large bowl, using a handheld mixer set on medium-high speed, cream together the peanut butter, cream cheese, and the remaining 1 teaspoon of vanilla. Gradually beat in the sugar. In a chilled bowl with a chilled beater, beat the remaining 1 cup of cream just until stiff peaks begin to form. With a rubber spatula, stir one-third of the whipped cream into the peanut butter mixture until smooth. Gently fold in the remaining whipped cream until mixed. Spread evenly over the chocolate layer in the pie shell. Refrigerate for at least 2 hours, or until the peanut butter mousse becomes firm. You can top the pie with whipped cream, chopped peanuts, or chocolate curls. Makes 8 to 10 servings.

ROBERT DITZEL
TRINITY UNITED METHODIST CHURCH
YORK, PENNSYLVANIA

BLUE RIBBON ARKANSAS STATE PECAN PIE

1 cup brown sugar
1 cup white corn syrup
1 tablespoon all-purpose flour
1/2 teaspoon salt
1/2 cup melted butter
1 teaspoon vanilla extract
3 eggs, lightly beaten
1 cup chopped pecans
Several pecan halves for top (or chop fine
    and sprinkle on top)

CRUST:
1 cup all-purpose flour
1/2 teaspoon salt
1 teaspoon sugar
1/3 cup shortening
3 tablespoons orange juice

Mix sugar, syrup, flour, salt, butter, and vanilla. Add eggs, stir in chopped pecans. Preheat the oven to 350 degrees. Make the crust by combining flour, salt, sugar, shortening, and orange juice. Press this into a 9-inch pie pan. Arrange pecan halves on top and bake for about 45 minutes. Cover the crust edges to prevent over-browning during the last 15 minutes of baking.

BETTY CATON
WELLINGTON VILLAGE ASSEMBLY OF GOD
LITTLE ROCK, ARKANSAS

MICROWAVE PECAN PIE

1 (9-inch) unbaked pie shell (homemade or
   store-bought)
1/4 cup butter
3 eggs
1 cup dark corn syrup
1/3 cup brown sugar
1 tablespoon self-rising flour
1 teaspoon vanilla extract
1 1/2 cups chopped pecans

Bake the pie shell in the oven at 350 degrees for 10 minutes. Place the butter in a large glass mixing bowl and microwave on high for 1/2 to 1 minute, until it melts. Add the eggs to the melted butter and beat with a fork to mix well. Blend in the corn syrup, sugar, flour, and vanilla. Then stir in the pecans. Pour the filling into the pie shell. Microwave on medium for 12 to 15 minutes. (If the microwave is not equipped with a rotating dish, be sure to turn the pie a half turn after 5 minutes.) The pie is done when the top surface is dry and puffed and the filling has set.

PINEMOUNT BAPTIST CHURCH
MCALPIN, FLORIDA

CHESS PIE

1 1/2 cups sugar
1 tablespoon cornmeal
1 teaspoon vanilla extract
1 teaspoon vinegar
1/2 cup melted margarine
3 eggs
1/4 cup milk
1 (9-inch) unbaked pie shell (homemade or
   store-bought)

Preheat the oven to 400 degrees. In a large bowl, combine all the ingredients and mix well. Pour the mixture into the pie shell. Bake for 10 minutes at 400 degrees, then lower the temperature to 325 degrees and continue baking for 30 minutes longer.

MARTY ADAMS
HIGHLAND HEIGHTS PRESBYTERIAN CHURCH
CORDOVA, TENNESSEE

IMPOSSIBLE PIE (MAKES ITS OWN CRUST)

4 eggs
1/2 stick margarine, melted
1 3/4 cups sugar
1/2 cup self-rising flour
1/4 teaspoon salt
2 cups milk
1 teaspoon vanilla extract
1 cup shredded coconut

Preheat the oven to 350 degrees. In the bowl of an electric mixer, beat the eggs for 3 minutes. Add the butter, sugar, flour, salt, milk, and vanilla. Beat again until the ingredients are well blended. Stir in the coconut. Pour the mixture into a greased 10-inch glass pie plate. Bake for 40 minutes.

Note: The ingredients can also be mixed in a blender.

PENNY FRITZ
TRINITY UNITED METHODIST CHURCH
YORK, PENNSYLVANIA

SHOO-FLY PIE

1 1/2 cups all-purpose flour
1/2 cup packed brown sugar
1/4 teaspoon salt
1/4 teaspoon ground cinnamon
1/8 teaspoon ground cloves
1/8 teaspoon ground ginger
1/8 teaspoon ground nutmeg
1/4 cup margarine
1 cup boiling water
1/2 cup dark molasses
1 1/2 teaspoons baking soda
1 egg, slightly beaten
1 (9-inch) pie shell (homemade or store-
   bought)

Preheat the oven to 450 degrees. In a large bowl, combine the flour, brown sugar, salt, and spices. Cut in the margarine until the mixture resembles coarse cornmeal. In a separate bowl, combine the water, molasses, and baking soda; blend in the egg. Starting and ending with the crumb mixture, arrange alternate layers of the two mixtures in the pie shell. Bake at 450 degrees for 10 minutes, then reduce the temperature to 350 degrees and bake for 15 minutes longer, or until firm.

Note: This recipe was given to me many years ago by my good friend Anne Corbett, who now has her own Ice Cream Parlor & Cafe in New Hampshire, where Shoo-Fly Pie is featured on the menu.

SUE CALLESIS
UNITED BAPTIST CHURCH OF POULTNEY
EAST POULTNEY, VERMONT

HOLIDAY SWEET POTATO PIE

2 large sweet potatoes
Pastry for sweet pie dough
2 whole eggs
2 egg yolks
2/3 cup sugar
1/2 teaspoon salt
1 teaspoon ground cinnamon
1/4 teaspoon ground ginger, or 1 teaspoon
   freshly grated
1/4 teaspoon freshly grated nutmeg
1 1/4 cups light cream or half-and-half

Preheat the oven to 350 degrees. Bake the sweet potatoes for 1 hour, or until soft. Cool, peel, and puree in a food processor. Set a rack in the lowest level of the oven.

For the bottom crust, lightly flour a bread board and roll the dough out to a 12-inch disk. Fold the dough in half and place it in a pie plate; unfold the dough and press it firmly into the plates. Trim away all but 1/2-inch excess dough at the edge of the pie plate. Fold the dough under and flute the edge.

For the filling, scrape the potatoes into a bowl and whisk in the whole eggs and egg yolks. Whisk in the remaining ingredients in order, whisking the mixture smooth after each addition. Pour the filling into the prepared pie shell. Bake the pie for about 1 hour, or until the crust is baked through and the filling is set. Cool the pie on a rack.

PINEMOUNT BAPTIST CHURCH
MCALPIN, FLORIDA

Famous Pumpkin Pie

1 (9-inch) pie shell (homemade or store-
   bought)
2 eggs, slightly beaten
2 cups fresh pumpkin, or 1 (15-ounce) can
3/4 cup sugar
1/2 teaspoon salt
1 teaspoon ground cinnamon
1/2 teaspoon ground ginger
1/4 teaspoon ground cloves
1 (12-ounce) can evaporated milk

Preheat the oven and a baking sheet to 375 degrees. In a large bowl, combine the filling ingredients in order. Crimp the edge of the pie shell so that it extends 1/2 inch above the rim. Place the pie shell on a preheated baking sheet and pour the filling into it. Bake the pie in the center of the oven for 70 minutes, or until a knife inserted in the center comes out clean. Cool on a wire rack. Makes one 9-inch pie. (Fresh pumpkin is recommended.)

Diana Aday
First Baptist Church
Estância, New Mexico

Butterscotch Pie

4 1/2 tablespoons all-purpose flour
1 1/2 cups brown sugar
1/4 teaspoon salt
1 1/2 cups milk
4 1/2 teaspoons water
4 tablespoons margarine
1 1/2 teaspoons vanilla extract
2 egg yolks, beaten
1 (9-inch) baked pie shell (homemade or
   store-bought)

In a large saucepan over medium heat, combine the flour, sugar, salt, milk, water, margarine, and vanilla. Add the egg yolks while the mixture is cool. Stir constantly over the heat until the mixture thickens and comes to a boil. Pour the filling into the pie shell, cool slightly, and top with meringue.

Joyce Camac
Tower Hill United Methodist Church
Tower Hill, Illinois

Chocolate Silk Pie

3/4 cup butter, softened
3/4 cup plus 2 tablespoons sugar
3 eggs
1 teaspoon vanilla extract
3 squares unsweetened chocolate, melted
   and cooled
1/2 pint whipping cream
1 (9-inch) baked pie shell (homemade or
   store-bought)

In the bowl of an electric mixer, cream the butter and 3/4 cup of the sugar. Add the eggs, one at a time, beating well after each addition. Add the vanilla and chocolate, beating until the mixture is thick. Pour into a cooled pie shell and refrigerate for 15 minutes. In a small bowl, stir the remaining 2 tablespoons of sugar into whipping cream and add this to the filling. Chill until serving time.

Katrina Suthers
Mosca United Methodist Church
Mosca, Colorado

BOSTON CREAM PIE

CAKE:
1/4 cup butter, softened
1 cup sugar
3 large eggs
2/3 cup milk
1 teaspoon vanilla extract
1 3/4 cups all-purpose flour
2 teaspoons baking powder

CUSTARD:
2/3 cup sugar
1/3 cup cornstarch
1/4 teaspoon salt
2 1/2 cups milk
4 large egg yolks, lightly beaten
1 tablespoon vanilla extract

GLAZE:
3 ounces milk chocolate or semisweet
* chocolate*
1 tablespoon butter
1/3 cup powdered sugar
1/4 cup milk

For the cake: Preheat the oven to 350 degrees. Grease and flour two 9-inch round cake pans. In the bowl of an electric mixer on medium speed, beat the butter, sugar, eggs, milk, vanilla, flour, and baking powder until the mixture is thoroughly blended and smooth. Spoon the batter into the prepared pans and bake for 30 minutes, or until a wooden pick inserted into the center of each layer comes out clean. Remove the cakes to wire racks to cool completely.

For the custard: In a 2-quart saucepan, combine the sugar, cornstarch, and salt and stir until the mixture is thoroughly blended; slowly stir in the milk until smooth. Bring to a boil over medium heat, stirring constantly; cook for 1 minute, until the mixture boils rapidly and thickens. Remove the pan from the heat and very slowly pour the egg yolks into the hot mixture, stirring rapidly and constantly to blend and keep smooth. Return the mixture to low heat and cook for 1 minute longer. Do not allow it to boil. Remove the pan from the heat and stir in the vanilla. Cool completely, stirring frequently.

For the glaze: In a small heavy saucepan over very low heat, melt the chocolate and butter, stirring frequently, until blended and smooth. Remove the pan from the heat. Stir in the sugar and milk until blended and smooth. Cover and keep warm.

To assemble: Using a sharp serrated knife, carefully cut the cooled layers of the cake in half horizontally. Place one layer, cut side up, on a serving platter; spread with one-third of the cooled custard. Repeat with the remaining layers and custard, ending with a cake layer, cut side down. Spoon the warm glaze over the top of the cake, letting the mixture drip down the sides. Makes 12 to 16 servings.

FRANCES CHAMBLEE
CROSS IN THE DESERT UNITED METHODIST CHURCH
PHOENIX, ARIZONA

Amazing Coconut Pie

2 cups milk
3/4 cup sugar
1/2 cup biscuit mix
4 eggs
1/4 cup butter or margarine
1 1/2 teaspoons vanilla extract
1 cup Baker's Angel Flake coconut

Preheat the oven to 350 degrees. In a blender, combine the milk, sugar, biscuit mix, eggs, butter, and vanilla. Cover and blend on low speed for 3 minutes. Pour the mixture into a greased 9-inch pie plate. Let the mixture stand for about 5 minutes, then sprinkle with the coconut. Bake for 40 minutes. Serve warm or cool.

LAURA HESS
TRINITY UNITED METHODIST CHURCH
YORK, PENNSYLVANIA

Baklava

2 pounds finely chopped walnuts
1 cup sugar
2 teaspoons ground cinnamon
1 teaspoon ground nutmeg
2 teaspoons ground cloves
1 1/2 pounds butter, clarified
2 pounds phyllo pastry sheets

SYRUP:
4 cups sugar
2 cups water
1/2 lemon, sliced
1 cinnamon stick
1/2 cup honey

Preheat the oven to 350 degrees. In a large bowl, combine the walnuts, sugar, and spices. Brush the bottom of a 14 x 20-inch baking pan with the butter and line with 1 pastry sheet. Brush with more butter, repeating this process until 8 pastry sheets line the bottom of the pan. Brush with butter and sprinkle with the nut mixture. Add another pastry sheet, brush with butter, and sprinkle with the nut mixture, repeating this process until all the ingredients have been used. End with eight top layers (making sure you butter each layer). Cut diagonally into diamonds *halfway* through the layers. A clove bud may be placed in the center of each diamond pastry delight if desired. Bake for 15 to 20 minutes, or until the dough is slightly golden on top. Reduce the oven temperature to 250 degrees for at least 1 1/2 hours.

For the syrup, boil the sugar and water with the lemon slices and cinnamon stick to form a thin syrup. Stir in the honey and cool. Spoon the cooled syrup over the hot pastry.

BARBARA BLOOD
CROSS IN THE DESERT UNITED METHODIST CHURCH
PHOENIX, ARIZONA

PLUM PUDDING 1887
(IN MEMORY OF MY MOTHER, ALICE OWEN)

*To make plum pudding to Englishman's taste
So all may be eaten and nothing to waste,
Take of raisins and currants and bread crumbs,
   all round,
Also suet from oxen, and flour a pound.
Of citron well candied, or lemon as good,
With molasses and sugar, eight ounces
I would into this compound.
Next must be hasted a nugmeg, well grated,
Ground ginger well tasted*

*With salt to preserve it, of such a teaspoonful.
Then of milk half a pint,
And of fresh eggs, take six.
Be sure after this that you properly mix.
Next tie up in a bag, just as round as you can,
Put into a capacious and suitable pan,
Then boil for 8 hours just as hard as you can.*

INEZ DUNBAR
CALVARY UNITED METHODIST CHURCH
TAYLOR, NEBRASKA

OLD-FASHIONED BREAD PUDDING

*4 cups (8 slices) cubed bread
1/2 cup raisins
2 cups milk
1/4 cup butter
1/2 cup granulated sugar
2 eggs, slightly beaten
1/2 teaspoon ground nutmeg
1 teaspoon vanilla extract*

VANILLA SAUCE:
*1/2 cup granulated sugar
1/2 cup brown sugar
1/2 cup butter
1/2 cup whipping cream
1 teaspoon vanilla extract*

Preheat the oven to 350 degrees. In a large bowl, combine the bread and raisins. In a 1-quart saucepan, combine the milk and butter. Cook over medium heat until the butter melts, 4 to 7 minutes. Pour the milk mixture over the bread and let stand for 10 minutes. Stir in the remaining ingredients and pour the mixture into a greased 1 1/2-quart casserole dish. Bake for 40 to 50 minutes, or until the center of the pudding sets.

In a 1-quart saucepan, combine all the ingredients except the vanilla. Cook over medium heat, stirring occasionally, until the mixture thickens and comes to a full boil. Stir in the vanilla.

To serve, spoon the pudding into individual dessert dishes. Serve with the sauce. Refrigerate leftovers.

VERNAE MAY
ASSEMBLY OF GOD
ESTÂNCIA, NEW MEXICO

INDIAN PUDDING

1 quart milk
5 tablespoons cornmeal
1/2 cup molasses
1 teaspoon salt
1 teaspoon ground ginger
2 eggs, well beaten
1 cup cold milk

Preheat the oven to 350 degrees. Scald the milk in a double boiler. To the hot milk, gradually add the cornmeal. Cook the mixture for 15 minutes, stirring constantly. Add the molasses, salt, ginger, and eggs. Pour into a greased baking dish and add the cold milk, stirring only slightly. Place the dish in a pan of hot water and bake for 2 hours. Stir occasionally. Serve hot or cold.

WILLIE STEVENSON
EAGLES NEST CHEROKEE
FOREST AVENUE CONGREGATIONAL CHURCH
BANGOR, MAINE

BLACKBERRY PUDDING

PUDDING:
1 cup sugar
1/2 stick butter
2 teaspoons baking powder
2 cups all-purpose flour
1 cup milk

Cream the sugar and butter. Sift the baking powder and flour. Stir all together with the milk. Pour into a large 9 x 13-inch buttered baking dish.

FILLING:
3 cups or more blackberries
1 cup sugar
2 cups hot water
1/2 stick butter

Preheat the oven to 325 degrees. Stir all ingredients together and pour on top of batter. Bake 35 to 50 minutes. Serves 12.

ARLENE GLICK
TOWER HILL UNITED METHODIST CHURCH
TOWER HILL, ILLINOIS

Zabaglione

5 egg yolks plus 1 whole egg
2 tablespoons sugar
1/2 cup Marsala wine

In a double boiler, combine the egg yolks, whole egg, and sugar and cook over simmering water. Beat the mixture with a wire whisk or a rotary beater until it is pale yellow and fluffy. Gradually add the Marsala and continue beating until the zabaglione becomes thick enough to hold its shape in a spoon. This process may take as long as 10 minutes. Spoon the zabaglione into individual dessert bowls, compote dishes, or large-stemmed glasses and serve while it is still hot.

Lindsay Hill vonHunnius
Mattapoisett Congregational Church
Mattapoisett, Massachusetts

BESS TRUMAN'S PUDDING

1 egg
3/4 cup sugar
2 teaspoon baking powder
1/3 cup all-purpose flour
1/4 teaspoon salt
1/2 cup chopped apples
1/2 cup chopped pecans
1 teaspoon vanilla extract
Whipping cream

Preheat the oven to 325 degrees. Grease a 9-inch square pan. In the bowl of an electric mixer, beat the egg well. Add the sugar and beat until creamy. Add the baking powder, flour, and salt. Next, add the apples, nuts, and vanilla just until mixed. Bake for 30 minutes. Serve with whipped cream. Makes about 6 servings.

HELEN STOWERS
BUCKINGHAM UNITED METHODIST CHURCH
GARLAND, TEXAS

CHOCOLATE MOUSSE

1 pint heavy cream
1/2 cup sugar
1/2 cup water
4 eggs
12 ounces semisweet chocolate, chopped
Pinch of salt
1 teaspoon instant coffee

Whip the cream in a food processor until it's thick, about 30 to 40 seconds. Transfer the whipped cream to another bowl and wash out the processor. In a small saucepan, boil the sugar and water until the sugar dissolves. In the processor, place the eggs, chocolate, salt, and coffee. Process until smooth. Add the hot sugar-water mixture and process for about 20 to 30 seconds. (This hot liquid makes the eggs safe to eat.) Let the chocolate mixture cool for approximately 10 to 15 minutes. Fold in the whipped cream and refrigerate for 8 to 10 hours. Serve with freshly whipped cream and berries, if desired.

SUSAN JONES
NORTHBROOK UNITED METHODIST CHURCH
ROSWELL, GEORGIA

BAKED RICE PUDDING

2 large eggs
1/2 cup sugar
1/4 teaspoon salt
2 cups milk
Vanilla (optional)
2 cups cooked rice
1/2 cup seedless raisins (optional)
Ground nutmeg
Whipped Cream

Preheat the oven to 350 degrees. In a medium bowl, beat the eggs slightly; add the sugar and salt. In a small saucepan, scald the milk and pour it into the egg mixture. Add the vanilla, if desired. Add the rice and stir in the raisins, if desired. Sprinkle a little nutmeg over the top. Pour the mixture into a 1 1/2-quart casserole dish and set in a pan of hot water (1 inch deep). Bake for 1 hour and 15 minutes. Serve warm with whipped cream, if desired.

MADELYN FOGLER
MATTAPOISETT CONGREGATIONAL CHURCH
MATTAPOISETT, MASSACHUSETTS

CREAMY BANANA PUDDING

1 (14-ounce) can Eagle Brand condensed
   milk
1 1/2 cups cold water
1 package instant vanilla pudding mix
2 cups whipping cream, whipped
36 vanilla wafers
3 medium bananas, sliced and dipped in
   lemon juice

In the bowl of an electric mixer, combine the condensed milk and water. Add the pudding mix and beat well. Chill for 5 minutes. Fold in the whipped cream. Spoon 1 cup of the pudding mixture into a 2 1/2-quart serving bowl. Top with one-third each of the wafers, bananas, and pudding. Repeat this layering twice, ending with pudding. Chill and serve.

KIM JONES
NORTH MONROE STREET CHURCH OF GOD
MONROE, MICHIGAN

Baked Apples

Syrup:
1/2 cup sugar
1/2 cup syrup
2 tablespoons butter
1/4 teaspoon ground cinnamon
1/2 teaspoon ground nutmeg
1 cup water
Vanilla
Few red hots for coloring

Filling:
6 apples, peeled and cored
Butter
Sugar
Nutmeg
Pie dough

Preheat the oven to 425 degrees. In a medium saucepan, boil the syrup ingredients for 3 minutes.

Fill the hole in the apples with the butter, sugar, and nutmeg; wrap the apples in regular pie dough. Turn the apples upside down in a greased baking dish. Pour the syrup over the apples and bake for 45 minutes.

Dorothy Trent
Memorial Baptist Church
Tulsa, Oklahoma

COOKIES & CANDY

Thank you for the world so sweet
Thank you for the food we eat
Thank you for the birds that sing
Thank you God for everything.

CHILD'S MEALTIME BLESSING

SCOTTISH SHORTBREAD

1 pound sweet butter (no substitutes!)
1 cup sifted powdered sugar
3 cups all-purpose flour
3/4 cup sifted cornstarch

Preheat the oven to 375 degrees. In the bowl of an electric mixer, cream the butter, gradually adding the powdered sugar. Blend well, but don't overwork or let the butter become oily. Combine the flour and cornstarch and gradually work into the butter mixture. Turn the dough out directly onto a baking sheet dusted with flour and roll out carefully to fill the baking sheet. Prick the dough all over with a fork. Bake for 5 minutes, then reduce the oven temperature to 300 degrees and continue baking for 45 to 60 minutes. When done, the shortbread should be golden but not browned at all. Cut it into squares or rectangles while it's still warm.

MADELYN FOGLER
MATTAPOISETT CONGREGATIONAL CHURCH
MATTAPOISETT, MASSACHUSETTS

NEIMAN MARCUS COOKIES

5 cups oatmeal
2 cups granulated sugar
2 cups brown sugar
2 cups butter, softened
4 eggs
2 teaspoons vanilla extract
4 cups all-purpose flour
1 teaspoon salt
2 teaspoons baking powder
2 teaspoons baking soda
24 ounces chocolate chips
1 (8-ounce) Hershey bar, grated
3 cups chopped nuts

Preheat the oven to 375 degrees. In a blender, blend the oatmeal to a fine powder. In the bowl of an electric mixer, cream the sugars and butter, adding the eggs and vanilla. Beat in the oatmeal, flour, salt, baking powder, and baking soda. Fold in the chocolate chips and Hershey bar, then stir in the nuts. Turn the dough out onto a lightly floured bread board and roll into balls. Place the balls 2 inches apart on cookie sheets.

Bake for 10 minutes. Makes 112 cookies.

DENISE ORTON
TOWER HILL UNITED METHODIST CHURCH
TOWER HILL, ILLINOIS

Old-Fashioned Peanut Butter Cookies

1 cup creamy peanut butter
1 stick butter or margarine, softened
1/2 cup granulated sugar
1/2 cup brown sugar
1 egg
1/2 teaspoon vanilla extract
1 1/2 cups all-purpose flour
3/4 teaspoon baking soda
1/2 teaspoon baking powder

In the bowl of an electric mixer, cream the first 6 ingredients. In a separate bowl, sift together the dry ingredients and combine with the peanut butter mixture. The dough will be stiff. Chill for several hours. Preheat the oven to 375 degrees. Turn the dough out onto a floured bread board and roll it into balls. Place the balls on greased cookie sheets and flatten with the tines of a fork greased and dipped into sugar. Bake for 8 to 10 minutes. Makes 3 dozen cookies.

JAN WICKLIFFE
CROSS IN THE DESERT UNITED METHODIST CHURCH
PHOENIX, ARIZONA

Grandma's Best Gingersnaps

1 cup packed brown sugar
3/4 cup white Crisco
1/4 cup molasses
1 egg
2 1/4 cups all-purpose flour
2 teaspoons baking soda
1 teaspoon ground cinnamon
1 teaspoon ground ginger
1/2 teaspoon ground cloves
1/4 teaspoon salt

In a large bowl, combine the sugar, shortening, molasses, and egg and mix well. In a separate bowl, combine the dry ingredients and stir into the creamed mixture. Cover and chill for 1 hour. Preheat the oven to 375 degrees. Turn the dough out onto a lightly floured bread board and shape it into balls; dip the tops in granulated sugar. Place the balls on a greased baking sheet and bake for 10 to 12 minutes.

JOY STEWART
MEMORIAL BAPTIST CHURCH
TULSA, OKLAHOMA

GINGERBREAD MEN

1 cup butter or margarine
1 cup sugar
1 teaspoon ground cinnamon
1/2 cup dark molasses
1 teaspoon ground nutmeg
1 teaspoon ground cloves
1 teaspoon ground ginger
2 eggs, well beaten
1 teaspoon vinegar
5 cups all-purpose flour
1 teaspoon baking soda

In a saucepan, cream the butter with the sugar. Add the cinnamon, molasses, nutmeg, cloves, and ginger; mix well, stirring constantly. Bring to a boil. Remove from the heat and allow the mixture to cool. When lukewarm, stir in the eggs, vinegar, flour, and baking soda until a smooth dough is formed. Chill for several hours or overnight.

Preheat the oven to 350 degrees. Divide dough into 6 portions. Roll out on aluminum foil. Cut with a gingerbread man cutter. Remove and reuse excess dough. Bake cookies on foil on a cookie sheet for 8 to 10 minutes. Remove cookies and foil from cookie sheet and cool. Decorate with Confectioners' Glaze.

CONFECTIONERS' GLAZE:
2 cups powdered sugar
Half-and-half or evaporated milk

Add just enough milk to the powdered sugar to make a mixture that will go through a pastry tube. Use the glaze to make piping, eyes, buttons, and a mouth on each gingerbread man.

GERRY DOSS
TRINITY UNITED METHODIST CHURCH
HUDSON, NEW YORK

CHOCOLATE CHIP COOKIES WITH MACADAMIA NUTS

1/2 cup butter or margarine, softened
1/2 cup packed light brown sugar
1/2 cup granulated sugar
1 teaspoon vanilla extract
1 egg
1 cup all-purpose flour
1/3 cup cocoa
1/2 teaspoon baking soda
1/2 teaspoon salt
2 cups semisweet chocolate chips
3/4 cup macadamia nuts, coarsely chopped

In a large bowl, beat the butter, brown sugar, granulated sugar, and vanilla until creamy. Add the egg and blend well. In a separate bowl, stir together the flour, cocoa, baking soda, and salt. Gradually add to the butter mixture, blending well. Stir in the chocolate chips and nuts. Cover and refrigerate for 1 to 2 hours. Preheat the oven to 350 degrees. Very lightly grease a cookie sheet. Using an ice cream scoop or a 1/4 cup measuring cup, drop the dough onto the cookie sheet. Flatten slightly. Bake for 10 to 12 minutes. Do not over-bake. The cookies will be soft. They will puff during baking and flatten when cooled. Cool slightly before removing from the baking sheet. Makes 1 dozen cookies.

MACKIE CASSELS
HOLUM BAPTIST CHURCH
GRAYSON, LOUISIANA

CHOCOLATE COOKIES

just for kids!

Cookie dough
Chocolate chips

Put chocolate chips on top of cookie dough. Cook in the oven for 10 hours.

TAYLOR THAMES
5 YEARS OLD
HOLUM BAPTIST CHURCH
GRAYSON, LOUISIANA

TOLL HOUSE MARBLE SQUARES

1 cup plus 2 teaspoon all-purpose flour
1/2 teaspoon baking soda
1/2 teaspoon salt
1/2 cup butter, softened
6 tablespoons granulated sugar
6 tablespoons firmly packed brown sugar
1 teaspoon vanilla extract
1/4 teaspoon water
1 egg
1/2 cup chopped nuts
6 ounces chocolate chips

Preheat the oven to 375 degrees. Sift together the flour, baking soda and salt. In the bowl of an electric mixer, blend the butter, sugars, vanilla, and water. Beat in the egg and flour mixture. Stir in the nuts. Spread in a 13 x 9 x 2-inch baking pan. Sprinkle the chocolate chips over the top and bake for 1 minute. Remove the pan from the oven and run a knife through the dough to marbleize. Return to the oven and bake for 12 to 14 minutes longer. Cut into squares and serve.

BETTY GREEN
OAKMONT CHURCH OF GOD
SHREVEPORT, LOUISIANA

AMISH SUGAR COOKIE RECIPE

2 eggs
2 cups sugar
1 cup shortening or lard
1 cup milk
1/2 teaspoon baking soda
2 teaspoons baking powder
1 teaspoon vanilla extract
Pinch of salt
5 to 6 cups all-purpose flour

Preheat the oven to 350 degrees. In the bowl of an electric mixer, cream together one of the eggs, sugar, and shortening. Add the other egg, milk, baking soda, baking powder, vanilla, salt, and flour. Turn the dough out onto a floured bread board and cut into your favorite shapes. Bake for 8 to 10 minutes, then cool on a rack.

CAROLYN MYERS
OAKMONT CHURCH OF GOD
SHREVEPORT, LOUISIANA

BUTTERSCOTCH COOKIES

1/2 cup butter
1 1/2 cups brown sugar
2 eggs, well beaten
2 1/2 cups all-purpose flour
1/2 teaspoon baking powder
1 teaspoon baking soda
1/2 teaspoon salt
1 cup sour cream
1 teaspoon vanilla extract
2/3 cup coarsely chopped walnuts or pecans

BURNT BUTTER ICING:

6 tablespoons butter
1 1/2 cups powdered sugar
1 teaspoon vanilla extract
Hot water

Cream the butter; add the sugar gradually and cream thoroughly. Blend in the eggs. Sift the flour, baking powder, baking soda, and salt together; add to the creamed mixture alternately with the sour cream. Blend in the vanilla and nuts. Chill until the dough is firm. Preheat the oven to 400 degrees. Drop by teaspoonfuls onto a lightly greased baking sheet, about 2 inches apart. Bake for 10 to 15 minutes. When the cookies are cool, spread with Burnt Butter Icing.

Brown the butter over medium heat till it is golden brown. Blend in the powdered sugar and vanilla. Stir in about 4 tablespoons of water, or enough to get the mixture to spreading consistency.

JAN WICKLIFFE
CROSS IN THE DESERT UNITED METHODIST CHURCH
PHOENIX, ARIZONA

HERMITS (BAR COOKIES)

1/4 cup raisins
1/2 chopped nuts
2 cups all-purpose flour
1/4 cup shortening
1/2 cup sugar
2 eggs
1/2 cup molasses
1/2 teaspoon salt
1 teaspoon baking soda
1/2 teaspoon baking powder
1 teaspoon ground cinnamon
1/2 teaspoon ground cloves
1/4 teaspoon ground nutmeg
1/4 teaspoon ground mace

Preheat the oven to 350 degrees. Toss the raisins and nuts in 1/4 cup of the flour and set aside. In the bowl of an electric mixer, cream together the shortening and sugar. Add the eggs and molasses and beat well. Add the remaining flour and the rest of the dry ingredients to the creamed mixture and mix thoroughly. Fold in the nuts and raisins. Spread the batter in a 9 x 13-inch baking pan and bake for 15 to 20 minutes. Sprinkle with a mixture of cinnamon and sugar or glaze with maple cream.

RONNY WILLIAMS
UNITED BAPTIST CHURCH OF POULTNEY
EAST POULTNEY, VERMONT

Rich Brownies

3/4 cup cocoa
2 cups sugar
2 sticks butter, melted
4 eggs
1 teaspoon vanilla extract
1 1/4 cups all-purpose flour
1/4 teaspoon salt
1/2 cup chopped walnuts or chocolate chips
   (optional)

Preheat the oven to 350 degrees. In a mixing bowl, combine the cocoa and sugar. Add the butter, eggs, and vanilla and mix well. Now add the flour and salt and mix just until smooth. (If you are adding the walnuts or chips, now is the time.) Scrape the mixture into a greased 8- or 9-inch square baking pan and spread out in an even layer. Bake until the brownies just begin to pull away form the sides of the pan (or until a toothpick inserted into the center comes out clean), about 40 to 50 minutes.

Allison Bulkeley
Cross in the Desert United Methodist Church
Phoenix, Arizona

Blond Brownies

1/4 cup margarine
1 cup packed light brown sugar
1 egg
3/4 cup all-purpose flour
1 teaspoon baking powder
1/2 teaspoon salt
1/2 teaspoon vanilla extract
1/2 cup coarsely chopped nuts

Preheat the oven to 350 degrees. In a medium saucepan, melt the margarine over low heat. Remove from the heat and add the brown sugar, stirring until well blended; cool. Add the egg, mixing well. Stir in the dry ingredients, then add the vanilla and nuts. Spread the batter in a well-buttered 8-inch square pan and bake for about 25 minutes. Cool in the pan or on cake rack. Cut into 2-inch squares. Makes 16 servings.

Jan Wickliffe
Cross in the Desert
United Methodist Church
Phoenix, Arizona

Coffee Can Ice Cream

just for kids!

1 can heavy cream
1 cup milk
1/2 cup sugar
1/2 teaspoon vanilla
Nuts or small pieces fruit (optional)

Place all ingredients into coffee can, secure lid, tape onto can. Roll can under foot until solid. Enjoy!

Joanne Coons
Trinity United Methodist Church
Hudson, New York

Fudge-Topped Brownies

Brownies:
1 cup margarine or butter
2 cups sugar
1 cup all-purpose flour
2/3 cup cocoa
1/2 teaspoon baking powder
2 eggs
1/2 cup milk
1 1/2 teaspoon vanilla extract
1 cup chopped walnuts

Topping:
1 (12-ounce) package semisweet chocolate chips
1 (14-ounce) can condensed milk
1 1/2 teaspoons vanilla extract

Preheat the oven to 350 degrees. In the bowl of an electric mixer, beat together all the ingredients except the walnuts. Stir in the walnuts. Spread the batter in a greased 13 x 9-inch baking pan. Bake for 40 minutes, or until set.

Just before the brownies are done, in a saucepan over low heat, melt the chocolate chips with the milk and vanilla. Immediately spread over the hot brownies. Cool. Chill in the refrigerator until set. Cut into bars. Makes 36 to 40 brownies.

Tressa Mill
First United Methodist Church
Belleville, Michigan

Melt-in-Your-Mouth Cookies

1 cup granulated sugar
1 cup margarine, softened
2 eggs
1 cup vegetable oil
2 teaspoons vanilla
4 1/2 cups all-purpose flour
1/2 teaspoon salt
1 teaspoon baking soda
1/2 teaspoon cream of tartar
1 1/2 cups shredded coconut (optional)
1 cup powdered sugar

In the bowl of an electric mixer, cream the granulated sugar and margarine. Beat in the eggs, oil, and vanilla. Sift together the flour, salt, baking soda, and cream of tartar. Mix well. Add the coconut, if desired. Mix again. Chill the dough overnight. Preheat the oven to 350 degrees. On a lightly floured bread board, roll the dough into balls the size of walnuts and place on ungreased cookie sheets. Press the balls flat with the bottom of a glass greased and dipped in the powdered sugar. Bake for 10 to 15 minutes. Makes 6 1/2 dozen.

Mary Grace Petty
Highland Heights Presbyterian Church
Cordova, Tennessee

7-LAYER COOKIE

1/4 pound butter, melted
1 cup graham cracker crumbs
1/2 cup coconut
1 (6-ounce) package chocolate chips
1 (6-ounce) package butterscotch bits
1 can Eagle Brand condensed milk
1 cup chopped nuts

Preheat the oven to 350 degrees. Mix the melted butter and crumbs. Pat into a thin layer in a 9 x 13-inch pan. Add the remaining ingredients in order in separate layers: coconut, chocolate chips, butterscotch bits, milk, and nuts. Bake for 30 minutes. Cut into small pieces while still warm.

MARY EBERTS
TRINITY PRESBYTERIAN CHURCH
WILMINGTON, DELAWARE

THE BEST OATMEAL COOKIES

3/4 cup butter or margarine
1 3/4 cups all-purpose flour
1 cup packed brown sugar
1/2 cup granulated sugar
1 egg
1 teaspoon baking powder
1 teaspoon vanilla extract
1/4 teaspoon baking soda
1/2 teaspoon ground cinnamon
1/4 teaspoon ground cloves
2 cups rolled oats
1 cup raisins

Preheat the oven to 375 degrees. In the mixing bowl of an electric mixer, beat the butter on medium to high speed for 30 seconds. Add half the flour, the brown sugar, granulated sugar, egg, baking powder, vanilla, and baking soda. Stir in the cinnamon and cloves. Beat until thoroughly combined. Beat in the remaining flour. Stir in the oats and raisins. On a lightly greased cookie sheet, drop by rounded teaspoonfuls 2 inches apart. Bake for 10 to 12 minutes.

KIM WALDEN
NORTH MONROE STREET CHURCH OF GOD
MONROE, MICHIGAN

STAINED GLASS CRAYONS

just for kids!

Make good use of your broken crayons!

Remove all paper from crayons. Place pieces in a well-greased muffin pan or use foil to cover muffin pan. Place in a 400 degree oven for a few minutes, until completely melted. Remove from oven and cool completely before removing from muffin pan. If you mixed the colors, your crayon circles will have a pretty stained glass effect and are great fun to color with!

SUSI HANSON
BUCKINGHAM UNITED METHODIST CHURCH
GARLAND, TEXAS

MOLASSES COOKIES

2 cups all-purpose flour
2 teaspoons baking soda
1 teaspoon ground ginger
1/2 teaspoon salt
1 teaspoon ground cinnamon
2/3 cup Crisco
1 cup brown sugar
1/4 cup molasses
1 egg, beaten
Granulated sugar

Preheat the oven to 350 degrees. Sift together the flour, baking soda, ginger, salt, and cinnamon. In the bowl of an electric mixer, cream the shortening and brown sugar. Beat in the molasses. Add the egg, then the sifted dry ingredients, to the creamed mixture. Shape the dough into balls. Place on a greased cookie sheet and flatten with a fork dipped in granulated sugar. Bake for 12 to 15 minutes. Makes 4 dozen.

LOISTINE McSHEPARD GRADY
GRIFFIN CHAPEL UNITED METHODIST CHURCH
STARKVILLE, MISSISSIPPI

SNICKERDOODLES

1 cup shortening
1 1/2 cups sugar
2 eggs
2 3/4 cups all-purpose flour
2 teaspoons cream of tartar
1 teaspoon baking soda
1/4 teaspoon salt
1 teaspoon vanilla extract
Additional sugar and cinnamon

Preheat the oven to 400 degrees. Cream the shortening, sugar, and eggs until light and fluffy. Combine flour, cream of tartar, baking soda, and salt. Add to the creamed mixture. Stir in the vanilla extract. Shape into balls the size of walnuts. Roll each ball in cinnamon/sugar. Bake on a cookie sheet for 10 minutes; watch carefully so they don't burn. Makes 5 dozen cookies.

Note: kids love them!

MICHELLE GODDARD
MEMORIAL BAPTIST CHURCH
TULSA, OKLAHOMA

MA'S APPLE SQUARES

1 cup shortening
1 cup sugar
3 eggs
1/4 teaspoon salt
2 teaspoons baking powder
2 cups all-purpose flour
4 apples, peeled and sliced
Ground cinnamon
Sugar
Butter

Preheat the oven to 350 degrees. Cream the shortening, sugar, and eggs. Add salt, baking powder, and flour. Place one-half of the dough in a greased 8 x 8 or 10 x 10-inch baking pan. Cover with the apples. Sprinkle cinnamon and sugar over the apples. Dot with butter. Spread the rest of the dough on top. Bake until the dough is lightly browned and the apples are cooked. Test for doneness with a fork.

AURIEN PREISS
CROSS IN THE DESERT UNITED METHODIST CHURCH
PHOENIX, ARIZONA

PUMPKIN BARS

2 cups all-purpose flour
2 teaspoons baking powder
1 teaspoon baking soda
1/2 teaspoon salt
2 teaspoons ground cinnamon
1 teaspoon pumpkin pie spice
2 cups sugar
1 cup nuts, chopped (optional)
1 cup salad oil
4 eggs
1 (16-ounce) can of solid pack pumpkin

Preheat the oven to 350 degrees. Combine all the ingredients and mix until blended. Bake in a lightly greased 10 x 15-inch baking pan for 20 to 30 minutes.

FROSTING:
3 ounces cream cheese
6 tablespoons butter
1 teaspoon vanilla extract
2 cups powdered sugar
1 tablespoon milk, or more if needed

Combine all the ingredients except milk and beat until smooth. Add the milk if needed to thin to spreading consistency.

AURIEN PREISS
CROSS IN THE DESERT UNITED METHODIST CHURCH
PHOENIX, ARIZONA

LEMON BARS

CRUST:
1 cup margarine
1/2 cup powdered sugar
2 cups all-purpose flour
Pinch of salt

Preheat the oven to 350 degrees. In a large bowl, combine the ingredients and mix as you would for a pie crust. Press evenly into a 9 x 12-inch baking pan. Bake for 15 minutes.

TOPPING:
4 eggs, beaten thoroughly
4 tablespoons all-purpose flour
2 cups granulated sugar
6 tablespoons fresh lemon juice

In a large bowl, combine the eggs, flour, and sugar and add the lemon juice. Pour over the baked crust and bake for 20 to 30 minutes longer, or until the egg mixture is firm.

Note: Frozen lemonade is excellent in place of the fresh lemon juice.

LEOLA BRODINE
CALVARY UNITED METHODIST CHURCH
TAYLOR, NEBRASKA

RASPBERRY-ALMOND BARS

2 cups all-purpose flour
1 1/2 cups old-fashioned or quick oats
1 cup sugar
2 sticks butter, softened
1 teaspoon almond extract
1 cup raspberry preserves
2/3 cup chopped almonds

Preheat the oven to 350 degrees. In a large bowl, mix together the flour, oats, and sugar. Cut in the butter with a pastry blender until the mixture resembles coarse crumbs. Stir in the almond extract until blended. Reserving 2 cups of this mixture, press the remainder over the bottom of a 9 x 13-inch baking pan. Spread the preserves over the top within 1/2 inch of the edge. Mix the almonds with the reserved oat mixture. Sprinkle evenly over the preserves and then press down gently to slightly compact the oat-almond mixture into the jam. Bake for 25 to 30 minutes, or until the edges are golden. Cool in the pan on a wire rack. Cut into 2-inch bars. Makes 32 bars.

MEMORIAL BAPTIST CHURCH
TULSA, OKLAHOMA

RASPBERRY NUT BARS

2 1/4 cups all-purpose flour
1 cup sugar
1 cup chopped walnuts
1 cup butter, softened
1 egg
1 jar raspberry jam (I use Polaner seedless all fruit)
Semi-sweet chocolate chips (optional)

Preheat the oven to 350 degrees. In a large mixing bowl, combine the flour, sugar, walnuts, butter, and egg until mixture is crumbly, scraping the sides of the bowl often. Reserve 1 1/2 cups of mixture and set aside. Press the remaining mixture in the bottom of a greased 11 x 7-inch baking dish. Spread the raspberry jam evenly over mixture to within 1/2 inch of all sides of pan. Sprinkle chocolate chips over the jam if desired. Crumble the remaining mixture on top and lightly press. Bake 40 to 50 minutes or until lightly browned. Cool completely and cut into bars. Makes about 24 bars.

AMY MARRELLO
TRINITY UNITED METHODIST CHURCH
HUDSON, NEW YORK

SUGAR ON SNOW AND MAPLE CANDY

Snow
1 to 2 quarts maple syrup
Doughnuts
Sour pickles

First go outside and get some nice white fresh snow. Fill two or three roasting pans or large bowls with snow. Boil the syrup until a small amount of syrup hardens slightly when placed on snow. (This should be about 212 degrees on candy thermometer.) Give every one a fork and eat all you can hold.

This should be served the Vermont way, with homemade plain doughnuts and sour pickles. The sour pickles cut the sweetness and you can eat more sugar on snow.

Pour some syrup into a small bowl or coffee cup and start to stir. As the syrup is stirred, it will start to harden and turn a beige color when it is thick enough. Drop teaspoonfuls on the wax paper and let set. Now you have a delicious maple sugar candy.

I love this and so do my friends.

KASI WALKER
CAVENDISH BAPTIST CHURCH
CAVENDISH, VERMONT

MICROWAVE PEANUT BRITTLE

1 cup sugar
1/2 cup corn syrup
1 cup raw peanuts
1/4 teaspoon salt
1 tablespoon margarine
1 teaspoon vanilla extract
1 teaspoon baking soda

Combine sugar and corn syrup in a large 10-cup glass bowl. Microwave on high for 8 to 9 minutes. Stop after 5 minutes and stir, adding the peanuts and salt (if you're using roasted, salted peanuts, omit the salt), then continue cooking. Remove the bowl from the microwave and add the margarine and vanilla. Return to the microwave and cook on high for 2 minutes longer. Remove and stir in the baking soda. Spread quickly on a greased cookie sheet. When the brittle cools, break it into pieces.

Note: Always make candy when the outside humidity is less than 50 percent.

BETTY MULLENNIX
NORTHBROOK UNITED METHODIST CHURCH
ROSWELL, GEORGIA

Easy Fudge

18 ounces (1 1/2 packages) semisweet
   chocolate chips
1 can condensed milk
2 teaspoons vanilla extract

In a saucepan over low heat, combine the chocolate chips and condensed milk until the chips melt. Stir in the vanilla. Pour the mixture into a greased 9 x 13-inch baking pan. Refrigerate and cut into small squares.

KEN MURPHY
BUCKINGHAM UNITED METHODIST CHURCH
GARLAND, TEXAS

Buttermilk Pralines

1/2 cup buttermilk
1/2 teaspoon baking soda
2 cups firmly packed light brown sugar
2 tablespoons butter or margarine
2 tablespoons light corn syrup
1 cup toasted pecans, chopped
1 teaspoon vanilla extract

Stir together the buttermilk and baking soda in a large heavy saucepan until blended. Add the brown sugar, butter, and corn syrup. Cook over medium high heat 8 to 10 minutes or until candy thermometer registers 234 degrees (soft ball stage). Cool the mixture 10 to 12 minutes. Beat with a wooden spoon until the mixture thickens slightly. Stir in the pecans and vanilla extract. Working rapidly, drop by rounded tablespoonfuls onto lightly greased waxed paper. Let stand until firm. Yield: 2 dozen.

MERRY R. JONES
GRIFFIN CHAPEL UNITED METHODIST CHURCH
STARKVILLE, MISSISSIPPI

Maple-Sugar Fudge

1 1/2 cups maple syrup
2/3 cup condensed milk
2 cups sugar
1 to 2 tablespoons butter
1 cup walnuts

In a medium saucepan, combine the syrup, condensed milk, and sugar and cook for about 15 minutes, or until a candy thermometer registers between 235 degrees and 240 degrees. Remove from the heat and add the butter and nuts. Let the mixture sit until it has cooled slightly, then beat until thick. Pour into a greased pan and allow to cool completely.

IN MEMORY OF RENA SCRIBNER
UNITED BAPTIST CHURCH OF POULTNEY
EAST POULTNEY, VERMONT

"Wait Until You Smell It" Play Dough

2 1/2 cups all-purpose flour
1/2 cup salt
1 tablespoon alum
3 tablespoons cooking oil
2 packages unsweetened
   Kool-Aid mix (dry)
1 cup boiling water

In medium-sized bowl, mix together flour, salt, and alum. Add cooking oil and Kool-Aid; stir well. Add boiling water and stir until color is uniform. Store play dough in the refrigerator in plastic bag when not in use.

SARAH, KATIE AND NOELLE KUGLE
TRINITY UNITED METHODIST CHURCH
YORK, PENNSYLVANIA

Peanut Butter Fudge

Pinch of salt
3 cups sugar
1 cup evaporated milk
1 tablespoon butter or margarine
1/4 teaspoon vanilla
2 cups peanut butter

In a large saucepan, combine the first 3 ingredients and cook over medium heat for approximately 10 minutes. Turn off the heat and add the remaining ingredients, stirring until the mixture begins to harden. Spread on a buttered cookie sheet and refrigerate for 15 minutes. Cut into pieces.

JO ANN LAMBERT
NORTH MONROE STREET CHURCH OF GOD
MONROE, MICHIGAN

Peppermint Bark Candy

1 pound white chocolate
2 cups crushed candy canes
1 (16-ounce) package chocolate chips

In a double boiler or microwave, melt the white chocolate. Add the candy cane to the white chocolate. Pour the mixture onto a cookie sheet covered with wax paper. Melt the chocolate chips and pour them over the white chocolate mixture. Swirl with a knife or spatula. Cool and break into pieces.

EULA HAFT
FIRST UNITED METHODIST CHURCH
BELLEVILLE, MICHIGAN

BEVERAGES

Bless the food upon the dishes
as you blessed the loaves and fishes.
As the sugar hides in the tea,
let me hide myself in Thee.

FRUIT AND MINT ICED TEA

1 quart boiling water
8 tea bags
1/2 cup fresh mint leaves
1 1/2 cups sugar (less, if desired)
6 ounces frozen lemonade
6 ounces limeade
3/4 cup orange juice
3 quarts cold water

Pour the boiling water over the tea bags and mint. Cover and let steep for 30 minutes. Discard the tea bags. Add the sugar and the next 4 ingredients. Pour the tea through a strainer and chill.

DOROTHY ARCHER
HIGHLAND HEIGHTS PRESBYTERIAN CHURCH
CORDOVA, TENNESSEE

OLD-FASHIONED LEMONADE

1 1/2 cups sugar
1 1/2 cups water
1 tablespoon lemon rind, finely grated
1 1/2 cups lemon juice (6 to 7 lemons)
1 lemon, thinly sliced
Mint sprigs

In a small saucepan, stir together the sugar, water, and lemon rind. Bring to a boil, stirring constantly. Boil for 5 minutes. Remove from the heat and let cool. Stir in the lemon juice and transfer the syrup to a jar. Cover and refrigerate for up to 3 weeks.

For individual servings, place 2 ice cubes in a tall glass. Add 1/4 cup of the syrup and 3/4 cup of ice water; stir well. Garnish with a lemon slice and a mint sprig.

AVIS
FOREST AVENUE CONGREGATIONAL CHURCH
BANGOR, MAINE

GINGER LEMONADE

1 3-inch piece fresh ginger
1 cup sugar
1 cup tap water
4 cups cold seltzer, club soda, or mineral
    water
1 cup fresh lemon juice, unstrained
1 lemon, thinly sliced
Fresh mint leaves for garnish

Peel and crush the ginger. In a medium-sized saucepan, mix together the ginger, sugar, and tap water. Bring to a boil over high heat, stirring to dissolve the sugar. Reduce the heat and simmer until the ginger is aromatic and the liquid is syrupy, about 10 to 15 minutes. Remove from the heat and allow to cool. Discard the ginger and pour the liquid into a large, 2-quart pitcher. Add the soda water, lemon juice, and lemon slices. Refrigerate until well chilled. Fill tall glasses with ice, pour in lemonade, and garnish with a sprig of mint.

PAT FAST
UNITED BAPTIST CHURCH OF POULTNEY
EAST POULTNEY, VERMONT

HOT MULLED CIDER

2 quarts sweet apple cider
1/2 cup brown sugar
1/4 teaspoon salt
Dash of nutmeg
1 teaspoon whole cloves
1 teaspoon whole allspice
1 (3-inch) cinnamon stick
1/2 lemon, thinly sliced

Boil all the ingredients in a saucepan over medium heat for about 20 minutes. Strain and serve hot. (For easy removal after boiling, tie the spices and lemon in a piece of cheesecloth.)

SUE CLAIRE CALLESIS
UNITED BAPTIST CHURCH OF POULTNEY
EAST POULTNEY, VERMONT

ORANGE AND BANANA SLUSH

1 cup orange juice
1 cup sherbet
1 banana

Combine the first 2 ingredients in a blender and whip. Add the banana and whip again. Pour into glasses and serve immediately.

FREDIA B. GOON
GRIFFIN CHAPEL UNITED METHODIST CHURCH
STARKVILLE, MISSISSIPPI

WATERMELON FRAPPÉ

4 cups diced (seeded) watermelon
2 tablespoons lemon juice
1 teaspoon lemon rind, grated
12 ounces ginger ale

Put the first 3 ingredients into a blender and mix until frothy. Pour the mixture into a pitcher. Add the ginger ale and stir. To serve, pour into glasses filled with ice. Makes 5 cups.

4-H FAVORITE
FOREST AVENUE CONGREGATIONAL CHURCH
BANGOR, MAINE

Berry-Banana Buttermilk Smoothie

2 large bananas, sliced and frozen
3/4 cup frozen apple juice concentrate, thawed
2 1/2 cups buttermilk
2 teaspoons vanilla extract
10 large fresh strawberries, frozen
Fresh strawberries for garnish (optional)

Process the first 4 ingredients in a blender until smooth. Add the strawberries, 2 at a time, pulsing until the mixture is smooth. Pour into glasses. Garnish with fresh strawberries, if desired, and serve immediately. Makes 5 cups.

Merry R. Jones
Griffin Chapel United Methodist Church
Starkville, Mississippi

Berry Warm-Up

3 tablespoons Lipton instant tea powder
1/2 cup 100 percent pure lemon juice
1/2 cup orange juice
1/2 cup sugar
1/4 teaspoon ground cinnamon
1/4 teaspoon ground nutmeg
4 cups water
2 cups cranberry juice cocktail

In a large saucepan, combine all the ingredients and heat through. Serve in cups or mugs and garnish, if desired, with lemon or orange slices. Makes about 6 servings.

Merry R. Jones
Griffin Chapel United Methodist Church
Starkville, Mississippi

Strawberry Yogurt Frost

1 (10-ounce) carton frozen, sweetened, sliced strawberries
1/3 cup instant nonfat dry milk
1 cup plain yogurt
3/4 cup water
1 teaspoon vanilla extract

Cut the frozen block of strawberries in half. Combine the strawberries, dry milk, yogurt, water, and vanilla in a blender and process until smooth. Makes 3 1/2 cups.

Banana Yogurt Frost: Substitute 2 large ripe bananas and 2 tablespoons of sugar for the sliced strawberries. Proceed as above.

Dianne Duke
Holum Baptist Church
Grayson, Louisiana

MOCK CHAMPAGNE

4 cups sugar
4 cups water
4 cups grape juice or pineapple juice
2 cups orange juice
8 pints ginger ale, chilled

Boil the sugar and water for 3 minutes and cool. Add the juices and chill. Just before serving, add the chilled ginger ale. Makes 50 servings.

CHRISTINE WALTER
CAVENDISH BAPTIST CHURCH
CAVENDISH, VERMONT

COFFEE LOVERS' FREEZE

3/4 cup sugar
1 1/2 cups milk
1 1/2 cups cold coffee
1 teaspoon vanilla extract
2 cups whipping cream

In a heavy saucepan, combine the sugar and the milk. Bring the mixture to a boil, stirring until the sugar dissolves. Remove the pan from the heat and let cool. In a bowl, combine milk mixture, coffee, vanilla, and 1 cup of the whipping cream; mix well. Pour the mixture into a loaf pan and freeze until it has the consistency of slush, 1 to 2 hours. Beat the remaining whipping cream until stiff peaks form. Don't overbeat. Just before serving, stir the slush mixture into dessert dishes, filling them two-thirds full. Top with the whipped cream. Makes 6 (1-cup) servings.

VICKI
FOREST AVENUE CONGREGATIONAL CHURCH
BANGOR, MAINE

CRANBERRY PUNCH WITH CRANBERRY ICE WREATH

FOR THE ICE WREATH:
2 cups water
2 cups cranberry juice
Cranberries
Mint leaves

FOR THE PUNCH:
2 quarts water
6 cups Earl Grey tea
4 cups cranberry juice
1 (12-ounce) can frozen orange juice
   concentrate, thawed
1 (12-ounce) can frozen pineapple juice
   concentrate, thawed
1 (12-ounce) can frozen lemonade
   concentrate, thawed
1 quart ginger ale

To make the ice wreath, combine the water and cranberry juice in a large bowl. Place the cranberries and mint leaves in the bottom of a 1-quart ring mold. Add just enough of the juice mixture to cover them, and refrigerate the rest of the juice. Freeze the ring until solid; that will anchor the decorations and keep them from floating to the top when you add the remaining juice. Add the remaining juice and freeze until solid.

To make the punch, combine the water, tea, cranberry juice, and citrus concentrates in a punch bowl that holds at least 2 gallons. Just before serving, stir in the ginger ale.

To unmold the ice wreath, dip the mold briefly in hot water. Invert it and ease out the frozen wreath. Float the wreath in the punch. Makes about 1 1/2 gallons of punch.

FATHER ROUGHAN
ST. PAUL CHURCH
WATERFORD, CONNECTICUT

ROSY MULLED PUNCH

SYRUP:
2 cups water
1 cup sugar
1 teaspoon whole cloves
1 teaspoon whole allspice
2 cinnamon sticks
1 lemon, sliced (optional)
1 orange, sliced (optional)

PUNCH:
3 quarts raspberry-cranberry drink

In a small saucepan, combine all syrup ingredients. Cook the mixture over medium heat until it comes to a boil, stirring constantly. Reduce the heat and simmer for 10 minutes. Strain and cool. Refrigerate the syrup until serving time.

At serving time, place the syrup in a large saucepan. Add the cranberry-raspberry drink and simmer over low heat until heated through. Serve hot with cinnamon sticks and slices of citrus, if desired. Serves 28.

FATHER ROUGHAN
ST. PAUL CHURCH
WATERFORD, CONNECTICUT

CHRISTMAS EGGNOG

12 egg whites
1 1/2 cups sugar
12 egg yolks
1 quart heavy cream, chilled
1 quart cold milk
1 quart whiskey or cognac
1/2 cup rum
Nutmeg

Beat the egg whites until foamy; add the sugar gradually, beating until each addition is dissolved. Beat the egg yolks until thick; fold in the egg white mixture. Gradually add the heavy cream, milk, whiskey and rum. Pour the mixture into a chilled punch bowl. Sprinkle each serving with nutmeg. Serves 30.

PRINCE OF PEACE CHURCH
GRANTSVILLE, WEST VIRGINIA

HOLIDAY AROMA

(Not for Drinking—Just Makes Your House Smell Good!)

1 quart pineapple juice
1 quart water
1 quart apple cider
4 cinnamon sticks
16 cloves
1/2 teaspoon pickling spices
4 teaspoons ground ginger

Mix all the ingredients together in a pot. Simmer.

REMEMBER: *Do not drink.* Just enjoy the aroma!

MARCIA B. RUSSELL
HIGHLAND HEIGHTS PRESBYTERIAN CHURCH
CORDOVA, TENNESSEE

WASSAIL

2 1/2 cups sugar
1 cup water
3 cinnamon sticks
1 lemon, sliced
1 quart pineapple juice
1 quart orange juice
1/2 cup lemon juice
5 1/2 cups Chablis or apple cider

In a medium saucepan, combine the sugar, water, cinnamon sticks, and lemon slices. Bring to a boil and cook for 5 minutes, stirring constantly. In a separate, larger saucepan, combine the juices, wine or cider. Bring the mixture to a boil, then reduce the heat and simmer for 10 minutes. Combine both mixtures and heat together. Remove the cinnamon sticks and serve hot.

KATHY GEEHRENG
DAMASCUS UNITED METHODIST CHURCH
DAMASCUS, MARYLAND

KIDS' FRUIT SHAKES

just for kids!

1 cup orange juice
1 banana, sliced
1 clementine, peeled and sectioned
5 strawberries
1 slice cantaloupe, cut into pieces
4 to 6 ice cubes

Place the orange juice and the fruits in a blender. Blend until well mixed. Add the ice cubes and blend for a few seconds just to chop the ice. Serve in small glasses. Makes 3 cups.

Experiment with different fruits or use greater or smaller amounts.

HEIDI SCHNEIDER
MATTAPOISETT CONGREGATIONAL CHURCH
MATTAPOISETT, MASSACHUSETTS

FRUIT SMOOTHIE OR FROZEN POP

1 cup low-fat yogurt
1/2 cup apple juice
1 cup fresh or frozen strawberries
1 banana

Blend all the ingredients in a blender or food processor until smooth. Drink as is or frozen in Popsicle molds or paper cups. Makes 3 cups, or 10 pops.

MARY WHITE
OAKMONT CHURCH OF GOD
SHREVEPORT, LOUISIANA

ROSY FRUIT PUNCH

just for kids!

1 (128-ounce) bottle cranberry juice, chilled
1 (64-ounce) carton orange juice, chilled
6 cups cold water
3 cups pineapple juice, chilled
3 cups sugar
3/4 cup lemon juice

In a large punch bowl, combine all the ingredients; stir until the sugar is dissolved. Makes about 8 1/2 quarts.

BETTY GRAMLING
OAKMONT CHURCH OF GOD
SHREVEPORT, LOUISIANA

MUD PIE SHAKE

6 ounces coffee ice cream
2 ounces half-and-half
2 ounces chocolate syrup
2 Oreo cookies
Whipped cream
Maraschino cherry, for garnish

Combine the ice cream, half-and-half, chocolate syrup, and cookies in a blender. Blend to combine. Serve in a pint glass or a martini glass. Top with whipped cream and a cherry. Makes 1 serving.

JAN WICKLIFFE
CROSS IN THE DESERT UNITED METHODIST CHURCH
PHOENIX, ARIZONA

Contributors

Bethel AME Church, Augusta, Georgia

Buckingham United Methodist Church, Garland, Texas

Calvary United Methodist Church, Taylor, Nebraska

Cavendish Baptist Church, Cavendish, Vermont

Cross in the Desert United Methodist Church, Phoenix, Arizona

Damascus United Methodist Church, Damascus, Maryland

First United Methodist Church, Belleville, Michigan

Forest Avenue Congregational Church, Bangor, Maine

Griffin Chapel United Methodist Church, Starkville, Mississippi

Highland Heights Presbyterian Church, Cordova, Tennessee

Holum Baptist Church, Grayson, Louisiana

Hungarian Presbyterian Church, Albany, Louisiana

Mattapoisett Congregational Church, Mattapoisett, Massachusetts

McClave United Methodist Church, McClave, Colorado

Memorial Baptist Church, Tulsa, Oklahoma

Miracle Deliverance Holiness Church, Columbia, South Carolina

Mosca United Methodist Church, Mosca, Colorado

Northbrook United Methodist Church, Roswell, Georgia

North Monroe Street Church of God, Monroe, Michigan

Oakmont Church of God, Shreveport, Louisiana

Pinemount Baptist Church, McAlpin, Florida

Pitt Community Church, Baudette, Minnesota

Prairie Chapel United Methodist Church, Urbana, Missouri

Prince of Peace Church, Grantsville, West Virginia

St. Paul Church, Waterford, Connecticut

Tower Hill United Methodist Church, Tower Hill, Illinois

Trinity Presbyterian Church, Wilmington, Delaware

Trinity United Methodist Church, Hudson, New York

Trinity United Methodist Church, York, Pennsylvania

United Baptist Church of Poultney, East Poultney, Vermont

United Methodist Church, Estancia, New Mexico

Wellington Village Assembly of God, Little Rock, Arkansas

Westside Baptist Church, Antlers, Oklahoma

TABLE OF EQUIVALENTS

BREAD CRUMBS

1 cup fresh bread crumbs = 2 ounces or 60 grams
1 slice bread with crust = ½ cup breadcrumbs,
1 cup dried or toasted bread crumbs = 4 ounces or 110 grams
1 pound of bread = 14 to 20 slices, or 454 grams
1 cup saltine soda crackers crushed = 28 crackers
1 cup graham cracker crumbs = 7 to 10 crumbled crackers, 4 ounces or 110 grams
1⅓ cups graham cracker crumbs = 16 crumbled crackers,
1 cup vanilla wafer crumbs = 30 wafers, 4 ounces, or 110 grams
2 cups vanilla wafer crumbs = 8 ounces
1⅔ cups chocolate wafer crumbs = 22 wafers
1½ cups gingersnap crumbs = 20 snaps
2 cups zwieback crumbs = 24 slices, 6 ounces, or

DAIRY PRODUCTS

CHEESE

8-ounce package cream cheese = 1 cup or 16 tablespoons
3-ounce package cream cheese = 6 tablespoons
1 pound cheese = 4 cups grated cheese

CREAM

½ pint heavy cream = 1 cup or 2 cups whipped cream
1 cup whipping cream = 2 to 2½ cups whipped cream

MILK

1 cup dry skim milk = 1 quart skim milk when mixed.
1 cup whole milk = 8 ounces weight
1 cup heavy cream = 8⅜ ounces weight
1 6-ounce can evaporated milk = ⅔ cup evaporated milk
1 14½-ounce can evaporated milk = 1⅔ cups evaporated milk
1 cup sweetened condensed milk = 10½ ounces weight
1 14-ounce can sweetened condensed milk = 1½ cups sweetened condensed milk
⅓ cup evaporated milk = ⅓ cup dry milk plus 6 tablespoons water

SOUR CREAM

1 8 ounces carton sour cream = 1 cup sour cream

EGGS

1 large whole egg = 3 tablespoons, 2 ounces, or 60 grams
1 cup large whole eggs = approx. 5 eggs
1 large egg yolk = 1 generous tablespoon
1 cup large egg yolks = approx. 12 egg yolks
1 large egg white = 2 tablespoons, or ⅛ cup
2 large eggs = scant ½ cup, 3 medium ages, or 180 grams
1 cup large eggs = 4 to 5 large eggs
1 cup eggs = 5 to 6 medium eggs
1 cup egg yolks = 12 to 14 large egg yolks
1 cup egg whites = 7 to 10 large egg whites
1 large egg = 2 egg yolks in the recipe
1 large fresh egg = ½ tablespoon dry plus 2½ tablespoons water
3 large egg whites stiffly beaten = 3 cups meringue

FATS

½ ounce butter = 1 tablespoons or ⅛ stick
1 ounce butter = 2 tablespoons or ¼ stick
2 ounces butter = 4 tablespoons or ½ stick
1 pound butter = 2 cups, 4 sticks, 32 tablespoons, or 454 grams
½ pound = 1 cup, 1 stick, 8 tablespoons, or 227 grams
¼ pound = ½ cup, 1 stick, 4 tablespoons, or 113 grams
1 cup butter or margarine = ⅞ cup of lard
1 cup hydrogenated fat = 6⅔ ounces
2 tablespoons = ¼ stick, 2 tablespoons, or 1 ounce

DRY INGREDIENTS

ARROWROOT

1 teaspoon arrowroot = 1 teaspoon all-purpose flour or 1 teaspoon cornstarch
1 tablespoon arrowroot = 3 tablespoons all-purpose flour or 2 tablespoons cornstarch
1 tablespoon arrowroot = 1 tablespoon all-purpose flour plus 1 teaspoon cornstarch

BAKING POWDER & BAKING SODA

2 tablespoons baking powder or soda = 1 ounce
1½ teaspoons = ¼ ounce
1 tablespoon = 0.5 ounce
1 teaspoon = 0.17 ounce

CORNMEAL

1 cup cornmeal = 3 to 4 ounces cornmeal
1 cup uncooked cornmeal = 4 cups cooked cornmeal

CORNSTARCH

1 pound sifted cornstarch = 4 cups
1 cup sifted cornstarch = 4 ounces
1 ounce sifted cornstarch = 4 tablespoons, or ¼ cup
1 tablespoon sifted cornstarch = 0.29 ounce
1 pound unsifted cornstarch = 3½ cups
1 cup unsifted cornstarch = 4.5 ounces
1 ounce unsifted cornstarch = 3½ tablespoons
1 tablespoon unsifted cornstarch = 0.2 ounce

CREAM OF TARTAR

4 tablespoons = 1 ounce or 30 grams
1 tablespoon = ¼ ounces or 7 grams
1 teaspoon = 0.08 ounce

FLOUR

3 tablespoons all-purpose flour = ¼ cup
6 tablespoons all-purpose flour = ⅓ cup
9 tablespoons all-purpose flour = ½ cup
12 tablespoons all-purpose flour = ⅔ cup
15 tablespoons all-purpose flour = ¾ cup
18 tablespoons all-purpose flour = 1 cup
1 pound all-purpose flour = 4 cups
1 cup bleached white all-purpose flour = 1 cup unbleached white all-purpose flour
1 cup bleached all-purpose flour = 1 cup whole wheat flour
1 cup bleached all-purpose flour = ⅞ cup stone ground whole wheat flour
1 pound of sifted bread flour = 4 cups
1 cup sifted bread flour = 4 ounces
1 pound unsifted bread flour = 3½ cups
1 cup unsifted bread flour = 4.75 ounces
1 pound sifted cake flour = 4¼ cups
1 cup sifted cake flour = 3.75 ounces
1 pound unsifted cake flour = 3½ cups
1 cup unsifted cake flour = 4.5 ounces

SALT

5 teaspoons salt = 1 ounce or 30 grams
1¼ teaspoons = ¼ ounce or 7 grams
1 teaspoon = 0.2 ounce

FRUITS AND VEGETABLES

APPLES
4 medium sized apples = 4 cups peeled and sliced
1 pound medium apples = 2 whole apples or 3 cups sliced apples

APRICOTS
1 pound dried apricots = 3 cups dried apricots

BANANA
1 pound banana = 3 medium or 1⅓ to 2 cups mashed

BERRIES
1 pint fresh berries = 1¾ cups of fresh berries

CARROTS
1 cup sliced = 2 medium size carrots
1 cup shredded = 1½ medium size carrots

COCONUT
1⅓ cups desiccated flaked coconut = 3½ ounces
1⅓ cups desiccated shredded coconut = 4 ounces or 115 grams

CHERRIES
1 pound candied cherries = 3 cups candied cherries

DATES
1 pound pitted dates = 2 to 2½ cups chopped dates

FIGS
1 pound whole figs = 2⅔ cups chopped figs

LEMON
1 medium sized lemon = 2 tablespoons lemon juice
1 medium sized lemon = 2 teaspoons lemon zest
1 teaspoon lemon juice = ½ teaspoon lemon extract

LIME
1 large sized lime = 2 tablespoons lime juice

ORANGE
1 medium sized orange = ⅓ cup orange juice
1 medium sized orange = 2 tablespoons orange zest

POTATOES
1 pound potatoes = 3 medium potatoes
1 pound new potatoes = 10 small new potatoes

PRUNES
1 pound unpitted prunes = 2¼ cups pitted prunes

RAISINS
1 pound seedless raisins = 2¾ cups raisins
1 pound seeded raisins = 3¼ cups raisins

STRAWBERRIES
1 quart fresh strawberries = 4 cups sliced

GELATIN
1 envelope unflavored gelatin = 1 scant tablespoon, enough to hard set 2 cups liquid
3 tablespoons = 1 ounce or 30 grams
2¼ teaspoons = ¼ ounce or 7 grams
1 tablespoon = 0.33 ounce
1 teaspoon = 0.11 ounce

GRAINS

OATS
5 ounces rolled oats = 1 cup
1 cup uncooked oats = 1¾ cups cooked

RICE
1 cup uncooked rice = 7½ ounces
1 cup uncooked rice = 2 cups cooked rice

NUTS

ALMONDS
1 pound almonds in shell = 1¼ cups nutmeat
1 pound almonds shelled = 3 cups nutmeat or 454 grams
¼ pound almonds shelled = 1 cup nutmeat
1 pound slivered almonds = 5⅔ cups nutmeat or 454 grams

BRAZIL NUTS
1 pound Brazil nuts in shell = 1½ cups nutmeat
1 pound Brazil nuts shelled = 3¼ cups nutmeat or 454 grams

CASHEWS
4½ ounces cashews, shelled = 1 cup nutmeat or 130 grams

CHESTNUTS
1 pound chestnuts, unshelled = 1½ cups nutmeat

HAZELNUTS
1 pound hazelnuts, unshelled = 1½ cups nutmeat
1 pound hazelnuts, shelled = 3½ cups nutmeat
4½ ounces hazelnuts, shelled = 1 cup nutmeat or 130 grams

MACADAMIA NUTS
4 ounces macadamia nuts, shelled = 1 cup nutmeat or 110 grams

PEANUTS
1 pound peanuts, unshelled = 2 to 2½ cups nutmeat
1 pound peanuts, shelled = 3 cups nutmeat or 454 grams

PECANS
1 pound pecans, unshelled = 2¼ cups nutmeat
1 pound pecans, shelled = 4 cups nutmeat or 454 grams

PISTACHIO NUTS
5 ounces pistachio nuts, shelled = 1 cup nutmeat or 150 grams

WALNUTS
1 pound walnuts, unshelled = 2 cups nutmeat
1 pound walnuts, shelled = 4 cups nutmeat or 454 grams

SUGAR

BROWN SUGAR
1 pound firmly packed brown sugar = 2½ cups

GRANULATED
1 pound granulated sugar = 2¼ cups
1 cup granulated sugar = 7 ounces
1 cup granulated sugar = 1 cup packed brown sugar
1 cup granulated sugar = 1¾ cups confectioners sugar
1 tablespoon granulated sugar = 1 tablespoon maple sugar

HONEY
1 cup honey = 12 ounces

MOLASSES
11 ounces of molasses = 1 cups

POWDERED
1 pound sifted powdered sugar = 4 cups
1 cup sifted powdered sugar = 4 ounces
1 pound unsifted powdered sugar = 3½ cups
1 cup unsifted powdered sugar = 4.5 ounces

WEIGHT
¼ ounce = 07 grams
½ ounce = 17 grams
1 ounce = 28 grams
2 ounces = 57 grams
5 ounces = 142 grams
8 ounces = 227 grams
12 ounces = 340 grams
16 ounces = 454 grams
32 ounces = 907 grams
64 ounces = 1.8 kilograms

VOLUME
¼ teaspoon = 1.25 ml
½ teaspoon = 2.5 ml
1 teaspoon = 5 ml
1 tablespoon = 15 ml
¼ cup = 59 ml
⅓ cup = 79 ml
½ cup = 119 ml
¾ cup = 177 ml
1 cup = 237 ml
1 pint (2 cups) = 473 ml
1 quart (4 cups) = 946 ml
1 gallon (4 quarts) = 3.78 litres

LENGTH
¼ inch = 5 millimeters
½ inch = 1 centimeter
¾ inch = 2 centimeters
1 inch = 2.5 centimeters
2 inches = 5 centimeters
4 inches = 10 centimeters
1 foot (12 inches) = 30 centimeters

HEAT
very cool = 250–275 F. = 130–140 C.
cool = 300 F. = 150 C.
warm = 325 F. = 170 C.
moderate = 350 F. = 180 C.
moderate hot = 375–400 F. = 190–200 C.
hot = 425 F. = 220 C.
very hot = 450–475 F. = 230–250 C.

INDEX